White Identity Politics

Amidst discontent over America's growing diversity, many white Americans now view the political world through the lens of a racial identity. Whiteness was once thought to be invisible because of whites' dominant position and ability to claim the mainstream, but today a large portion of whites actively identify with their racial group and support policies and candidates that they view as protecting whites' power and status.

In *White Identity Politics*, Ashley Jardina offers a landmark analysis of emerging patterns of white identity and collective political behavior, drawing on sweeping data. Where past research on whites' racial attitudes emphasized out-group hostility, Jardina brings into focus the significance of in-group identity and favoritism. *White Identity Politics* shows that disaffected whites are not just found among the working class; they make up a broad proportion of the American public – with profound implications for political behavior and the future of racial conflict in America.

Ashley Jardina is Assistant Professor of Political Science at Duke University. She studies the nature of racial attitudes and group identities and their influence on public opinion and political behavior. Her research has been featured in the *New York Times*, *Vox*, and the *Washington Post*'s Monkey Cage.

Cambridge Studies in Public Opinion and Political Psychology

Series Editors
Dennis Chong, *University of Southern California and Northwestern University*
James H. Kuklinski, *University of Illinois, Urbana-Champaign*

Cambridge Studies in Public Opinion and Political Psychology publishes innovative research from a variety of theoretical and methodological perspectives on the mass public foundations of politics and society. Research in the series focuses on the origins and infl uence of mass opinion, the dynamics of information and deliberation, and the emotional, normative, and instrumental bases of political choice. In addition to examining psychological processes, the series explores the organization of groups, the association between individual and collective preferences, and the impact of institutions on beliefs and behavior.

Cambridge Studies in Public Opinion and Political Psychology is dedicated to furthering theoretical and empirical research on the relationship between the political system and the attitudes and actions of citizens.

Books in the series are listed on the page following the Index.

White Identity Politics

Ashley Jardina
Duke University, North Carolina

CAMBRIDGE
UNIVERSITY PRESS

CAMBRIDGE
UNIVERSITY PRESS

University Printing House, Cambridge CB2 8BS, United Kingdom

One Liberty Plaza, 20th Floor, New York, NY 10006, USA

477 Williamstown Road, Port Melbourne, VIC 3207, Australia

314-321, 3rd Floor, Plot 3, Splendor Forum, Jasola District Centre, New Delhi - 110025, Indi

79 Anson Road, #06-04/06, Singapore 079906

Cambridge University Press is part of the University of Cambridge.

It furthers the University's mission by disseminating knowledge in the pursuit of education, learning and research at the highest international levels of excellence.

www.cambridge.org
Information on this title: www.cambridge.org/9781108475525
DOI: 10.1017/9781108645157

First published 2019
Reprinted 2019

A catalogue record for this publication is available from the British Library

Library of Congress Cataloging in Publication data
Names: Jardina, Ashley, author.
Title: White identity politics / Ashley Jardina, Duke University, North Carolina.
Description: Cambridge, United Kingdom: New York, NY, USA: Cambridge University Press, [2019] | Includes bibliographical references and index.
Identifiers: LCCN 2018049097 | ISBN 9781108475525 (hardback) | ISBN 9781108468602 (paperback)
Subjects: LCSH: Identity politics – United States. | Whites – United States – Politics and government. | Whites – Race identity – United States. | United States – Race relations – Political aspects.
Classification: LCC JK1764.J37 2019 | DDC 320.56/909073–dc23
LC record available at https://lccn.loc.gov/2018049097

ISBN 978-1-108-47552-5 Hardback
ISBN 978-1-108-46860-2 Paperback

To my Michigan family

CONTENTS

FIGURES

TABLES

ACKNOWLEDGMENTS

I wrote much of this book in the comfort of an old sweatshirt, its block "M" on the front almost entirely faded from many washings. By my side, I had the steadfast company of Maize, my sweet golden retriever named, of course, after one of the University of Michigan's school colors. My own social identity is deeply tied to the University of Michigan, and for good reason. Over the years, I have received incredible support, advice, and friendship from my advisors, colleagues, and dear friends from my alma mater. This book exists because of my Michigan family, and it is dedicated to them.

My deepest gratitude goes to Ted Brader and Vincent Hutchings. They served as the co-chairs of my dissertation committee, but their role extends well beyond the development of this particular project. Together, they shepherded me through college and graduate school. I owe much of who I am as a person and scholar to their guidance and support. They have set a tremendously high bar as mentors, scholars, and friends. They both also saw value in this project early on, when many expressed doubts about the notion of a white identity. I am thankful that they encouraged – and still encourage – me to take risks in my work.

Ted has bestowed on me tremendous wisdom, wit, and support. He has helped shape this research significantly, and I am grateful for his attention to detail, his generosity, and his patience. His work has been some of the greatest inspiration for my own, and I continue to strive to be as careful and thorough of a scholar as he is. Ted has also expertly, and slyly, been the mentor who has challenged me the most over the years, pushing my work to be better. He has often raised the bar in his expectations without me even realizing it, in part because he has also been such a first-rate sounding board and so quick with encouraging words. He is also a truly great friend, and many of my fondest moments in Ann Arbor entail outstanding dinner conversations with Ted and his brilliant wife, Valerie, always over fine wine and excellent food.

Vince, as he has done for so many, has given me countless hours of his time over many years. From him, I learned how to design experiments and surveys. He has shown me how to ask interesting questions and how to add clarity to my arguments. He has given me careful feedback, teaching me not only when work is subpar, but also when it is good. Vince is a model scholar, but more importantly, he is the kind of person I strive to be. He is kind, generous, compassionate, and deeply patient. He has an unwavering belief that his students belong in academia, and that they have the ability to succeed in graduate school and beyond. For most of my adult life, Vince has been my cheerleader and my champion, and I am so proud to be one of his students. I will be forever grateful that over a decade ago, both he and Ted saw something in me as an earnest undergraduate, and I would not be where I am today without them.

Nancy Burns has been one of my most important mentors. She offered me a position as her research assistant during my second year in graduate school and since then, I have benefited tremendously from her brilliant advice, excellent cooking, and the time I have been able to spend with her extraordinary family – Scott, Sef, and Tate. Nancy is one of the kindest and bravest people I know, and a great deal of what I have learned about doing good social science work is from her. I am indebted for the incredible opportunities she has given me, and I am as much a student of hers as I am of the members of my formal graduate dissertation committee.

So much of the work here is a reflection of what I have learned from Nicholas Valentino. Nick initially possessed a healthy skepticism of this project, and it is better for it. He pushed me to shore up my theoretical account, and to address alternative theories thoroughly. In the end, he has been one of my strongest supporters, and I am thankful for all his time, advice, and feedback that undoubtedly improved my work immensely.

In many ways, this book would not have been possible without Donald Kinder. My project builds off his brilliant and far-reaching groundwork in race and public opinion. His work, along with that of David Sears', has been deeply influential to my own thinking about racial attitudes. Much of this book was written with several of Don's books near at hand, their pages now dog-eared, underlined, and filled with notes. I have been tremendously fortunate to have worked with Don and to have had him on my dissertation committee. When I was a graduate student, he pushed me to think more deeply about the historical implications of my research, to provide stronger evidence for my claims, and to expand the scope of my work. This book is far richer for that advice.

Along the way, many others at the University of Michigan served as important mentors and gave me the tools and guidance to complete this project. Elleanor Crown was one of the first to support and encourage my academic interests when I was an undergraduate. Skip Lupia provided valuable feedback on this project's framing. Rob Mickey offered excellent advice and encouragement. Over the years Michael Traugott, Ken Kollman, Charles Shipan, Mark Tessler, Mika LaVaque-Manty, Hanes Walton, Jr., and Allen Hicken have been wonderful counselors and friends. I am also grateful to many of the staff at the Center for Political Studies in the Institute for Social Research.

One benefit of the Michigan network is that it is vast and filled with brilliant, obliging scholars. To that end, I was fortunate that Ismail White, Frank Baumgartner, and Taeku Lee – all Michigan grads – generously took the time to read an early version of this manuscript. They spent an entire day in Durham going through a draft with me, and their insights were crucial to the development of the book.

My friends from graduate school, who are like family, encouraged me and kept me grounded. I am especially grateful to Andrea Benjamin, Papia Debroy, and Alex Jakle. Much of the daily grind of writing this book was done with the company, reassurance, and feedback of my dear friend Alexander Von Hagen-Jamar, whose tireless support carried me through the finish line. Spencer Piston read many drafts of many pieces of this project over the years, and his feedback and support have been especially important to me. Yanna Krupnikov, Adam Seth Levine, and Antoine Banks have served as important mentors and models. My friendships with Emily Bosk, Katie Brown, Logan Casey, Chinbo Chong, Jennifer Chudy, David Cottrell, Allison Dale-Riddle, Rob Garlick, Keith Gibson, Cassandra Grafstrom, Eric Groenendyk, Hakeem Jefferson, Andrea Jones-Rooy, Nathan Kalmoe,

Kristyn Karl, Pam McCann, Erin McGovern, Jennifer Miller-Gonzalez, Fabian Neuner, Vanessa Cruz Nichols, Davin Phoenix, Rachel Potter, Molly Reynolds, Katherine Gallagher Robbins, Ethan Schoolman, David Smith, LaFleur Stephens-Dougan, Jessi Streib, Stacey Tsibulsky, Alton Worthington, and Nicole Yadon have brought me so much good advice, guidance, peace of mind, and joy.

My Michigan family provided the foundation of support for this project, but I am equally thankful to the community of colleagues and friends who have helped me and have contributed to my work in the years since I left Ann Arbor. First and foremost, this project exists only because of the truly brilliant David Sears, whose groundbreaking and now canonical research laid the foundation for the study of white racial attitudes in political science. My work here not only builds off David's important scholarship, but it is also much better thanks to his invaluable feedback. I am so fortunate to have benefited not only from David's careful reading of an early version of the manuscript, but also from his kindness and encouragement.

Many of my colleagues at Duke University provided important feedback on this project, including John Aldrich, Kerry Haynie, Sunshine Hillygus, and Christopher Johnston. I am also thankful for the comments I received from Kyle Beardsley, Pablo Beramendi, Joseph Grieco, Melanie Manion, Scott de Marchi, David Rohde, and David Siegel. I am especially grateful to Georg Vanberg, not only for his helpful comments and support, but also for generously providing me with the resources to host a book conference.

Many other dear friends and colleagues have given helpful advice, offered encouragement, and shared commiseration. I am thankful for Cameron Ballard-Rosa, Nicholas Carnes, Lauren Davenport, Christopher DeSante, Christopher Federico, Lorrie Frasure-Yokley, Shana Gadarian, Leonie Huddy, Michael Jones-Correa, Jane Junn, Alexander Kirschner, Samara Klar, Corrine McConnaughy, Lucy Martin, Tali Mendelberg, Christopher Parker, Brian Schaffner, Deborah Schildkraut, Paul Sniderman, Joe Soss, Lester Spence, Michael Tesler, Ali Valenzuela, Lynn Vavreck, Vesla Weaver, and Cara Wong. I am also grateful to Trey Boone, for offering welcome distractions, input, support, and so much to look forward to during the publication process.

I owe the finishing touches of this project to some exemplary research assistance from graduate students at Duke University. Much gratitude goes to Arvind Krishnamurthy and Katelyn Mehling. I am especially indebted to Victoria Dounoucos and Bailey Sanders, who are amazing, and who worked tirelessly until the end.

I was lucky to be able to work with the fabulous Sara Doskow at Cambridge University Press. She has been a wonderful editor. I appreciate her enthusiasm for the project, and her patience. She has not only been incredibly accommodating, but she has expertly shepherded this project from manuscript to print, and I am very glad to have worked with her.

Survey research is expensive, and the work in the pages that follow would not have been possible without the financial support I received from a number of sources. Much of the data in the book here are from the American National Election Studies (ANES), which are funded by the National Science Foundation. This project would be much less than what it is if it were not for the fact that the 2012 ANES included a question on white identity. It is even more substantial because the ANES board included on the 2016 ANES Pilot and the 2016 Time Series the white identity and white consciousness items I proposed. While I was at the University of Michigan, I received the generous support of the National Science Foundation Graduate Research Fellowship. Many of the surveys used in this book were funded by the Gerald R. Ford Fellowship, and the Rackham Graduate School. I am also thankful for funding received through the University of Michigan Department of Political Science and Duke University, which supported several of my studies.

Finally, I am grateful to my parents, Michael and Marie, for their love and support. They have made many sacrifices for me over the years, and I am thankful that they have supported so many of my endeavors. I am especially indebted to my mother, who has given me a great deal of her time so that I can have more of my own.

This book is a product of the hard work of many people. Its weaknesses are entirely mine, but its strengths are the result of so much time and energy from dear friends, family, and colleagues. To each of you, I am sincerely grateful.

1 THE NEW AMERICAN MINORITY

> An identity is questioned only when it is menaced, as when the
> mighty begin to fall, or when the wretched begin to rise, or when
> the stranger enters the gates, never, thereafter, to be a stranger: the
> stranger's presence making you the stranger, less to the stranger
> than to yourself.
>
> JAMES BALDWIN (1976)

In 1998, President Bill Clinton gave the commencement address at Portland State University in Portland, Oregon. Standing before the crowd of graduating students, he told them he wanted to speak about the America of their future – an America that was changing and becoming more diverse at a breathtaking rate. The driving force behind this increasing diversity, he stated, was a new and large wave of immigration that was changing the face of the country. He described how in places like Hawaii, Houston, and New York City, there was currently no majority race. "No other nation in history has gone through demographic change of this magnitude in so short a time," he said. Then, he paused, and posed a question to the crowd, "What do the changes mean? They can either strengthen and unite us, or they can weaken and divide us. We must decide."

Eighteen years later, the changes Clinton described are upon us. In many more cities, whites, once the numerical majority, are now a minority. According to recent population projections, by 2043, whites will no longer comprise a majority of the country.[1] Our increasingly diverse nation elected its first black president in

2008. The first justice of Hispanic heritage was appointed to the US Supreme Court in 2009.[2] The 115th Congress, which began its meeting in January 2017, was the most racially and ethnically diverse in history.[3] Within the walls of our political and economic institutions, individuals of different backgrounds, heritages, and experiences have joined the ranks.

These changes have not come to pass without protest. In numerous ways, some white Americans have expressed their dismay at the changing racial composition of the country and at the strides racial and ethnic minorities have made in achieving political, social, and economic power.[4] Over the past decade, several predominantly white state legislators have moved to enact strict immigration laws. They have challenged ethnic studies courses, diversity programs, and college courses on race – particularly those perceived as derisive toward whites (Delgado 2013).[5] They have also proposed legislation requiring presidential candidates to produce birth certificates, and enacted voter identification laws, making it potentially more difficult for racial and ethnic minorities to participate in elections (Bentele and O'Brien 2013).[6]

During these legislative battles, racial tensions flared. In 2006, hundreds of thousands of Latinos gathered in cities across the United States to protest restrictive immigration legislation and to demand policies that would provide immigrants with pathways to citizenship (Voss, Bloemraad, and Lee 2011). More fuel was added to these fires in the aftermath of Barack Obama's election as the nation's first African American president in 2008. Many heralded Obama's victory as a sign of our nation's racial progress. But Obama's election also appears to have brought to the fore more insidious forms of racism and ethnocentrism (Kam and Kinder 2012; Kinder and Dale-Riddle 2012; Piston 2010; Tesler 2012a; Tesler and Sears 2010). It also did little to mend the vast divide between white and black Americans over racial policy. Americans today remain more polarized around issues of race than ever (Goldman 2012; Hutchings 2009).

These tensions took center stage during the 2016 presidential election, with the Republican candidacy and election of Donald Trump. Over the course of his campaign, Trump spoke disparagingly of Muslim and Mexican immigrants. He proposed a halt to refugees entering the country and promised to build a wall along America's southern border to stop the flow of immigrants from Mexico. Vowing to "put America first," Trump warned of the dangers of globalization. Outside of Trump's campaign rallies, protestors, many of whom were black or Latino, clashed, sometimes violently, with white Trump supporters. Hostilities mounted even further when, only days after taking office, President Trump signed an executive order banning citizens from seven Muslim-majority nations from entering the country. Much of Trump's first year as president was marked by public outcry over immigration policies many regarded as draconian.

It appears, to answer Clinton's earlier question, that our increasingly diverse nation has in many ways divided us. What explains these rifts? Why are white Americans mobilizing en masse around issues of racial and ethnic diversity? And why were so many white Americans drawn to a candidate like Donald Trump, who was often derisive of racial and ethnic minorities, and whose campaign focused on curbing immigration and rejecting international trade agreements? Why do we now seem to be witnessing a backlash to globalization, a widespread desire to close our nation's borders, to restrict immigration, and to stay out of foreign affairs? And why have hostilities between whites and other racial and ethnic minorities grown in recent years?

Some of this backlash is rooted in prejudice, racism, and ethnocentrism. But as I will show, a great deal of many whites' reactions to our country's changing racial landscape do not simply manifest in outward hostility. Amidst these changes, many whites have described themselves as outnumbered, disadvantaged, and even oppressed. They have voiced their anxiety over America's waning numerical majority, and have questioned what this means for the future of the nation. They have worried that soon they may face discrimination based on their own race, if they do not already (Norton and Sommers 2011).[7] These sentiments hint at the fact that the growing non-white population, the pending loss of whites' majority status, and the increasing political and economic power of people of color in the United States has a second consequence. For a number of whites, these monumental social and political trends – including an erosion of whites' majority status and the election of America's first black president – have signaled a challenge to the absoluteness of whites' dominance. These threats, both real and perceived, have, as I will demonstrate, brought to the fore, for many whites, a sense of commonality, attachment, and solidarity with their racial group. They have led a sizeable proportion of whites to believe that their racial group, and the benefits that group enjoys, are endangered. As a result, this racial solidarity now plays a central role in the way many whites orient themselves to the political and social world.

In the pages that follow, I examine the rise and consequences of white identity politics. My argument is rooted in the notion that an identity – a psychological, internalized sense of attachment to a group – can provide an important cognitive structure through which individuals navigate and participate in the political and social world (Conover 1984; Huddy 2003; Lau 1989; Miller et al. 1981). A great body of evidence indicates that as humans, our need to belong, to see ourselves as similar to others with whom we share common goals, is innate. We are, so to speak, primed to adopt group attachments around our social groupings, whether they be based on religion, occupation, or something else. Not surprisingly, these identities can profoundly influence our political preferences and behavior.

As we will see, this solidarity, and whites' desire to protect their group's interests, plays a key role in today's most important and pressing political and social issues. Over the course of this book, I will show that mass opposition to immigration, to government outsourcing, and to trade policies are a function of white identity. What is more, we will learn that white identity undergirds significant support for social welfare spending. Contrary to popular perceptions, many whites are supportive of more government assistance, but primarily when they believe that assistance is directed at their group. Indeed, desires to preserve Social Security and Medicare are rooted in white racial solidarity.

Most importantly, white racial solidarity is a pivotal factor in contemporary electoral politics. A great deal of work on race in political science over the past decade has focused on the profound role racial prejudice played in opposition to Barack Obama and his political agenda. But this work has overlooked the relationship between Obama's electoral success and whites' racial in-group attitudes. Perhaps because of this oversight, many social scientists and pundits were surprised by the successful presidential campaign Donald Trump mounted in 2016. This work offers a comprehensive and systematic way for us to understand support for Trump, a candidate who effectively mobilized whites around their racial identity.

For social scientists, this work makes a number of additional contributions. The theory and evidence I present expand our account of intergroup relations more broadly, demonstrating when and in what ways dominant group identities are salient and consequential. Much of the work on racial conflict in the United States has focused on white *out-group* attitudes in the form of racial prejudice and racial resentment. I look at a whites' *in-group* attitudes, and make a strong case that such attitudes are not synonymous with prejudice, nor do strong out-group animosities necessarily follow from a strong sense of in-group identity (Brewer 1999).[8] Many whites identify with their racial group without feeling prejudice toward racial and ethnic minorities, and many more whites possess some degree of negative affect toward racial and ethnic minorities without also identifying with their racial group.

I also unpack the nature of white racial solidarity, demonstrating that many whites in the United States not only identify with their racial group, with great political consequence, but a sizeable subset also possesses a sense of group consciousness. That is, some whites not only feel a strong attachment to their racial group, but for some, that attachment is also coupled with a set of beliefs about the need for whites to work together to achieve their political goals. Furthermore, I introduce valid and reliable ways to measure both forms of white racial solidarity on public opinion surveys.

Finally, this book reconsiders our prevailing understanding of race relations in the United States. The evidence here makes clear that race is central to American politics, and pays careful and renewed attention to how the hierarchical arrangement of racial groups profoundly influences our nation's politics. This work joins a long line of research, which argues that racial conflict and racial inequality in the United States are not merely the product of learned racial prejudice; such disparities are also the product of white efforts to protect their power and status (Blumer 1958; Bobo 1999; Klinkner and Smith 1999; Masuoka and Junn 2013; Parker and Barreto 2013). Indeed, many of the whites in my account are seeking to reassert a racial order in which their group is firmly at the top.

The history of race relations in the United States has been an unsteady, often wavering, climb toward racial equality, with steps taken both forward and backward. The issues I take up in the pages to come are part of another chapter in the story of how Americans choose to confront new challenges to the nation's racial hierarchy. Ultimately, these matters cut to the core of how Americans define what it means to be citizens, the extent to which we as a nation embrace multiculturalism, and how well we choose to live up to democratic values. These questions are complicated and knotty, but fundamental to American social and political life. This work is part of an effort to untangle them, and to better understand what divides and what unites us.

Overlooking White Identity

To political scientists, the claim that whites possess a racial identity should come as a surprise. Historically, the study of identity, especially as it has pertained to race or ethnicity, has often been one-sided, focusing on the concept's development and its role among subordinate or minority groups. Hughes (1948) noted how common it was "to study ethnic relations as if one had to know only one party to them" (p. 479). But, as he put so eloquently, we cannot fully understand group relations through the study of one group anymore "than a chemical combination by study of one element only, or a boxing bout by observation of only one side of the fighters" (p. 479).[9]

And yet racial identity among whites has been especially ignored or rejected by social scientists. When considering whether white Americans feel a sense of anxiety about the status of their racial group, or whether whites possess a sense of racial identity that has political consequences, for the past fifty years, the answer generally has been "no." For the most part, scholars have argued that racial solidarity among whites has been invisible and politically inconsequential. Whites, by nature of their dominant status and numerical majority, have largely been able to take their race for granted. Sears and Savalei (2006) describe this position well:

> In general, whites remain dominant in American society – numerically, socially, economically, and politically – and overt, explicitly racial conflict is now relatively rare. As a result, whites' whiteness is usually likely to be no more noteworthy to them than is breathing the air around them. White group consciousness is therefore not likely to be a major force in whites' political attitudes today.
>
> *(2006, p. 901)*

The scholarly consensus has been that whites do not, by and large, think about their whiteness – at least not in a way that is politically meaningful. They are not, according to the conventional wisdom, influenced by an inward attachment to their racial group, or by a sense of group identity. Whiteness, according to this line of reasoning, for all intents and purposes, is invisible. Thus, for whites, our perspective on their attitudes and behavior when it comes to race has been almost exclusively outwardly focused; it attends to the nature and consequences of racial prejudice, resentment, and animus among whites, particularly that which is directed toward blacks.

I argue, however, that now is the time to reconsider the scope of racial attitudes associated with whites' political evaluations, preferences, and behaviors. Most of the scholarship concluding that white racial solidarity is generally invisible or without consequence was conducted between the 1970s and the early 2000s. During this time, the nation looked quite different than it does today. The United States was far less diverse, and most racial conflict was situated primarily between black and white Americans. There was also little doubt that whites constituted an overwhelming numerical majority of the American population and fully controlled government institutions at all levels.

Today's racial and ethnic landscape is vastly different than it has been at any other time in our nation's history. Due to immigration and differences in birth rates across racial and ethnic groups, the relative size of the white population is shrinking. The United States is now one of the most racially and ethnically diverse countries in the Western world. Because of the rapid racial and ethnic diversification of the country, we must reevaluate our theories about the nature of racial conflict and racial attitudes, many of which were established under a black–white paradigm. Issues of race, of diversity, of globalization, and of immigration are fundamentally altering our political parties, our political attitudes, and our political institutions (Abrajano and Hajnal 2015; Hajnal and Lee 2011). Our theories must be updated and reconstructed to account for a much greater array of groups under changing circumstances.

This book offers a framework for understanding racial conflict in today's more racially and ethnically diverse nation. I contend that, today, whites' racial attitudes are not merely defined by prejudice; many whites also possess a sense of racial identity and are motivated to protect their group's collective interests and to maintain its status. As well shall see, whiteness is now a salient and central component of American politics. White racial solidarity influences many whites' worldview and guides their political attitudes and behavior.

White Nationalism

The backlash to our nation's growing diversity has undoubtedly contributed to the rise of more insidious groups, often associated with white supremacy, such as the Ku Klux Klan, neo-Nazis, skinheads, white nationalists, and some militia movements.[10] It has almost certainly fostered the rise of individuals calling themselves members of the "alt-right," a somewhat amorphous, reactionary group that supports white nationalism, and whose members generally endorse efforts to protect the white race.[11] Many argue that these groups have become more mainstream, and they certainly gained significant media attention during the 2016 presidential campaign when they vehemently supported Trump.[12]

Understanding the rise and the consequences of these movements is important. But that is not the aim of this book. The whites I describe here are not marginalized extremists who actively participate in the production of a white, masculine, and patriarchal ideology – one that advocates for the separation of groups and the superiority of whites (Ferber 1998). The whites in my account are a much broader group and far greater in number. In fact, whites high on racial solidarity comprise approximately 30–40 percent of the white population and, like most whites, the vast majority of those who identify with their racial group reject assertions of white supremacy and racism. And while these whites may share some of the same political views as their more extremist counterparts, they are not one and the same. This sizeable portion of white Americans are not especially interested in the separation of groups and the denigration of other races and ethnicities. Instead, as we shall see, they are primarily concerned with their in-group and desire to protect its status. Nevertheless, this work may provide somewhat of a cautionary tale. With evidence in hand that elites can appeal to whites' racial interests explicitly and successfully, there is potential for the ranks of white nationalists to grow.

The White Working Class

In response to today's political and social upheaval, many pundits and academics have turned their attention squarely on the white working class (Gest 2016; Hochschild 2016; Vance 2016). By their account, many of these whites have been left behind by the consequences of globalization, their jobs shipped overseas or displaced by immigrants. Angry and disenfranchised, they are lashing out and are susceptible to political appeals by elites espousing more protectionist policies and who promise to restore manufacturing jobs. For some commentators, the politics of white identity is the politics of the white working class.

There is, however, far more to the story. Many whites who possess a racial identity are, by some measures, members of the working class. But the phenomena I describe are not limited to whites situated in blue-collar jobs. This is, therefore, not merely a tale about the white working class. A much wider swath of whites view their racial group as dispossessed, persecuted, and threatened by America's changing racial dynamics. The politics of white identity is not wholly or even primarily rooted in economic disenfranchisement; it is far broader and more pervasive.

From Where We Have Come

To understand the role of white racial solidarity today, we must go back in time. From the country's very beginnings, race, particularly whiteness, was intricately connected to America's national identity. One year after the US Constitution was adopted and a year before the Bill of Rights was ratified, the US Congress passed the Naturalization Act of 1790. It was the first statute in the country to codify laws regarding national citizenship.[13] The Act explicitly limited naturalization to any "free white persons" who had lived in the United States for at least two years, excluding American Indians, slaves, free blacks, and indentured servants from citizenship. In subsequent years, as the immigrant population in the United States began steadily to tick upward, racial restrictions on citizenship were left intact, and naturalization laws became increasingly restrictive.

Between the 1840s and 1850s, America experienced one of its first significant, postcolonial waves of immigration. An oppressive caste system and a potato crop decimated by blight encouraged three million Catholic Irish to flee their home country for the United States.[14] In recent decades, the Irish have generally been subsumed under the umbrella of whiteness, but in the early decades of the nineteenth century their racial status was far more ambiguous (Ignatiev 1995). In fact, according to Jacobson (1999), the vagueness of the term "white people" as first written into the Naturalization Act of 1790 contributed to a new set of ideological tensions in the nation in the 1840s and 1850s. While "established codes of whiteness" were initially inclusive of all Europeans (p. 72), the influx of Catholic Irish at least temporarily prompted an effort to restrict the boundaries around race. The foreignness, lower economic status, and Catholicism of this group of immigrants challenged the religious and ethnic composition of the United States, engendering hostility among old-stock Americans (Billington 1938).[15] This animosity gave way to a pervasive nativism in the 1850s known as the "Know-Nothing" movement.[16] Supporters of this movement formed a political party called the American Party, which was anti-Catholic and anti-immigrant. The party's leaders demanded more restrictive naturalization laws.

The Know-Nothings did not obtain enough power to accomplish their political goals with much rigor, and political divisions, particularly over slavery, fueled the party's decline after 1856. But the sentiments espoused by the Know-Nothings have reverberated over the course of the nation's history. Each subsequent wave of immigration has provoked national conversations around the preservation of America's identity as a white nation, and one in which whites maintain political, social, and economic power.

By the early part of the twentieth century, such sentiments reached new heights, with significant political consequence. In F. Scott Fitzgerald's famous novel, *The Great Gatsby*, in which one of the central characters, Tom Buchanan, remarks to his wife, "[t]he idea is if we don't look out the white race will be – will be utterly submerged … It is up to us, who are the dominant race, to watch out or these other races will have control of things." Fitzgerald's book is set at the beginning of the Roaring Twenties, in the aftermath of World War I, and following intense domestic racial tensions resulting in the race riots of 1919's Red Summer. It was published in 1925, just after the passage of the American Immigration Act of 1924, which slowed down to a trickle the massive waves of European immigrants who had arrived during the previous two decades. The Act established strict immigration quotas, sharply curtailing "non-white" immigrants from Asia and Southern and Eastern Europe. Many proponents of this law embraced the argument espoused by Tom Buchanan; they were supremely interested in controlling the ethnic composition of the US population and believed in the racial superiority of Northern Europeans. They also saw the law as part of a larger effort to establish a distinct American identity – an identity biased toward Anglo-Saxon culture and which privileged "whiteness" (King 2000).

For nearly a century, the Immigration Act of 1924 had its intended effect. It was not until the passage of the Immigration and Nationality Act of 1965 that national quotas were lifted. Many scholars argue that policymakers were motivated to eliminate the national origins system by the Civil Rights movement, viewing the restrictions as counter to the country's democratic ideals (Chin 1996; King 2000). Others, however, have expressed skepticism that support for the legislation revealed the better angels of our nature when it comes to race. For one, congressional reports on the 1965 legislation noted that the quota system put in place by the 1924 Act never achieved its goals of maintaining the ethnic balance of the US population (King 2000). Very few immigrants came from the Nordic countries from which immigration was preferred. Furthermore, by the 1960s, the narrative around race and ethnicity had transformed. "Race relations" had become a squarely black–white issue, and the alarm that some Americans had felt in the 1920s around a broader array of racial and ethnic groups altering the demographic composition of the United States had faded. Immigrants from parts of Europe who were viewed as undesirable in the 1920s had become part of a new American myth about immigration – one that cast the assimilation of European immigrants and their economic mobility as a standard against which blacks were judged and found wanting (Jacobson 1999). In fact, the 1965 legislation, some argue, was intended to increase the number of immigrants from Southern and Eastern Europe – immigrants who were now considered white (White 1982).

In reality, the 1965 Act opened the door for the sweeping demographic changes we are witnessing today, allowing massive immigration from Asia and Latin America.[17] But it would still be decades before immigration levels would reach a critical mass. In the meantime, white Americans remained dominant over the political, economic, and social institutions in the United States. By a landslide, they have comprised the majority of the country's residents. In each decade between 1790 and 1990, whites, as defined by the US Census, made up over 80 percent of the US population. At the federal level and in most locales, they have held the vast majority of elected offices. More white people have served as heads of America's most powerful companies and corporations than people of color, and whites have captured a disproportionate share of the nation's wealth. They have been, for all intents and purposes, securely positioned atop the country's racial hierarchy, maintaining their status as the dominant group in American society (Kim 2000).[18]

Scattered throughout these decades there have, of course, been moments of racial unrest and upheaval, particularly as African Americans fought to end discrimination and demanded equality. Racial integration and the Civil Rights movement chipped away at white hegemony. But for the most part, whites' power has been resolute, and they have therefore never suffered what W.E.B Du Bois called double consciousness – the internal conflict, or sense of twoness, experienced by blacks in the United States, who must reconcile their own oppressed racial identity with their American identity. Whites have, in contrast, been able to cast and maintain the identity of the nation as their own.

The Study of Racial Attitudes and Racial Conflict in the United States

These circumstances have profoundly structured how we have thought about and studied race in America. In the latter half of the nineteenth century, moving into the early twentieth century, anthropologists, biologists, and other scientists relied on pseudoscientific techniques to claim that humans could be organized into distinct racial groups with different capabilities and capacities rooted in biological differences. Greatly influenced by Charles Darwin, American and European thinkers promoted the theory of Social Darwinism in an effort to prove European and white American superiority over Native Americans, Asians, Africans, and Latin Americans. As Richard Hofstadter describes, "The measure of world domination already achieved by the 'race' seemed to prove it the fittest" (Hofstadter 1992, p. 173).

These theories, which we have now come to refer to as scientific racism, were used to justify eugenics programs and anti-miscegenation laws. Proponents of these claims also favored the use of intelligence tests to "demonstrate" the inferiority of non-white races. In fact, these tests were eventually administered to immigrants arriving in the United States through Ellis Island in the early 1900s. With little command of English, many of these newcomers fared poorly on the tests, but the results were interpreted as evidence that immigrants from Russia, Hungary, Italy, and elsewhere were mentally inferior. The findings were used to justify the quotas put in place by the Immigration Act of 1924 (Franco 1985; Gould 1981).

During the 1930s, the Nazi Party used scientific racism as a means to justify the superiority of the German people and of the Aryan race. But in the 1940s, the advances of science, coupled with horror over the atrocities committed in the name of the Nazi ideology, marked a turning point for scientific racism. In the wake of World War II, prominent social scientists argued that America needed to denounce doctrines of racial superiority and confront racism and inequality in order to live up to the nation's democratic ideals (Benedict 1945; Montagu 1942; Myrdal 1944). Scholars took up this call and turned their attention to the study of racism and white racial prejudice in earnest. Today, our attention to the role of whites' racial animus in understanding racial conflict has not wavered. When it comes to explaining race relations in the United States, research continues to focus heavily on whites' out-group prejudices and hostilities.

As social scientists began to uncover further the nature of whites' racial prejudice, they also took up understanding the consequences of racial conflict. Some of this work, inspired by Marxism, focused on the effects of groups in society seeking to protect their group's interests, either real or imagined (Blumer 1958; LeVine and Campbell 1972).[19] Other work focused on the development and role of group cohesion and solidarity among blacks, especially during and immediately after the Civil Rights movement. Much of this work drew on psychological theories of group identity – ones that were developed, independent of the study of racial conflict, in order to understand the role of group cohesion and identities as they mattered for political beliefs, behavior, and group conflict more generally (Berelson, Lazarsfeld, and McPhee 1954; Tajfel 1974; Tajfel and Turner 1979). Many argued that the feelings of group threat, racial alienation, and group subordination experienced by blacks in the United States were important ingredients in the development of a strong sense of group attachment and racial consciousness among blacks in America (Bobo and Hutchings 1996; Dawson 1994; Matthews and Prothro 1966; Miller et al. 1981).

Over this same period, beginning in middle of the twentieth century, researchers noticed a decline in whites' explicit expression of racial prejudice toward blacks (Kinder and Sanders 1996; Kluegel and Smith 1982; Schuman et al. 1985). Whites' racial attitudes, scholars argued, were transforming (Kinder and Sanders 1996; Kinder and

Sears 1981; McConahay and Hough 1976). In the midst of the Civil Rights movement, whites' egalitarian ideals were joined with a sense of racial sympathy. They supported racial equality, and civil rights were regarded as the nation's most important problem. This support motivated the passage of monumental civil rights legislation. But in the days following the passage of the Voting Rights Act of 1965, an intense three-day race riot broke out in the Watts neighborhood in Los Angeles. Blacks looted and set fire to the city. Other riots across the country followed, and in their wake, white sympathy for blacks faltered.[20]

Moving into the 1970s, the importance of civil rights in the minds of whites waned, and many seemed to believe that the passage of the Civil Rights Act of 1964 meant that legal barriers to black equality had all but disappeared. The persistence of race riots and violence in inner-cities made whites apprehensive. Conservative politicians exploited these fears and accused blacks of failing to live up to American values. If racial equality had not been achieved, they argued, it was because of the moral failing of blacks. As political scientists Donald Kinder and Lynn Sanders write, these politicians, like Richard Nixon and Ronald Reagan,

> did not promote biological racism; they did not promise a return to segregation; they did not imply that blacks were second-class citizens or that they should be treated differently than anyone else. Their message was subtle, rather than blatant; it was that blacks should behave themselves. They should take quiet advantage of the ample opportunities now provided them. Government had been too generous, had given blacks too much, and blacks, for their part, had accepted these gifts all too readily.
>
> *(1996, p. 105)*

This rhetoric breathed life into a new type of racial prejudice – one that is subtle, and a combination of anti-black affect and the belief that blacks do not adhere to traditional American values associated with the Protestant work ethic.

This theoretical framework is the dominant paradigm for how we think about whites' racial attitudes today. In political science, we refer to this collection of attitudes as symbolic racism, modern racism, or racial resentment (Kinder and Sanders 1996; Kinder and Sears 1981; McConahay 1983; Sears and Henry 2005). This form of racial animus is considered a socialized predisposition. That is, whites are taught to subscribe to these beliefs as children, and they then carry these attitudes into adulthood, where they inform political judgments. The evidence for their import is compelling. Racial resentment predicts whites' opinions toward a wide range of racialized political policies and has a profound impact on political candidate evaluations. It is, quite clearly, a central component to the way in which whites interpret the political and social world.

The theories of symbolic racism and racial resentment are not without their critics (e.g., Sniderman and Carmines 1997; Sniderman and Piazza 2002). One common complaint is that because the theories' architects define the concept as a combination of anti-black affect and more conservative values, they rely on a measure that confounds these two constructs (Feldman and Huddy 2005; Sniderman and Tetlock 1986; Tetlock 1994). Thus, in work examining the associations between racial prejudice and political preferences, many scholars instead focus on the negative racial stereotypes about blacks (Piston 2010). Nevertheless, this alternative approach shares, with racial resentment, an emphasis on the negative out-group attitudes whites possess toward blacks.

A New Framework for Understanding Whites' Racial Attitudes

If we step back and think about how we understand racial politics in the contemporary United States, we have white racial prejudice, on the one hand, driving white opposition to policies that benefit racial and ethnic minorities. On the other hand, we have a sense of racial solidarity or consciousness among blacks, motivating their political preferences and voting behavior. You will notice that this arrangement focuses on just two groups in American society: blacks and whites. Because for most of our nation's history these were the two predominant racial groups in conflict, our theories about race are derived primarily from the interactions between these two groups. But our changing racial landscape means not only that existing theories might need to be modified, but also that they cannot necessarily help us fully understand racial dynamics today.

In this book, I offer a new framework for thinking about racial attitudes. It is one that does not dismiss the power of white racial resentment, but that does reassess existing theories of group dynamics. It reconsiders how white Americans might be responding to growing racial and ethnic diversity, and to the political, social, and economic success of a myriad of racial and ethnic groups. Many whites, I argue, are anxious about these changes. They are worried about what such changes mean for the status of their group and its future in American society. These concerns have driven some whites to turn inward, to circle the wagons, and to see their racial group as one that is threatened, with members who have shared political interests. In short, in reaction to threats to their group, whites are bringing their racial identity to bear on their political attitudes and behavior in important ways. White identity has real consequences.

Understanding the nature of whites' racial attitudes and their consequences is crucial to understanding the dynamics of American politics and to achieving a more racially egalitarian society. Recognizing that when it comes to race, whites are motivated not merely by racial animus, but by in-group favoritism, suggests the need for a shift in understanding how individuals might work to change whites' attitudes. The import of white identity indicates that whites' racial attitudes are not merely a function of socialization, but that they are also rooted in perceptions about their group's status and its potential loss of power or privileges. Modifying such beliefs may require new and different strategies.

The distinction between white prejudice and white identity also has implications for the types of political messages elites may use to persuade whites. Politicians need not appeal to racial animus to be politically successful under this framework; instead, they might campaign to preserve the status quo, or to protect whites' collective interests. Such efforts might on their face seem less problematic than overt racial bigotry, but nonetheless serve, in a broader scheme, to preserve racial inequality. By stoking concerns about their racial group's status, politicians might also encourage whites to believe further that whites experience racial discrimination; consequently, whites may become even less sympathetic toward policies that promote racial equality for other groups and more inclined to support policies that disproportionately benefit their own group, thereby exacerbating racial inequality. White biases may also transform, marked less by a dislike of racial out-groups than by a defense of collective interests – a position potentially as problematic, but perhaps more insidious and easily cloaked in a façade of legitimacy (Effron and Knowles 2015). In short, the future of white racial attitudes in American politics may be defined by both racial prejudice and racial solidarity.

Where We Are Headed

In moving forward with a new theory about the nature of racial attitudes in today's contemporary social and political environments, I start by taking a step back. A long line of work in the social sciences has considered how socio-demographic groups have influenced individuals' political beliefs and behavior. They have examined how one's occupation, union membership, religion, and other group memberships have been integral to the policies people endorse and the political candidates for whom they cast their ballots (Berelson, Lazarsfeld, and McPhee 1954; Lazarsfeld, Berelson, and Gaudet 1944). A second, tangential, and enormously influential body of work in social psychology has focused on intergroup behavior and the sources of intergroup conflict (Sherif 1961; Tajfel 1974; Tajfel and Turner 1979). Many of the theories in this domain propose that individuals are intrinsically motivated to see themselves as members of distinct social groups. A natural consequence of this behavior is the expression of in-group favoritism. People are inclined to think more positively of their in-group, and they are more likely to share resources with other group members, sometimes at the expense of out-groups.

In Chapter 2, I borrow insights from these lines of scholarship to develop a theory of dominant group identity. Because dominant groups usually co-opt the cultural mainstream of the larger society, their group identity is often taken for granted or is seen as invisible. I describe when we would expect this type of identity to become salient and politically consequential. My main claim is that such identities are reactionary – they are activated in response to group threat. I also consider when and in what circumstances we might expect white identity to inform public opinion.

With this groundwork laid, I turn in Chapter 3 to measuring white identity and white consciousness. I show that in the United States, a sizeable proportion of white Americans identify with their racial group, and I demonstrate that both white racial identity and white consciousness are distinct from other political predispositions.

In other words, white identity is not merely a proximate measure of other attitudes or values that we consider important fixtures or antecedents of contemporary public opinion. Perhaps more importantly, I show that both identity and consciousness are not merely alternative measures to racial animus. Both measures of group solidarity are distinct from our most common conceptualizations of racial prejudice.

In Chapter 4, I examine the antecedents of white identity and white consciousness, exploring the demographic characteristics, economic circumstances, geographic contexts, and personality dimensions associated with higher or lower levels of white identity. Many might find the results surprising, as they challenge conventional expectations about who among whites might be more predisposed to adopt a white identity or possess a sense of consciousness. For instance, white identifiers are not overwhelmingly among those residing in the South, or the economically disaffected. But those whites who are older, with lower levels of education, who live in rural areas, and who are more inclined toward dispositions like authoritarianism, are in fact likely to have a stronger racial identity and to possess higher levels of white consciousness.

From here, I move on to explore the confluence of attitudes white identifiers possess; I demonstrate that white racial solidarity is not without content. Whites who identify with their racial group share beliefs about their place in society, about national identity, racial conflict, group competition, and group privilege. These beliefs are part of the content of white identity, which Chapter 5 describes in more detail. High white identifiers tend to possess more exclusionary views about American identity, perceive greater competition between their own racial group and others, and possess a greater sense of racial alienation – the belief that their group has been or is currently being treated unfairly in society. At the same time, white identifiers recognize and enjoy their group's privileged status and express little collective guilt.

White identity and white consciousness play a powerful and distinct role in a number of domains, but one of the key places these constructs exert their influence is with regards to immigration opinion. Just as in the 1920s, ideas about race, whiteness, and national identity are significantly implicated in contemporary conversations about immigration. Accordingly, we see in Chapter 6 that white identity and consciousness are remarkably strong and consistent predictors of immigration attitudes. This racial attachment is one of the most central components of immigration opinion. Whites who possess higher levels of racial identity and consciousness are far more supportive of restrictive immigration opinion. They are also more likely to believe that immigration has especially negative consequences for the United States.

The reach of white identity and consciousness exceeds the domain of immigration. As we see in Chapter 7, it also influences attitudes about policies like Social Security and Medicare – programs viewed as disproportionately benefiting whites. There are other places where it makes a difference; whites who feel a stronger attachment to their racial group are also more opposed to many of the consequences of globalization, like the outsourcing of jobs. This chapter also examines the important, but distinct role of white identity as compared to racial prejudice. While whites are interested in protecting their group and maintaining its privileged status, they are not especially invested in opposing policies that benefit racial and ethnic minorities. White identity and consciousness, it seems, are usually unrelated to attitudes toward programs like affirmative action and welfare.

The consequences of racial identity go well beyond these policy domains. White identity plays a central role in one of our most fundamental and important political activities: vote choice. The analysis in Chapter 8 reveals that even after accounting for the range of factors we usually believe motivate electoral outcomes, it is clear that white identity is a key component in support or opposition of candidates in recent presidential elections. In 2012, the evidence is straightforward; whites high on racial identity were far more supportive of Mitt Romney. Even more significantly, in 2016, we can explain the unconventional, yet successful candidacy of Donald Trump through the lens of white identity and consciousness. Trump, who ran on an anti-immigrant, pro-Social Security platform, in many ways uniquely appealed to whites who were anxious about their group's waning status. It is, perhaps, entirely unsurprising that white identity and consciousness were two of the best indicators of support for Trump.

Taken together, the evidence I have amassed across these different domains demonstrates the significance of white racial identity and consciousness in American politics. In the book's conclusion, I lay out some important observations. I describe how the vastly changing demographic landscape, which has brought white identity to the fore, is here to stay for the foreseeable future. White identifiers are not likely to be politically marginalized by these changes but are instead likely to be a key constituency targeted by political elites. The import of white identity has, therefore, significant consequences for the future of racial inequality in the United States. As whites seek to maintain the racial status quo, they are fighting to maintain a racial hierarchy, one that privileges their group, often at the expense of other racial and ethnic groups. These struggles are likely to define American politics for years to come.

The issues taken up here are not trivial. We cannot, I argue, understand contemporary racial attitudes or modern American politics, without turning our attention to the role of white racial solidarity. And so, let us begin.

2 MAKING THE INVISIBLE VISIBLE

The fish does not see the water, and whites do not see the racial nature of a white polity because it is natural to them, the element in which they move.

CHARLES MILLS (1997)

If you just put everything aside and talk about it rationally, it's not racism when you're trying to maintain a way of life and culture.

MAN AT POLITICAL RALLY FOR DONALD TRUMP, RALEIGH,
NORTH CAROLINA, NOVEMBER 7, 2016

When you're accustomed to privilege, equality feels like oppression.

UNKNOWN

The concept of race has a complicated history. Historians believe the word emerged as a folk idea in the English language between the sixteenth and eighteenth centuries. It was used as a categorizing term like *type* or *sort*, but its initial meaning was unclear (Allen 1997; Hannaford 1996; Smedley 1998; Smedley and Smedley 2004). As the English began to interact more with various populations and settled in North America in greater numbers toward the end of the seventeenth century, the term race slowly came to be used more frequently as a way to refer to different groups. It was widely employed by the eighteenth century, having been transformed into a way of justifying the European and American enslavement of Africans.

Today, we know the view that there are distinct groups of humans each belonging to different species is not a biological reality. Nevertheless, the social implications of race are significant and durable. We continue to organize our social and political world by dividing individuals into different racial groups, with hefty consequences. In the United States today, there are vast and persistent racial differences when it comes to socioeconomic status, political power, and wealth (Oliver and Shapiro 2006; Shapiro 2004). These disparities have been a tremendous source of intergroup conflict, as blacks and other ethnic minorities have struggled to achieve equality and whites have worked to maintain their power.

Despite the significant progress blacks and other racial and ethnic minorities have made toward achieving greater equality over the course of America's history, the nation today remains marked by an enduring racial hierarchy, one in which whites are at the top, blacks are at the bottom, and other racial and ethnic groups fall somewhere in between (Bobo 2004; Dawson 2001; Kim 2000).[1] This hierarchy is powerful and pervasive; it profoundly influences the life chances of individuals depending on where they are located (Massey 2007; Sidanius and Pratto 1999). I join others in arguing that this hierarchy continues to shape race relations in the United States, especially as new groups have entered a racial landscape that was once largely dominated by white and black Americans (Bobo 2004; Klinkner and Smith 1999; Masuoka and Junn 2013).

My argument is as follows: The hierarchical arrangement of racial and ethnic groups fundamentally structures the way Americans understand their own group, their identification with that group, and their group in relation to others. These group orientations subsequently organize and frame the way individuals view the political and social world. White Americans benefit tremendously from their position at the top of the hierarchy. Their group, on average, receives greater material benefits, social esteem, and political accommodation. This dominant status also means that whites have come to accept this arrangement as "normal"; they view themselves as the "default category." When these cherished privileges – ones that whites regard as almost natural – are challenged, many whites react defensively, condemning and resisting changes to the racial status quo.[2]

Over the past two decades, threats to the racial status quo have come in several forms. Massive waves of immigrants, mostly from

Central America and Asia, have changed the demographic composition of the nation. America's political, social, and economic institutions are becoming more racially and ethnically diverse, as more people of color gain access and power within these spaces. Most symbolically, America elected its first black president. The nation has also become more integrated globally. Many American jobs have moved overseas, some barriers to trade have been lifted, and the United States took new interventionist roles in the affairs of other nations. Each of these factors has challenged whites' dominant status, threatening the security of their position atop the nation's racial hierarchy.

Not all whites are reacting to these threats uniformly. I argue that it is whites who are most attached to their group, who identify with it most strongly, and who recognize their group's privileges that are most interested in preserving the racial order and most reactive to threats to whites' status. These whites are responding to these challenges by increasingly viewing the political world through the lens of their racial group identity. They are proud of their group, but are also worried that group members are experiencing discrimination, and that they have not been given their fair share in life. They also believe their group experiences competition with other racial and ethnic groups, and that whites have too little political and economic influence. They are seeking to protect whites' collective interests by opposing immigration and by supporting social welfare policies that disproportionately benefit their group. They are attempting to maintain the racial status quo by opposing political candidates they believe are threatening their group, like Barack Obama, and supporting those, like Donald Trump, they see as restoring their group's power.

Today, white identity deeply influences American politics. In what follows, I explain how this came to be and describe the nature and consequences of white racial identity. I illustrate how as a dominant group identity, white identity is sometimes latent, but it is also *reactive* – made salient by threats to the dominance of whites as a group. In making this argument, my work here challenges the leading paradigm in the study of race and American politics – namely, that the problem of racial conflict lies almost exclusively in the individual and irrational hostilities of white Americans. My framework takes up the calls of several scholars of race and public opinion, who argue that we need new ways of understanding race relations in the United States, ones that take seriously the idea that race is a fundamental organizing principle of American society, and that "racial attitudes capture aspects of the preferred group positions and those patterns of belief and affect that undergird, mobilize as needed, and make understandable the prevailing racial order" (Bobo 2004, p. 27).

Approaches to Intergroup Relations

The landscape of theories on intergroup relations is vast, but the numerous theoretical approaches to understanding group conflict and cooperation can be boiled down into roughly two categories. The first approach treats intergroup hostility as a product of the attitudes held by individuals, which are learned or adopted through socialization. In what follows, I refer to these theories as "individual oriented." The second approach considers group categories, group interests, and identities as powerful determinants of attitudes and behavior. Throughout this text, I will refer to the broad range of theories falling into this domain as "intergroup oriented."[3]

Individual Oriented Theories

Individual oriented theories focus on out-group hostility and animosity, which they see as a product of individual-level, stable characteristics that compel people to hold negative or prejudicial intergroup attitudes. They do not posit that individuals are motivated in their behavior and attitudes by group identities, interests, resources, or status. Some of these theories begin with the assumption that these out-group attitudes are acquired, usually through socialization, observation, and experience. Others argue that out-group animosity is a product of particular personality traits and is therefore somewhat learned but also somewhat innate.

One of the earliest and most prominent theories of this sort is authoritarianism. The theory of the authoritarian personality was originally conceived in the 1950s by Adorno and his colleagues as an explanation for the broader syndrome of attitudes that contributed to anti-Semitism, but that also condoned prejudice, fascism, and ethnocentrism (Adorno et al. 1950; Duckitt 1989, 2003). It generated a great deal of attention and initial enthusiasm, but excitement waned over the next several decades, in part because of flawed properties of the construct's original measure and a larger rejection of the theory's Freudian foundation.[4] In recent years, the concept of authoritarianism has been revived, with updated measures, and has been strongly linked to a number of political, social, and ideological phenomena (Feldman and Stenner 1997; Hetherington and Weiler 2009; Stenner 2005). Today, authoritarianism is more commonly conceived of as a need for social conformity accompanied by an intolerance toward those seen as challenging the social status quo (Feldman 2003; Stenner 2005). It is also characterized by a need for order, and a proclivity to view the world in black and white, rather than in shades of gray (Hetherington and Weiler 2009).

In the 1990s, Social Dominance Theory (SDT) emerged as another perspective on ethnocentrism, intolerance, and group conflict (Sidanius and Pratto 1999; Sidanius et al. 2004). Arguably, this theory bridges the divide between intergroup and individual oriented theories. The theory itself is intergroup oriented – it describes the hierarchical arrangement of groups within a society and seeks to understand the development and maintenance of such an arrangement. According to SDT, conflict is mitigated within societies by the promotion of ideologies that legitimize inequality and discrimination. Yet the theory is also individual oriented in that it proposes that individuals within societies vary along a personality dimension called social dominance orientation (SDO) (Pratto et al. 1994).[5] Those at one end of this scale prefer hierarchy and want their in-group to be dominant and superior to out-groups. Individuals at the opposite end desire more egalitarian relationships between groups in society. Like authoritarianism, SDO predicts a range of political and intergroup phenomena, as well as prejudice more generally.[6]

Symbolic politics theory offers another framework. It argues that intergroup dynamics are a function of the symbolic predispositions that individuals acquire early in life, and that then serve as powerful and enduring influences on political attitudes in adulthood. That is, attitudes toward groups in society are acquired through socialization. Whether specific symbolic attitudes are brought to bear on political preferences is a function of the salience of particular political symbols at a given time (Sears 1993; Sears and Henry 2005). Theories in this domain, like racial resentment, symbolic racism, and modern racism, elaborate on this framework, applying it specifically to race relations between blacks and whites in the United States (Kinder and Sanders 1996; Kinder and Sears 1981; McConahay and Hough 1976).[7] According to these theories, in recent decades, a new form of racism replaced more overt racial attitudes like "old-fashioned" or "Jim Crow racism," which were defined by the erroneous belief that blacks are biologically and innately inferior. Today, white prejudice toward blacks is characterized by anti-black affect coupled with the belief that blacks do not subscribe to traditional American values associated with the Protestant work ethic, like hard work and patriotism. These attitudes developed in the wake of the Civil Rights movement, facilitated by elite efforts to reframe black demands for equality as unfair attempts to acquire unearned privileges.[8]

Symbolic racism clearly plays a central role in motivating whites' political attitudes and behavior. Indeed, as I will show throughout the analyses to come, racial resentment and racial animus are significant components of white public opinion.[9] The theory, however, features an important shortcoming when it comes to contemporary race relations in the United States. Like many theories of racial conflict, it was developed specifically to explain conflict between blacks and whites. Indeed, the theory of racial resentment is very much situated in the socio-political development of modern race relations between these two groups, and it is not intended to account for whites' attitudes toward Latinos, Asians, or other minorities. This focus was not without good reason. The relationship between blacks and whites in the United States historically has been exceptional, and for many decades, prior to significant immigration in the 1990s and early 2000s, these two groups were at the center of racial conflict. What is more, many have argued that the relationship between blacks and whites is, and perhaps will remain, exceptional (Sears and Savalei 2006).[10] Nevertheless, scholarship on intergroup relations has not kept up with the nation's rapid growing racial and ethnic diversity. There are, today, few theoretical accounts that help us quantify and understand white attitudes in relation to other minority group members, including Latinos and Asians, in the same vein as those that exist to explain whites' attitudes toward blacks. Now is the time to reconsider whether predispositions are part of a more complicated portrait of intergroup relations, one in which identity plays a role alongside racial hostility. As Bobo (1983) argues, racial attitudes are likely multidimensional, and which factors matter depends on the issue at hand or the object of evaluation, in addition to context and circumstances. My account here helps fill this gap by explaining the nature of whites' racial attitudes amidst a much more racially diverse landscape.

Intergroup Oriented Theories

Much of the work in the domain of intergroup oriented theories begins with the premise that individuals categorize themselves and others into groups automatically and often unconsciously (Allport 1954; Duckitt 2003; Gaertner and Dovidio 2005). When we encounter people in the world, we immediately sort them into salient social groupings, often based on characteristics like race, gender, age, and so forth. These groups matter politically; they organize people's feelings of obligation and antagonism, drawing boundaries around who people believe should receive benefits or pay costs. When people think about the political world, social identities often are the "who" in political scientist Harold Lasswell's famous refrain that politics is about "who gets what, when, and how" (1936).

Social identity theory is one of the foundational theories under this umbrella. It posits that individuals' self-concepts are derived by their membership in various groups (Tajfel 1978; Tajfel and Turner 1979). The theory claims that individuals fundamentally desire a positive social identity. This need motivates people to make social comparisons that then give way to in-group favoritism and that enhance perceptions of the status of the group to which one belongs.[11] In other words, when individuals feel that their group is positively distinct from out-groups, their self-image as a group member is subsequently heightened. What is more, this behavior can happen under even the most minimal of circumstances. One of the tenets of social identity theory was established via a series of studies, which encompass what we now know as the minimal group paradigm, demonstrating that merely categorizing individuals into arbitrary groups in a lab setting is sufficient to elicit in-group favoritism (Tajfel 1974; Tajfel and Turner 1979).

Some of the work by students of social identity theory focuses on competition between groups over status and prestige (Tajfel and Turner 1979). Realistic group conflict theory and power theory add another element by incorporating conflict and competition over tangible resources into the study of intergroup relations (Blalock 1967; Giles and Evans 1985; Giles and Hertz 1994; LeVine and Campbell 1972; Sherif and Sherif 1953). Other theories build off this foundation but focus specifically on racial groups. In particular, group position theory argues that white hostility and prejudice are a function of the perception that racial and ethnic minorities are challenging whites' status and resources (Blumer 1958; Bobo and Hutchings 1996).[12] Similarly, the "racialized social system" theory views white prejudice as a defense of the group's privileged position in society, and argues that whites use the discourse of "color-blind" racism as a tactic to maintain their status (Bonilla-Silva 2010). And the theory of "reactionary conservatism," embodied by attitudes toward the Tea Party movement, posits that some people fear change, especially if it threatens their way of life. Whites susceptible to this predisposition want to restore the nation to a time when their group was dominant (Parker and Barreto 2013). Implicit in each of these approaches is that conflict between groups, particularly racial groups, is an inevitable and natural by-product of in-groups attempting to protect their disproportionate share of power and resources from demanding out-groups.

Racial and Ethnic Minority Group Identity

Some of the earliest work on American public opinion drew attention to the way in which social identities can powerfully shape individuals' political attitudes and behavior (Berelson, Lazarsfeld, and McPhee 1954; Campbell et al. 1960; Verba and Nie 1972). This work paid particular attention to the political importance of groups when it came to religion and union membership. But the intergroup orientated framework has been especially central to understanding the political attitudes and behavior of racial and ethnic minorities in the United States. Scholars have argued that an enduring racial hierarchy and a legacy of discrimination and oppression have led to the development of a strong racial identity among racial minorities, particularly blacks.[13] Racial identity is an important driver of black political participation and engagement (Chong and Rogers 2005; Dawson 1994; Miller et al. 1981; Shingles 1981; Tate 1993). It also motivates support for more redistributive political policies (Dawson 1994). Recent work has extended this line of thinking to explain political evaluations and engagement among Latinos and Asian Americans as well (Barreto and Pedraza 2009; Junn and Masuoka 2008; Sanchez 2006; Schildkraut 2005; Stokes-Brown 2012; Wong, Lien, and Conway 2005; Zepeda-Millán and Wallace 2013).

The Invisibility of White Identity

One implication of intergroup oriented theories should be that like racial and ethnic minorities, whites also possess a racial identity. The framework of theories like social identity theory and group position theory certainly make this inference. They suggest that demands on the part of non-whites ought to threaten whites' status, increasing the salience of white group identity or consciousness and its subsequent relevance in political decision-making. Some scholarship does, at least implicitly, make this claim. For instance, work in the vein of power theory argues that the racial context in which whites live can trigger feelings of group threat. Whites who live in more racially diverse areas should, by these accounts, feel that their group is more threatened by racial out-groups. These studies assume the importance of white racial identity, although often they do not mention or actually measure it (for an exception see Giles and Evans (1985)).[14]

Intergroup oriented theories, however, have not gained much traction among social scientists seeking to explain whites' racial attitudes. Despite the broader attention to intergroup theories in the social sciences, only a few studies have directly examined the prevalence and potential political influence of in-group attitudes among whites.[15] As sociologist Ashley Doane notes, one "major shortcoming of much of the existing literature on whiteness is its lack of empirical grounding" (Doane and Bonilla-Silva 2003, p. 17).[16] There have, however, been a handful of political scientists, most of whom are advocates of individual oriented theoretical approaches to understanding racial conflict in the United States, who have compared the effects of white identity to the effects of white racial animus on racialized policy preferences. For proponents of intergroup oriented approaches to the study of white racial attitudes, the results have been disappointing. Previous work has repeatedly demonstrated the superior predictive power of individual predispositions like racial resentment and often finds few, if any, effects when it comes to white group interests or white in-group attitudes.

Political scientist David Sears and his colleagues have engaged in some of the most rigorous efforts in political science to empirically examine the political role of white racial identity. For instance, Sears and Kinder (1985) explored whether whites' opposition to racial busing was rooted in the belief that blacks pose tangible threats to whites' interests (a claim consistent with realistic group conflict theory), or if opposition to busing was instead determined by racial resentment.[17] They uncovered no significant evidence for the claim that hostility to change in the racial status quo stems from personal or group threat. Rather, whites' lack of support for busing was significantly associated with higher levels of symbolic racism.

In another study, Kinder and Winter (2001) examined the underpinnings of the opinion divide between blacks and whites over policies related to race and social welfare. They considered a range of possible explanations for vast differences in opinion between the two groups, including racial solidarity, measured with a question from the American National Election Study (ANES) that asks individuals how close they feel to other members of their racial group. Their analysis demonstrates a powerful association, for blacks, between racial identity and policy preferences. For whites, however, they find that white in-group solidarity has almost no effect on attitudes, and therefore does little to account for racial differences in opinion. While blacks seem highly influenced by their racial identity, whites, they posit, appear primarily motivated by their out-group attitudes, and by racial resentment in particular.

In more recent work, Sears and his colleagues directly compared the political power of white identity to that of symbolic racism (Citrin and Sears 2014; Sears and Henry 2005; Sears and Savalei 2006). They make use of the Los Angeles County Social Survey (LACSS), spanning several years in the 1990s, to examine the relationship between white identity and racial policy. The measures of identity available on the LACSS are straightforward and direct. They capture the strength of white identity and are in keeping with many of the items I will use to measure white identity in the analyses to come. Nevertheless, there is little evidence from their analysis that white identity undergirds opinion on racial policies. What is more, Sears and his co-authors argue that white identity is not only politically inconsequential, but that few whites possess a racial identity in the first place, especially when compared to the degree to which blacks embrace a racial identity.

Wong and Cho (2005) undertook an extensive examination of white identity using data from the ANES Time Series spanning eight years between 1992 and 2000. To capture white racial identity, they also use a group closeness measure, and find that racial identity is quite common among white Americans, parting ways with the findings of

Sears and colleagues. In keeping with the work of Sears and others, however, Wong and Cho find little support for the notion that white racial identity is politically consequential, at least when it comes to support for federal aid to minorities, opinion on Civil Rights progress, attitudes toward government guaranteeing jobs, or support for government spending for services.

In short, the results of prior investigations of the political consequences of white racial identity have been remarkably consistent. Time and again, the same conclusion has been reached: white Americans' attachment or identification with their racial group is not a strong or significant predictor of their political preferences or behavior.

The Wrong Time and the Wrong Measures

Previous efforts to examine the potential political influence of white identity, while certainly valuable, have faced some important challenges. For one, previous scholars were constrained by data limitations. Prior to 2012, most national and publicly available opinion surveys, like the ANES, did not include a direct measure of white racial identity. For example, Wong and Cho (2005) rely on a proximate item – a measure of group closeness that was included on ANES Time Series studies between 1992 and 2000. As I will discuss in more detail in the next chapter, there is reason to worry that the closeness item may not accurately capture a sense of group attachment; instead it likely assesses feelings of sympathy or social distance. Thus, relying on the closeness item may not allow scholars to completely investigate the political power of white identity.

Sears and his co-authors do not face this measurement problem in their analysis using the LACSS. This survey included several items that more reliably measure group identity than the closeness item. But Sears and others face another important constraint; their studies were conducted with data from the 1990s and early 2000s – years before the country would recognize the diversifying effects of massive immigration, demographic change, and other factors I argue are likely to have made white identity politically salient. And if, as I and others have suggested, whites' whiteness is relevant primarily when they no longer feel as if their group's dominant status is secure, it would be years before significant challenges to whites' status would be widely perceived. In short, the conclusion that white identity is not politically consequential may very well be an artifact of the time in which such research was conducted. Today, amidst a much more diverse nation, we might reach different conclusions.

Too Narrow a Focus

When it comes to the study of race relations in the United States, both the individual oriented and intergroup oriented approaches have, as sociologist Mary Jackman argues, been driven by answering one question in particular: "how can whites' hostility to blacks be reduced, possibly even eliminated" (1994, p. 33)? Both schools of thought have paid abiding attention to white hostility and to prejudice, which they see as either an irrational antipathy (Allport 1935; Kinder and Sanders 1996; Kinder and Sears 1981; Sears 1993) or as the product of conflict over tangible resources.[18]

This emphasis on white hostility is well intentioned and important; it grew out of a desire to eliminate racial inequality and was rooted in sentiments like those expressed by Gunnar Myrdal: that the problem of race relations in the United States is really a "white man's problem" and that racial disparities are a function of white racial discrimination (Myrdal 1944). But this enduring attention to white prejudice has led to a somewhat myopic approach to the study of race in American politics. Work in this domain has not fully embraced the possibility that intergroup attitudes are partly a function of whites' efforts to defend their group's interests, and that these attitudes can be independent of individual-level expressions of anti-black animus. Even proponents of theories that take group interests more seriously have fixated on whites' prejudices and outward hostilities. Blumer's (1958) notion of a "sense of group position," for example, focuses on prejudice as a function of status threat. As I will explain more fully throughout this chapter, however, a more comprehensive treatment of white racial attitudes needs to also focus on whites' inward-looking interests, attitudes, and behaviors.

This focus on white racial animus has also guided empirical efforts to examine the political impact of white identity. The work of Sears, Wong and Cho, and others, has attended almost entirely on the relationship between white racial identity and white opinion on racialized policies associated with blacks. They have looked at whether white identity predicts opinion on minority-targeted policies like affirmative action programs, government assistance to minorities, and government efforts to ensure equal opportunity in jobs, to no avail (Sears and Savalei 2006; Wong and Cho 2005). The expectation has largely been that white racial identity should behave like white racial prejudice. What this work has found, however, is that white racial identity is largely unrelated to public opinion in the domain of minority-targeted policies; instead, whites' racial animosities, usually conceived of as racial resentment, are the primary drivers of opinion on these policies. The subsequent conclusion has been, therefore, that white racial identity is simply unimportant politically.

In what follows, I argue that we need to expand the scope of political preferences and evaluations we expect are associated with white racial identity. Rather than treating white identity as yet another expression of racial prejudice, we need instead to conceive of it as an in-group attitude, one that motivates whites to support policies and political candidates that whites see as protecting their group, but not necessarily exclusively vis-à-vis opposition to policies targeted at racial and ethnic minorities.

In-Group Favoritism and Out-Group Animosity

The expectation that white identity predicts hostility toward blacks or opposition to minority-targeted policies follows from both Blumer's group position theory and from power theory, both of which argue that perceived threats from minorities to whites' power, privileges, or resources ought to generate white hostility (Blalock 1967; Blumer 1958; Key 1949). This idea – that there's a reciprocal relationship between white identity and white racial animosity – also derives from Sumner's theory of ethnocentrism, which argues that positive feelings toward one's in-group are directly correlated with contempt toward out-groups (1906). Furthermore, some work under social identity theory has also proposed a similar interplay between in-group attitudes and out-group hostilities. Indeed, according to Brewer, "most contemporary research on intergroup relations, prejudice, and discrimination appears to accept, at least implicitly, the idea that ingroup favoritism and outgroup negativity are reciprocally related" (Brewer 1999, p. 430). Accordingly, in-group and out-group attitudes have generally been studied interchangeably, as if favoritism toward in-groups and discrimination toward out-groups are two sides of the same coin.

Brewer and others, however, have made a strong case that in-group favoritism and out-group derogation are separate phenomenon (Struch and Schwartz 1989b). Generally, evidence indicates that positive in-group attitudes and strong in-group identities do *not* systematically correlate with out-group bias or negativity (Brewer 1979). Rather, in-group identification is more strongly associated with in-group favoritism than with intergroup differentiation (Hinkle et al. 1989). In other words, group bias is routed through enhanced evaluations and support for one's in-group, rather than through out-group derogation (Brown 2000). Nevertheless, the focus on white racial prejudice, I argue, has led scholars specifically applying an intergroup oriented framework to the study of race relations to overlook these claims. This work has sought to find a direct relationship between white identity and expressions of out-group hostility, with only tepid results.

This perspective has not, however, been extended to the study of group identities among blacks. For the most part, when social scientists consider the consequences of racial solidarity among racial and ethnic minorities, they do not generally expect that such identification underlies support for policies that are detrimental to whites.[19] Instead, they anticipate, for example, that black racial identity predicts support for policies or political candidates that benefit blacks, and that is generally what research demonstrates (Herring, Jankowski, and Brown 1999; Sniderman and Piazza 2002).[20] Part of my argument, then, is that we must, to some extent, think about white identity in the way we think of black identity. To do so, we need to consider that white identity is associated with different political outcomes than we have before. White identity, I argue, ought to be strongly tied to policies and candidates that benefit whites and protect their group's status, rather than merely those that are more clearly framed as derogating out-groups.

A Theory of Dominant Group Identity

The study of both intergroup relations and racial attitudes has provided important insights into the nature of racial conflict. My approach here synthesizes many of the claims of existing theories to create a new framework, one that helps us understand when, why, and in what ways white political behavior is a function of an effort to preserve the racial hierarchy. Current theories of intergroup relations often have strikingly little to say about the behavior of dominant groups. Many either ignore dominant groups or take them for granted (Doane 1997). As Phinney (1990) noted just two decades ago, "ethnic identity among members of a dominant group in society, although it can be conceptualized, has apparently not been studied empirically" (p. 500).

Here, I seek to fill this theoretical and empirical lacuna. I begin with the concept of group identity. According to social identity theory, we, as humans, not only divide the world into groups, but we have a psychological tendency to develop strong attachments to many of the ones to which we belong. We also express favoritism toward these groups, and are motivated to achieve and maintain a positive social identity, which in turn boosts self-esteem (Tajfel 1974; Tajfel and Turner 1986). This in-group favoritism results from efforts to achieve a favorable evaluation of one's own group relative to other groups. What is more, the stronger one's identification with a group, the more meaningful that group membership is to one's self-image.

The second foundation of my approach is that, consistent with social dominance theory and group position theory, racial groups in American society are arranged hierarchically, with whites at the top, as the dominant group. Regardless of whether whites identify with their racial group, their objective categorization into the group imbues them with considerable status and privilege. Some whites might be motivated to identify with their racial group because of the sense of positive group distinctiveness they achieve by doing so. In fact, some work suggests that group identities emerge among members of high-status groups because such membership positively distinguishes group members from outsiders (Bettencourt et al. 2001). Nevertheless, the common expectation is that the status of whites as the dominant group has served as an obstacle to the development of a strong, salient group identity (Gurin 1983). As Doane explains, "The combination of existing domination with transparency enables 'whiteness' to be cast – but not named – as the larger society, the cultural mainstream, and the nation" (2003, p. 12). The experience of being white, compared to racial and ethnic minorities, means that whites are less likely to suffer prejudice, discrimination, or disadvantages due to their race. Furthermore, groups that are dominant in societies often experience the normalization of their group identities (Rosaldo 1989). White Americans reside in a cultural environment where their group is considered "mainstream." Thus, "to be white in America is not to have to think about it" (Terry 1981, p. 120). Accordingly, existing literature has generally characterized whiteness as invisible, hidden, or unmarked (Doane 1997; Frankenberg 1993, 2001; Roediger 1994).

Put another way, whites have the luxury of not thinking about their racial group and its collective interests when their status at the top of the racial hierarchy is secure. Under these circumstances, white identity likely plays only a minimal role in informing whites' political attitudes and evaluations. Instead, when whites feel secure, we are likely to see that to the extent that whites' racial attitudes inform their political preferences, it is almost exclusively via whites' individual animosities and prejudices, most likely in the form of racial resentment.

What happens, however, when whites are unable to take this racial identity for granted? How do some whites react when they feel like their privileges are being challenged or the dominant status is eroding? When many whites perceive these threats, I argue, they become more aware of their racial identity. It becomes more noticeable and important, and more likely to influence the way some whites engage with the political and social world. My claim, in simplest terms, is that dominant group identities can become salient and politically meaningful when the conditions that facilitate their invisibility are disturbed; that is, when the group believes that its status is sincerely challenged. In short, the salience and assertion of a dominant group identity is reactive; it is an effort to defend the group's position within a stratified system (Doane 1997; Perry 2007).

Making Whiteness Visible: The Role of Group Threat

Many of my expectations are consistent with Blumer's theory of group position (1958). According to Blumer, feelings of racial prejudice among dominant group members are accompanied by feelings of natural superiority, a belief that subordinate groups are "fundamentally different stock" and should be excluded from the dominant group, attitudes of entitlement and a proprietary claim to certain rights and privileges, and a fear that subordinate groups will threaten – or are threatening – these rights (Perry 2007). Blumer especially highlighted the role of threat in activating a sense of group position. Like many social scientists, his aim was to account for the roots of white hostility. He saw white identity and white prejudice as directly related.

My work here, however, steers Blumer's expectations in a different direction. I focus on the way in which the activation of in-group identity via threats to the racial hierarchy affects whites' interest in protecting their in-group and its collective interests, above and beyond out-group animus.

Threat and Identity Salience

In keeping with the claims of Blumer and other scholars of intergroup relations, I argue that threat plays an important role in the acquisition and activation of group identities. External threats, either real or perceived, can increase in-group solidarity and can distinguish the boundaries between groups (Coser 1956; Grant and Brown 1995; Kinder and Sears 1981; LeVine and Campbell 1972). For instance, Baker (1975) demonstrates that cohesion among whites in South Africa was driven by threats to their cultural distinction. Giles and Evans (1985), using data from the 1972 ANES, find that white respondents who perceived blacks as too influential and who believed that the Civil Rights movement was moving too quickly were more likely to rate their own in-group more favorably. Lau (1989) demonstrates that liberals and conservatives felt much closer to their ideological group when residing in a district with a contested election.

Threat also increases the salience or importance of a group identity.[21] By salience, I mean the relevance of an identity to a given situation. According to social identity theory – and consistent with Blumer's group position theory – a social identity should become especially evident when intergroup relations are unstable or insecure (Tajfel 1974, 1978). When a social hierarchy is unstable, the identity of low-status groups become particularly relevant to realizing change, and the identity of high-status groups become salient in resisting challenges to the status quo (Doosje, Spears, and Ellemers 2002; Ellemers, van Knippenberg, and Wilke 1990). Evidence for this claim is fairly consistent. Some work has even found that threats in the form of changes to the status quo actually elevate the blood pressure of members of high-status groups (Scheepers and Ellemers 2005). Thus, we should expect that threats to the racial hierarchy ought to make whites' racial identity more salient.

Threat does not simply make group identities more relevant, however. It also promotes in-group cohesion by fostering group norms that serve to protect the in-group from perceived out-group threats

(Brewer 1999). Furthermore, strong group identifiers are more likely to respond to threats collectively, rather than individually (Doosje, Spears, and Ellemers 2002). In other words, they tend to view challenges to the group via their group's collective interests, rather than their own self-interests. And feelings of threat or deprivation also make strong group identifiers more inclined to engage in collective social protest activity (Grant and Brown 1995). Accordingly, we would expect that strong white identifiers are most reactive to threats to their group, and this threat fosters white identifier's proclivity to view the world through the lens of their group identity, and to be more attuned to the interests of their in-group.

From Group Identity to Political Behavior

The authors of one of the most canonical books in political science, *The American Voter* (Campbell et al. 1960), paid special attention to the role of groups in political behavior. A group, they argued, is "a psychological reality that exerts greater or lesser attractive force upon its members" (p. 306). They hypothesized that "the higher the identification of the individual with the group, the higher the probability that he will think and behave in ways that distinguish members of his group from non-members" (p. 307). Today, there is now a mass of evidence that strong, subjective group identities are closely tied to higher levels of political cohesion (see Huddy 2013 for a review). For an identity to matter for political attitudes and behavior, however, it must be relevant. Threat to one's group, I argue, activates one's group identity, making it more readily accessible, and more likely to influence the way one engages in politics. It follows, therefore, that when their racial identity is activated, whites are more likely to consider whether political policies and candidates help or harm their racial group. Strong group identifiers, in turn, should be more supportive of policies or candidates they believe benefit their group and preserve its interests (Knowles et al. 2014; Lowery et al. 2006; Sidanius et al. 1997; Tate 1993; Weller and Junn 2018). They should also display greater levels of in-group bias and pride (Jackson and Smith 1999; Mullen, Brown, and Smith 1992) and be more inclined to participate in group-oriented political action on behalf of their group.

  Previous work on identity and threat has often made a distinction between realistic group interests and symbolic interests. For example, according to realistic group conflict theory, group threats come in the form of real, tangible resources. But I join others in arguing that threat need not be real – it can simply be perceived – nor does it need to occur with respect to economic or physical resources. Outgroups may also threaten the dominant group's symbolic interests (Kinder and Sanders 1996; Sniderman, Hagendoorn, and Prior 2004; Stephan and Stephan 1996).

There is some debate in the intergroup relation literature over whether realistic threats matter more for political cohesion than symbolic threats.[22] Parsing which types of threats might be more likely to politically mobilize white identifiers is an important avenue for future work, but the distinction between real tangible threats and symbolic threats is less important for my interests here. My argument merges symbolic and realistic approaches by suggesting we consider perceived realistic threats as a potential source of status threat. Prior work certainly supports the claim that a sense of realistic group deprivation, relative to other groups, influences political behavior. For example, in 1968, whites who felt their group was doing worse relative to blacks were more inclined to support George Wallace's presidential candidacy (Vanneman and Pettigrew 1972). Important for my argument is that not all group members tend to react to this sense of relative deprivation; rather, it is the most strongly identified members of a group who are most likely to react to a sense of relative deprivation by demonstrating political cohesion and politically mobilizing (Struch and Schwartz 1989a).[23]

Group Consciousness

There is strong evidence that group status threat promotes collective action among group members. It also orients groups toward political solutions to threat. Politicians can facilitate this process by making group members aware of their grievances, thus increasing the link between social identities and politics (Huddy 2003). In other words, threat can *politicize* a group identity. It therefore follows that threat might be instrumental in the promotion of a concept called group consciousness – a sense of group attachment defined by the belief that group members should work together to improve the position of their group (Chong and Rogers 2005; Conover 1988; Gurin, Miller, and Gurin 1980; Miller et al. 1981). It is, as McClain et al. (2009) put it succinctly, "in-group identification politicized by a set of ideological beliefs about one's group's social standing, as well as a view that collective action is the best means by which the group can improve its status and realize its interests" (p. 476). If dominant group members feel that their group's status is in jeopardy, one consequence may be the development and activation of not merely group identity, but a group consciousness as well.

It is important to clarify the distinction between white identity and white consciousness. White identity is also politicized; it is a lens through which many whites interact and engage in the political world. It influences political attitudes and behaviors. Consciousness is comprised of group identity along with a very specific set of political beliefs about one's in-group. It requires that individuals not only feel attached to their group, but that they also believe their group experiences some type of deprivation and should work collectively within the political system to address the group's grievances. It is, in short, a *mobilized* political identity.

We can think about the distinction between group identity and group consciousness by considering an example outside the domain of race. One might, for instance, have an identity as a college student, and maybe even a student at a specific university. One's position as a college student may make one inclined to adopt particular policy positions on issues related to student loans, state curricula, or university funding. But at the same time, one may see little need to organize collectively with other college students to protest the treatment of college students or their circumstances. You could imagine, however, how a threat to cut funding from one's campus, or the introduction of a policy directly targeting university students, might encourage a group of college students to want to act collectively to address the group's concerns. In short, a social identity can develop into a sense of consciousness when a group feels sufficiently threatened or particularly concerned about their group's position within a hierarchy. Consciousness has often been applied to understanding the political behavior of subordinate groups, but the architects of the concept of group consciousness argued that for high-status groups, political consciousness can matter as well. For high-status groups, group consciousness ought to be aimed at justifying and maintaining a group's advantage (Gurin, Miller, and Gurin 1980).

Part of my effort here is not merely to determine whether whites identify with their racial group, but also whether they possess a sense of group consciousness. Given the theoretical dimensions of group consciousness, we would expect racially conscious whites to identify with their group, feel that their group experiences some type of relative deprivation, and support their group working together to improve or maintain the status of their group. Furthermore, because consciousness is an especially politicized attachment, my expectation is that relative to white identity alone, consciousness ought to be more deeply tied to political attitudes and behavior. It should more strongly predict support for policies and candidates that benefit whites' collective interests, and it should be closely tied to greater levels of political participation among whites.

The Importance of "Big Events"

I have established that threat is an important component to the activation of dominant group identities. Next, we must consider the nature of threats that might challenge the racial order and the dominant status of whites in the United States. For threats to trigger identity at the mass level, they need to be prevalent, identifiable, and significant.[24] Blumer offers important insight regarding the type of threats that might activate white identity. He argues that "big events" in the public arena are what trigger attention to a group's relative and potentially waning position – those events that are "momentous, that touch deep sentiments, that seem to raise fundamental questions about relations, and that awaken strong feelings of identification with one's racial group" (1958, p. 6).[25]

If we think back over the span of US history, there are moments that seem quite clearly to meet these criteria. For instance, in the early 1850s, a wave of immigrants from Germany and Ireland stoked anxiety among American citizens. In response to this influx of immigrants, the Native American Party, later known as the Know Nothing Party, gained a modicum of support among citizens who wanted to limit the influence of these newcomers. The Civil War marked an especially clear challenge to the racial hierarchy, particularly for white southerners. The Great Migration of blacks out of the rural South to the Northeast, Midwest, and West elevated racial tensions in major US cities. Around the same time, in the 1920s, the racial order was challenged as the country wrestled with the rapid demographic changes brought about by waves of immigrants from Eastern and Southern Europe. Thirty years later, whites likely perceived the events of the Civil Rights movement as a clear effort to upend the racial order. Unfortunately, due to data limitations, we are unable to investigate fully the possibility that during these moments, white identity was salient and politically potent. If we could go back in time, however, we very well might find that white racial solidarity was especially politically relevant around these moments.

Today's political and social climate has raised new challenges regarding the nation's racial dynamics. The first is the significant change in the racial and ethnic composition of the United States facilitated by a massive wave of immigrants that, according to Census projections, will result in whites becoming a numerical minority by 2044 (Abrajano and Hajnal 2015; Colby and Ortman 2014; Craig and Richeson 2014a; Hajnal and Rivera 2014). These phenomena are associated with both the loss of numerical status, and the introduction of Latinos and Asians as additional groups in a system stratified by race. Indeed, work has already demonstrated that many white Americans are especially threatened by these demographic changes (Abascal 2015; Craig and Richeson 2014a, 2014b; Danbold and Huo 2015; Major, Blodorn, and Major Blascovich 2018; Norton and Sommers 2011; Outten et al. 2012). The second momentous event was the election of the nation's first African American president, Barack Obama – one especially symbolic of whites' loss of political dominance (Parker, Sawyer, and Towler 2009).

My argument is that this confluence of events, beginning with immigration, combined with demographic change and the election of Obama, have all served as powerful threats to whites' dominant status. As a result, white identity is now activated and politically relevant. In fact, in some domains, it is *chronically salient*. That is, whites bring their racial identity to bear on certain political preferences relevant to protecting their group readily, automatically, and consistently.

As is the case with other identities and political predispositions, however, we ought to find that white identity is not always the lens through which whites view the landscape of political policies or candidates. White identity is not, in other words, always politically consequential, nor would we expect it to matter in all domains. For instance, it seems hard to imagine that white identity predicts opinion on an issue like climate change, which has not been markedly framed as harming or benefiting whites as a group. We would not necessarily expect white identity to consistently predict evaluations of political candidates, either. But we should consider the possibility that politicians can activate white identity, either by way of their own race if they are not white, or by drawing attention to potential threats to whites' status and by campaigning to protect that status.

The Political Consequences of White Racial Solidarity

What might we anticipate to be the effects of threats to a dominant identity? For one, dominant group members ought to engage in behaviors intended to maintain the strength, cohesiveness, and security of the group (Wohl, Branscombe, and Reysen 2010). The assertion of this identity should manifest as a preservation of the status quo – an effort to maintain political, social, and economic systems under the control of the dominant group (Levin et al. 1998). As I described earlier, the expectation of previous work, especially that which examined white identity, is that efforts to protect the group should generate out-group hostility. Yet I argue that instead we should consider the ways in which status threat motivates whites to turn inward, amplifying in-group bias and motivating whites to support policies and politicians they see as preserving their group's privileged status and minimizing threats. White racial solidarity should also, in turn, be linked to opposition to policies and political elites that whites see as harming their group's collective interests.

In making this claim, I am not suggesting that threats to dominant groups, like whites, do not also generate some degree of out-group hostility. Instead, I argue that we should follow the expectations of a long line of work in social identity theory, which demonstrates that in-group favoritism and out-group hostility are separate phenomenon, rather than two sides of the same coin (Brewer 1979). Group threat directed at whites may indeed generate some out-group animus, but my interest here is the effect of white in-group identity net prejudice. In other words, how does white racial solidarity matter politically above and beyond the effects of racial hostility? My claim is that white racial solidarity is far more consequential for policies that benefit whites, and considerably less associated with policies that benefit or harm racial and ethnic minorities.

My approach rests on the foundation of previous studies of intergroup relations, which demonstrate that in-group favoritism and out-group hostility are distinct. There are several reasons why we might expect white racial solidarity to be more tightly linked with efforts to protect one's group, as opposed to greater levels of racial hostility. For instance, many whites might see efforts to protect their group and secure its interests as a more normatively acceptable response to status threat than overt racial hostility. It may also be cognitively easier for whites to understand how policies benefit or harm their own group, than it is for them to consider how policies that are explicitly tied to racial and ethnic minorities might subsequently affect whites. Furthermore, most racialized policies in the United States are not framed as harming or coming at the expense of whites, making it even less likely that whites see minority-targeted policies as helpful or harmful to their group.

Where, then, and in what ways might we expect white racial solidarity to matter? First, we should find that white identity is intimately tied to American identity. Part of the preservation of whites' dominant status lies in their ability to cast their group as mainstream American. White identifiers should therefore prefer a more exclusionary American identity, one whose features closely mirror the characteristics of most whites. We should also expect that white identity should operate like other social identities. Strong identifiers should possess a sense of pride in their group. But, as Blumer posits, the racial hierarchy should also significantly structure whites' attitudes; we should therefore also expect that members of the dominant group, in the face of threat, express a confluence of attitudes that suggest they are concerned about their group and its status. White identifiers should recognize their group's privileged status and feel entitled to the advantages their group members possess. At the same time, they should also express a sense of grievance over the apparent challenges to their status, expressing the belief that whites are in competition with other racial groups, that whites experience discrimination, or that whites are being treated unfairly.

If, as I argue, whites see immigration as a serious challenge to whites' dominance, then white racial solidarity ought to be especially linked with opposition to immigration. It should also be tied to support for policies that I argue disproportionately benefit whites and are associated with whiteness, like Social Security and Medicare spending, and with more favorable views on legacy college admissions. At the same time, if I am correct and white identity is not another manifestation of out-group hostility, we should find, as others have, little to no relationship between white racial solidarity and opposition to black-targeted policies like affirmative action or welfare spending.

Finally, if white identity is truly central to the way in which many whites view the political world, it ought to be associated with evaluations of certain political candidates. The authors of *The American Voter* (Campbell et al. 1960) noted that politicians have to help establish the link between groups and political evaluations. They argued that in some instances, these links are already "built into" the object of orientation by way of the political candidate being a member of the group – or in the case of Barack Obama – being so obviously *not* a member of the group. As the first black president, Obama represented a serious challenge to whites' dominance. White identity should therefore be associated with opposition to Obama, and to non-white political candidates more generally, whose race makes whites' racial identity a salient component of their political evaluations. But we might also find that white political candidates who have appealed to whites' desire to protect their group should also activate white identity. Politicians like George Wallace, Richard Nixon, Patrick Buchanan, and of course, Donald Trump, have all arguably signaled to whites that they intend to maintain the racial hierarchy. As a result, we ought to find that white in-group attitudes have been significantly related to support for these candidates as well.

The Nature of White Identity

When, how, and among whom strong social identities are adopted is an important research question. It is also a question that is difficult to address with cross-sectional observational data, or even single-shot experimental data, where one can only get a sense of individuals' levels of group identification at a particular moment. Truly studying the development and adoption of a group identity would be better done over time and is not the primary aim of this book. I hope future work takes the findings here as the beginning of an effort to understand which whites are more likely to adopt strong racial identities and why. Here, however, the principal goal is of equal, if not greater importance: to understand when and in what ways white racial solidarity is politically consequential.

Nevertheless, in the pages to follow, I will consider what characteristics and personality traits are associated with higher levels of white identity. I examine whether white racial solidarity is linked with certain demographic characteristics, including levels of education, where one lives, and the racial composition of one's community. I also examine whether levels of white identity or consciousness are a function of real or perceived economic deprivation. And I consider the extent to which certain personality traits underlie the propensity to adopt a strong racial identity.

Whites as an Oppressed Minority

Whites who identify with their racial group today do not do so in a vacuum. Their decision to identify with their racial group, the content of that identity, and the way they choose to express it is also likely a function of the way in which whites perceive racial identity to matter among other racial groups. Whites today have watched racial and ethnic minorities develop strong racial identities aimed at protecting their own groups' interests, and many whites – willfully unaware of the long and significant legacy of racial oppression experienced by people of color – may think it is appropriate for them to do the same. They might therefore adopt not just a sense of grievance about the loss of their group's status, but may also co-opt the language of subordination and oppression. Many of these whites may feel as if their group is not getting its fair share, perhaps because those benefits are going to another group. They may wonder why they, too, cannot get government aid or assistance directed at their group, and they may also seek to celebrate and express pride in their racial group in the way they believe other racial groups choose to do. In other words, white identity may be, in part, a reaction to the development of other strong racial identities in American society, and its nature may be, to some extent, modeled after these other identities.

It is also important to note that while I anticipate that a sizeable number of whites do indeed identify with their racial group, we certainly would not expect white racial identity to approach the levels of identity we observe among blacks. Indeed, the long history of racial subordination and discrimination blacks have experienced, coupled with black elite efforts to foster a strong group consciousness among their group, has undoubtedly contributed to the development of strong and widely adopted racial identity among blacks (Dawson 1994; Gurin, Miller, and Gurin 1980). Whites as a group have not, by and large, faced similar experiences, and therefore we would not expect their levels of identity to approach those of blacks in the United States. Nevertheless, we should find that white identity is far from undetectable. As we will see, a substantial proportion of whites possess a strong racial identity. What is more, levels of white racial identity have not changed much among the larger white American population in the past seven years, suggesting a strong degree of stability.

White Identity as a Recognition of White Privilege

A growing body of work in the social sciences under the auspices of "whiteness studies," has focused, from a normative perspective, on critiquing the reproduction and maintenance of systems of racial inequality (Hartigan Jr. 1997).[26] A great deal of this research has noted the invisibility of whiteness or the notion that whites do not think about their racial group in a meaningful way (Delgado and Stefancic 1997; Lipsitz 1998; Perry 2001). Ethnographic work has consistently found that individuals described being white as "nothing" or "normal" (Jackson II and Heckman 2002; Perry 2002, 2007).[27]

"Whiteness" studies also focus on the construction of social privilege and power from which whites primarily benefit, all while whites deny that such stratification has a racial basis (Frankenberg 1993). Some of this research explains how whites actively try to minimize or deny their privileged status, often through subscription to ideologies like color-blind racism (Doane and Bonilla-Silva 2003; Lipsitz 1998; Lowery, Knowles, and Unzueta 2007). And with social justice intentions, some have started a "new abolitionist movement" aimed at eliminating "whiteness" (Ignatiev and Garvey 1996; Mazie et al. 1993; Roediger 1994). Work under this vein emphasizes whiteness as a means by which to justify systems of oppression and privilege and argues that this identity should be deconstructed and eliminated.

Social psychologists and sociologists have also tackled the issue of whiteness from a similar perspective. This work was largely pioneered by Helms (Helms 1984, 1995), who developed a five-stage model of identity formation. Her model led to the construction of the White Racial Attitude Identity Scale (WRAIS).[28] Unlike the way in which I describe racial identity throughout this book – as a conscious favoritism for one's in-group and recognition that one's group has shared interests – Helms defines racial identity as a progression from abandonment of racism to the adoption of a nonracist, positive identification. In other words, this identity is viewed as a normative, psychological process resulting in a "healthy nonracist identity."[29] This scale has been primarily used by psychologists as a way to understand how behavioral predispositions produce psychological counseling outcomes. In short, the common thread tying together much of this work is an emphasis on the need for whites to become aware of their racial identity and the privileges that accompany being white as part of a move toward social justice and change.

While important, this work takes an approach to the study of identity distinct from that detailed in this book. Unfortunately, most of the whites who possess high levels of white identity in my analyses are not racially conscious in a way that is intended to promote greater racial equality. Nevertheless, my work here still shares many of the same broader goals of the research being conducted in the domain of "whiteness" studies; the aim is to understand how white racial solidarity helps maintain systems of inequality – an important step in working toward a more racially egalitarian society.

Conclusion

I have now argued that white racial solidarity ought to be an important component to the way in which whites arrive at their opinion on a range of important political policies and candidates. Some whites, I argue, possess a strong sense of attachment to their racial group. When their group's dominant position is secure, whites' racial identity is not especially politically consequential. But when "big events" in the political environment signal a threat to whites' dominant status, white racial solidarity can become politically relevant, influencing whites' political attitudes and behavior. Namely, in the face of status threat, white racial solidarity predicts support for policies and political candidates that whites perceive as benefiting their racial group and preserving its privileges. In other words, whites high on racial identity seek to preserve the racial hierarchy, and to protect the status quo.

Part of my contribution lies in my ability to demonstrate that white racial solidarity matters above and beyond existing and dominant explanations for white public opinion. We should, for instance, find that whites' desire to preserve their group's interests is more politically consequential than individual self-interest (Bobo 2004). We should also find that white racial solidarity remains politically powerful even after accounting for symbolic predispositions, like racial resentment. Furthermore, white identity should matter above and beyond standard elements in political decision-making, like partisanship, political ideology, and demographic characteristics. In the analyses to follow, I test these expectations, and demonstrate that white racial solidarity is indeed an important element in contemporary public opinion.

3 THE MEASUREMENT AND MEANING OF GROUP TIES

> I seize the word identity. It is a key word. You hear it over and over again. On this word will focus, around this word will coagulate, a dozen issues, shifting, shading into each other.
>
> ROBERT PENN WARREN (1965)

It seems hard to imagine, but the idea of an identity, as we conceive of it today, is relatively new. The word comes from the Latin root *idem*, meaning "the same," and while its English usage can be traced to the sixteenth century, it did not enter the common parlance of the social sciences until the 1950s (Gleason 1983). It was then that it appeared as a way to characterize the role of organized religion and ethnicity in American life (Herberg 1955). From there, during the political and social turmoil of the 1960s, the term identity gained further traction as a means to explain the nature and attachment to region, to nation, and to race (Erikson 1966; Morton 1961; Woodward 1958).[1]

Today, the study of group identities is flourishing. Scholarly attention to the topic has grown exponentially.[2] Despite the ubiquity of work on the concept, however, students and observers of group identities and identity politics face criticism about a dearth of conceptual clarity and consensus in the discipline. As Abdelal et al. note, there is a "lack of precision about what 'identity' actually means" (2001, p. 6) – so much so that some scholars have advocated for abandoning the concept entirely (Brubaker and Cooper 2000).[3]

Such a recommendation, which would surely lead social scientists to throw out the proverbial baby with the bathwater, is becoming less pertinent today as political and social psychologists have come much closer to a consensus about the meaning and role of group identities. Generally, they have circled around the notion of an identity as a psychological attachment to a group. Nevertheless, this history of conceptual ambiguity has facilitated some crucial challenges to my examination of white identity today. A lack of agreement over the meaning of identity and how to study it means there is still some disagreement over how to measure it (Abdelal et al. 2009; McClain et al. 2007; Sniderman and Piazza 2002). Since there is no standard set of measures upon which to draw, part of my endeavor will be to develop and advocate for a measure of white racial identity. I will also proceed with developing a measure of white racial consciousness – of which identity is a component – that is guided by existing work.

My efforts are not intended to add more noise to the landscape of identity measures. On the contrary, I will draw on theories of social identity, existing efforts to arrive at consensus in the identity literature, and a series of studies, which have adopted similar measures to one another, in constructing my own measure – one that is intended to be straightforward and universal. With some modifications, I employ a measurement strategy that has been increasingly used by scholars to measure a range of group identities. The result is a reliable, valid measure of group identity that can readily be employed in future studies.

Social scientists have employed a variety of methodological approaches to the study of group identities.[4] I rely on survey measures – the backbone of public opinion research – as a means to examine white identity straightforwardly and accessibly. Some might argue that such an approach is a too limited and confined means by which to study something as complicated and nuanced as group identity. Part of the analysis here, however, will demonstrate that the close-ended survey questions I put forth are actually capturing the sentiments of group identity as intended. In other words, people mean what I think they mean when they self-report their level of racial identity on a public opinion survey.

The measures I propose are *explicit* measures of white racial identity. They purposefully and directly ask whites about their racial identification. Some previous work sought to measure white identity under the assumption that it is an *implicit* or subconscious identity; this work used an adaptation of the Implicit Association Test, where study participants are timed as they associate certain words on a computer screen with specific racial groups (Knowles and Peng 2005).[5] While important, this research was conducted under the prevailing assumption that white identity is latent, invisible, and hard for whites to articulate. Part of my aim is to challenge these conventions and to demonstrate that dominant group identities, like white identity, are not always hidden. White identity is an overt social identity, held consciously by whites, and it can be measured reliably and validly using explicit survey questions.

From here, I will describe the different components that measures of group identity and group consciousness ought to capture, while laying out the survey items that correspond to these dimensions. Then, I will show the extent to which white Americans subscribe to a racial identity and racial consciousness, and discuss how respondents describe and justify, in their own words, their responses to survey items intended to capture these constructs. Finally, for those interested in the psychometric properties of these measures, including an empirical examination of their reliability and validity, the latter half of the chapter will be devoted to such analyses.

We will make a number of important discoveries as part of this endeavor. The first is that a noteworthy number of white Americans do identify with their racial group – on the order of 30 to 40 percent. A somewhat smaller, but still significant percentage of whites possess a sense of racial consciousness. We will also see that white identity is not merely party identification, ideology, racial prejudice, or some other political attitude or social predispositions by another name. It is also not, as I will demonstrate, a proxy for white supremacy or extremism. What is more, the measures are demonstrably reliable and valid, and we can move forward, examining the political consequences of white identity, with confidence.

Sources of Evidence

In the pages to come, I rely on evidence gleaned from multiple public opinion surveys to measure white racial solidarity and investigate its political power. I frequently employ the gold standard of public opinion data – the American National Election Studies (ANES) Time Series. The ANES has been conducted among nationally representative probability samples of American citizens in every presidential election year, as well as many mid-term years, since 1952. We can be reasonably confident that the results from the ANES can be extrapolated to the white American population more generally. For most of the history of the ANES, interviews were conducted in person both before and after the election. The ANES asks a wide range of questions on electoral participation, public opinion, political and social attitudes, and voting behavior; thus, it will be especially valuable for my purposes.

At several points throughout this book, I will make use of a number of the ANES Time Series studies, although primarily those conducted in 2012 and 2016, both of which included a key measure of white identity that I will describe in more detail later in this chapter. The 2012 ANES was conducted in two waves, the first of which was completed before the election, beginning in early September 2012. Post-election interviews were conducted beginning November 7, 2012, and continuing into January 2013. For the first time in the history of the ANES Time Series, the 2012 face-to-face study was supplemented with a study conducted on the Internet among an entirely separate sample. Because the study designs vary, the samples are different, and because of the potential for different modes – or ways of administering the survey – to influence how participants respond to questions on the surveys, I treat the two modes as separate studies. The face-to-face sample was comprised of 2,054 respondents, 916 of whom are non-Hispanic whites. The Internet sample consisted of 3,860 participants, 2,593 of whom are non-Hispanic whites.

The 2016 ANES Time Series was also conducted in two waves, both in person and online, beginning in the two months prior to the 2016 election in November. Respondents were re-interviewed starting on November 9, 2016. The face-to-face survey had 1,181 respondents, including 797 non-Hispanic whites. The online supplement consisted of 3,090 respondents, 2,242 of whom are non-Hispanic whites.

In addition to the ANES Time Series studies, I rely on an additional study conducted among a nationally representative probability sample. In 2010, my colleagues and I at the University of Michigan fielded a survey among 758 non-Hispanic white adult US citizens via the firm Knowledge Networks (KN) (now GfK).[6] The KN survey included a central measure of white identity, as well as a range of questions gauging political attitudes and preferences. KN recruited participants using an address-based probability sampling frame, and participants receive free Internet access and a computer, if needed, in exchange for responding to the firm's surveys. This method produces high-quality national probability samples, and includes households that did not initially have Internet access or a computer.

I also bring to bear evidence from the 2016 ANES Pilot Study, which was conducted between January 22 and January 28, 2016. The sample consisted of 1,200 individuals, 875 of whom were non-Hispanic white. These respondents were part of an opt-in Internet panel housed by the survey firm YouGov. While designed to pilot questions for later use on the 2016 Time Series Study, given that the pilot was conducted around the 2016 presidential primaries, it is especially useful. It included not only a core measure of white identity, but also measures of white consciousness.[7] What is more, the study allows me to investigate attitudes and behavior at a much earlier point in the election process. While not a probability sample, it is comprised of a large and diverse population of respondents who volunteer to complete online surveys. Respondents are selected into the panel by sample matching, which effectively creates a pool of respondents who resemble the US population with respect to gender, age, race, and education (Rivers 2006).

To supplement these studies, I fielded two of my own surveys among nationally diverse convenience samples. The first was undertaken with a sample recruited by the firm Survey Sampling International (SSI) in July of 2013. SSI recruits individuals to their Internet-based panel via opt-in methods, and provides a census-balanced sample by selecting respondents based on demographic attributes within their large panel.[8] This study was conducted among 798 non-Hispanic whites. It was administered to respondents in two waves, with the span of a week separating wave 1 and wave 2 to reduce the possibility that responses to questions in wave 1 might subsequently bias responses to items in wave 2. The 2013 SSI Study included measures of white identity and white consciousness.

I fielded a second two-wave study via the survey firm YouGov. Wave 1 was collected in October 2016, prior to the US presidential election, and included 1,467 non-Hispanic white adult US citizens. Wave 2 re-interviewed 600 of the respondents from wave 1, and was conducted just after the presidential election in November of 2016.[9] This study also included measures of both racial identity and racial consciousness.

Altogether, I provide evidence for my claims from six primary sources spanning six years.[10] I am therefore able to demonstrate that my results are robust over time and across multiple sources, conducted in multiple modes.[11] There are some constraints to my approach; I am not always able to measure racial identity and consciousness with the full range of appropriate questions, which I describe below. I also do not have the luxury of testing the predictive power of white identity or consciousness over a much broader span of time, or before and after key political events like the election of Barack Obama. Nevertheless, in the analysis to come, we shall see that even with truncated and at times proximate measures of identity and consciousness, it is clear that whites' in-group attitudes are powerfully linked to their political attitudes and behavior.

Measuring Group Identity

As originally conceived by Tajfel (1978), a social identity is "that part of an individual's self-concept which derives from his knowledge of his membership of a social group (or groups) together with the value and emotional significance attached to that membership" (p. 63). From this definition, scholars have gleaned that social identities have both a cognitive and affective component (Brubaker and Cooper 2000; Citrin, Wong, and Duff 2001; Ellemers, Kortekaas, and Ouwerkerk 1999). As the field has grown, there have been a number of attempts to define and distinguish between additional identity dimensions but, generally, efforts to measure group identity reflect this common conception.

The cognitive dimension of identity entails the most basic act of self-categorization. It is the response to the question, "Who am I?" We routinely answer this question, grouping ourselves into nationalities, religions, occupations, and so forth. In the United States, categorizing ourselves into a racial group is second nature. We identify as black or white, bi-racial or multiracial, in the same way we think of ourselves as men or women. Americans frequently and deliberately engage in racial self-categorization, checking the box for their corresponding race or ethnicity on forms, applications, and surveys. In the analysis throughout this book, each study participant will have marked themselves as a non-Hispanic white person on a public opinion survey.

Yet not all groups into which we might self-categorize are important to our self-concepts. We often place ourselves into groups toward which we do not feel especially attached or about which we do not feel strongly. One can identify as an American without feeling especially patriotic. A person might think of themselves as Jewish without being especially religious. Someone may have attended a college or university without possessing much in the way of school spirit.[12] It is not until we have a stake in our group identities, when they acquire emotional significance, that such attachments influence behavior (Tajfel 1974). In other words, as Citrin, Wong, and Duff (2001) note, identifying *as* a group member is not the same as identifying *with* a group. It is this latter component – the strength and significance of a social identity – that the affective dimension of group identity addresses. It is also this dimension that is of special interest in efforts to understand the relationship between group identity and political behavior.

Under the umbrella of this affective component, political psychologists have employed measures of group identity intended to capture several subscales. They include (1) the subjective importance of a social identity, (2) the valence of feelings one has toward group members, and (3) a subjective sense of belonging or commonality with the group. These elements have been used to measure a range of group identities, including national identity (Citrin, Wong, and Duff 2001; Huddy and Khatib 2007; Sniderman, Hagendoorn, and Prior 2004; Theiss-Morse 2009), ethnic identity (Junn and Masuoka 2008), partisanship (Greene 1999; Huddy, Mason, and Aarøe 2015), religious identity (Winter 1996), and even artificially assigned identities in laboratory settings (Patterson and Bigler 2007). My proposed measure of white identity contributes to the convergence around these measures. I turn now to describing the individual components of a white identity measure.

Identity Centrality

First and perhaps foremost, a measure of group identity ought to capture the *centrality* and significance of membership in a group (Cameron 2004; Leach et al. 2008; Morris, Stryker, and Serpe 1994; Sellers et al. 1998).[13] Fortunately, one of the oldest and most direct survey measures of group identity assesses centrality quite clearly. In 1976, political scientist Michael Hooper introduced a general measure of identity, which drew on the methods the Survey Research Center at the University of

Michigan had developed to measure attachment or identification with a political party. He adapted the structure of this measure to create a survey item that would assess individuals' level of identification with any number of social groups (Hooper 1976). It asks respondents how *important* it is for them to identify with a specific group.[14]

Adapting this question for whites, we can assess the centrality of white identity with the following question: "*How important is being white to your identity?*" Response options range from "extremely important" to "not at all important" on a five-point scale. This is the measure most frequently employed throughout the analysis that is to come. It is a straightforward and direct survey item that captures the degree to which race is a significant identity for whites. It also has the virtue of having been included on each survey analyzed throughout this book, including three national, publicly available surveys – the 2012 ANES, the 2016 ANES Pilot Study, and the 2016 Time Series Study.

Group Evaluations

Most theoretical treatments of group identity acknowledge that psychological attachments to groups are accompanied by an emotional valence (Cameron 2004; Luhtanen and Crocker 1992; Sellers et al. 1997). In other words, people might feel positively or negatively toward the group with which they identify. This expectation is partly derived from the original architecture of social identity theory, which posits that one of the key functions of a group identity is to maintain an individual's positive self-regard (Tajfel 1978; Tajfel and Turner 1979). Accordingly, most measures of identity contain items that assess how individuals evaluate their group.

When it comes to racial identity among whites, assessing this aspect of identity seems especially important. As a dominant identity, whiteness carries some hefty baggage. White identity has been associated with the oppression and subordination of other racial or ethnic groups. Overt identification with other whites has been tied to white supremacist hate groups, including the Ku Klux Klan and neo-Nazi organizations. In less extreme terms, many whites might recognize the extent to which their race influences the way they are treated in broader society, and the opportunities or benefits they are afforded, perhaps unfairly. In short, many whites might see their identity as having an effect on their lives, but they may not view this identity in a positive light. It therefore seems prudent to parse out the white identifiers who view their group positively from those who do not. One approach is to assess the extent to which whites feel proud of their group. I therefore ask whites, "To what extent do you feel that white people in this country have a lot to be proud of?" with five response options ranging from "a great deal" to "none at all."

A third element of social identity concerns the ties that bind an individual to a social group. One way to think about in-group ties is as a sense of belonging or commonality. Individuals are more likely to feel attached to a particular group, or believe that the group represents them well, if they feel they have a lot in common with other group members.[15] Some might consider this dimension to be a high bar for whites to surpass when it comes to group identification. If the group's dominant status has afforded its members the ability to take racial identification for granted, it may also have fostered the belief that whites are a diverse, heterogeneous group, sharing few universal and distinct qualities, interests, or beliefs. In other words, as an "invisible" identity, whiteness may not have a distinct set of narratives, traits, or cultural components readily associated with it, making it more difficult to agree that whites have much in common with one another. To assess this component of racial identity, respondents are asked, "How much do you think whites in the United States have more in common with one another than they do with racial and ethnic minorities?" Response options range, on a five-point scale, from "A great deal more in common" to "Nothing at all in common." An alternative variation asks, "How much would you say that whites in this country have a lot in common with one another?"

To summarize, my proposed measure of white identity is comprised of the following items:

- *How important is being white to your identity?*
- *To what extent do you feel that white people in this country have a lot to be proud of?*
- *How much would you say that whites in this country have a lot in common with one another?*

A Single-Item Measure of White Identity

As is often the case in social science work, we cannot always measure white identity with the ideal set of survey questions I have put forth.

In fact, throughout much of this book, due to the limited availability of a white identity measure on national surveys, I will often rely on just a single question – the racial importance item.[16] From a measurement perspective, single-item measures are suspect. One cannot, for instance, calculate the internal reliability of a single-item measure, and such a measure is more vulnerable to the sort of random measurement error that is often canceled out with the use of multiple items. By using a single item, we can expect to introduce more statistical noise into the analysis that follows, and are likely to find weaker relationships between white identity and political attitudes and behavior than we might otherwise find with a more robust measure. From this perspective, much of the empirical analyses to follow are a conservative test of the relationships I purport to uncover. In other words, the risk I run here is understating my case, rather than overstating it.

There are, however, several reasons why we can employ this item with confidence. For one, the racial importance item has considerable face validity. It directly and plainly asks respondents to report the significance of their racial identity. What is more, as we shall see in the analysis to come, the measure displays impressive stability. The distribution over many years among a national sample of whites is roughly the same. Lastly, the analysis throughout the rest of this book will serve as a testament to the value of this single measure, which as we shall see, has remarkable and consistent predictive power with respect to key political variables of interest.[17]

Measuring White Consciousness

Group identity alone can influence individuals' political attitudes. We might also expect that when conditions are ripe, identity can lead to group consciousness among some whites. Thus, we will need a way to measure racial consciousness among whites as well. This task requires a bit of work. While methods to measure consciousness have evolved somewhat over time, they have done so primarily to account for consciousness among subordinated groups, particularly blacks and women (Gurin 1983; Gurin and Townsend 1986; Gurin, Miller, and Gurin 1980; Miller et al. 1981). Many of these measures are therefore specific to these groups, making it difficult or nonsensical to merely replace the words "blacks" or "women" with "whites." As a consequence, I will have to craft my own survey measures.

Recall that previously, I described how consciousness is a more politicized form of group attachment. It entails not only an investment in the group, but also an awareness of the group's position in society and a commitment to collectively working to attain what is in the best interest of the group (Miller et al. 1981). It is, to state plainly, group identity coupled with an additional set of beliefs about the group and its orientation toward the political world. Accordingly, there are multiple dimensions to consciousness, the first of which is identity. The second component of consciousness assesses the degree to which group members see their circumstances as a function of some external, unjust force, like the encroachment of another group on the racial hierarchy. For whites, we might expect such a position to be couched in terms of racial or ethnic minorities receiving some benefit at the expense of whites. In keeping with this sentiment, white respondents are asked, *"How likely is it that many whites are unable to find a job because employers are hiring minorities instead?"* On a five-point scale, whites indicate a response ranging from "extremely likely" to "not at all likely."

Individuals high on group consciousness do not merely believe their group experiences some illegitimate disparities; they are also inclined to want to work together with other group members to eliminate challenges to their group's dominance. This third component of consciousness – collective orientation – is measured by asking whites, *"How important is it that whites work together to change laws that are unfair to whites?"* Respondents again answer on a scale with five options ranging from "extremely important" to "not at all important." These three items were included on the 2013 SSI Study, the 2016 ANES Pilot Study, the 2016 ANES Time Series, and the 2016 YouGov survey.[18] Scaled together, these items comprise a measure of white racial consciousness.[19] To summarize, combined with the measures of racial identity, the consciousness items are as follows:

- *How likely is it that many whites are unable to find a job because employers are hiring minorities instead?*
- *How important is it that whites work together to change laws that are unfair to whites?*

Unfortunately, measures of group identity and group consciousness are not available uniformly across each of the data sources I employ

Table 3.1 *The Availability of White Solidarity Measures across Data Sources*

	KN 2010	ANES 2012	SSI 2013	YouGov 2016	ANES Pilot 2016	ANES 2016
Single-item measure of white identity (racial identity importance question)	•	•	•	•	•	•
Three-item measure of white identity (importance, pride, commonality)				•		
Three-item measure of white consciousness (importance, employers hiring minorities, whites should work together)			•	•	•	•
Five-item measure of white consciousness (three items from identity, hiring minorities, whites should work together)				•		

throughout this book. At times, I will only be able to investigate the relationship between white identity and political preferences, and often only with the single measure. As a guide of the analysis to come, I describe in Table 3.1 the measures available across each data source.

The Presence and Prevalence of White Racial Solidarity

What do these measures reveal about levels of racial identity and racial consciousness among whites in the United States? Do white Americans think about their race in these terms? Do sizeable proportions view their racial identity with some degree of importance? According to Sears and Savalei (2006), given whites' dominant status, we ought to observe very low levels of racial identification among whites. In their own examination of white identity from a sample drawn from the Los Angeles County Social Survey (LACSS) in the 1990s, Sears and Savalei find that when asked about the importance of their racial identity, they report that only 15 percent of whites appear to be strong identifiers. How do levels of identification compare when we look at data from more contemporary sources?

The Importance of One's Racial Identity

Table 3.2 presents the distribution of the primary measure of white identity – the racial importance item – across six sources of evidence: the 2010 KN Study, the 2012 ANES, the 2013 SSI Study, the 2016 YouGov Study, the 2016 ANES Pilot, and the 2016 ANES. If we consider the percentage of respondents who are clustered into the two highest response options, it is immediately clear from the table that sizeable portions of white Americans possess a racial identity. Between 30 and 40 percent of white Americans indicate that their racial identity is very, if not extremely, important to them.[20]

We can also see that between 2010 and 2016, among both convenience samples and with nationally representative data, levels of white identity, as measured by the "importance" item, do not appear dramatically different. Despite the growing importance of white racial identity in American politics, it is not necessarily the case that more whites are identifying with their racial group. These trends lend support for the possibility that while the political significance of white identity might wax and wane, levels of identity have stayed fairly consistent.

Can we conclude, however, that levels of white identity have changed since the time of Sears and Savalei's investigation? Or can we argue that white identity levels are notably different among a national sample of whites as opposed to only those within LA County? Not necessarily. Note that if we follow Sears and Savalei and pay attention only to the most extreme category of the importance item ("extremely important") in Table 3.2, the percentages look quite similar to what these scholars uncovered in the LACSS data from the 1990s. Between 11 and 21 percent of respondents across the three surveys in Table 3.2 place themselves at the highest level of racial identity – values consistent with the 15 percent Sears and Savalei report.

But the assumption that racial identity among whites was previously limited is, I argue, somewhat overstated. If we go review the full distribution of the white racial importance item in the LACSS, it turns out that 29 percent of whites chose the next highest level of racial identity, indicating that their identity as a white is "somewhat important."[21] Combining those who chose "somewhat important" with those who selected "very important," we can conclude that even in the 1990s, approximately 44 percent of whites claimed that their racial identity had some degree of significance.[22]

Table 3.2 *The Distribution of the White Racial Identity Importance Item*

	KN 2010 (%)	ANES 2012 (%)		SSI 2013 (%)	YouGov 2016 (%)	ANES 2016 Pilot (%)	ANES 2016 (%)	
		(Face-to face)	(Web)				(Face-to-face)	(Web)
Not at all important	8	23	22	19	16	25	31	29
A little important (KN = "Not very important")	27	18	20	12	11	14	18	17
Moderately important (KN = "Somewhat important")	38	25	28	28	31	25	22	26
Very important	27	20	19	21	21	16	18	17
Extremely important	–	14	11	19	21	20	12	11
Observations	752	860	2,821	797	1,460	875	649	2,087

Note: Percentages are rounded. KN, ANES, and YouGov data are weighted.
Sources: 2010 KN, 2012 ANES, 2013 SSI, 2016 YouGov, 2016 ANES Pilot, 2016 ANES.

Scholars have also dismissed the import of white racial identity on the premise that levels of white identity do not approach the degree of racial identity we observe among racial and ethnic minorities. It is indeed the case that levels of white identity are not nearly as prevalent as racial identity among blacks and Latinos. If we consider levels of identity among these two groups, measured with the racial importance item in the 2012 and 2016 ANES, we find that between 45 and 61 percent of blacks indicate their racial identity is extremely important. If we combine the next category ("very important"), between 69 and 85 percent of blacks possess high levels of identity. Levels of identity among Hispanics, measured in this way, are also notably higher. Between 49 and 75 percent of Hispanics report that their ethnic identity is very, if not extremely, important.[23]

In short, levels of racial identity among whites are notably lower than what we observe among blacks and Hispanics in the United States. Of course, for the reasons outlined in the previous chapter, we would not necessarily expect levels of racial solidarity among whites to approach that of racial and ethnic minorities in the United States. Whites' dominant status and the fact that their racial group has not systematically experienced oppression and discrimination have meant that the ingredients for the development of strong group identities have not been as present or as potent as they are for other groups. Nevertheless, the percentage of whites who do identify with their racial group is still sizeable. Furthermore, as we shall see in the chapters that follow, racial solidarity, while not as widespread for whites as it is for other racial and ethnic minorities, still shapes whites' political preferences in profound and important ways.

Pride in One's Group

Having established that a sizeable percentage of whites in the United States believe that their racial identity is important, I next examine the extent to which whites feel proud of their race. In the 2016 YouGov survey, respondents were asked about the extent to which they feel that whites have a lot of which to be proud. From the first column in Table 3.3, we can see that 26 percent selected the second highest category – "a lot" – and another 28 percent said that whites have a great deal of which to be proud. Taken together, it is apparent from

Table 3.3 *The Distribution of the Racial Identity Pride and Commonality Items*

	Racial pride (%)	Racial commonality (%)
None at all	4	2
A little	8	15
A moderate amount	33	42
A lot	26	27
A great deal	28	14
Observations	1,460	1,457

Note: Percentages are rounded. Data are weighted.
Source: 2016 YouGov.

responses to these questions that sizeable portions of white Americans associate their racial group with feelings of pride.

Commonality with One's Group

Lastly, I examine levels of commonality among whites in the United States. The second column in Table 3.3 presents the distribution of the survey item in the 2016 YouGov Study. Approximately 14 percent of respondents indicated that whites have a great deal in common with one another. An even greater percentage – roughly 27 percent – claim that whites have a lot in common with one another. It turns out, despite concerns that most whites might be inclined to view their group as heterogeneous, this dimension has notable degrees of variation. A minority – but a sizeable minority – of whites fall into the upper categories of this measure, suggesting that whites do feel some sense of shared ties or commonality with other members of their racial group.

The three items are intended to be scaled together by averaging them to create a single measure of white identity. I will discuss the properties of this measure later in this chapter, but for now, let us look at the distribution of this scaled item as measured in the 2016 YouGov Study and presented in Figure 3.1. I have coded the combined white identity scale to range from zero to one, with higher values indicating stronger levels of racial identity. We can see that the figure is skewed left, indicating that a sizeable proportion of whites score at the middle to high end of the scale. Roughly 35 percent of whites have scores in the upper quartile of the scale. These are whites we would

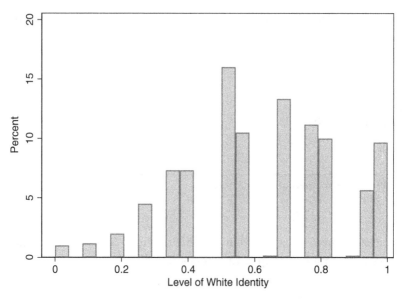

Figure 3.1 The Distribution of the White Identity Scale

The graph shows frequency of responses across range of three-item white identity scale, which is coded to range from zero to one, with higher values indicating higher levels of group identity. Mean of white identity=0.62.

Source: 2016 YouGov.

consider high on group identity. When using the single item measure of white identity, we would consider those who choose one of the top two response options (either "very" or "extremely" important) to have high levels of white identity. At this point, it should be clear that many whites do possess a sense of racial identity.

White Consciousness

Perceptions of Deprivation

Having examined levels of white identity, I move on to determining the extent to which white Americans also possess a sense of racial consciousness. First, let us look at the measure's constituent items, starting with the question assessing beliefs about the group's perceived disparities. How many whites believe that members of their racial group are denied jobs because employers are hiring minorities instead? The distribution of responses to this question, presented in Table 3.4, indicates

Table 3.4 *The Distribution of the Racial Consciousness Perceptions of Discrimination*

	SSI 2013 (%)	YouGov 2016 (%)	ANES 2016 Pilot (%)	ANES 2016 (%)	
				(Face-to-face)	(Web)
Not at all likely	14	13	21	25	18
Somewhat likely	23	24	27	28	33
Moderately likely	23	27	24	27	27
Very likely	21	22	16	14	14
Extremely likely	19	14	12	7	8
Observations	793	1,459	875	696	1,877

Note: Percentages are rounded. YouGov and ANES data are weighted.
Source: 2013 SSI, 2016 YouGov, 2016 ANES Pilot.

that between 7 and 19 percent of whites think this scenario is extremely likely. Another 14–22 percent believe it is very likely.

Collective Orientation

Next, I consider the extent to which whites subscribe to a sense of collective orientation. What percentage believe it is important for members of their group to work together in order to change laws unfair to whites? In Table 3.5, we can see that 15–26 percent of whites agree it is extremely important for members of their group to work together. An additional 19–26 percent agree that it is very important to do so.[24]

Scaled together, what do these items reveal about levels of racial consciousness among whites in the United States? Respondents with a consciousness score of zero report no racial identity, think it is not at all likely that whites are unable to find a job because employers are filling jobs primarily with minority applicants, and believe it is not at all important that whites work together to change laws unfair to their group. Those with a score of one possess the highest levels of identity, believe minorities are obtaining jobs at the expense of whites, and strongly support working together to change laws unfair to their group. Figure 3.2, which draws from the 2016 YouGov Study, shows that the measure is relatively normally distributed, with an average score of 0.59 on the zero to one scale.[25] Not all whites have high levels of racial consciousness. Nearly 38 percent score at 0.5 or below on the

Table 3.5 *The Distribution of the Racial Consciousness Collective Orientation Item*

	SSI 2013 (%)	YouGov 2016 (%)	ANES Pilot 2016 (%)	ANES 2016 (%)	
				(Face-to-face)	(Web)
Not at all important	16	12	23	23	21
Somewhat important	11	11	15	13	12
Moderately important	22	26	24	27	30
Very important	26	28	19	21	21
Extremely important	26	23	19	15	16
Observations	796	1,454	873	697	1,866

Note: Percentages are rounded. YouGov and ANES data are weighted.
Source: 2013 SSI, 2016 YouGov, 2016 ANES Pilot, 2016 ANES.

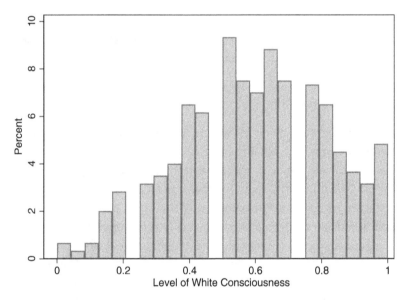

Figure 3.2 The Distribution of White Racial Consciousness
The graph shows frequency of responses across range of five-item white consciousness scale, which is coded to range from zero to one, with higher values indicating higher levels of group consciousness. Mean of White Consciousness=0.59.
Source: YouGov 2016

zero to one scale. Just over 26 percent, however, possess scores in the upper quartile. These whites are who we would consider to be high on group consciousness.[26]

With both measures of white identity and white consciousness in hand, the next part of this chapter turns in greater detail to unpacking the psychometric properties of these measures. For methodologists and those interested in empirical demonstrations of the properties of these measures, please read on. Others, however, may wish at this point to move on to Chapter 4, where I examine the demographic characteristics of whites who possess higher levels of white identity and white consciousness.

Assessing Measures of Identity and Consciousness

In an ideal world, social scientists would be able to measure concepts of interest like identities, attitudes, preferences, and personalities with perfect precision. In reality, our efforts are messy and imprecise. When we aim to measure a construct like identity with a survey, our ability to accurately capture any individual's true level of said identity is at the whim of any number of factors. The order in which the question appears on the survey, distractions the respondent experiences in the background while answering questions, a news segment he or she watched earlier in the day, and perhaps even what the person ate for breakfast that morning could influence the response a survey-taker gives when asked a question.

The goal of social scientists is to minimize factors that introduce bias into the measurement of a construct. Our aim in constructing a measure, then, is to maximize two properties: reliability and validity. A measure is reliable to the extent that it is free from random error; that is, when it is consistent. It is valid to the extent that it measures what it is intended to measure (King, Keohane, and Verba 1994).

Mode Effects and Social Desirability Bias

The fact that the racial importance item has a consistent distribution over time and across surveys is one demonstration of the reliability of this item.[27] There are other factors that may influence the reliability of the measures employed throughout my analysis, however. For one, we might observe differences in responses depending on the survey mode – that is, the way in which the survey was administered to participants. Several of the surveys employed throughout this book were conducted over the Internet, but the portion of the 2012 and 2016 ANES Time Series used in much of the analysis, as well as older ANES

Time Series that make their way into some of the empirics throughout, were conducted via face-to-face interviews. Different survey modes can introduce measurement error for a number of reasons. Of special interest with regards to measuring white identity is the possibility of social desirability concerns biasing the measures.

The historical association of this identity with supremacy and hate groups, or even just a reluctance to talk about race, may cause some whites to be more reticent in reporting their racial identity on public opinion surveys, especially when asked to do so in the presence of a survey interviewer. As a result, my measure might be underestimating levels of white identity in some modes. Fortunately, it is relatively easy to determine whether the white identity measure is sensitive to what we call mode effects, or differences in responses that might be the result of the way in which the survey was administered. To see if white identity is sensitive to these effects, we can compare the distribution of responses to the white identity question across survey modes using the 2012 and 2016 ANES.[28] This is not a completely clean test of mode effects, as respondents were not randomly assigned to one mode or another, and participants in the online study opted in to participate. Thus, there may be some selection effects at work here as well. Nevertheless, if some social desirability effects are influencing responses, we ought to find that levels of identity in the face-to-face mode will be lower than in the Internet mode, where respondents might feel more comfortable expressing their racial identity privately and anonymously.[29]

We can go back to Table 3.2 to compare the distribution of white identity, measured with the racial importance item, across the two survey modes. Comparing the columns in Table 3.2 for both the 2012 and 2016 studies reveals that the distribution of this measure in the face-to-face mode is not significantly different from the Internet mode.[30] If anything, respondents taking the survey via the Internet are more likely to temper their responses to the identity question; a slightly smaller percentage indicated that their identity is extremely important to them. At the same time, however, slightly *fewer* of the whites in the Internet sample were clustered in the lowest end of the identity measure, reporting that their identity is "not at all important." Across both modes, a majority of the respondents indicated that their racial identity is "moderately important." In short, the similarity in responses across the two survey modes suggests that social desirability bias is not necessarily affecting individuals' willingness to claim a racial identity.

Race of Interviewer Effects

Even if many whites possess a racial identity and usually feel comfortable revealing their identification on anonymous opinion surveys, it may still be the case that in specific circumstances, whites might feel reluctant to express their identity. For instance, it is possible that *to whom* they are reporting this identity matters. Some whites may feel comfortable revealing their white identity to fellow whites, but may be uncomfortable doing so in the presence of non-white individuals. One way to uncover this potential bias is by comparing whites' responses to the racial identity question on the 2012 ANES survey when their interviewer was white to responses given when the interviewer was black or of some other race or ethnicity.

Comparing mean levels of white identity (measured with the racial importance item rescaled to range from zero to one) among respondents who got either a white or black interviewer (or one reported as "other") reveals some important differences in respondents' willingness to express an identity.[31] When white respondents are interviewed by a white individual, their average reported level of white identity is 0.45 (on a zero to one scale), which is roughly equivalent to a response of "moderately important." Whites interviewed by an interviewer who self-identifies as "other" report nearly the same level of white identity (0.46). In comparison, whites interviewed by a black individual report significantly lower levels of white identity, on average.[32] The mean level of racial identity among whites interviewed by blacks is 0.36, which falls between "only a little" and "moderately" important.[33]

A robust line of research has documented the fact that the race of the interviewer can significantly affect survey-takers' responses to questions on face-to-face surveys (Finkel, Guterbock, and Borg 1991; Hyman 1954; Krysan 1998). Some work demonstrates that in the presence of interviewers of the same race, respondents are more likely to be open or honest. Other times, however, respondents attempt to save face with interviewers of their own race by giving what they believe is the "correct" or most socially desirable response (Anderson, Silver, and Abramson 1988). Comparing the average level of white identity among whites who had a white interviewer to those white respondents who took the survey over the Internet sans interviewer, there appears to be no difference in levels. Thus, it seems that white respondents were not over-reporting their racial identification among white interviewers, but they may have been under-reporting their true attitudes in the presence of black interviewers.

A number of studies have also demonstrated that whites tend to give more racially liberal responses to race-related questions when their interviewer is of a different race or ethnicity – or in the case of telephone surveys, perceived to be non-white (Hatchett and Schuman 1975; Hyman 1954; Krysan 1998). Similarly, the fact that whites tend to report lower levels of racial identity in the presence of blacks suggests that some degree of self-monitoring is occurring, and that a meaningful percentage of white respondents feel uncomfortable declaring that their racial identity is important to a black interviewer. Furthermore, while the interviewer remained present when respondents answered the racial identity questions, these items were actually self-administered; respondents were handed a portable device and asked to complete the questions privately. Yet the presence of the black interviewer alone affected results, even when respondents could feel somewhat confident that their responses were anonymous. Thus, it appears that the expression of white identity may be conditioned on circumstances, and that under certain conditions, some whites feel that it is inappropriate to proclaim an identification with their race.

What we can glean from the analysis thus far is, first, that the measures of white identity and white consciousness I employ here demonstrate important consistency in their distributions across time and within different survey modes. At the same time, there is a notable caveat. Efforts to measure white identity or consciousness may be susceptible to social desirability biases under some circumstances. We can see that some whites were reluctant to claim a sense of racial identity when interviewed by a person of color. To account for this effect, I control for the race of the interviewer when analyzing data collected via face-to-face interviews in the 2012 ANES. At the time of this writing, information about the race of the interviewer in the 2016 ANES study was not available, and so we must be slightly more cautious when it comes to some of the conclusions we can draw from those results. It is important to note, however, that this source of measurement error is fairly limited. Only a subset of whites (approximately 24 percent) were interviewed by non-whites in the 2012 ANES, and much of the evidence throughout this text draws from surveys conducted over the Internet, where no interviewer was present and surveys were self-administered.

Construct Validity: What Does It Mean to Say You Identify as White?

With strong evidence that the measures of white identity and white consciousness are reliable, I turn next to assessing their validity. A measure can be highly reliable, but it might otherwise fail to measure the concept we intend for it to measure, making it invalid. There are several different approaches to assessing validity. First, I consider the content validity of white identity. Does the measure described here capture the substantive content of what we expect white racial identity to embody? In other words, do respondents mean what I think they mean when answering the identity questions?

I asked respondents, with open-ended questions, about their racial identity, and had them explain why they chose a particular response option to the close-ended racial importance identity question.[34] How do whites at varying levels of racial identity conceive of this identity in their own words? When asked about the importance of their racial identity, what comes to mind? I draw first on a survey that is not among the six I described above. This study was conducted for the sole purpose of understanding whites' thought process when answering the racial identity question. It was conducted among 373 white US adult citizens in November of 2013 via Amazon's Mechanical Turk (MTurk) service. MTurk samples are not nationally representative, but they routinely replicate results from nationally representative surveys (Berinsky et al. 2012; Mullinix et al. 2014). The second set of responses come from the 2016 YouGov Study described above and used throughout this text. In this analysis, I consider whites high on identity to be those who reported that their identity is either very or extremely important to them.[35]

When reviewing the explanations for their response to the identity importance item, it is immediately clear that many whites high on identity see their race as central to who they are. Several put this perception quite plainly: "Its who I am. It's something I cannot change no matter what." Another respondent said, "Because it is who I am and who I represent."

Others explained their response with more detail, and one sentiment emerged repeatedly from their answers. Whites who see their racial identity as important often noted that they feel proud to be white. They wrote, "I am white and proud of it" or "I am very proud of who I am, and my people's history as inventors, explorers, and creators." Others commented on their ancestry or heritage: "As I've never been anything else, I cannot imagine being different. I am proud of my heritage, as I assume anyone else would be of theirs." Within the MTurk sample, 10 percent of white identifiers indicated they were proud to be white. Among the YouGov sample, approximately 15 percent used "pride" or "proud" to describe their response.

Many also described their choice as simply a natural response given the importance of their heritage, their families, and the people with whom they associate. About 13 percent of the YouGov sample of white identifiers described their identity in this way. One strong identifier from the YouGov sample said, "It is the family that I was born in." Another wrote, "I am white. My entire family is white." Many also mentioned that being white is part of their culture. For instance, one respondent from the MTurk study wrote:

> Even in today's more educated times, a person's race is a big part of who they are. Most my friends are white, and the majority of my co-workers are as well. I have friends of other races, but feel like I identify more with other white people. For the most part, we have similar upbringings and beliefs. Furthermore, our skin color is one of the few things we can never change nor hide.

Another said,

> I mean that it is who I am. I identify as a white person and so it has become just a part of who I am. Most applications and government paperwork include what race someone is, when looking into my family I think we all feel the same way. It was a little annoying when applying for scholarships as it was very hard to find something for just white people but I enjoy my race.

These examples characterize the general set of sentiments expressed by respondents quite well. What is more, in describing their response to the racial importance item, respondents mentioned many of the components of identity captured by the three-item scale. They indicated pride in their racial group and discussed a sense of commonality. In short, these open-ended responses provide important evidence that the close-ended measures are capturing the concept of identity as intended.

Discriminant Validity: Is White Identity Another Concept by Another Name?

The second component of validity that is of concern here is discriminant validity.[36] This endeavor would not be especially fruitful if instead of identity or consciousness, I was merely measuring racial animus, or any number of other political attitudes and identities central to public opinion and political behavior. If I am to argue successfully that white identity and white consciousness are powerful forces in contemporary American politics, I need to demonstrate that they are distinct from other predispositions and that they have predictive power above and beyond other variables we think are traditionally associated with political preferences. Therefore, I next examine the relationship between white identity, white consciousness, and other social and political predispositions.

Specifically, I look at the extent to which white identity and consciousness are *correlated* with these other variables of interest. Correlation coefficients, which range from negative one to one, indicate the degree to which two variables are linearly related. In other words, they provide a measure of the extent to which one variable increases or decreases as the other variable increases or decreases. We expect attitudes or predispositions that trend together to have correlations close to positive one, and those that trend closely but in opposite directions to have correlations close to negative one. For instance, we would expect that among whites, political ideology and partisan identification are quite highly correlated. That is, those who say they are ideologically conservative should also be more inclined to identify with the Republican Party. And they are. The correlation among whites in the 2012 ANES face-to-face study between party identification and ideology is 0.70 (p=0.00).

My aim here is to demonstrate that white identity and consciousness are not so strongly correlated with other political and social predispositions that we would consider them one and the same. Thus, the correlation coefficients should not approach the level we might expect to find between items that are in fact highly correlated, like party identity and ideology. It would not be surprising, however, to find that white identity and consciousness are at least somewhat associated with other political and social predispositions. In fact, we would expect them to be to some degree. But if both white identity and white consciousness are distinct attitudes, they should not be interchangeable with other political predispositions, racial attitudes, or identities.

I begin with racial identity alone, measured with the racial importance item, examining first its relationship with standard political predispositions across the ANES 2012 Time Series, the 2016 YouGov Study, the 2016 ANES Pilot, and the 2016 ANES Time Series. I look first at the most central and significant political predisposition – partisanship.[37] Political science scholarship has long recognized party identification as a durable, stable attachment, and most Americans think of themselves as either Democrats or Republicans (Campbell et al. 1960; Green, Palmquist, and Schickler 1998). Because party identification plays an important role in informing Americans' political preferences, it will be included in many of the forthcoming analyses. We must know, therefore, that the role white identity plays in informing political preferences is independent of partisanship. Turning to Table 3.6, we can see that white identity is not just party identity by another name. In 2012, the correlation is close to zero and statistically insignificant. A weak but significant correlation appears in 2016, such that white identifiers lean more Republican.

What about the relationship between white identity and ideological identification? Many Americans readily categorize themselves as liberal or conservative, and these distinctions often influence public opinion on a range of social and economic issues (Conover and Feldman 1981; Levitin and Miller 1979). Perhaps white identity is simply another expression of an individual's ideological position. We can see in Table 3.6. that it is not, but ideological distinctions do seem to matter somewhat for white identifiers; they tend to be slightly more conservative, although not overwhelmingly so.

Is identity more strongly associated with views about the size and role of the government? Americans tend to prefer a more limited government, and attitudes about the scope of government correspond to opinions across a range of policies (Markus 2001). We can see from Table 3.6 that the relationship between the two constructs is underwhelming. Higher levels of white identity are more often

Table 3.6 *The Relationship between White Identity and Political and Social Predispositions*

	ANES 2012		YouGov 2016	ANES Pilot 2016	ANES 2016	
	(Face-to-face)	(Web)			(Face-to-face)	(Web)
Party identification (Republican)	0.06 (851)	0.01 (2,389)	0.15* (585)	0.11* (839)	0.11* (644)	0.11* (1,886)
Ideological identification (conservative)	0.07* (859)	0.05* (2,390)	0.18* (595)	0.18* (817)	0.13* (649)	0.14* (1,888)
Limited government	-0.04 (855)	-0.05 (2,385)	0.08 (596)			
Egalitarianism	0.06 (859)	0.002 (2,390)	-0.20* (600)		-0.15* (649)	-0.15* (1,888)
Racial resentment	0.13* (858)	0.13* (2,390)	0.23* (600)	0.19* (874)	0.22* (649)	0.18* (1,888)
Anti-black stereotype index	0.35* (852)	0.32* (2,379)	0.25* (600)	0.31* (871)	0.28* (690)	0.27* (1,865)
Black feeling thermometer	-0.09* (846)	-0.13* (2,378)	-0.14* (587)	-0.22* (873)	-0.17* (636)	-0.15* (1,870)
Hispanic feeling thermometer	-0.09* (844)	-0.12* (2,379)		-0.25* (874)	-0.19* (633)	-0.17* (1,864)
Asian feeling thermometer	-0.08* (846)	-0.08* (2,380)			-0.16* (640)	-0.12* (1,868)
Muslim feeling thermometer	-0.15* (831)	-0.14* (2,373)		-0.30* (873)	-0.20* (638)	-0.23* (1,762)
Ku Klux Klan feeling thermometer			0.30* (559)			

Notes: Table entries are the Pearson correlation coefficients. Number of observations appears in parentheses. Data are weighted.

* p<=0.05.

Source: 2012 ANES, 2016 YouGov, 2016 ANES Pilot, 2016 ANES.

associated with *less* support for limited government, but the correlation is small and statistically insignificant.

Next, I consider white identity's relationship to beliefs about equality. Egalitarianism is central to debates over many social programs, especially welfare, and there is some evidence that beliefs about whites' power and status might be significantly related to support for racial inequality (Branscombe, Schmitt, and Schiffhauer 2007; Feldman and Zaller 1992). We might, therefore, expect that whites with higher levels of racial identity are less likely to adopt egalitarian beliefs. The coefficients in Table 3.6 reveal that white identity is tied to more inegalitarian beliefs, but only modestly so.

How do these trends hold up when we consider the relationship to each of these items and white racial consciousness? Consciousness is a *politicized* form of group attachment. Thus, we might anticipate that its association with other political attitudes is much stronger than what we observed with respect to identity. The strength of the correlations between consciousness and these political and racial predispositions is in fact greater than when we look at identity alone.[38] I find that those high on white consciousness tend to lean Republican and they are more ideologically conservative. They are more supportive of limited government, and less egalitarian. Yet the larger point of this endeavor is not subverted. In no case is the correlation so overwhelming that we would consider consciousness to be interchangeable with any of the predispositions considered here. Thus, we can move forward confident that both identity and consciousness are independent of these other attitudes.

In-Group Love and Out-Group Hate

One of the arguments central to my theory is that white identity is not merely another expression of out-group animus. It is very much in-group oriented, rooted in a desire to protect group members' privilege and status. White identity should not be another proxy for racial resentment, for anti-black stereotypes, or for dislike toward other racial or ethnic minorities. At the same time, we still might expect white identity to be somewhat related to out-group animosity, given that some previous work under the umbrella of social identity theory has posited that in-group favoritism is often associated with out-group derogation (Brewer 1979).

In Table 3.6, I examine the relationship between identity and a host of different measures of out-group attitudes. I first consider whether white identity embodies racial resentment. The correlation is consistently positive, ranging from 0.13 to 0.23, but still modest in size. Not all white identifiers score high on racial resentment, and not all those who score high on racial resentment possess strong levels of white identity. Let us unpack these relationships further. Among all whites in the 2012 ANES face-to-face study, the mean level of racial resentment is 0.68 on a zero to one scale. Most whites in the United States are fairly racially conservative. Among whites high on racial identity (those who score at 0.75 or one on the white identity measure), approximately 60 percent score at or above the overall mean level of racial resentment for whites in the United States. At the same time, a sizeable segment of whites low on identity happen to score high on resentment; approximately 44 percent of whites who say their racial identity is either only a little or not at all important are at or above the mean level of white racial resentment. There are also many white identifiers who score rather low on the resentment scale; approximately 38 percent of whites high on identity have a racial resentment score at 0.50 or below.

What about the relationship between white identity and anti-black stereotypes? These attitudes are measured as the difference between where whites rate their own group and where they rate blacks on two seven-point scales, the first assessing how hardworking or lazy each group is thought to be, and the second assessing how intelligent or unintelligent group members are thought to be. The association is somewhat stronger than what we observed between identity and racial resentment. The correlation coefficient ranges from 0.25 to 0.35.[39] This slightly larger effect is not surprising, however; the stereotype index is comprised of assessments of both the out-group (blacks) *and* the in-group (whites). While the expectation is certainly not that in-group attitudes are entirely unrelated to out-group assessments, I do expect that white identity is more strongly associated with in-group evaluations. To find out, I deconstruct the stereotype measure, and calculate the correlation between white identity and where whites place their own group on the stereotype measures versus where they place blacks. Doing so provides some evidence not only of the measure's discriminant validity, but also of its convergent validity. That is, white identity should be more closely associated to an arguably related measure – positive in-group evaluations – than with a theoretically less-related concept – negative out-group animosity.

I find, among 2012 ANES respondents, that the correlation between white identity and the average rating whites give blacks on the lazy/hardworking and intelligent/unintelligent scale is fairly small, although still significant: 0.14 ($p<0.05$). The correlation between white identity and where whites place themselves on these dimensions, on average, however, is nearly twice that, at -0.27. Whites with higher levels of identity rate their in-group far less negatively (and far more positively) on these two dimensions. In short, we can see that the relatively stronger correlation between white identity and the stereotype index appears to be driven somewhat more by the in-group evaluation component of the measure.

The next rows of Table 3.6 reveal that white identity is also correlated with more negative affective evaluations of racial and ethnic out-groups. Whites with higher levels of racial identity tend to rate blacks, Hispanics, Asians, and Muslims lower on feeling thermometer measures. Again, however, in no case is the correlation so large that we would consider the relationships either directly reciprocal, nor would we conclude that white identity is merely capturing out-group animus.

Finally, I examine whether white identity is mainly capturing more extreme views by examining the correlation between white identity and attitudes toward one of the most notorious white supremacist groups, the Ku Klux Klan (KKK). Given the KKK's extreme brand of racism, we should feel somewhat confident from the other correlations in Table 3.6 that the relationship between white identity and affect toward the KKK will not be especially strong. Nevertheless, we want to make sure that white identifiers are not primarily KKK sympathizers, especially given the recent rise in white supremacist and white nationalist movements in the United States. At the same time, we should still expect a positive relationship between white identity and support for an extremist group like the KKK. While not all white identifiers associate with these groups, bona-fide white supremacists are nevertheless likely among my respondents and presumably inclined to report high levels of white identity.

I measured attitudes toward the KKK using a 101-point feeling thermometer among respondents on the 2016 YouGov Study. To be clear, the KKK is deeply unpopular. The average thermometer rating all whites give members of the KKK in 2016 is a chilly 13 degrees – much colder than the average, but still cool, rating of 26 degrees whites gave the KKK on the 1964 ANES. We can also see, however, from

the last row in Table 3.6, that there is a modest, positive, and significant correlation between white identity and attitudes toward the
KKK. Those who evaluate the KKK more positively also report higher
levels of racial identity. This relationship is troubling but should not
be overstated. White identifiers are hardly uniform KKK supporters.
As expected, white supremacists are a small subset of white identifiers.

To illustrate this point more clearly, I consider how many
whites high on white identity evaluate the KKK positively. Out of the
244 whites in the 2016 YouGov Study who report that their racial identity is very or extremely important, 45 (18 percent) rate the KKK above
50 degrees. Only 25 (10 percent) of white identifiers rate the KKK
above 70 degrees. By comparison, 52 (21 percent) white identifiers
give the KKK a thermometer score of zero. A total of 199 (82 percent)
rate the KKK at or below 50 degrees. Whites supremacists are among
the ranks of white identifiers, but they are not the overwhelming
majority of them.

What about the relationship between each of these items and
white consciousness? The measure of consciousness takes into account
beliefs about out-group threat, measured with the survey item that
asks whites whether they believe it is hard for their group members
to find jobs because positions are going to minorities instead. We may
therefore also observe stronger relationships between consciousness
and racial animus.[40] Whites high on consciousness do tend to possess
higher levels of racial resentment, subscribe to more anti-black stereotypes, and evaluate Hispanics and Muslims more negatively. They, too,
rate the KKK somewhat more warmly, on average. But the magnitudes
of the correlations, in each case, are only slightly greater than what we
observed when looking at identity alone. In no instance is the relationship so great that we might question whether consciousness is merely a
stand-in for one of these other attitudes or predispositions.

Exposing the Extremists

Before moving on, let us take this analysis one step further. What percentage of white identifiers might we sincerely consider to be white
supremacists, or at least likely to share the views of such groups? Such
individuals ought to score very high on white identity *and* possess a
strong sense of out-group animus. Let us begin with racial resentment –
a more subtle and conservative measure of racial attitudes. Among

respondents in the 2012 ANES who say their racial identity is extremely important, 24 percent have the highest possible score on the racial resentment scale. This set of whites – those that score at the highest level of racial identity and racial resentment – are few in number; they amount to approximately 3 percent of all whites in the sample.

What about when it comes to a more overt, disparaging form of racial animus? What percentage of white identifiers evaluate their racial group very positively when it comes to the stereotypes of hardworking and intelligent, but rate blacks very unintelligent and lazy? In other words, how many white identifiers score, on the stereotype index, at the maximum point on the scale? Among 2012 ANES respondents, approximately 6 percent of white identifiers rate their group as positively as they rate blacks negatively. And an even smaller number of white identifiers also feel especially warm toward the KKK. Among white respondents in the 2016 YouGov Study, a total of two whites who reported that their racial identity is extremely important gave the KKK a thermometer rating of 100 degrees. A total of seven (or approximately 5 percent) rated the KKK above 80 degrees. There are some especially racist whites who also identify strongly with their racial group, but not many.

The racially prejudiced are undoubtedly found among those who identify with their racial group, and higher levels of white identity are somewhat linked to higher levels of racial animosity. These sentiments, however, are not one and the same. White identity is not merely an alternative measure of racial animus, nor are white identifiers overwhelmingly racially hostile. A small percentage of white identifiers score quite high on measures of racial prejudice or resentment, but many more white identifiers possess average and even low levels of racial prejudice. In other words, white identity is not defined by racial animus, and whites who identify with their racial group are not simply reducible to bigots.

Other Measures of Group Solidarity

An Alternative Measure of White Identity: The Feeling Thermometer

Until recently, the racial importance item was not frequently included on large, publicly available public opinion surveys.[41] But many surveys conducted in the past several decades have routinely measured attitudes toward a range of groups using what is called a feeling thermometer. This type of measure first made its way onto the ANES in 1964, and has been used in subsequent years to measure attitudes toward religious groups, racial groups, ideological groups, candidates, other political figures, and so forth. The measure asks respondents to rate how warm or cold they feel toward a group or individual, with a score ranging from 0 to 100. Higher values indicate warmer, more positive feelings.

The thermometer item has some advantageous properties from a measurement perspective. The measure does not impose any framework or boundaries on respondents. It simply asks them to make whatever evaluation comes readily to them (Weisberg and Rusk 1970). The thermometer item also allows researchers to capture the strength of attitudes toward a group. Nevertheless, while it is sometimes used as a measure of identity, the thermometer does not truly capture the essence of a social identity. It is instead a measure of group affect. One can, after all, feel warmly toward a group without identifying with said group.

At the same time, the thermometer item is not a terrible proximate measure for group identity when no other measure is available (Giles and Evans 1985).[42] We would, after all, expect whites high on white identity to also feel quite warmly toward their in-group, and one of the foundational claims of social identity theory is indeed that group identity gives way to in-group favoritism.[43] If we compare the average score whites who are high on racial identity give their racial group on the feeling thermometer compared to those low on white identity using the 2012 ANES, we see evidence for this relationship. High white identifiers rated whites 13 degrees more warmly than low identifiers.[44] Thus, it seems reasonable to assume that the thermometer measure is in fact tapping some degree of in-group attachment. I will, therefore, use the white feeling thermometer as a rough measure of group identity in some of the analysis to come, with the caveats described here in mind.

Interdependence

Under the umbrella of work on group identity, researchers have also examined another sentiment known as linked fate or interdependence.

This concept captures the belief that one's individual fate or outcome is inextricably tied to the fate of the group to which one belongs. Much of the theoretical development and empirical application of linked fate has been with respect to African Americans. Political scientists like Michael Dawson (1994) and Katherine Tate (1993) have argued that day-to-day encounters with discrimination and racial oppression make blacks aware that they are treated as members of a group, rather than as individuals. As a result, black Americans recognize their own fate as tied to that of their racial group, and this belief significantly informs their political beliefs and behaviors (Brown and Shaw 2002; Simien 2005). Linked fate is usually measured on surveys with a question that asks respondents how much they think what happens generally to members of their group in this country will have something to do with what happens in their own life.

Do some whites also possess a sense of linked fate? If so, is this sentiment related to white identity or white group consciousness, and does it have similar predictive power? A majority of white respondents in the 2012 ANES do report some degree of linked fate; 52 percent agreed that their own life chances depend, at least somewhat, on the fortunes of their racial group.[45] Work by Dawson (2009), however, suggests we ought to proceed with caution when employing measures of linked fate as an alternative (or in addition to) to white group identity or consciousness as conceived here.[46] He examined linked fate among whites using data from a nationally representative probability sample in 2004, and finds that approximately 17 percent of whites (compared to 45 percent of blacks) had adopted a strong sense of linked fate.[47] To be sure, this is a noteworthy percentage of whites. When Dawson dug deeper and examined the correlates of linked fate among whites, however, his results were surprising. Many of the antecedents of white linked fate were contrary to what one might expect. For instance, he finds that education is *positively* and significantly related to a sense of interdependence among whites. That is, more educated whites were more likely to possess some degree of racial interdependence. As we will see in the next chapter, this relationship runs counter to what I find when it comes to the relationship between education and identity or consciousness. More educated whites are less compelled to adopt a racial identity or a sense of group consciousness.

To complicate matters even further, Dawson finds that to the extent linked fate matters politically, higher levels of white linked fate are associated with racially liberal positions on racialized policies like offering apologies and reparations for slavery. Dawson was certainly surprised by these relationships; he remarked that "these results are *so* counterintuitive that we went back to the raw data to make sure there were no coding mistakes" (2009, p. 193).

While many whites may report a sense of linked fate with their racial group, Gay, Hochschild, and White (2016), in an extensive analysis of linked fate across racial groups, find that the construct is rarely associated with political attitudes or engagement, even among blacks. They find little evidence that a sense of linked fate is related to perceptions of group discrimination or to group affect measured with feeling thermometers. If anything, they conclude, linked fate seems primarily to be capturing some underlying sense of social connectedness. Individuals who report a strong sense of linked fate with their racial group are likely to feel connected to other types of groups, like those related to class or religion, but this attachment does not translate into predictable political outcomes.

I extend these inquiries into racial linked fate among whites, examining the relationship between this sentiment and the same social and political predispositions I consider above. I use the 2012 ANES Time Series, which included the standard measure of linked fate asked among whites.[48] Is white racial linked fate correlated with these other attitudes in the same way as white identity or linked fate? For the most part, it is not. While white linked fate is positively associated with Republican Party identification (Pearson $r=0.01$) and conservative ideology (Pearson $r=0.02$), the relationship is not statistically significant and the correlation is close to zero. White linked fate is also not substantively or significantly correlated with attitudes about the size of government (Pearson $r=0.07$), nor with egalitarianism (Pearson $r=-0.01$).

Perhaps, however, white linked fate is more strongly associated with racial out-group attitudes, as was the case with both white identity and consciousness. Again, there is little evidence for these associations. Higher levels of white linked fate are not correlated with racial resentment (Pearson $r=0.04$), the stereotype measure of racial prejudice (Pearson $r=0.04$), nor with feeling thermometer evaluations of blacks (-0.01), Hispanics (Pearson $r=0.03$), Asians (Pearson $r=0.03$), or Muslims (Pearson r=-0.01). It appears, then, that the correlates of white linked fate are notably different than they are for identity and consciousness.[49]

Dawson's analysis suggests that white linked fate may in fact be associated with a more progressive outlook on race and American politics. My own analysis, however, is more consistent with that of Gay, Hochschild, and White (2016). Among respondents in the 2012 ANES, I find that white linked fate bears little on political preferences. Unlike white identity, white linked fate is unrelated to vote choice. It has no effect on many of the other attitudes and preferences I find are associated with white identity in the chapters to come.[50] I recommend, therefore, that researchers avoid using it as a proximate measure of racial group solidarity in the same way I conceive of group identity and group consciousness here.

Estimating the Effect of White Identity

One of my primary goals throughout the rest of the book is to estimate the effect of white identity on public opinion. To do so, I must take into account the relative importance of other influences on political preferences, making sure that the effect of white identity or white consciousness is independent of other political, social, and demographic factors, held constant. Accordingly, I employ multiple regression analysis, which allows me to consider alternative explanations for the political outcomes and attitudes of interest. It also permits me to determine whether survey data are consistent with the claim that white racial solidarity influences a range of political attitudes and behavior, and how large the effect is.

In the analysis ahead, I use what I refer to as a "standard model" of public opinion. Of course, there is no single agreed upon model in public opinion research, but there is at least some conventional wisdom about the ingredients that make up public opinion in any one domain. Throughout my analysis, I use a basic set of controls. My main interest is in uncovering the effect of white identity or white consciousness after considering two competing explanations for whites' political preferences: economic self-interest and racial animus. The additional controls test for robustness and account for other explanations that are relevant to the matter of opinion at hand. I keep the model specifications relatively parsimonious, which allows me to determine the magnitude of the effect of identity and consciousness while considering only the most central alternative accounts.

In each model, I control for *partisanship*. The attachments Americans have toward one political party or another profoundly influence how they view the political world. Partisanship helps individuals make sense of politics, and it is one of the most important variables within American political science. No other variable is more paramount to understanding American political behavior (Campbell et al. 1960; Green, Palmquist, and Schickler 2002). In the models that follow, I therefore account for partisanship, measured on a seven-point scale ranging from strong Democrat to strong Republican.

Americans do not just sort themselves by political party. Many also claim to adopt either liberal or conservative ideologies and willingly describe themselves in these terms. Of course, the truth about the extent to which these ideologies represent genuine commitments to points of view or core beliefs is somewhat disappointing; most Americans are rather ideologically innocent, even though many are willing to sort themselves into one ideological category or another (Converse 1964; Kinder and Kalmoe 2017). Nevertheless, to the extent that some Americans do possess sincere and meaningful political ideologies, I also account for *political ideology*, measured on a seven-point scale ranging from extremely liberal to extremely conservative.[51]

The authors of the canonical *The American Voter* explained that many American's political views could be explained by "primitive self-interest" (Campbell et al. 1960, p. 205). Yet evidence that Americans vote with their pocketbooks is rather scarce. To the extent that economic indicators routinely predict people's political judgments, it is usually via what Kinder and Kiewiet (1981) call *sociotropic information* – or individuals' assessment of the national economy. I control for such evaluations in my models by including individuals' reports of whether the national economy had gotten better, worse, or stayed the same over the past year. Still, despite evidence to the contrary, the notion that citizens are moved in their political views by their economic circumstances continues to be a powerful narrative. I therefore account for the potential influence of *economic self-interest* in two ways. First, I include an indicator of whether respondents in my study are unemployed, a reasonable proxy for objective economic vulnerability.[52] Second, I take into consideration the possibility that some white Americans might feel economically insecure, even if they are not objectively so. Accordingly, I include a measure of the extent to which whites feel that their family has been doing better, worse, or about the same financially compared to a year ago.[53]

Another powerful predictor of public opinion is *education*. More educated individuals are more equipped to understand and interpret the political world. They also tend to be more politically interested and engaged, more liberal in their political positions, and more tolerant (Almond and Verba 1963; Hyman and Wright 1979). Thus, I include education in my analysis to be sure that the effect of white racial solidarity is independent of this factor.

My models also include controls for both *age* and *gender*. Life experiences, variation in socialization, and generational differences mean that older citizens sometimes have different preferences than younger ones, and women sometimes hold different views than men. In the analysis to come, I therefore control for these characteristics.

Individuals also arrive at their political views via matters of principle. Many Americans oppose particular policies or candidates because they support a more limited role for government, preferring fewer interference or government oversight. To determine that white racial solidarity matters above and beyond these attitudes, I also include a measure of individuals' preferences about the *scope of government* (Markus 2001).

Finally, my expectation is that white racial solidarity matters for opinion above and beyond racial animus. If white identity and white consciousness are independent constructs, capturing in-group sentiments, they should have an effect on opinion even after taking into account whites' racial out-group attitudes. In the analyses that follow, I include what has become the standard measure of whites' racial attitudes in political science: racial resentment. As I described in the previous chapters, resentment embodies the belief that blacks in the United States do not subscribe to traditional American values like hard work and patriotism (Kinder and Sanders 1996). For some of the political preferences of interest in the pages ahead, however, whites' attitudes specifically with respect to blacks are not always appropriate. There are instances in which I am more interested in how whites feel about Hispanics, and therefore I replace the measure of racial resentment with a measure of affect toward Hispanics.

Formally, the standard model I employ can be written as follows:

$$y = \beta_0 + \beta_1 \text{ White Racial Solidarity} + \beta_2 \text{ Partisanship} + \beta_3 \text{ Ideology}$$
$$+ \beta_4 \text{ Unemployed} + \beta_5 \text{Economic Self Interest}$$
$$+ \beta_6 \text{ Sociotropic Evaluations} + \beta_7 \text{ Education} + \beta_8 \text{ Age} + \beta_9 \text{ Gender}$$
$$+ \beta_{10} \text{ Limited Government} + \beta_{11} \text{ Racial Resentment} + \varepsilon$$

In the expression above, y represents opinion on a range of political preferences and attitudes that will be taken up in the chapters to come.

Conclusion

This chapter serves as an important bridge between the theory of dominant group identity salience laid out in the previous chapter and the empirical applications of white racial identity and consciousness that I take up in subsequent chapters. I introduced measures of both racial identity and racial consciousness. The ideal measure of racial identity is comprised of three items that assess the importance whites ascribe to their racial identity, how proud they are of their group, and how much in common they think group members have. When possible, this three-item measure is employed in the empirical analysis throughout this book. Often, however, we are limited to only a single measure of racial identity – the racial importance item. While a single item is less reliable than a three-item measure, this one survey question gets at the core of a social identity. It measures the strength and centrality of one's attachment to the group, and will be the measure used most often in ensuing analysis. The empirics that follow will be a testament to this single item's remarkable predictive power; it proves to be a capable and consistent measure of racial identity.

The original measure of racial consciousness I introduced is comprised, at a minimum, of three items. The first component of this measure is group identity, but the measure also accounts for two other dimensions of consciousness: the belief that the group suffers illegitimate disparities, and subscription to the notion that the group should work together to overcome these disparities. As a politicized sense of group solidarity, consciousness ought to be more closely and strongly linked to political attitudes and behavior.

Throughout this chapter, I demonstrated that the proposed measures of racial identity and racial consciousness are reliable and valid. Both demonstrate consistency over time in their distributions. Furthermore, they are indeed distinct constructs, and not merely some other political attitude or predisposition in disguise. Even more importantly, we now know that neither racial identity nor consciousness are proximate measures of racial animus, nor are they merely capturing extreme expressions of white supremacism.

White identity and consciousness are clearly tapping a much broader and more widely held set of attachments toward the in-group. The measures of both identity and consciousness provide compelling evidence for the presence of white racial solidarity – evidence that defies conventional expectations about the racial attitudes and attachments of whites. Across numerous sources of data, collected over the span of several years, we can see that a sizeable portion of white Americans do identify with their racial group. In short, between 30 and 40 percent of whites believe being white is important to their identity. A smaller – but still sizeable – proportion of whites are racially conscious; approximately 20 percent are high on white racial consciousness.

With these measures in hand, I will next turn my attention to understanding the characteristics of individuals who are more likely to adopt a racial identity and to possess a sense of group consciousness. From there, I delve deeper into the set of attitudes and beliefs possessed by white identifiers. Finally, I focus squarely on the political consequences of white identity and white consciousness. As we shall see, both are profoundly implicated in contemporary American politics.

4 WHO IDENTIFIES AS WHITE?

When Republican candidate Donald Trump won the 2016 presidential election, it came as a surprise to many journalists, pundits, and political scientists. Pre-election polling and most prominent election forecasters projected a clear victory for Democratic candidate Hillary Clinton. In a rush to offer an explanation for the election's outcome, many of these individuals latched onto a compelling narrative. They argued that Trump was carried to victory by a large, unexpected, and unprecedented wave of support by the white working class. They described this subset of white voters as aggrieved, their economic security ripped away by a loss of manufacturing jobs through outsourcing, immigration, and the broad consequences of globalization. These whites, and white men especially, experts argued, were alienated, forgotten by the political establishment on both sides of the partisan aisle, their status challenged by the country's growing racial diversity.

This account should sound familiar. It echoes many – but not all – of the claims I have made about the factors that have contributed to the rise of white identity in contemporary American politics. As I will go on to show in Chapter 8, white identity is indeed strongly linked to support for Donald Trump. But are white identifiers primarily comprised of working-class whites? Are they worried about their economic circumstances, situated in blue-collar jobs, and more likely to be men? One might wonder, too, whether high levels of white identity are more prevalent among southerners, on the assumption that race is more salient in the South, with its long history of racial tensions. Or perhaps white identifiers are found among the evangelical Christians, given the group's strong ties to Anglo-Saxon Protestantism and their own waning population. In short, who are the white identifiers and the racially conscious?

My primary goal in this book is to show the import of white identity as it relates to public opinion. Understanding the factors that lead to the development of a social identity could fill the pages of a separate book, and done well, entails observing individuals over an extended period of time. Identity acquisition is a protracted process, and the result of multiple factors. Nevertheless, I offer an at least rudimentary account of the origins of white identity, with the caveat that I cannot make robust claims about what may or may not cause an individual to adopt a racial identity in the first place. My principal aim is to understand what characteristics are correlated with strong levels of racial identity and racial consciousness among whites. By the end of this chapter, we will have, in hand, a portrait of white identifiers.

For the most part, for the sake of parsimony, I highlight comparisons across two sources of evidence – the 2012 ANES and the 2016 ANES. I supplement with analyses from the other available data sources when it is fruitful, and consider the relationships across each of my primary data sources to confirm the robustness of the results.[1] I rely on these two studies because both were conducted among nationally representative samples. What is more, the four-year difference between them allows us to draw some conclusions about the stability of the associations uncovered here, but I note that differences in time, survey modes, and samples can still yield idiosyncrasies.

Demographic Characteristics

What compels individuals to adopt strong group identities? Social psychologists have argued that an important ingredient in identity acquisition is the nature of an identity. The status, size, and permeability of a group, for instance, can affect individuals' inclination to associate with that group (see Huddy (2013) for a review). Of course, not everyone possesses a strong group identity, even when they can be objectively categorized into a particular group. We know that a majority of white Americans, for instance, do not possess a strong racial identity. What motivates some to identify with their racial group? In what follows, I consider a range of possible dispositional and contextual factors that might be associated with the propensity to adopt a white racial identity and to possess a strong group consciousness.

Age

The authors of *The American Voter*, the seminal work in American public opinion, argued that the strength of an individual's group identification is primarily a function of the length of one's time as a group member (Campbell et al. 1960). It is not inconceivable that as one progresses through life, the costs or benefits a person encounters as a function of his or her race may become more apparent, potentially fostering a greater sense of group attachment. Perhaps older whites therefore possess stronger racial identities or higher levels of racial consciousness simply by way of having been an objective group member for longer.

Age may also matter for a different reason. If we do observe higher levels of white identity and consciousness among older whites, such a relationship may have nothing to do with one's time as a group member, but instead be a function of generational effects. That is, the social and political experiences of one's cohort may make some whites more or less likely to adopt a group identity. For example, we might speculate that the racial turmoil of the 1960s, or the prevalent and socially acceptable beliefs about racial order in the United States prior to the Civil Rights movement, may have made some of the oldest generation of whites today more racially conscious and more likely to possess a racial identity.

Gender

The notion that much of today's political turmoil has been promulgated by white *men* is now deeply ingrained into contemporary political mythology. After all, they are the group most likely to feel aggrieved by the social, economic, and political gains achieved by women, immigrants, and racial and ethnic minorities over the past several decades.

What is more, there is some truth to the claim that white men's economic success and security is not what it used to be. After 1967, the median income of white men, adjusted for inflation, stagnated. Over this same period, however, the median income for women nearly doubled. Today, when it comes to median earnings, white men are slightly worse off than they were in 1996.[2] To be clear, white men are still markedly better off economically than are white women or blacks of either gender, but their stalled earnings may nevertheless contribute to the perception of economic hardship. Subsequently, we may find that white men possess stronger levels of racial solidarity than white women, especially if men find that associating with their race affords them some status or, as social identity theory would predict, preserves their self-esteem.

It is not unreasonable, however, to speculate that women may in fact possess higher levels of racial identity than men. Women tend to be more prosocial, possibly increasing their overall proclivity to adopt a group identity (Van Lange et al. 1997). Consistent with this expectation, in their analysis of white racial identity using the group closeness item, Wong and Cho (2005) find that white women report higher levels of closeness with other whites than do men.

Education

Education powerfully influences the way in which individuals interact with the political and social world (Kinder and Kam 2010; Stouffer 1955). Higher levels of education impart the skills, resources, and values that motivate people to be more deliberate in their interactions and evaluations. Education also exposes individuals to new ideas, cultures, and groups. It is, so to speak, the antidote to parochialism. One might not be surprised, therefore, to learn that higher levels of education are associated with reduced prejudice, lower levels of ethnocentrism, and greater levels of tolerance (Bobo and Licari 1989; Feldman 2003; Hetherington and Weiler 2009).

How might education be related to levels of solidarity among members of a dominant group? There are several possibilities. For one, individuals with higher levels of education might be more attuned to the different experiences of racial groups in the United States and may therefore be more likely to reject the idea that whites are a threatened group with shared interests, relative to blacks or other minorities. Levels of education are also related to certain types of worldviews – that is, to attitudes, beliefs, and behaviors – that might influence the adoption of a dominant group identity. For instance, lower levels of education are highly predictive of authoritarianism, a personality trait that leads individuals to view the world in black-and-white terms, to be inclined to see distinctions between in-groups and out-groups, and to be motivated to protect existing social norms (Feldman 2003; Hetherington and Weiler 2009). According to Stenner (2005), "there is no more important determinant of authoritarianism than (lack of) education" (p. 154).

Similarly, Gabennesch (1972) argues that lower education levels give way to higher levels of authoritarianism because a lack of education results in an insular worldview he calls "reificiation." This outlook is characterized by absolutism, adherence to conventionalism, and conformity to authority. As Feldman and Stenner (1997) explain, we can expect such individuals to "be threatened and disturbed by any events that challenge the self-evident truth of established beliefs and the integrity of the social order" (p. 767). In short, lower levels of education may foster a proclivity to identify more readily with a dominant group because of the belief structure that less educated individuals are more likely to adopt.[3]

There is also some reason to be skeptical of this relationship. Jackman challenges the proposition that higher education leads to an "enlightened" worldview and a greater commitment to tolerance. By her account, dominant groups develop ideologies that legitimize the existing hierarchical status quo (Jackman and Muha 1984), and "the well-educated members of these dominant groups are the most sophisticated practitioners of their group's ideology" (Jackman and Muha 1984).[4] Sidanius, Pratto, and Bobo (1996) make a similar prediction. They argue that the better-educated members of dominant groups, like whites, are more capable of understanding how social policy affects their group's material and symbolic interests. These more educated group members are also more likely to comprehend how ideologies of in-group superiority help maintain their group's relative dominance. Thus, we might expect that the *most* educated individuals are also the most likely to subscribe to a white identity.[5]

Table 4.1 compares whites low and high on white identity by average age, gender, and levels of education.[6] White identifiers are, on average, in their early fifties. The same is true of those high on white consciousness.[7] Compared to those low on identity, they are just slightly older, and across each of my data sources, the correlation between age and white identity (Pearson $r=0.10$ in 2012 ANES face-to-face study) is positive and often statistically significant.[8] I note, however, that the

Table 4.1 *The Relationship between White Identity and Age, Gender, and Education*

	ANES 2012 (Face-to-face)			ANES 2016 (Web)		
	Low ID	High ID	All whites	Low ID	High ID	All whites
Age (mean)	47 years	51 years	50 years	48 years	52 years	49 years
Male	54%	43%	48%	49%	44%	48%
Female	46%	57%	52%	51%	56%	52%
High school graduate (only)	35%	42%	37%	21%	40%	28%
College graduate	34%	29%	33%	38%	27%	34%
No college	65%	71%	67%	62%	73%	66%

Note: Percentages are rounded. Data are weighted.
Source: 2012 ANES, 2016 ANES.

magnitude of the coefficient is fairly small. There is a slight tendency for white identity to increase as individuals get older, but it is not an especially powerful trend.[9]

We can also see in Table 4.1 that despite the popular suggestion that white men are especially aggrieved or have been left behind by changes in American society, men do not appear to be more inclined to adopt a racial identity. In fact, 57 percent of women, compared to 43 percent of men, scored high on racial identity in the 2012 ANES, and the distribution is nearly identical in the 2016 ANES. There are also more women high on white consciousness than men. Again, just as was the case with age, however, the correlation between gender and white identity (Pearson r=0.07 in 2012 ANES face-to-face study) is quite modest. Women, for the most part, are more inclined to adopt a racial identity or a racial consciousness, but the relationship is not especially strong, nor does it appear across every data source.

The table reveals notable differences between high and low white identifiers with respect to education. Among 2012 ANES respondents, 42 percent of whites high on racial identity graduated high school, but received no further education, compared to 35 percent of whites low on identity. The separation between groups is most notable when it comes to having graduated from college. The vast majority – 71 percent – of whites high on identity do not have a college degree, compared to 67 percent of whites generally and 65 percent of those low on identity. We can see that the distribution is similar in the 2016 ANES. The differences are even more marked when it comes to racial consciousness. In the 2016 ANES (face-to-face study), 81 percent of whites high on consciousness did not graduate college (39 percent had graduated high school). In short, many whites who possess a high level of identity or consciousness have graduated high school, but the most did not complete college. Across each of my datasets, education is consistently correlated (Pearson r=-0.09 in the 2012 ANES face-to-face) with levels of identity, such that more educated respondents are less likely to report high levels of white identity.

The association between education and racial identity is in keeping with the notion that whites who are motivated to develop an explicit attachment to their racial group are also potentially more likely to adopt a reified worldview. It is also contrary to Jackman's argument about the role of education in providing the cognitive sophistication important to possessing a dominant group identity. More educated whites may be more capable of perpetuating the dominant group's ideology and status, but those efforts are not manifest in a proclivity to adopt a strong racial group identity or racial consciousness. It is less educated whites who are more inclined to identify with their racial group.

Geography

The South

There are a number of reasons to suspect that whites in different parts of the country or who live in more or less racially diverse locales may also have higher or lower levels of racial solidarity. For instance, we might expect that white racial solidarity is strongly socialized in the South, which has historically, and overtly, celebrated whiteness (Blalock 1956; Key 1949). Furthermore, a long line of work in political science has suggested that whites in more racially or ethnically diverse areas feel threatened or perceive greater racial competition, possibly influencing levels of racial solidarity (e.g., Giles and Evans 1985; McKee and Teigen 2016; Taylor 1998). Thus, in addition to expecting higher levels of solidarity in the South, we might also predict that whites in the western part of the United States, which has a large Latino population, possess higher levels of identity or consciousness. Furthermore, we might observe that whites who reside in locales with a greater

Table 4.2 *The Relationship between White Identity and Geographic Context*

	ANES 2012 (%) (Face-to-face)			ANES 2016 (%) (Web)		
	Low ID	High ID	All whites	Low ID	High ID	All whites
"Confederate" South	24	29	27	20	23	21
Deep South	4	10	6	7	9	7
Northeast	15	21	20	18	19	19
North central	28	27	28	–	–	–
South	30	33	32	25	31	27
West	26	18	20	25	19	23
Rural	16	28	20	–	–	–

Note: Percentages are rounded. Data are weighted.
Source: 2012 ANES, 2016 ANES.

percentage of blacks, or Latinos, or non-whites more generally, might be more inclined to identify with their racial group.

I explore these possible relationships in Table 4.2. I look first at whether whites in the South – defined here as the eleven former states of the Confederacy – tend to have higher levels of identity or consciousness. We can see that 29 percent of whites high on identity are in the Confederate South, compared to 27 percent of whites generally and 24 percent of whites low on racial identity. The percentages among whites in the 2016 ANES study are slightly lower, but the difference between the groups is essentially the same. There is also a positive correlation between southern residence and white identity, but the effect is small and statistically insignificant (Pearson $r=0.06$ in 2012 ANES face-to-face study).[10]

The differences by geography are somewhat more noteworthy when it comes to consciousness.[11] In the 2016 ANES (web), 26 percent of whites high on consciousness resided in the South, compared to 21 percent of all whites and 19 percent of those low on consciousness. The correlation between consciousness and southern residence is positive and significant (Pearson $r=0.05$ in 2016 ANES web), although not especially large.

More whites with high levels of racial identity are found in the South, but this trend is modest. One reason for these tepid results is that my approach is not actually distinguishing individuals who were raised and socialized in the South from those who moved their later in life. It is possible that "true" southerners are more likely to adopt a white identity, but significant in-migration to the South in recent decades makes it difficult to parse those who were socialized in the South from those who are relative newcomers with survey data that simply ask about current place of residence (Hillygus, McKee, and Young 2017). In one effort to sidestep these limitations, I examine the relationship among survey respondents residing in the deep South – Georgia, Alabama, South Carolina, Mississippi, and Louisiana – which has experienced less in-migration (Walsh 2012). The results, however, are not markedly different. I find that in the 2012 ANES (face-to-face), 10 percent of whites high on racial identity can be found in the deep South, but most white identifiers live elsewhere. A slightly greater percent (12 percent) of those high on consciousness live in the deep South (among 2016 ANES respondents), but again, most of these whites can be found in other parts of the country. The evidence that southerners tend to possess greater levels of racial solidarity than those outside the South is suggestive, but weak.

Across the Nation

Next, I compare the association between racial solidarity and residence in each of the four Census regions.[12] White identifiers are relatively dispersed across these areas, although somewhat more likely to be found in the Midwest and the South. Counter to expectations, we can also see that those whites in the western part of the country are actually less apt to possess high levels of white identity or consciousness. Approximately 18 percent of whites high on identity live in the West, compared to 26 percent of those low on identity and 20 percent of all whites (ANES 2012 face-to-face).[13]

Rural America

Political scientist Katherine Cramer (2016) makes a compelling case that many rural Americans possess a "rural consciousness," defined by perceived distributive injustices and a resentment toward elites and urban residents. Rural consciousness shares many of the same sentiments I argue are associated with white identity – a sense of perceived injustice and alienation. Could rural residence, therefore, be related to a sense of white identity as well? To find out, I matched respondents' county of residence with USDA rural–urban continuum codes, categorizing counties into metro or non-metro (rural).[14] I find that at least among respondents in the 2012 ANES, rural residence is slightly associated with levels of white identity; 28 percent of white identifiers live in a rural area, compared to 20 percent of whites generally and 15 percent of whites low on racial identity. The correlation between white identity and rural residence (Pearson $r=0.12$ in the 2012 ANES face-to-face) is also significant. The effect is not large, but there does appear to be some positive relationship between rural residence and greater levels of white identity.

I also turn to the 2010 KN and 2012 ANES studies to examine whether whites who reside in counties with different racial and ethnic characteristics tend to possess higher or lower levels of racial solidarity.[15] The results are somewhat inconsistent across the two studies, but there is some very slight evidence from the 2012 ANES that whites in communities with a higher percentage of blacks (Pearson $r=-0.07$), or a higher percentage of non-whites generally (Pearson $r=-0.08$), actually possess *lower* *l*evels of racial identity – although I note the relationship is substantively quite small.[16] Meanwhile, the percentage of Latinos in one's county seems to have little relation to levels of white identity. Furthermore, while I have argued that immigration is powerfully linked to the *activation* of white identity, there is little evidence from this analysis that it is associated with different *levels* of identity. Neither the overall percentage of foreign-born residents in communities, nor the change in the foreign-born population is significantly correlated with white identity.[17]

Economic Evaluations and Circumstances

Social scientists have long been interested in the political preferences and behavior of the white working class (Berelson, Lazarsfeld, and McPhee 1954; Lane 1959). This interest has reached new heights in recent years, and not only among academics; journalists and pundits are turning their attention to this group in earnest as well. Books like Arlie Hochschild's *Strangers in their Own Land* and J.D. Vance's *Hillbilly Elegy*, which dive deep into the lives of America's working class, made their way onto bestseller lists.[18] Their accounts seemed even more relevant after the 2016 presidential election, when many argued that Donald Trump was handed the presidency by the country's disaffected, white, blue-collar workers, whose experience with deep economic stagnation and the loss of manufacturing jobs to outsourcing had left them politically, socially, and economically aggrieved (Gest 2016). Trump's promise to restore manufacturing jobs was, according to accounts, especially enticing to this bloc of voters.

Are the political trends we are witnessing today less a story about race, and more a story of economics? Possibly. But political scientists have looked far and wide for evidence that economic self-interest significantly influences public opinion, with little to show for it (Kinder and Kiewiet 1981; Sears and Funk 1990). Today, the general consensus is that group interests and national – not personal – economic evaluations are far more potent predictors of Americans' political preferences.

In keeping with these findings, the evidence that economic factors are what best explain Trump's victory are slim (Mutz 2018). In one of the most comprehensive studies of Trump support at the time of this writing, economists at Gallup found that whites who live in places where manufacturing jobs have declined since 1990 did not view Trump more favorably (Rothwell and Diego-Rosell 2016). Furthermore, his supporters were not more likely to have lower incomes, nor to be unemployed, compared to voters that opposed Trump. They were however, living in places with low economic mobility, and tended to be blue-collar workers with less education.

Of course, I do not expect perfect overlap between support for Trump and white racial solidarity. The working-class narrative is, however, important to investigate to the extent that conventional wisdom now presumes that it is this subset of whites who are most reactive to the threats to the racial order that I have described. It is an enticing and logically compelling perspective. Surely, as realistic group conflict theory would lead one to hypothesize, the whites most vulnerable to the effects of globalization, the ones most likely to have their job shipped overseas, or to be displaced by immigrants willing to work for lower wages, ought to be more inclined to rally around their collectively threatened racial group than those more insulated from these challenges. I therefore examine the relationship between white identity, white consciousness, and a number of different measures of economic circumstances and evaluations. The results are presented in Table 4.3.

Table 4.3 *The Relationship between White Identity and Economic Evaluations and Circumstances*

	ANES 2012 (Face-to-face)			ANES 2016 (Web)		
	Low ID	High ID	All whites	Low ID	High ID	All whites
Income (mean)	$55,000–59,999	$50,000–54,999	$55,000–59,999	$60,000–64,999	$50,000–54,999	$55,000–59,999
Unemployed	3%	2%	3%	6%	6%	6%
Own home	77%	79%	78%	66%	67%	67%
Union	18%	17%	17%	15%	14%	16%
Working class	38%	42%	38%	36%	42%	36%
Middle class	72%	62%	69%	64%	58%	64%
Family worse off than year ago	40%	41%	37%	30%	33%	31%
Professional occupation	34%	24%	31%			
Clerical occupation	17%	20%	21%			
Semi-skilled occupation	33%	42%	35%			
Laborer occupation	9%	10%	7%			
Other occupation	7%	4%	6%			
Very/extremely worried about current financial situation	20%	21%	21%	10%	14%	11%
Knows someone who lost job in past 12 months	55%	51%	54%	43%	42%	44%
Economic mobility harder today	–	–	–	70%	73%	71%

Note: Percentages are rounded. Data are weighted.
Source: 2012 ANES, 2016 ANES.

I begin first with income. Do whites with lower incomes tend to possess higher levels of racial solidarity? The first row in Table 4.3 suggests that there is a weak, but apparent relationship between income and racial solidarity; higher white identifiers have mean incomes slightly below the average found among all whites in the data. In the 2012 ANES, as well as across several other studies, the correlation between income and white identity or white consciousness is small, but significant (Pearson r=0.08 for white identity).[19] Nevertheless, it is important to note that the majority of white identifiers are not what we might consider poor. Approximately 54 percent of them report incomes at or above the US Census Bureau's estimate of the 2012 US median household income of $51,371.[20]

But what about the most economically vulnerable – those who are unemployed. Are white identifiers disproportionately among this group? They are not. Only 2 percent reported being unemployed in the 2012 ANES (face-to-face), compared to 3 percent of all whites and those low on identity. Furthermore, the correlation between identity and employment is insignificant and essentially zero. White identifiers are also overwhelmingly homeowners. Among 2012 ANES respondents high on white identity, 79 percent reported owning a home, suggesting that these whites are not especially struggling financially.

Maybe these whites are more likely to live in areas where unemployment grew over time, or where manufacturing jobs declined. I examined this possibility as well, and found no significant effect. Among 2012 ANES respondents, levels of white identity were not associated with living in a county where unemployment grew between 2007 and 2012, nor was it associated with a decrease in manufacturing jobs in one's county over that same period.[21]

Much of the narrative about whites' economic struggles focuses on class. To some extent, we can capture class with income, but often what people mean when they refer to the working class is those individuals situated in blue-collar jobs that entail manual labor. The 2012 ANES allows me to assess the relationship between identity and class, defined this way, with several different approaches. First, I consider whether white identifiers are more likely to be union members or live in households with a union member, given that unions in the United States represent a disproportionate number of workers situated in more blue-collar occupations.[22] We can see in Table 4.3 that they are not. Approximately 17 percent in the 2012 ANES (face-to-face) are union members, or live in a household where someone belongs to a union, but this rate is nearly identical to the percentage of low identifiers that belong to union households. These trends are essentially the same for whites high on racial consciousness.

The 2012 ANES also asked respondents with which class group they most identify. Questions of subjective class membership are notoriously skewed; most Americans identify with the middle class, and most are not well-informed enough about income distributions in the United States to accurately place themselves into objective class categories.[23] Furthermore, no particular income level qualifies one as middle class, making these class identities highly subjective. Nevertheless, there do appear to be some small differences when it comes to how low and high identifying whites think about their class group. From Table 4.3, we can see that most white identifiers – 62 percent – place themselves in the middle class. That percentage is slightly lower than what we find among all whites (69 percent), and ten percentage points lower than where low identifiers place themselves. Relative to all whites and white identifiers, a slightly greater percentage – 42 percent – of white identifiers identify as working class. The trends for individuals high and low on consciousness in the 2016 ANES (web) are roughly the same. There is, then, a slight tendency for white identifiers to see themselves as working class. Most whites high on identity, however, place themselves in the middle class.

The 2012 ANES also asked individuals, via an open-ended question, to state their occupation. I coded respondents' stated occupation into one of the following categories: professional or managerial, clerical worker, semi-skilled worker, laborer, or other (a category which includes students and homemakers).[24] Are white identifiers disproportionately found among one of these occupational categories? To some extent, yes. Most white identifiers – 42 percent – are in semi-skilled positions. By comparison, 35 percent of all whites fall into this occupation category, and only 33 percent of low identifiers do. Fewer white identifiers have professional occupations. Only 24 percent are in this category, compared to 31 percent of all whites and 34 percent of low identifiers. Still, when we take clerical occupations into account, about equal numbers of white identifiers are in professional or clerical occupations as are in semi-skilled jobs. Approximately 10 percent are in laborer positions. By these accounts, we can roughly place about half of white identifiers in jobs that might be considered blue-collar, which is just slightly more than the white population generally.

Perhaps racial solidarity is more strongly linked to subjective economic evaluations, rather than objective circumstances. In the 2012 ANES study, respondents were asked whether their family was doing better, worse, or about the same financially as they were in previous years. Do white identifiers have a more negative personal financial outlook? Not compared to those low on identity. The correlation between white identity and negative personal economic evaluations is essentially zero and insignificant. Perhaps they are not more or less worried than in previous years, but are nonetheless concerned about their current financial situation. They are not, as it turns out. Approximately 21 percent express some worry about their economic circumstances, but that is no more than low identifiers or all whites more generally. Another 51 percent say they know someone who lost a job in the past 12 months, but that's slightly fewer than whites low on identity. In short, whites high on identity do not report being any more economically troubled or vulnerable than whites low on identity.

Results from the 2016 ANES, however, do suggest that whites high on racial consciousness may be somewhat more concerned about their economic circumstances. Approximately 38 percent of whites high on consciousness reported that their family was worse off than a year ago, which is eight percentage points more than those low on consciousness. The same percentage also reported being very or extremely worried about their current financial situation, compared to just 20 percent of whites low on consciousness and 24 percent of all whites. Furthermore, 53 percent claimed to know someone who lost a job in the past month, which is more than the 41 percent of those low on consciousness and 44 percent of all whites. Finally, 79 percent of whites high on consciousness claimed that it is harder to get ahead economically today than it was twenty years ago, which is slightly more than the 70 percent of whites low on consciousness who complained about economic mobility. Thus, there is some evidence that while those high on consciousness are not necessarily objectively worse off compared to other whites, they are at least more inclined to feel that their economic circumstances could be better.

Religion

Part of the narrative about the threat posed to American identity by immigration and increasing racial and ethnic diversity is about

Table 4.4 *The Relationship between White Identity and Religion*

	ANES 2012 (%) (Face-to-face)			ANES 2016 (%) (Web)		
	Low ID	High ID	All whites	Low ID	High ID	All whites
Mainline Protestant	14	15	14	2	3	3
Evangelical Protestant	14	19	19	9	8	8
Roman Catholic	20	23	24	24	23	25
Undifferentiated Christian	17	16	16	–	–	–
Not religious	25	20	22	13	17	9
Bible is word of God	24	35	28	22	30	25

Note: Percentages are rounded. Data are weighted.
Source: 2012 ANES, 2016 ANES.

religion. It is not merely that white dominance is challenged by demographic change, but that white *Christian* America is in decline. Between 2008 and 2016, the percentage of Americans who identify as both Christian and white fell 11 percentage points. The nation went from a majority (54 percent) to a minority (43 percent) white Christian nation (Huntington 2004). In response to these trends, conservative elites have appealed to their white Christian base, especially Protestants and evangelicals, warning them that demographic changes pose a threat to the group's political power and their ability to elect conservative Republicans who align with their policy positions.

Religion is also deeply entrenched in the character of American identity. The dominant culture in the United States is not merely white; it is Anglo-Protestant. The influx of immigrants, particularly from Latin America, may not threaten America's Christian identity, but they may be seen by some as posing a challenge to the nation's Anglo-Protestant culture (Sears and Savalei 2006; Wong 2018). For these reasons, we might expect an association between Protestant or evangelical identity and white identity.

In Table 4.4, I examine these possible relationships. Approximately 15 percent of white identifiers are mainline Protestant, and 19 percent identify as evangelical. Another 23 percent are Roman Catholic. About 16 percent are other Christian denominations and 20 percent say they are not religious. I also inquire as to whether white identifiers are more likely to believe in biblical inerrancy – or the belief that the bible is the literal word of God. Here, we do see somewhat of a distinction. Approximately 35 percent of white identifiers subscribe to biblical inerrancy, compared to 24 percent of whites low on identity. We see similar trends among whites in the 2016 ANES when it comes to both racial identity and racial consciousness.[25] White identifiers, like most whites in America, are Christian, and while no Christian denomination is especially over-represented among this group, a sizeable minority of these whites do adopt evangelical beliefs.

Partisanship and Ideology

Most Americans have an attachment to one political party or the other, and parties today tend to reflect our nation's social cleavages, including those with respect to race. Today, blacks in the United States are more likely to identify with the Democratic Party and white Americans slightly favor the Republican Party. Given these trends, we might expect that white identifiers are more at home among the Republican Party, especially if they believe that Democrats cater more to the political interests of racial and ethnic minorities. We saw in the previous chapter that there is a slight but significant correlation between white identity and partisanship. That relationship is confirmed in Table 4.5. Among whites high on racial identity, 55 percent identify as Republican compared to 50 percent of those low on identity. Another 31 percent identify as Democrats compared to 43 percent of those low on identity. These distributions are largely the same when we compare whites high and low on racial consciousness.[26] Interestingly, a notable 14 percent claim they are independents – twice that of low-identifiers and slightly more than the white population as a whole.

A majority of those high on identity also consider themselves ideologically conservative. Among respondents in the ANES, 57 percent of white identifiers lean conservative, compared to 51 percent of those low on identity and 54 percent of all whites. Only 28 percent call themselves liberal, far fewer than the 40 percent of low identifiers who indicate they are ideologically liberal, and the 34 percent of all whites who lean left. Among whites high on consciousness, this number is even lower. Only 19 percent say they are ideologically liberal, while most (51 percent) identify as conservative in the 2016 ANES (web).

Table 4.5 *The Relationship between White Identity and Partisanship and Political Ideology*

	ANES 2012 (%) (Face-to-face)			ANES 2016 (%) (Web)		
	Low ID	High ID	All whites	Low ID	High ID	All whites
Democrat	43	31	39	44	33	39
Republican	50	55	52	41	55	47
Independent	7	14	9	15	12	14
Liberal	40	28	34	34	24	29
Conservative	51	57	54	41	50	45

Note: Percentages are rounded. Data are weighted.
Source: 2012 ANES, 2016 ANES.

Personality

As Aristotle observed, we, as social animals, have a fundamental need to belong. Perhaps, therefore, our propensity to adopt particular group identities is deeply rooted, so ingrained that it is a function of our personalities. Social scientists are paying increasing attention to the role of personality in guiding individual behavior, including the propensity to develop strong group attachments (Mullin and Hogg 1999).

Much of the research on how personality influences politics rests on the assumption that personality traits are further back in a causal chain, in which certain characteristics or contextual factors are more proximate to political preferences than others. In other words, the ideological beliefs, racial attitudes, or group identities we adopt, and that then influence our political beliefs and behaviors, are likely a function of our personality traits. Thus, we might expect personality to have less of a direct effect on political behavior and to instead work through attitudes and identities more proximate to political preferences and behavior.

Before proceeding, I want to again remind readers of the limitations presented by the analysis that lies ahead. When it comes to examining the factors that predict adopting a group identity, our ability to draw conclusions about causality is limited. Just as I do here, most existing research on the matter dabbles in associations using observational data, and the link between individual traits and group attachments is therefore muddied; some scholars make claims that individual traits drive the adoption of identities, and others suggest that some of these same traits arise as a result of strong group attachments. In the analysis that follows, I remain cautiously agnostic about the direction of relationships. I also recognize that some work has uncovered a direct association between some of the traits I investigate and political attitudes and behavior.

At the same time, I want to reiterate the group-centric nature of politics. Politicians, policymakers, and other political elites craft their appeals around major social cleavages and social identities. And people think about politics in these terms, too (Converse 1964; Nelson and Kinder 1996). For these reasons, we would expect that people's political preferences are likely organized and influenced by their group attitudes more readily and more powerfully than by their less-proximate personality traits. This speculation does not mean that white identity, for instance, does all the work of channeling the influence of personality traits into political attitudes and behavior. Instead, I recommend we proceed with the following explanation in mind: certain individual traits may go hand in hand with a penchant for adopting a racial identity – a racial identity that, as we will see, affects how individuals interact with the political world. Many of these traits may also have separate, independent effects on political preferences, as prior work has shown. Thus, while we want to know the extent to which they are associated with white identity, in analysis in chapters to come, we may also look to see the extent to which identity is related to political attitudes above and beyond these traits, when appropriate.

The Big Five Personality Dimensions

Some work has already begun to explore how personality traits might influence the propensity to adopt a group identity. Qualities like the need for certainty about the world (Neuberg and Newsom 1993), one's level of cognitive complexity (Goodwin and Friedman 2006), and other dimensions of personality may be related to the development of in-group identification and bias. Similarly, it could be that different personality traits can help account for variation in the propensity to adopt a strong racial identity among a dominant group, like whites. To explore this possibility further, I turn to one branch of personality research, which posits that core personality traits can be conceived of along five dimensions. These dimensions are measured with survey questions that ask respondents to evaluate how well a range of different qualities describe themselves.

The first of the five dimensions, extraversion, is associated with sociability and assertiveness. The second, agreeableness, is linked to a tendency to be cooperative and harmonious with others. The third, conscientiousness, is a tendency to be dependable, dutiful, and to adhere to social norms. The fourth, emotional stability, sometimes referred to as neuroticism, is linked with low levels of negative emotions like anxiety and anger. Lastly, openness to experience is associated with intellectual curiosity and independence. Work in this domain has found that these "Big Five" personality traits predict a wide range of attitudes, behaviors, and life circumstances, including overall health (Borghans et al. 2008) and income levels (Gerber et al. 2010, 2012; Mondak 2010). These traits are also associated with variables of greater interest to political scientists, including political ideology, policy preferences, partisanship, and political behavior (Gerber et al. 2010, 2012; Mondak 2010). Gerber et al. (2012), for instance, find that extraversion and agreeableness are associated with stronger partisan identities. These dimensions might very well be associated with a general proclivity to adopt a strong group identity.

I turn to the 2012 ANES to consider whether some of these personality dimensions are associated with higher levels of white racial identity. The inherent sociability of extraverted individuals may make group identities more appealing, but it is not obvious that greater levels of racial identity among whites promote more social interactions between group members. Thus, while extraversion might be associated with higher levels of political participation, it is less clear that this dimension will matter for the adoption of white identity. When it comes to agreeableness, individuals who score high on this dimension are also likely to be drawn into pro-social behavior. As Mondak (2010) argues, however, agreeable individuals desire to maintain positive relations with others, avoid group conflict, and tend to express lower levels of prejudice.[27] If identifying as white is rooted in group conflict and perceptions of threat, then we might expect agreeableness to be negatively related to a strong sense of in-group identification.

Emotionally stable people tend to be calm, relaxed, and exhibit greater self-control. Individuals at the opposite end of this dimension tend to be anxious and nervous. If stronger white identities are associated with the maintenance of privilege and activated in response to threat, then individuals more sensitive to threats may be more likely to cling to their racial identity. Thus, we would expect emotional stability to be negatively related to white identity. Further, individuals who score higher on the openness to experience dimension are more likely to seek information, to expose themselves to new cultures, and to try new activities and meet new people. It seems reasonable that individuals with these traits may be less threatened by other racial or ethnic groups, or by demographic changes. Therefore, we might expect this trait to be negatively associated with white identity. Finally, conscientious individuals tend to favor personal responsibility and tradition. They prefer the status quo. These individuals may be more prone to find demographic change, or the election of Obama, as a disruption to the traditional norms of American society. Thus, perhaps conscientiousness is positively related to white racial identity.

I look at the relationship between white identity and these personality dimensions both via the correlation between the individual items, and by including all of the items together into a single multivariate regression model to account for the possibility of a common, latent, dimension underlying each factor. For each personality trait, the correlation is in the expected direction. Those higher on white identity display higher levels of extraversion (Pearson $r=0.04$ 2012 ANES face-to-face), lower levels of agreeableness (Pearson $r=-0.04$), and higher levels of conscientiousness (Pearson $r=0.01$). They are also less emotionally stable (Pearson $r=-0.07$) and less open to new experiences (Pearson $r=-0.05$).[28] The correlation is only statistically significant with respect to emotional stability, however, and the strength of the correlations in each case is relatively small.

Multivariate analysis paints a clearer picture. Accounting for each factor simultaneously, I find that white identifiers and whites high on consciousness tend to be more extraverted and less emotionally stable. The strongest and most consistent relationship appears to be with respect to openness, which is negatively associated with levels of identity.[29] The less open to new experiences individuals are, the more inclined they are to adopt a white identity. These traits are consistent with the notion that whites high on identity are more insular, and potentially less agreeable to outsiders, to immigrants, and to perceived changes in their culture and communities.

Authoritarianism and Social Dominance Orientation

There are additional personality traits beyond the Big Five, which have the potential to powerfully influence political attitudes and behavior. One of these traits in particular has received renewed attention in political science: authoritarianism. The theory of the authoritarian personality, originally conceived by Theodor Adorno and his colleagues (1950), has loomed large in psychology. It describes a personality syndrome thought to be, in part, the product of strict socialization and punitive parenting. The resulting repressed hostility toward parents and authority figures manifests as a broader hostility toward out-groups. Today, one way we measure individual levels of authoritarianism is with survey questions that ask about child-rearing practices. Individuals are asked to choose, for instance, whether it is more important for children to be independent or to respect their elders, or whether they should display curiosity above good manners.

As a construct, authoritarianism is very much out-group oriented. Karen Stenner calls it a predisposition of intolerance (Stenner 2005). It is therefore perhaps unsurprising that authoritarianism is associated with ethnocentrism, anti-Semitism, and prejudice (Perreault and Bourhis 1999). Authoritarianism, however, is also thought to be associated with stronger in-group identities – even artificial groups in labs – including attachments with dominant social groups (Feldman and Stenner 1997; Stenner 2005). Duckitt (1989), for instance, argued that authoritarian behavior might be explained by a tendency for some individuals to identify with dominant social groups. Furthermore, much in the same way I argue white identity is activated by perceived group threat, so too is authoritarianism (Pratto et al. 1994; Sidanius and Pratto 1999). It seems reasonable, therefore, to postulate that white identity and authoritarianism are related.

I also consider the possibility that white identity is a product of another trait: social dominance orientation (SDO). The architects of social dominance theory argue that individuals vary in the extent to which they possess an SDO. This personality trait, which they claim is normally distributed across individuals, is a significant factor in the acceptance or rejection of ideologies that foster inequality (Levin and Sidanius 1999; Pratto et al. 1994). Individuals who score high on SDO desire that their in-group dominate and be superior to out-groups. They also prefer that groups be arranged hierarchically, and they eschew equality. Because strong group identities and in-group favor-itism reinforce their group's position in the social hierarchy, members of high-status dominant groups are thought to possess higher levels of in-group identification. Existing empirical work supports this claim (Levin and Sidanius 1999; Sidanius, Pratto, and Mitchell 1994).

How does white identity relate to both authoritarianism and SDO? The Pearson r correlation between authoritarianism and white racial identity in the 2012 ANES is 0.16.[30] In 2016, the correlation is 0.19. In both cases, the relationship is significant, but the size of the correlation is modest. We can say that that there is a tendency for those high on white identity to score higher on authoritarianism, but they are not one and the same.

The picture with regards to SDO is slightly different. I measured SDO with four standard items on the 2013 SSI Study.[31] Compared to authoritarianism, there is a more notable correlation between identity and SDO (Pearson $r=0.42$); whites with higher levels of SDO are also more inclined to adopt a white racial identity. This finding is consistent with several studies, which have documented a strong correlation between SDO and in-group identification among high-status groups (Levin and Sidanius 1999; Sidanius et al. 1997; Sidanius, Pratto, and Rabinowitz 1994). To be clear, the magnitude of the coefficient does not suggest we should conclude that white identity is merely a proxy for SDO. Indeed, Sidanius and his students have argued that SDO is associated with strong group identities, but is also complementary, serving as a crucial ingredient linking in-group identification to out-group discrimination (Levin and Sidanius 1999).

The correlational analyses have left us with several impressions. There is a slight – and I emphasize slight – tendency for those whites who possess higher levels of white identity and white consciousness to be older, to be women, to have lower levels of education, and to occupy more blue-collar jobs. For the most part, whites high on identity are not objectively more economically vulnerable than other whites in the United States. Most own homes, and white identifiers, at least, do not report that they are more economically fragile than other whites. There is, however, some indication that whites high on racial consciousness do feel somewhat more troubled financially. Consciousness, as a con-struct, in part embodies a sense of aggrievement, and these whites do in fact feel aggrieved. Among whites high on identity and conscious-ness, there is also a small association with evangelicalism, southern residence, and living in a rural locale. Personality traits also seem markedly linked as well, especially authoritarianism and SDO.

Competing Factors

We have in hand a profile of white identifiers, but by looking only at correlations, it is difficult to tell whether some of these relationships are spurious. For instance, the association between white racial solidarity and occupation may just be a function of the fact that both are correlated with levels of education. To account for this possibility, I turn to multivariate analysis, modeling white identity and consciousness as a function of many of these factors simultaneously.

I find, across surveys and over time, that age is often a small but significant predictor of identity, all else equal.[32] Older whites are somewhat more inclined to identify as white. Education matters, too. More educated whites have lower levels of identity. Region, rural residence, and religion, however, do not stand out as predictors once we account for the other predictors described throughout this chapter. Economic factors are not especially important, either. Neither income, employment status, union membership, occupying a blue-collar job, nor feeling negatively about one's current financial situation are significantly predictive of white identity. But the personality measures, including authoritarianism and SDO, do hold up to controls. Both are indicative of higher levels of white identity.

The results are similar when it comes to white racial consciousness. Whites with higher levels of consciousness tend to be older, they are more likely to be women, and they have lower levels of education. Both authoritarianism and SDO are predictive of white consciousness as well. In addition, just as is the case with respect to white identity, personal economic circumstances and religion have little effect.[33]

Conclusion

In this chapter, I have considered whether a range of demographic characteristics, contextual factors, and personality traits are associated with levels of identity and consciousness. While my efforts here are not, primarily, to understand *why* someone adopts a strong racial identity, we can get a sense of who among the white American population comprises the white identifiers and the racially conscious.

All else equal, white identity and white consciousness tend to be consistently linked to levels of education and to certain personality traits. There is also a notable association with age, and to a lesser extent, gender. That higher levels of education are linked to lower levels of racial solidarity is a finding counter to at least some previous empirical work on white identity, measured with the closeness item (Wong and Cho 2005).[34] It is also contrary to the claims of Jackman (1994) and others that the most educated are more adept at perpetuating the racial status quo. The finding is, however, consistent with the notion that white racial solidarity is more likely to be embraced by individuals with a particular personality profile – those who cling to tradition, who are less open to new experiences, who support hierarchy and authority, and who are resistant to interruptions of the status quo. Those who are lower in education, higher in authoritarianism, and with greater levels of SDO are inclined to possess such a worldview.

I also explored whether geographic context is associated with white racial solidarity. Are whites in the South, where they were perhaps socialized to hold their racial group in high esteem, more inclined to adopt an identity or sense of consciousness? To some extent, yes. There is evidence that southern residence is tied to slightly higher levels of white racial solidarity. The effect, however, is not overwhelmingly consistent or strong in magnitude, nor does it hold up well to controls for other factors in a multivariate model. That is, whites with high levels of racial solidarity are found in *and* outside of the South.

What of whites in more racially diverse areas, or who live in places that have experienced significant changes in the foreign-born composition of their communities? A long line of work on racial threat might predict that whites in these places – where race ought to be more salient and perceptions of inter-group threat greater – should have adopted stronger group identities. There is, however, little evidence that greater diversity leads to higher levels of white identity. These analyses should not necessarily be taken as the final word on the matter; there is more work to be done in the future examining the effect of context on the development of group identities. But what we can see here is that to the extent to which one's community is associated with levels of group solidarity, the relationship is better captured by the rural/urban divide. In keeping with Walsh (2012), rural residents are somewhat distinct; whites in these counties are somewhat more likely to adopt a strong group identity, but it is unclear whether there is something unique about rural residence, or if instead that relationship appears because whites in those areas are likely to be less educated and older.

I also took up in earnest the idea that a subscription to white identity or consciousness is a working-class phenomenon. Are such attachments found in great levels among the ranks of the more economically aggrieved, those with lower incomes, those who perceive their families to be struggling financially, those who are unemployed, and those who work blue-collar jobs? This narrative carries a little weight, but we should be cautious in concluding that white identity politics is the politics of the white working class. Whites high on identity and consciousness are not, for the most part, objectively economically vulnerable. Most own houses, have average incomes similar to most whites in the United States, are employed, and identify as middle class. There is some tendency among those high on racial consciousness to report a greater degree of financial despair when asked about how their family is doing economically, but those evaluations do not necessarily map onto objective economic circumstances. The evidence presented here suggests that the pervasive narrative about class is *not* a story about realistic group conflict, in which the most objectively economically vulnerable whites are aggrieved and now politically conscious, uniquely airing their grievances at the ballot box. Indeed, there are many whites who possess high levels of racial consciousness who are financially secure and situated in white-collar jobs.

We should also keep in mind that class, geography, status, and education, together, are a confluence of circumstances and characteristics whose effects are difficult to untangle. White Americans in blue-collar jobs in more rural areas of the United States may comprise a slightly greater share of those who are high on identity and consciousness. We should nevertheless be hesitant to conclude that their politics are driven by economic self-interest. An alternative explanation is that these whites, given their circumstances, are also likely to have lower levels of education, to have lived more insular lives, and to be more inclined toward parochialism. It is not, therefore, necessarily their economic circumstances motivating their beliefs, and multivariate analyses corroborate this point; education, which tends to correlate highly with occupation, geography, and worldviews, is also significantly associated with white racial solidarity.

We might also consider the small effects of class as indicative of another way in which the racial hierarchy in the United States
influences attitudes and behavior. Many whites may not be directly
motivated by economic self-interest but working-class whites may
nevertheless find race to be an attractive social identity. While many
of these whites possess similar economic interests as blacks and other
minorities in the United States, the nation's racial hierarchy has generally prevented working-class whites from seeing themselves as sharing
the same fate as these other groups. Instead, working-class whites have
been able to use race as a means to elevate and distance their own
group from those at the bottom of the racial order.

Writing about class during Reconstruction, W.E.B. Du Bois
described working-class whites' ability to make these distinctions as the
"psychological wage" they were paid, relative to working-class blacks:

> They were given public deference and titles of courtesy because
> they were white. They were admitted freely with all classes of
> white people to public functions, public parks, and the best
> schools. The police were drawn from their ranks, and the courts,
> dependent upon their votes, treated them with such leniency as
> to encourage lawlessness. Their vote selected public officials, and
> while this had small effect upon the economic situation, it had
> great effect upon their personal treatment and the deference shown
> them. White schoolhouses were the best in the community, and
> conspicuously placed, and they cost anywhere from twice to ten
> times as much per capita as the colored schools. The newspapers
> specialized on news that flattered the poor whites and almost
> utterly ignored the Negro except in crime and ridicule.
>
> (1935, p. 700)

One could imagine that for many whites, especially those without
college degrees and in more rural areas, that their race may be an
important marker of their status – an identity they are more likely to
adopt in the midst of growing resentment about a changing nation
and changing world, in which they perhaps feel their group is being
left behind. If whites – particularly working-class whites – see value
in these privileges for their group, then they ought to be especially
reactive to threats to the advantages and status they accrue from being
white. One can certainly see how the nation's increasing diversity, and
the perceived political, economic, and social success of people of color,
might be viewed by some as a challenge to these wages.

5 THE CONTENT AND CONTOURS OF WHITENESS

According to sociologist George Lipsitz, whiteness is everywhere, but it is hard to see. He writes that as "the unmarked category against which difference is constructed, whiteness never has to speak its name, never has to acknowledge its role as an organizing principle in social and cultural relations" (1998, p. 1). This perspective captures the way most scholarship has described white identity over the past twenty years (Delgado and Stefancic 1997; Flagg 1993; Frankenberg 1993; Perry 2001). As the dominant group in American society, so the argument goes, whites are less likely to experience discrimination or to be reminded of social or cultural differences, making their identity hidden or invisible (Doane 1997).

Prior to conceptualizing whiteness in this way, much of the scholarly work on the identities of white Americans in the twentieth century focused on the role and nature of white *ethnic* identities (e.g., Berelson, Lazarsfeld, and McPhee 1954). By the 1990s, however, scholars had argued that European immigrants had completely assimilated into American culture, and Italian, Irish, Polish, and other ethnicities were no longer salient for white Americans (Alba 1990; Kaufmann 2004; Waters 1990).

Today, many scholars agree that the "American culture" into which these groups assimilated was narrowly defined in the nineteenth century as Anglo-Protestant (Allen 1997; King 2000). Individuals of European descent who were not initially considered white by early nineteenth-century terms were eventually subsumed under the umbrella of whiteness, in part by distancing themselves from blacks in the United

States and by abandoning their European ethnic identities (Brodkin 1998; Ignatiev 1995; Jacobson 1999; Roediger 2006). This process of assimilation, coupled with the way in which group dominance shapes group identities, means that whiteness became largely characterized not merely as invisible, but as contentless and indistinguishable from national identity. In this sense, white identity has been defined as the loss of identity, or as "mainstream," and therefore without identifiable qualities or mores.

In this chapter, I reevaluate the claim that white identity has no content. I examine how whites understand their race and consider the attitudes and beliefs that accompany the adoption of a white racial identity. Via a series of survey questions, and by asking whites to explain their attitudes about their identity in their own words, we can see that whites who identify with their racial group share a set of common ideas about their group and attach meaning to their race.

The discoveries here reinforce my argument that white identity is a meaningful social identity, and like other identities, there emerges a consensus among group members about the qualities and characteristics of the group and its status. I find that the construction of whiteness is based largely around three themes: its relationship with a particular conception of American identity, the adoption of a sense of pride and entitlement, and the prevalence of a sense of grievance and deprivation. Each of these elements influences the way in which white identifiers understand and interpret the political and social world.

Racial Identity Imbued with National Identity

One need not look with much scrutiny to recognize that America's culture and traditions have been deeply influenced by the nation's Anglo-Saxon Protestant heritage. This conception of American identity was crafted deliberately and can be traced to the very founding of the nation (Kaufmann 2000; King 2000). In 1790, when the US Congress passed the first law concerning the granting of national citizenship, it limited naturalization to immigrants who were "free white persons" of good character.[1] It would be 162 years later, with the passage of the Immigration and Nationality Act of 1952, before Congress would abolish the racial restrictions placed on immigration and naturalization that began in 1790.

This is just but one of many examples of the ways in which race has been constructed and codified, both subtly and overtly, by America's laws and institutions (Haney-Lopez 2006; Harris 1993). As part of this process, American identity has been rendered by its racial identity. Whiteness in America is often viewed as synonymous with "American," and the dominant identity of America is, in turn, defined by whiteness (Masuoka and Junn 2013). Today, this association is so tightly bound that it pervades whites' subconscious. Psychologists Devos and Banaji (2005) demonstrate through a series of implicit association tests that Americans automatically and unconsciously associate "American" with "White." The greater the extent to which whites demonstrated this "American = White" association, the stronger was their reported national identity.

Most white Americans see themselves as archetypal members of the nation. Whites have, after all, been able to set the standard for what it means to be a prototypical American (Theiss-Morse 2009). We should expect, however, that white identifiers are especially likely to view themselves as prototypical, in part because what imbues their group with privileges and status is, in fact, this ability to define what it means to be American. Thus, the relationship between national identity and racial identity should, therefore, be somewhat symbiotic, and higher levels of white identity should be associated with stronger levels of American identity. Further, when whites talk about their racial identity, they are likely to tie its content to the symbols and traditions of the nation, or to describe their group as prototypical.

To determine whether whites who feel attached to their racial group are also more inclined to identify strongly as American, I turn to the 2010 KN survey, the 2012 ANES, the 2013 SSI Study, and the 2016 ANES. Each survey measured American identity similarly to how I measure white identity – by asking respondents the extent to which being an American is important to their identity on a five-point scale ranging from "not important" to "extremely important." I present, in Table 5.1, the pairwise correlation between white identity, white consciousness, and American identity across each survey. In each case, the correlation is significant and positive. Whites with higher levels of racial solidarity are indeed somewhat inclined to identify more strongly as Americans. It is important to note, however, that the correlations are not enormous. White identity and American identity are not one and the same.

Table 5.1 *The Correlation between White Identity and American Identity*

	KN 2010	ANES 2012		SSI 2013	ANES 2016	
		(Face-to-face)	(Web)		(Face-to-face)	(Web)
White identity	0.28*	0.24*	0.18*	0.31*	0.41*	0.38*
	(747)	(856)	(2,386)	(797)	(698)	(1,886)
White consciousness				0.40*	0.43*	0.40*
				(798)	(700)	(1,891)

Note: Table entries are pairwise correlation coefficients. Number of observations in parentheses.
* p<0.05.
Source: 2010 KN, 2012 ANES, 2013 SSI, 2016 ANES.

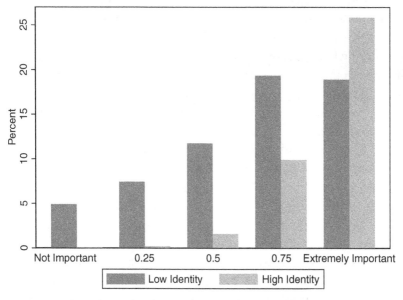

Figure 5.1 The Relationship between White Identity and American Identity
Note: The bars present the percentage of respondents at each level of American identity. Whites "low" on racial identity are those who reported their identity as "a little important" or "not at all important." Those high on identity are those who said their racial identity is "very important" or "extremely important."
Source: 2016 ANES (web).

To provide a better sense of this relationship, I present in Figure 5.1 the distribution of responses to the American identity item among low and high white identifiers.[2] We can see that whites high on racial identity are clustered at the high end of the American identity scale. Nearly 26 percent of respondents scored high on both racial identity and on American identity. Viewing the distribution this way, however, still obscures an important point, which is that close to 69 percent of whites high on racial identity indicated that their American identity is extremely important to them. To the extent that the correlation between racial identity and American identity is not overwhelming, it is because, as we can see from the figure, there are many whites who score low on racial identity but still high on American identity. In other words, we can say this about the relationship between American identity and white identity: there are many white Americans who do not identify with their racial group but do identify strongly as American. At the same time, of course, notable percentages of white Americans reject both identities. Most whites who do identify with their racial group, however, also possess a strong national identity.

When whites high on racial solidarity think about their racial group and what it means to identify with it, is their thinking interlaced with conceptions of America? To find out, I return to the open-ended surveys I introduced in Chapter 3.[3] Recall that, on a 2013 Mechanical Turk survey and on the 2016 YouGov Study, I asked whites to explain their response to the racial importance identity question. On the MTurk survey, I also asked fifty-six white respondents the following: "When you think about white people, what comes to mind? Are there any symbols, events, things of cultural significance that you think best represent most whites?"

Their responses were notably infused with references to American identity and the symbols that accompany it. Many wrote that they thought of the American flag. Others said that the Founding Fathers came to mind. They drew on many of the tropes associated with American culture. One person wrote, "Generally I think about middle class families, baseball, hot dogs." Several discussed our national holidays and mentioned European ancestry. A number of respondents simply described white as synonymous with American, invoking the notion of prototypicality. One person said, "Just average, white people are average in America." Another wrote, "Mainstream America, the way that people of every race who have money choose to live," and still another said, "America. America as a whole is a good representation. The whole idea and meaning behind it." In the minds of whites with high racial solidarity, the characteristics of the white identity and American identity are intimately linked.

Racial Identity and the Boundaries of National Identity

The associations white identifiers make between their racial group and their national identity have broader implications. According to Theiss-Morse (2009), strong national identifiers, who are more likely to view themselves as prototypical group members, also have an incentive to establish distinct boundaries around their national group. These boundaries are more likely to be exclusive, meaning that some Americans might maintain a particular normative idea of who represents a "true" American (Citrin, Reingold, and Green 1990; Schildkraut 2007; Wright, Citrin, and Wand 2012). Theiss-Morse differentiates between "hard" and "soft" boundaries when it comes to American identity. Hard boundaries, she argues, are those characteristics that people are born into or are difficult to change, like being Christian, being born in the United States, living in the United States for a long period of time, speaking English, and being white. In contrast, soft boundaries exist around qualities that are easier to adopt, like obtaining American citizenship, feeling American, and respecting the nation's laws and institutions.[4] Do whites with higher levels of identity adopt more exclusive, hard boundaries around their conceptualization of American identity, ones that prioritize their white, Christian, English-speaking heritage?

To find out, I asked whites on the 2013 SSI survey a series of questions that capture these different attitudes toward being a "true American." Respondents were asked to what extent having American citizenship, being Christian, speaking English, feeling American, having American ancestry, having been born in America, having lived in America for most of one's life, respecting America's political institutions and laws, and being white are important for being truly American on a five-point scale from "extremely important" to "not at all important."

What is the relationship between white identity and each of these different aspects of American identity? To obtain a closer view, we can examine Figure 5.2, which compares the distribution of responses for each of the nine items by high and low identifiers.

The chart is revealing. It is immediately obvious, as one pans across the panels, that there is a divide in opinion between whites with low levels of racial identity and those with higher levels. For instance, a greater number of the people who say that having American citizenship is extremely important to being truly American are high

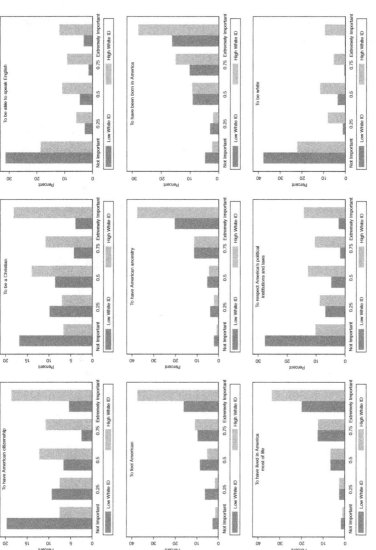

Figure 5.2 White Identity and Different Features of American Identity

Note: Bars represent the percentage of respondents who gave each answer to each survey question. Whites "low" on racial identity are those who reported their identity as "a little important" or "not at all important." Those high on identity are those who said their racial identity is "very important" or "extremely important."

Source: 2013 SSI Study

identifiers. The vast majority of those who say American citizenship is not at all important score low on racial identity. We can also see that white identifiers are disproportionately represented among those who think that being Christian is important to being American, and they are slightly more inclined to be among those who think that speaking English is important. Interestingly, both high and low identifiers seem to be in greater agreement that speaking English is not as important for being an American.

White identifiers are over-represented among those who think having American ancestry, having been born in America, and living in America for most of one's life are important for being truly American. Perhaps not surprisingly, while "being white" is not an especially popular criterion for being American, those who think it is are more likely to identify as white. But white identifiers do not just comprise the lion's share of those with hard boundaries around American identity; they also are found among those who endorse soft boundaries as well.[5] Of the individuals who believe feeling American and respecting America's political institutions and laws are important to being American, more score high on identity than low.[6]

Another interpretation of these results is that Americans high on racial identity do not emphatically embrace each more exclusionary attribute of Americanness, but they do not vehemently reject these attributes either. They are, compared to low identifiers, less inclined to reject the idea that boundaries of prototypicality should be placed around national identity.

While the distribution of these different components of American identity is noteworthy, they cannot tell us whether white identity is strongly associated with the endorsement of more exclusionary attitudes about who is a "true American," all else equal. Perhaps negative attitudes toward non-whites primarily underlie support for this flavor of American identity. Alternatively, it might be that having a stronger national identity generally is what primarily promotes this preference, as Theiss-Morse would argue. To explore this, I examine the relationship between white identity and attitudes about being a "true" American in two different ways. I look at the relationship between racial identity and the endorsement of these boundaries as separate scales representing "hard" and "soft" boundaries, and then together by creating an additive index of all nine of the above survey items to serve as a single measure of American exclusionism, ranging from most inclusive to most exclusive.[7] I regress each of these scales on white identity, party identity, ideology, employment status, personal and national economic evaluations, education, age, gender, racial resentment, and importance of American identity.[8]

In Figure 5.3 I focus specifically on the relationship between white identity, racial resentment, and American identity for each of the three scales. The results are consistent no matter how I slice the boundaries of American identity; whites with higher levels of racial identity are more supportive of exclusionary boundaries. What is more, although I do not present the results here, I find that among those high on racial consciousness, the pattern is substantively identical.[9] In these models, racial out-group attitudes and American identity matter as well, but each of these factors is related to support for opinions on what it means to be a "true" American in roughly equal degrees. In short, white racial identity is an important component of adopting particular beliefs about who is a "true" American and who is not.

This relationship between white identity and this specific conception of American identity is reflective of a long history in which national identity was explicitly tied to race in order to help create and maintain a certain racial order – an order from which white Americans today implicitly and explicitly benefit. The nation's rapid diversity challenges this definition of America and threatens the mythology and character of the nation that helps maintain whites' power and privilege. Thus, part of the loss many whites may feel as a result of the nation's changing racial and ethnic landscape may very well be the ability to think of America as white.

Pride and Privilege

One of the central tenants of social identity theory is that individuals display in-group favoritism toward the groups with which they identify – even when those groups are minimal and arbitrarily assigned (Tajfel 1970). In-group favoritism takes on many forms; it can mean evaluating one's group more positively, liking one's group more, or allocating more resources toward one's group (Brewer 1979; Brewer and Kramer 1985; Tajfel 1982). These preferences make sense when we consider the arguments of social identity theory and its cousin, self-categorization theory, both of which posit that individuals are

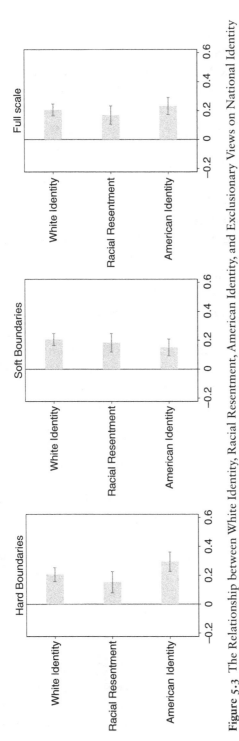

Figure 5.3 The Relationship between White Identity, Racial Resentment, American Identity, and Exclusionary Views on National Identity

Note: Bars represent the coefficient for each variable in the OLS model. The lines represent the 95 percent confidence intervals. Model also controls for party identification, ideology, employment status, negative personal and national economic evaluations, education, age, and gender. Estimates from full model appear in Online Appendix 5A.

Source: 2013 SSI.

motivated to maintain a high level of collective self-esteem and to establish a sense of positive distinctiveness by seeking comparisons with out-groups that paint their own group more positively (Abrams and Hogg 1988; Crocker and Luhtanen 1990; Turner 1975).

If white racial identity and white consciousness follow these same patterns we observe with respect to other social identities, then we would expect white identifiers to express a sense of group favoritism when they describe their racial identity. We already have some evidence that white identifiers express positive sentiments about their group. I noted in Chapter 3 that when white people talk about why their racial identity is important to them, they often mention that they are proud of their group and of the accomplishments of group members. As the dominant group, however, we might also expect that whites talk about their race in ways that more directly reflect their group's status and the privileges that status affords.

We can glean some sense of how whites think about the benefits that accompany their race by returning to the follow-up open-ended question featured on the 2013 MTurk survey, where respondents were asked what comes to mind when they think about white people in the United States. We already know that many responses tied white identity to American identity. Other whites, however, listed features associated with economic, social, and political status. For instance, one person wrote, "Station wagons. Quiet neighborhoods. Nuclear families. Gifted children. Pea coats. Office jobs. Advanced degrees. Chevrolet vehicles." Another said, "I associate 'yuppie' things, like Volvos and Starbucks and Apple laptops with white people, generally." A third person wrote, "Clean neighborhoods, safe neighborhoods, families, parades, NASA."[10] Finally, several associated whiteness with political power. One person simply wrote "government." Another said, "a higher likelihood of achieving political office." And yet another said, "I think of history, founding fathers, etc. Leaders of industry and government." When some whites talk about their identity, we can see they do so by linking it to certain markers of status.

White Privilege and White Guilt

The whites quoted above described certain advantages their group is afforded, but they did not make many overt references to power or privilege. One body of academic work has focused on a specific conceptualization of the privilege possessed by whites, defined as the unearned advantages whites in Western societies have received by way of their race. One of the more popular ways of conceiving white privilege is attributed to Peggy McIntosh (1989), who described the benefits whites possess as "an invisible weightless knapsack of special provisions, maps, passports, codebooks, visas, clothes, tools, and blank checks" (p. 11). For instance, whites can go shopping and feel confident they will not be harassed. They can turn on the television or open the newspaper and see their race widely represented. They can expect that if a traffic cop pulls them over, they will not be singled out because of their race.

Some social scientists have turned their attention to examining the extent to which whites are aware of these privileges and their attitudes toward them (Branscombe, Schmitt, and Schiffhauer 2007; Knowles et al. 2014). One line of work even uses the terms "white identity" or "white consciousness" to describe how whites can be made aware of white privilege, from the perspective that recognizing white privilege is an important step in combatting racial inequality (Flagg 1993; Helms 1995; Tatum 1992). As part of this process, some scholars have argued that one effect of recognizing white privilege is the development of a sense of white guilt, or an awareness of the collective wrong minorities have experienced. Steele, for example, describes white guilt as a result of the juxtaposition of the knowledge of whites' "ill-gotten advantage" with their inevitable gratitude for being white, rather than black, in America (1990, p. 499).

The way in which I conceive of white identity and white consciousness, as social identities, is very different from the way in which these scholars have thought about the idea of white privilege and white guilt. How might white racial solidarity, as considered here, be related to these two concepts? Do some whites think about their racial identity in this way? That is, do those whites with a sense of racial solidarity also critically recognize their group's privileges? Do they accept or reject a sense of racial guilt?

The open-ended responses from the YouGov and MTurk surveys provide some answers. Many whites high on racial identity use the framework of privilege to explain their sense of group identity.[11] One respondent, who reported that his or her identity is "extremely" important, described their racial circumstances in this way: "Because I identify and am proud to be white. I see all the struggles that minorities go through and I thank god every day that I do not have to face those

types of situations." This person was somewhat of an exception, however, in that most white identifiers described the privileges they accrue
as a result of their race with little accompanying sympathy for other
groups. As social identity theory would predict, many of these whites
recognize the benefits this privileged status has for their positive self-
regard. One respondent put this quite plainly: "I feel that, as a white
person, my standing in society is a little higher, due to perceptions of
race. Therefore, I feel a little better about myself and my overall identity."
Another MTurk subject explained, "Being white automatically gives me
the right to be the leader in America." Another said, "I don't like to think
of race as very important but the fact is that the successful in the world
are primarily white males. Going off that I would say I am lucky." Or, put
even more plainly by one YouGov respondent, "Why would I want to be
any other race?" These sentiments appeared time and again:

> I can't imagine being another race. I feel like if I was born black
> or Middle Eastern I would badly wish I was white. I am most
> comfortable around other white people. All my friends are white,
> and I have only dated white girls. Most of my hobbies and
> interests are those probably most popular among white males. If
> I was a different race, I would be a completely different person.
>
> *(MTurk)*

> Our society treats people other than a white identity different.
> I believe it is very important to me to fit in with the rest of my
> community. African and Hispanic Americans are treated differently
> in terms of jobs, education, and general social situations.
>
> *(MTurk)*

> Being white opens up more opportunities than any other race.
>
> *(YouGov)*

> White is not minority.
>
> *(YouGov)*

> Being white makes me safer in general.
>
> *(YouGov)*

> I am happy to be a white American. As we know, being white
> confers certain privilege and I do not need to fear if I am stopped
> by a police officer.
>
> *(YouGov)*

> It's important because every little bit in this life can help you
> out. I'm the first to say that though I'm not rich or driving some

nice sports car, I hit the jackpot by being born a white male in
the suburbs of middle america. I don't look down on anybody
but I see how much more adversity other groups go through.
My wife's family, second generations Mexicans in America, has
struggled to fit in and make a comfortable life here. They've seen
members of their family deported. It seems like every day on the
news, either black or muslim people are being railed about or
unjustly judged with tragic consequences. My life is simpler and
easier being white. I'm not better than anybody, but I can get by
easier in this life than others and for that I'm grateful.

(MTurk)

Others coupled their feelings of privilege with their belief that whites
have historically made important contributions:

My identity is tied to my family, my profession, my
accomplishments. If I will be demonized for my skin color by
the media proclaiming it somehow a privilidge I abuse, though
it denied me scholarships and promotions, I'll take pride in
the accomplishments of my ancestors. Going to the moon,
the industrial revolution, antibiotics and other hallmarks of
civilization don't belong to anyone else.

(MTurk)

I feel white people are given more privileges in the US. They make
up the majority and have always been strong leaders and in the
wealthier class, which is where I'd like to be, so that's why I like
to identify as white.

(MTurk)

I was raised in the time when being white made us superior.
There are still abuses within the white communities, but it is still
better than being any other color. Though the young people of
today are trying to be more accepting, I think that is not true.

(YouGov)

I value my white background. we are known to be more driven
business savvy and educated.

(YouGov)

These individuals clearly recognize that being white affords them
advantages. In fact, all told, 34 percent of high white identifiers
mentioned that their group is somehow privileged, and another 28 percent of the moderate identifiers describe their group in this way in the

MTurk sample. But their recognition of privilege is not couched in the racially progressive language that sociologists hope will lead to the recognition and then rejection of white privilege as part of a path toward racial equality. These whites are, to put it pedantically, glad to be white. They recognize that their circumstances could be different – that they could be worse off. It is this very position that makes these whites especially vulnerable to perceptions of threat. They acknowledge that they potentially have something to lose.

Measuring White Privilege and White Guilt

Social scientists like Swim and Miller (1999) have sought to measure with surveys the extent to which whites possess a sense of racial privilege and of racial guilt. To more clearly understand the extent to which feelings of guilt or privilege relate to white identity, I included measures of these items on the 2013 SSI Study. One important distinction from previous work is that I measure white guilt and white privilege among a nationally diverse adult sample of white Americans, rather than a college student sample like previous work. I also measure guilt with four of their survey items (as opposed to eleven). These questions ask about how often individuals feel guilty about being white given the treatment of non-whites in the country, how often they feel guilty about the inequalities between white and black Americans, and how often they feel guilty about privileges they receive as a white person. I scaled these together to create a single measure of guilt.[12]

Figure 5.4 presents the distribution of the White Guilt Scale (coded to range from zero to one) among the SSI respondents. Like Swim and Miller (1999), I find that most whites do *not* report feeling a sense of collective racial guilt.[13] The figure is skewed right, with a sizeable proportion of the respondents (22 percent) scoring at zero on the scale.

I also adapted Swim and Miller's (1999) measure of white privilege, comprised of five survey items averaged together into a single scale.[14] Respondents were asked the extent to which they feel that white Americans have certain advantages over minorities, the extent to which being white grants them unearned privileges, whether having white skin opens certain doors for them, whether they have privileges due to their race, and whether being white is an asset in their everyday lives. Figure 5.5 presents the distribution of scores on the White Privilege Scale. It is immediately obvious that compared to the Guilt

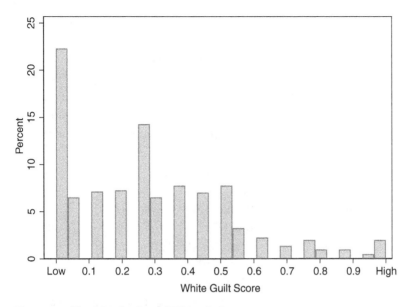

Figure 5.4 The Distribution of White Guilt

Note: Bars represent the percentage of respondents at each level of white guilt. The measure is a scale of four survey items.

Source: 2013 SSI.

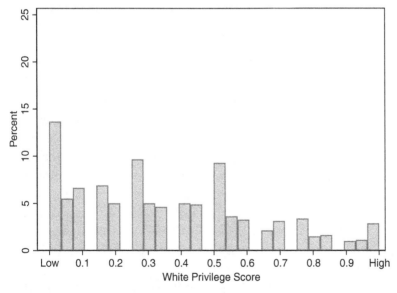

Figure 5.5 The Distribution of White Privilege

Note: Bars represent the percentage of respondents at each level of white privilege. The measure is a scale of five survey items.

Source: 2013 SSI.

Scale, a greater number of whites do report feeling some sense of privilege due to their race.

Like others, Swim and Miller adopt the perspective that whites' recognition of privilege is part of a process that engenders racial equality; their proposal is that the realization of unearned privilege is significantly related to white guilt, which then leads to more egalitarian positions on racialized policies like affirmative action. For many whites, their expectation might be correct. In the SSI Study, white guilt and white privilege are significantly correlated; the pairwise correlation coefficient is 0.50 and is statistically significant. Whites who possess higher levels of racial guilt also tend to believe whites have more advantages.

When it comes to the relationship between white identity, white guilt, and white privilege, however, my expectations are quite different, especially given the responses white identifiers provided to the open-ended survey items. I anticipate that white identity is largely unrelated to greater levels of white guilt, but strongly associated with the adoption of white privilege. Most white identifiers, I argue, embrace their privileged status. It is, after all, the feature of their group they desire to maintain and protect. Furthermore, prior work has demonstrated that when high-identified group members are reminded of their group's past negative treatment of another group, these individuals felt far less collective guilt than low-identified group members (Doosje et al. 1998). Thus, we might not expect that strong white identifiers possess particularly high levels of white guilt.

Figure 5.6 shows the relationship between white identity, white guilt, and white privilege, controlling for party identification, ideology, economic circumstances and evaluations, education, age, gender, and racial resentment. The bars represent the coefficients on each variable in the model and illustrate their magnitude. We can see from the figure that white identity is associated with *both* a sense of guilt and privilege. The effect of white identity on white guilt is, however, small and not especially meaningful. By comparison, the relationship between identity and privilege is notably larger. Higher levels of white identity are associated with believing that whites are privileged. Substantively, the effect of white consciousness is the same.[15]

What else explains the propensity to adopt a sense of white guilt or to believe whites are privileged? Conservative whites are far less likely to adopt either position. Interestingly, we do see some small effect for economic self-interest when it comes to white privilege; whites who

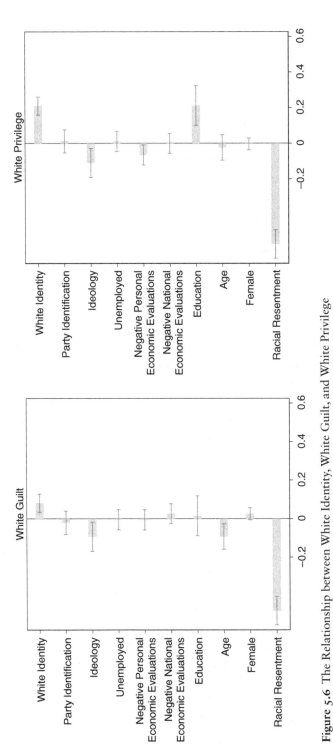

Figure 5.6 The Relationship between White Identity, White Guilt, and White Privilege

Note: Bars represent the coefficient for each variable in the OLS model. The lines represent the 95 percent confidence intervals. Estimates from full model appear in Online Appendix 5B.

Source: 2013 SSI.

say their family is not faring as well financially are also less inclined to say that members of their group have certain advantages. The size of the effect is, however, relatively small. Levels of education are also associated with a greater sense of white privilege. There is no relationship, however, between education and white guilt. Age, on the other hand, matters somewhat for white guilt but not white privilege. Older whites are less likely to feel guilty about racial inequalities or injustices. Finally, we can see that racial resentment emerges as the most powerful predictor of adopting either sentiment. Resentment also has the opposite effect on these two attitudes as white identity. More racially resentful whites are much *less* likely to feel a sense of group guilt or privilege.

The relationship between white privilege and white racial identity comport with what we gleaned from the open-ended responses. Many white identifiers recognize that their group has certain advantages, they are happy to have such advantages, and they have no desire to relinquish them. At the same time, we can see that there is some very slight tendency among white identifiers to feel guilty about these benefits. This analysis provides further evidence that white identity and racial animus are distinct attitudes and, in this case, pull whites in opposite directions. White identifiers recognize their group's advantages and may want to protect their group's privileges, but recognize – and even feel slightly guilty – that they have some group privileges. Whites high on racial resentment, however, wholly reject any sense of racial guilt.

Celebrating Whiteness

In the spring of 2015, Jim Boggess taped a sign to the window of his business, Jimbo's Deli, in Flemington, New Jersey. The sign read, "Celebrate your White Heritage in March. White History Month." His sign generated some controversy. When subsequently interviewed by the local paper, Boggess explained, "No matter what you are – Muslim, Jewish, black, white, gay, straight – you should be proud of what you are. I shouldn't have to feel bad about being white."[16] Boggess was criticized for his posting. Some members of the community complained that it was racist. He was baffled. "If there's any racial discrimination going on, it's by people who are objecting to the sign because I'm white." He noted that other groups have their own celebrations. "I just wanted to be included," he said. "Why is this such a big deal? I don't get it."

In response to the open-ended items on my surveys, many white identifiers shared similar sentiments. They appeared resentful of that idea that expressing their identity would be seen, unfairly, as problematic or even racist. They seemed to feel attacked for their position, and defensive of this identity:

> All of my family is white so obviously i'm proud of being white just like any other race is proud of their color. Only problem is if you say that you are proud of being white people think it's some sort of racist thing. When im really just proud of being half Finnish and American.
>
> *(MTurk)*

> How being white these days seem to be frowned on and we are to blame for everything and how we are to blame for the blacks who were slaves which was a very long time ago and should be dropped and left in the past. How white people are sick of hearing this.
>
> *(YouGov)*

> With all the unrest today being White is considered a racist regardless of your beliefs.
>
> *(YouGov)*

> The way white people are being treated and discriminated against in his country both by non-whites AND our Government.
>
> *(YouGov)*

> How its considered racist to say you're proud to be white, while other ethnicities are praised for their cultural pride.
>
> *(YouGov)*

> My pride will be seen as hate in this distorted reality media obsessed world.
>
> *(YouGov)*

> Since I am white and answered the way I did I am sure some would consider me as being racist. If I was black and answered that it was important to me to self-identify as black then that would be just fine in the eyes of many.
>
> *(YouGov)*

It is apparent that many whites have adopted similar attitudes as the deli owner from New Jersey. They have observed other racial groups organize around their race, establish race-based student organizations on college campuses, and honor their racial heritage. Some whites

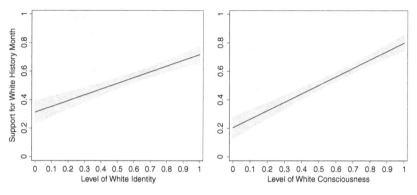

Figure 5.7 White Racial Solidarity and Support for Congress Passing a Law Creating a White History Month

Note: The line represents the predicted level of support for a White History month at each level of white identity or consciousness. The shaded area represents the 95 percent confidence intervals. Predicted values are generated by holding gender constant at female and all other variables in the model at their mean. Model also controls for party identity, ideology, employment status, personal and national economic evaluations, education, age, gender, and racial resentment. Estimates from full model appear in Online Appendix 5C.

Source: 2016 YouGov.

wonder why they cannot openly celebrate their race in the way they believe blacks and other racial minorities are able to do. A common refrain during February is, "Why is there an African-American History month, but not a White History month?" Many whites seem to ask this question with sincerity, and not because they align themselves with white nationalists, white supremacists, or KKK members. Instead, they think that racial equality means that they, too, ought to be able to recognize their racial group. These whites complain that the very rejection of whites' ability to do so is yet another example of the way in which whites are unfairly maligned in the United States.

On the 2016 YouGov survey, I asked whites to what extent they would support or oppose Congress passing a law that would designate one month of the year as White History month. Approximately 29 percent of all whites reported that they would support this proposal either "a great deal" or "a moderate amount." Only 22 percent said they would oppose it, with the rest of respondents falling somewhere in between these points.

If white identifiers feel a sense of pride in their group, we may find that they especially want to celebrate their race. Figure 5.7 indicates that they do. The lines plot the predicted level of support for a White History month across levels of white identity and white consciousness from models that also control for party identity, ideology, economic considerations, education, age, gender, and racial resentment. The effect of white racial solidarity on opinion here is enormous. Among white identifiers, moving from the lowest level of identity to the highest produces an increase from 0.32 to 0.72 on the scale of support for white history month. For those on white consciousness, the difference is between 0.20 and 0.80. Whites who identify with their group are an order of magnitude more supportive of a white history month, and their levels of support are, on average, near the top of the scale.

Grievance and Alienation

On November 9, 1963 *New York Times* columnist Russell Baker published a column on the "problem of the white Anglo-Saxon Protestant" in the "era of rampant minorities." He remarked that, "in the span of a few cruel years he has seen his comfortable position as the 'in' man of American society become a social liability as the outcasts and the exploited have presented their due bills on his conscience." Baker goes on. "Now the white Anglo-Saxon protestant is asking for sympathy, and no one will listen. His basic complaint is that he has become a second-class citizen and finds it harder and harder to keep his self-respect."

The year 1963 was a defining one for the black Civil Rights movement. Less than three months before Baker's piece appeared in the *New York Times*, Martin Luther King Jr. stood in the shadow of the Lincoln Memorial and delivered his famous "I have a dream" speech. In the preceding ten weeks, blacks participated in 758 demonstrations in seventy-five cities (Patterson 1996). The movement for black equality was gaining considerable traction, and Baker's writing suggests that some whites felt threatened by these changes. This notion – that whites felt as if their own group was losing its first-class status – is remarkably familiar.

Such sentiments reflect much of the discourse we can observe among whites in the contemporary political environment, particularly in response to the country's growing diversity. For example, in the midst of Barack Obama's first term as president, as the excitement over Obama's historical achievement waned and conversations about a post-racial America dissipated, new language entered the fray. In 2011, CNN published a story with the headline, "Are whites racially oppressed?"[17]

Like Baker's piece quoted above, the CNN story highlighted the idea that many whites in the United States viewed their own group as a dispossessed minority. It argued that whites in the United States felt overlooked when it came to opportunities for college scholarships, that they worried about the loss of their numerical majority, and were dismayed by immigration.

We now know that whites feel proud of their group, they recognize that they enjoy a privileged status, and they feel entitled to the advantages they possess. But in the face of threats to their group and its status, the content of white racial solidarity, I argue, should also reflect a sense of grievance and alienation, as well as perceptions of threat. What might such attitudes look like? As part of understanding the sources of intergroup conflict, both realistic group conflict theory and group position theory draw our attention to perceived group competition or zero-sum access to power and resources (Blumer 1958; Bobo 1999; Bobo and Hutchings 1996). Note that the emphasis is on *perceived* competition. Threat need not be the product of real, objective, or material conditions. If whites feel that their status is threatened by racial and ethnic minorities, we should find evidence of these beliefs. Furthermore, it should be whites with higher levels of racial solidarity who are more likely to believe that more political or economic power for out-group members, like blacks and Latinos, means less power for their group. I note that previous work has often expected to find a strong relationship between racial prejudice and perceptions of racial competition (Bobo and Hutchings 1996). If my argument is correct, however, the relationship between white racial solidarity and beliefs about group competition should be robust to controlling for out-group animus.

To test this claim, I turn to the 2010 KN Study, which included measures designed to assess perceptions of zero-sum competition between whites and other racial or ethnic groups.[18] Survey respondents were asked the extent to which they believe that more good jobs for blacks mean fewer good jobs for members of other groups, and whether the more influence blacks have in politics, the less influence members of other groups have. They were asked identical but separate questions about their belief in these outcomes with respect to Hispanics as well.[19]

I turn first to perceptions of economic competition – measured by asking whites the extent to which they think more good jobs for blacks or Hispanics means fewer good jobs for their own group.

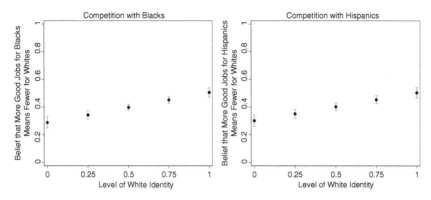

Figure 5.8 The Relationship between White Identity and Perceptions of Zero-Sum Economic Competition

Note: Points represent the predicted level of perceptions of economic competition at each level of white identity. Bars represent the 95 percent confidence intervals. Predicted values are generated by holding gender constant at female and all other variables in the model at their mean. Model also controls for party identification, ideology, employment status, personal and national economic evaluations, education, age, gender, and either racial resentment or affect toward Hispanics. Estimates from full model appear in Online Appendix 5D.

Source: 2010 KN.

Figure 5.8 shows the predicted degree of subscription to these attitudes, across levels of white identity, from a model controlling for party identity, ideology, economic circumstances and evaluations, education, age, gender, and either racial resentment or affect toward Hispanics. Even after accounting for these factors, white identity emerges as a strong and significant predictor, across both datasets, of perceptions of zero-sum competition over jobs. The effect of consciousness, although not illustrated here, is even more powerful.[20] These effects hold regardless of whether the out-group in question is black or Hispanic.

Other variables predict these attitudes as well. More educated whites are less likely to perceive zero-sum economic competition. Notably, however, being unemployed or facing personal economic circumstances are only weakly and inconsistently related to these attitudes. Attitudes toward blacks and Hispanics are the only items that compete with racial identity in terms of the magnitude of their effect on perceptions of competition. Whites who are more resentful toward blacks or who feel more coldly toward Hispanics are also far more likely to report that more good jobs for these groups mean less for others. Moving from the lowest level to the highest level of identity

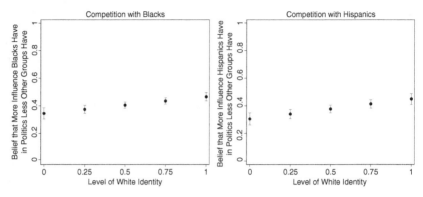

Figure 5.9 The Relationship between White Identity and Perceptions of Zero-Sum Political Competition

Note: Points represent the predicted level of perceptions of economic competition at each level of white identity. Bars represent the 95 percent confidence intervals. Predicted values are generated by holding gender constant at female and all other variables in the model at their mean. Model also controls for party identification, ideology, employment status, personal and national economic evaluations, education, age, gender, and either racial resentment or affect toward Hispanics. Estimates from full model appear in Online Appendix 5E.

Source: 2010 KN.

produces a shift toward perceptions of greater competition with blacks from 0.28 to 0.51. The predicted level of competition with Hispanics goes from 0.30 among the lowest identifiers to 0.50 among the highest.

Do we observe the same effect with respect to political competition? Do whites with higher levels of identity believe that more political influence for blacks or for Hispanics means less influence for other groups? I test whether we observe these relationships, again using the 2010 KN Study and the same set of controls.[21] We can see in Figure 5.9 that white identity is associated with the belief that greater political influence for blacks and Hispanics comes at the expense of others' political power, and the magnitude of this effect is fairly similar to what we observed with respect to perceptions of economic competition. Moving from the lowest level of white identity to the highest results in a shift in the belief that blacks' political influence comes at the expense of other groups of 0.34 when identity is low to 0.47 when it is high on a zero to one scale. For attitudes toward Hispanics' political influence, the predicted effect among low-identifying whites is 0.31, and it leaps to 0.45 among those highest on white identity. In short, even accounting for out-group attitudes, white in-group identity is strongly linked to perceptions of group competition. The implication of these results, of

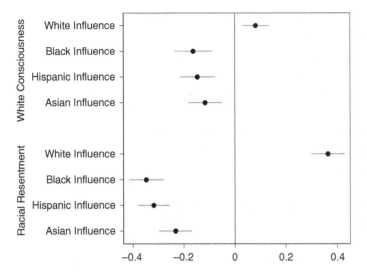

Figure 5.10 The Relationship between White Consciousness and the Belief that Groups Have Too Little Influence in US Politics

Points represent the coefficients on white consciousness and racial resentment for each model. The lines represent the 95 percent confidence intervals. Model also controls for party identity, ideology, negative personal and national economic evaluations, education, age, and gender. Estimates from full model appear in Online Appendix 5F2.

Source: 2016 ANES (web).

course, is that as racial out-groups gain political and economic power, whites high on racial identity may very well see this as an encroachment on their own group's status and privileges. What is more, we can see that beliefs about zero-sum competition are about out-group *and* in-group attitudes among whites; that is, they are associated with both whites' racial animus and with their racial identity.

We can also turn the question of political influence on its head, asking not merely whether whites with higher levels of racial solidarity believe that blacks or Hispanics have too much or too little political influence, but whether whites are more likely to endorse the notion that their own group has too much or too little political influence. We might be especially likely to find a relationship between the belief that whites have too little influence and racial consciousness, since theoretically, consciousness ought to be associated with discontent about the status of one's group.

The 2016 ANES asked whether whites believe their own group has too much or too little political influence. In Figure 5.10, I compare the relationship between white consciousness and perceptions of group influence with respect to whites, blacks, Hispanics, and Asians. Again, I model support for this belief just as I did above, with the expectation that whites with higher levels of racial consciousness are also more likely to buy into the idea that their group has less political influence than they would like. The results, presented in Figure 5.10, confirm this expectation. Whites with higher levels of consciousness are more likely to think that their group has too little influence. The coefficient on white consciousness is positive and significant. These whites are also *less* likely to agree that other racial groups have too little influence.

We can also see from the chart that racial resentment is driving opinion here as well. More racially resentful whites also feel that their group has too little influence. Like the effect of white consciousness, the effect of resentment when it comes to attitudes about the influence of other racial groups is negative. While consciousness and racial resentment both push whites' opinion about their group's influence in a similar direction (although I note that the magnitude of the effect is greater for racial resentment), the important conclusion for our purposes is that white consciousness remains a strong and significant predictor of these attitudes even after taking racial animus into account. In short, beliefs about the influence of their own racial group and that of racial out-groups are driven both by identity and resentment.

Racial Discrimination

In recent years, social scientists have uncovered an interesting phenomenon when it comes to white attitudes about race. Apparently, many whites in the United States now believe that their racial group experiences significant discrimination (Gallagher 1997). In fact, by some accounts, whites argue that they experience more discrimination or "reverse racism" based on their race than do blacks in the United States (Norton and Sommers 2011). Results from the 2016 ANES Pilot confirm that many whites subscribe to the notion that there is considerable discrimination against their group. On the survey, nearly 18 percent of whites said that their racial group faces "a great deal" or "a lot of" discrimination. To be clear, many more whites (over 30 percent) agreed that blacks experience significant discrimination. Just a slightly smaller percentage – 24 percent – report that Hispanics face considerable discrimination.

This finding is consistent with my argument that many whites are seeking to protect their group's dominant status. Claims of discrimination on the part of high-status groups serve to reinforce the social hierarchy (Levin et al. 1998; Sidanius and Pratto 1999; Wilkins, Wellman, and Kaiser 2013). Which whites, however, are most likely to believe their own group experiences discrimination? If white racial solidarity is associated with a sense of grievance, then we ought to find that whites high on racial consciousness are more likely to adopt such views about their group. In Table 5.2, I explore what factors might predict whites' beliefs about the degree of racial discrimination whites, blacks, and Hispanics encounter using the 2016 ANES Pilot Study.[22] In the first column, we can see that higher levels of white consciousness are indeed associated with a propensity to indicate that whites experience discrimination. Interestingly, sociotropic economic evaluations also play a role; whites who say the national economy is doing worse are also more likely to make such claims, perhaps reflecting some residual hostility toward Obama, who was president at the time these items were asked. And not surprisingly, more racially resentful whites claim their own group is discriminated against.

In the next two columns, we can see that white consciousness is unrelated to attitudes about the level of discrimination experienced by blacks and Hispanics. The coefficients are positive, but relatively small and statistically insignificant. In short, white consciousness is significantly associated with perceptions of discrimination experienced by whites, but it is not especially related to either the denial of discrimination experienced by blacks or Hispanics, or the belief that these groups also face racial discrimination. In contrast, racial resentment is significantly linked to the belief that whites experience discrimination, and to opposition to the notion that blacks are discriminated against. When it comes to Hispanics, however, out-group animus, at least measured with the Hispanic feeling thermometer, is unrelated to beliefs about the racial discrimination Hispanics experience.

Racial Alienation

In their canonical work on intergroup conflict, Lawrence Bobo and Vincent Hutchings (1996) argue that a concept closely allied with perceptions of zero-sum competition is that of racial alienation. Alienation, they posit, is a spectrum. At the one end, for dominant group members, racial alienation appears as a "profound sense of group

Table 5.2 *The Relationship between White Consciousness and Beliefs about Racial Discrimination*

	Whites experience discrimination	Blacks experience discrimination	Hispanics experience discrimination
White consciousness	0.181***	0.012	0.046
	(0.047)	(0.054)	(0.050)
Party identification (Republican)	–0.018	–0.073	–0.125***
	(0.046)	(0.048)	(0.042)
Ideological identification (conservative)	0.085	–0.044	–0.105**
	(0.066)	(0.061)	(0.053)
Employment status	–0.065	0.017	–0.021
	(0.041)	(0.060)	(0.051)
Negative national economic evaluations	0.133***	–0.033	–0.002
	(0.051)	(0.060)	(0.049)
Education	–0.071**	–0.038	–0.063*
	(0.035)	(0.037)	(0.035)
Age	–0.017	0.063	–0.003
	(0.051)	(0.055)	(0.056)
Female	–0.013	0.059***	0.038*
	(0.022)	(0.022)	(0.023)
Racial resentment	0.276***	–0.365***	
	(0.051)	(0.056)	
Hispanic feeling thermometer			0.066
			(0.052)
Constant	0.022	0.791***	0.545***
	(0.042)	(0.050)	(0.072)
Observations	793	792	793
R-squared	0.260	0.248	0.094

Note: Table entries are OLS coefficients. Standard errors in parentheses. All variables in model coded to range from zero to one.
***$p<0.01$, **$p<0.05$, *$p<0.1$, two-tailed.
Source: 2016 ANES Pilot.

enfranchisement and entitlement" (p. 956). The converse is true for subordinate group members, for whom racial alienation manifests as a "profound sense of group disenfranchisement and grievance" (p. 956). Alienated individuals believe that their group members are getting less than their fair share, that they have not been provided the opportunities they deserve, and that they are owed a better chance. According to Bobo and Hutchings, the more members of a group feel alienated – that is, the more they feel as if their group is oppressed or treated unfairly – the more they will perceive out-groups as competitive threats.

The logic of their claim is consistent with conventional expectations; racial and ethnic minorities in the United States have experienced significant discrimination. They also occupy social, political, and economic spaces that are considerably disadvantaged compared to whites. Over time, these experiences become a dimension of group members' collective memory, leading them to feel more alienated. In contrast, the more secure the power and status of a group, the less alienated and threatened group members ought to feel. Not surprisingly, in their empirical tests, Bobo and Hutchings found some evidence that a sense of racial alienation among whites is linked to perceptions of group competition with blacks, but that the levels of reported alienation among whites were far lower than what was observed among blacks, Latinos, and Asians.

For the same reasons today's political climate calls for revisiting the influence of white identity, we also ought to reconsider whether racial alienation is at notable levels among the white American population, and especially among those who identify as white. The data that Bobo and Hutchings brought to bear on their extensive analyses were from the 1992 Los Angeles County Social Survey – well before immigration brought significant demographic change to the US population. Today, in the midst of our attention to whiteness and white grievance or oppression, we may very well observe noteworthy levels of racial alienation among whites.

In keeping with Bobo and Hutchings' approach, I measured racial alienation on both the 2010 KN and 2013 SSI surveys with a series of questions. The first item asks respondents the extent to which they agree or disagree that American society owes white people a better chance in life than they currently have. The second gauged respondents' agreement or disagreement with the conclusion that American society has provided their group a fair opportunity to get ahead in life. The third question (not included on the SSI Study), measured their agreement with the sentiment that American society has not dealt fairly with white people. In both datasets, these items were scaled together to create a single measure of alienation.[23]

Do whites feel alienated? Figure 5.11 compares average levels of racial alienation by levels of racial identity. In this analysis, I compare whites to blacks, with the expectation that blacks should be more alienated than whites. And they are. Regardless of their levels of racial identity, blacks, on average, report greater levels of racial alienation than whites. Among high identifying whites, the average degree of reported alienation, on a zero to one scale, is 0.36. For high identifying

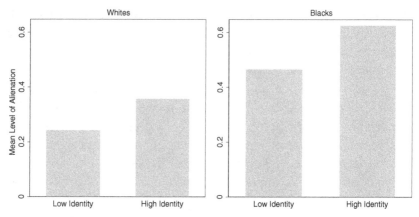

Figure 5.11 Average Levels of Racial Alienation among Whites and Blacks

Bars represent the mean level of racial alienation by levels of racial identity, among whites and blacks. "Low identifiers" are those that say their identity is "not at all important" or "not very important." High identifiers are those who indicated their identity is "somewhat important" or "very important." Alienation is a scale of three items recoded to range from zero to one.

Source: 2010 KN.

blacks, the average is almost twice that at 0.63. Nevertheless, the levels of alienation found here among whites, given whites' dominant status, are notable. Furthermore, these attitudes are moderated by white racial solidarity; whites with higher levels of racial identity and conscious-ness do, as expected, feel more alienated. This relationship holds even after taking into account the factors from our standard public opinion model and controlling for racial resentment.[24] And if racial alienation is, as Bobo and Hutchings posit, a product of perceptions of discrimin-ation and other feelings of subordination, then we might very well see an increase in whites' feelings of alienation moving forward.

White Ambivalence

Not all whites adopt a racial identity. Some, as previous work on whiteness has concluded, do not feel especially attached to their racial group, perhaps because being a member of the majority group has allowed them to take their race for granted. Responses to the open-ended questions, in which whites were asked to explain their response to the identity importance item, provide further insight into why some whites reject a racial identity. Just a few whites also openly rejected a white identity on the grounds that whiteness is associated with the subordination and oppression of out-groups:

> I have zero pride for being white. Thinking about whiteness to me, means thinking about white privilege and all the unfair unsubscribed benefits I have received for simply being born white. Being white is embarrassing. Often shameful.
>
> *(YouGov)*

> I thought about all the white supremicists that would think it was so important to be white and I was disgusted by the thought. I hate how white America bullies other races and I wish white people could acknowledge their racism.
>
> *(YouGov)*

> Maybe my identity as a member of specific European ethnicities is significant to me, but not the color of my skin. That's just asinine. The only people who are ever "proud" of being white are neo nazis, KKK members, or various unaffiliated hicks.
>
> *(MTurk)*

These sentiments were only rarely expressed, which may come as no surprise given the fact that so many whites willingly adopt a racial identity. Few associate this identity or consciousness with racism or white supremacy.[25]

For the most part, however, we should not assume that whites reject a racial identity for innocuous reasons. Many of the whites who reported low levels of identity did not report doing so because they adopted progressive, socially liberal views on race or because they seemed conscious of the legacy of discrimination people of color in the United States have experienced. If anything, many seemed annoyed by the broader discussion of race generally. They argued that we would be better off if we, as a nation, focused less on race:

> Society as a whole would be much better off if all of them hung up on what race they are would get over it. Grow up and move on. None of us can be equal as long as any group believes they are better than all the rest and cannot forget and forgive past.
>
> *(YouGov)*

> I was thinking that if black people weren't so caught up in being black that racism would start to dissipate and would no longer

be an issue worthy of a survey question. You don't see Asians or other races so worried about the color of there skin.

(YouGov)

This country is too fixated on race we are all children of god brothers and sisters in christ Jesus son of the living god. I do not see skin color I see human beings we should all be this way.

(YouGov)

Others rejected a sense of racial identity on the grounds that race should not be anyone's defining characteristic. Approximately one quarter of the low-identifiers seem to have adopted this "color-blind" philosophy:

Because I don't judge people by what color they are. There are plenty of white people I don't like after all. It's all about what's in a person's head and heart. And I dislike generalizations such as all {fill in the ethnic or racial characteristic}. White people aren't all alike, black people aren't all alike, Asian people are not all alike, and so on.

(MTurk)

I want to be identified by who I am not what I am.

(MTurk)

So my body produces less melanin than some other guy. What's the big deal? Martin Luther King was exactly right: It's character that counts, not the color of one's skin.

(MTurk)

I think all men and women are created equal and it doesn't matter about what race they are. To me it is what is on the inside that counts.

(MTurk)

It doesn't matter what I look like. People will ultimately judge me by my actions.

(MTurk)

What defines someone is their personality, intelligence, how they treat others, accomplishments, goals, etc. I don't see how being white has anything to do with my identity except my physical traits. It's of little importance.

(MTurk)

Why would my skin color effect who I am as a person? The color of someone's skin does not define them.

(YouGov)

Race doesn't matter to me and I don't want to be judged why I am the way I am based on color.

(YouGov)

Color should never be a way to define ones identity. You're color has little to do with who you are as a person. Ones environment makes a bigger impact than skin color.

(YouGov)

We are all pink inside.

(YouGov)

As sociologist Eduardo Bonilla-Silva (2010) has pointed out, these views can be just as problematic and pervasive as overt racism. Color-blind racism allows whites to deny the existence of racial discrimination, and it legitimizes practices that maintain racial inequality.

Where then, one might wonder, are the racially progressive whites on my scale of white identity? Are there not some whites who are racially conscious in a way that recognizes their group's unearned privileges? Indeed, there are some whites who both outright dismiss racial identity and reject racism. These whites are located at both ends of the white identity scale, adding some noise to the measure.[26] We might recognize them as whites who either report high levels of identity but low levels of out-group animus, or whites who report low levels of both attitudes. Among respondents on the 2012 ANES who report that their white identity is extremely important, approximately 10 percent have racial resentment scores that are at the very low end of the scale (at 0.375 or below on the zero to one scale). Among whites who claim that their racial identity is not at all important, about 14 percent score very low on racial resentment. These whites make up a small fraction of all whites (about 21 percent), but they are present. They are also more likely to be highly educated and score low on racial resentment. Fortunately, the tools of multivariate analysis allow me to attenuate the effects they have on the measure of white identity. Controlling for education and resentment in my models helps reduce the noise these whites add to the measure.

Conclusion

The efforts in this chapter were aimed at understanding the confluence of attitudes to which white identifiers, by and large, subscribe. When whites, as the dominant group, describe their whiteness, they do so in ways that reiterate their status. They orient themselves as "mainstream," and they equate the traits of their group with those of the nation. We should not take the association of white with American here as an indication that whiteness has no inherent meaning, that it is simply a reflection of American culture. For one, white racial solidarity is associated with a particular notion about national identity. Whites high on racial identity are much more likely to adopt exclusionary boundaries around what it means to be American, and agree that traits like the ability to speak English, to have lived for most of one's life in America, and put plainly – being white, are important to being truly American. Their understanding of race and national identity is very much an affirmation of the dominant group's ability to capture and define the identity of the country. Such associations also serve to position many whites as vulnerable to threats that challenge this link. Immigration from non-European countries and increasing diversity have the potential to challenge whites' ability to see their own image as reflected in that of the nation.

Whites with higher levels of racial solidarity also clearly recognize the privileges their group is afforded. They describe the social, political, and economic power of their group. They are proud of their group's accomplishments and support the idea of celebrating their race just as other racial and ethnic groups do. Many also recognize that if they were to have been born another race, their life may have been more difficult. Yet, this recognition of privilege is not necessarily one that moves whites to adopt more racially egalitarian views overall. Instead, these whites seem more interested in maintaining these advantages.

At the same time, many of these same whites also feel that their group experiences discrimination. They are more likely to perceive economic and political competition with racial and ethnic minorities in zero-sum terms. They also feel alienated, and report that their group is not getting its fair share in society and has not been getting the opportunities it deserves.

How might we reconcile these seemingly inconsistent positions; one, that whites are not getting what they deserve, and two, that whites have a number of advantages? These two perspectives appear less contradictory when we consider the fact that whites view their privileges as proprietary. Thus, any challenge to these advantages feels unfair. Klinkner and Smith put this perspective eloquently:

> People who have grown up with arrangements in which their group regularly receives special social esteem as well as more material benefits, arrangements that seem so familiar as to be virtually natural, are always likely to find changes in those arrangements disquieting. Predictably, they will look for reasons to confine and condemn them. Our fellow white Americans, we firmly believe, are not people any more inherently prone to racism, selfishness, or evil than any other group in this or any other society. Their attachments to familiar ways are perfectly normal and human, and in many regards such attachments can rightly be cherished. But in American society, whites happen to be the group who have the upper hand; and so many of their understandable attachments to the status quo, often accompanied by genuine good will toward others, nonetheless have always worked against overcoming real and severe injustices.
>
> (Klinkner and Smith 1999, p. 7)

It is clear from the open- and close-ended survey results that whites recognize their advantages; it means they are aware that they have resources to protect, and to potentially lose. Their recognition that they are better off than racial and ethnic minorities ought only to exacerbate the anxieties they feel in the face of threat; they recognize and perhaps believe that their circumstances can – and very well may – be worse.

Interestingly, the open-ended items also revealed important characteristics about those whites who purport to reject a racial identity. Many argued that their identity was not important because they were not fond of judging others' attitudes or behaviors based on race. In short, they seemed to subscribe to the language of "color-blindness," which is often portrayed as ideological tool co-opted by conservatives in order to dismiss the existence of structural racism and racial inequality. The sentiment seems innocuous in that it proposes that individuals "ignore" race when making evaluations. Unfortunately, color-blindness allows individuals to disregard the very real disadvantages faced by racial and ethnic minorities and to deny the privileges enjoyed by whites. Indeed, some scholars have proposed that color-blindness is another manifestation of contemporary racism (Bonilla-Silva 2010; Haney-Lopez 2014). While this project is primarily focused on who identifies as white and what the political implications of this identity are, these results suggest that there is much to be learned about racial conflict by examining the individuals at the low end of the identity scale as well. It seems that a significant proportion of them have adopted a particular racial ideology that may also inform political attitudes.

Finally, we saw here several instances in which white identity and racial resentment play either similar or divergent roles in predicting attitudes. Both white identity and racial resentment are related to more exclusionary views on American identity. They are both also predictive of perceptions of political and economic competition with racial outgroups, and the belief that whites have too little political influence. But racial resentment pulls whites in the opposite direction when it comes to attitudes about white privilege. More racially resentful whites deny white advantages, whereas more racially conscious whites embrace this belief. In short, sometimes both in-group and out-group attitudes are working in tandem, driving white opinion, but here we also see further evidence that these are separate constructs with sometimes separate effects.

6 THE PRESERVATION OF WHITENESS

On April 9, 1924, Senator Ellison DuRant "Cotton Ed" Smith (D-South Carolina) stood before members of the US Congress and delivered an impassioned speech in favor of what would become the Immigration Act of 1924. The law proposed a quota system that would limit the number of new immigrants to the United States from any country to just 2 percent of the number of people from that country who were already residing in the United States. It was an unabashed effort to further restrict immigration to the United States from Southern and Eastern Europe, the Middle East, Asia, and India. There was little doubt that its intention was to reduce immigration from countries whose citizens were not considered "white" by the standards of the time. Arguing in support of the legislation, Smith proclaimed that it was time for America to "shut the door" to any further influx of foreigners, and for the nation to instead focus on increasing its population of "pure, unadulterated American" citizenry (Speech by Ellison DuRant Smith 1924). Smith's speech made clear the significance of race in defining such citizenship:

> Thank God we have in America perhaps the largest percentage of any country in the world of the pure, unadulterated Anglo-Saxon stock; certainly the greatest of any nation in the Nordic breed. It is for the preservation of that splendid stock that has characterized us that I would make this not an asylum for the oppressed of all countries, but a country to assimilate and perfect that splendid type of manhood that has made America the foremost Nation in her progress and in her power.

The legislation was passed into law with strong support; only six senators dissented. The majority view of Congress reflected the broader national discourse on citizenship and national identity of the time – a conversation that largely centered on the belief that Anglo-Saxon heritage should be the prevailing criteria for entry into the United States and whiteness the defining characteristic of American identity (Jacobson 1999).[1] In response to the passage of the Act, the *Los Angeles Times* published an article on April 13, 1924 with the headline "Nordic Victory is seen in Drastic Restrictions."

The history of immigration in the United States is intricately tied to the notion of whiteness. Americans have routinely resisted opening the country's borders to foreigners, especially when those arriving are not, by the current standards, considered white. But in contemporary debates, immigration opponents often frame the issue as an economic problem; immigrants, they argue, take jobs from American citizens, depress wages, and are a heavy burden on the social welfare system. In this chapter, I take up whether immigration attitudes are primarily about economic concerns – either personal or national in nature – or if, instead, immigration opinion is largely driven by group attitudes. In particular, I examine whether opposition to immigration and anti-immigrant sentiments are motivated, at least in part, by whites' sense of racial solidarity. My expectation is that immigration is an issue that cuts to the heart of whites' concerns about their group's status atop the nation's hierarchy. Consequently, white racial solidarity ought to strongly and consistently predict more negative attitudes toward immigration.

Challenges to America's Racial Identity

The immigration restrictions of the 1920s curtailed immigration to the United States for the next forty years. As the 1924 Act intended, many of the immigrants that did enter the United States between the 1920s and mid 1960s were from Western Europe and Canada. This preference for "Nordic stock" was mirrored among the American public. According to a poll conducted by Gallup in 1944, Americans were more than willing to let in some immigrants from England and Sweden. They were less welcoming of Mexicans and Jews.[2] Another poll from 1945 showed that Americans were quite content with immigrants from

Scandinavian countries, Holland, Belgium, and England. They were far less enthusiastic about the possibility of immigrants from Poland, Greece, and Russia – countries whose citizens were much less likely to be considered white by the American standards of the time.[3]

It was not until the passage of the Immigration and Nationality Act of 1965 (also known as the Hart-Cellar Act) that a path was laid for changes in immigration patterns. The law marked a radical shift in immigration policy. It abolished the quota system based on national-origins that had been put in place by the 1924 legislation, and it effect-ively opened the door to the waves of immigrants that arrived in the 1980s and 1990s. It is no coincidence that the law's passage coincided with the Civil Rights movement. It was framed by proponents as a national effort to end discriminatory practices. In 1964 Attorney General Robert F. Kennedy urged Congress to remove the quota system and declared, "Everywhere else in our national life, we have eliminated discrimination based on one's place of birth. Yet this system is still the foundation of our immigration law."[4]

The Hart-Cellar Act was widely supported in Congress, but after the legislation was introduced, many of the same debates about the racial composition of the United States that inspired the 1924 restrictions were again brought to the fore. Senator Sam Ervin (D-NC), argued that it was impossible for any new immigration policy to not favor one group over another, and so why not, he asked, create a preference for "national groups who historically had the greatest influence on the building of the nation?" Senator Robert Byrd shared Ervin's sentiments, and argued that immigrants from Western Europe could "more easily and readily assimilate into the American popula-tion." Furthermore, while the American public in 1965 was far less restrictive in their immigration preferences than they had been in pre-vious decades, public opinion polls showed that they still preferred immigrants from Canada, England, and Scandinavia. These same polls also reflected shifts in thinking about which immigrant groups were considered white; next on the list of preferred immigrants were Germans, the Irish, and the French.[5] In response to concerns from both American citizens and his elected colleagues, Senator Edward Kennedy assured potential detractors that "the ethnic mix of this country [would] not be upset."[6]

The Hart-Cellar Act was signed by President Lyndon Johnson at the foot of the Statue of Liberty on October 3, 1965. Quite contrary

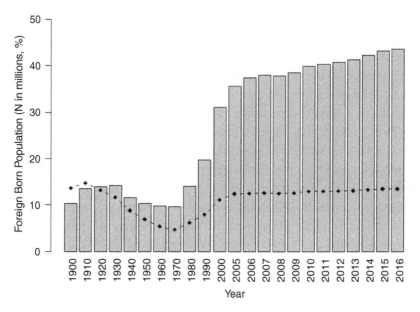

Figure 6.1 The Immigrant Share of the US Population, 1900–2015

Note: Bars represent the total number of foreign-born individuals living in the United States (in millions). Line represents the percentage of the total population that is foreign born. Data from 2000 to 2015 from www.census.gov. Foreign-born population includes anyone who is not a US citizen at birth, including those who become US citizens through naturalization. Percentage is the foreign-born population as a percent of the total population.

Source: Data from 1900 to 1990 from Gibson and Lennon. US Bureau of the Census (www.census.gov/population/www/documentation/twps0029/tab01.html).

to Senator Kennedy's expectations, the Act would eventually have an enormous impact on the racial and ethnic composition of the United States. As Figure 6.1 shows, with the national quotas lifted and the nation's doors more open, immigration began to increase notably in the 1980s and 1990s, before exploding in the early and mid 2000s. This growth was impressive. In 1979 the immigrant share of the population was just under 5 percent. By 1990, the percentage had increased to nearly 8 percent. In 2005, immigrants comprised 12.4 percent of the population, and today they make up 13.5 percent – just shy of the share in the early 1900s that preceded the restrictive immigration legislation of the 1920s. More than forty-one million immigrants live in the United States today – a number that is four times as many as was the case in the 1960s and 1970s.[7]

The wave of immigrants that arrived in the United States between the 1960s and today were mostly from Latin America and South or East Asia. These trends are quite a change from previous immigration patterns; most immigrants to the United States in the 1960s and 1970s were from Europe.[8] Today, immigrants from Mexico make up 28 percent of the foreign-born population and comprise the largest single share of immigrants. Those arriving from South or East Asia are not far behind, comprising 26 percent of the foreign-born population.[9]

As the population of immigrants has grown, it has become apparent that explicit discussion of whiteness, immigration, and citizenship, is not a relic of a distant era in which racial prejudice was more widely accepted. Such debates, it seems, are inevitably rehashed each time the United States experiences a new wave of immigration. The most recent period is no exception. Political scientist Samuel Huntington (2004), for example, warned that the influx of Latinos to the United States presents "the single most immediate and most serious challenge to America's traditional identity" (p. 2). Huntington left no doubt as to the exact nature of this identity when he asked, "[w]ill the U.S. remain a country with a single national language and a core Anglo-Protestant culture" (p. 2)? A number of other scholars and political pundits, including Victor Davis Hanson (2003), Francis Fukuyama (1993), Peter Brimelow (1996), and Patrick Buchanan (2011) have joined Huntington in lamenting what they argue are the dangers of multiculturalism, the rise of group identity politics, and the failure of new immigrant groups to assimilate to the dominant American culture.[10] They contend that bilingualism, the election of non-white politicians, population displacement, and even challenges to "racial purity" are all threats to white Americans posed by "the browning of America."

Many of these same individuals have predicted a backlash among white Americans in response to the changes spurred by immigration. Huntington claimed that initiatives against illegal immigrants, affirmative action, and bilingual education are just a few examples of whites' negative responses. He also foreshadowed what he saw as inevitable collective action on the part of whites: "If blacks and Hispanics organize and lobby for special privileges, why not whites? If the National Association for the Advancement of Colored People and the

National Council of La Raza are legitimate organizations, why not a national organization promoting white interests"?[11] Similarly, political scientist Carol Swain argued that a rise in white nationalism and white racial consciousness is a clear symptom of whites' concern over Latino immigration. She proposed that such a reaction would be "the next logical stage for identity politics in America" (Swain 2002, p. 423).

In this chapter, I put the claims of Huntington, Swain, and others to the test by investigating the extent to which contemporary white Americans perceive immigration as a threat to their cultural and racial dominance. If, as I have argued, white identity is now routinely salient, and if immigration is a source of threat to whites' status, then whites who identify with their racial group should be far more restrictive in their immigration opinion, and they should believe that the consequences of immigration are more negative than positive. In fact, white identity should be one of the most powerful and consistent drivers of immigration opinion today.

The Threat to White Dominance

Immigration is exceptional in the degree to which it may be perceived as a challenge to whites' dominant status. For one, some whites might view large influxes of foreigners with unfamiliar cultures and language as a realistic threat to the nation's status quo. In other words, the mass introduction of new languages, food, and cultural traditions may very well serve to displace the country's dominant culture. Today, immigration is framed as a threat. Immigrants, critics argue, take American jobs, raise crime rates in communities, and change American culture. But immigration is also a unique threat specifically because race has been so significantly implicated in citizenship policies over the course of the nation's history. Efforts to accommodate immigrants who are not part of the country's Anglo-centric culture may be viewed as directly threatening white Americans' cultural hegemony (Kaufmann 2004). Higham (1955) described how past nativistic responses among white Americans toward European immigrants were more common when immigrants challenged the order and dominance of Anglo-Saxon Americans. Furthermore, whiteness has been so central to American citizenship that previous immigrant groups, especially those from Southern and Eastern Europe, deliberately came to identify as "white" in order to distance themselves from Chinese immigrants and African Americans (Saxton 1975). The notion that immigrants adopted a white identity in order to gain political and social acceptance in America has now been broadly documented by historians (Brodkin 1998; Ignatiev 1995; King 2000; Roediger 2006). While today's Latino immigrants may eventually follow the path laid out by nineteenth- and early twentieth-century European immigrants, eventually becoming subsumed under a white identity, this transformation has not yet occurred.[12]

White Opposition to Immigration

Americans have never been especially enthusiastic about immigration. In 1965, pollsters began asking what became an ongoing time-series question about whether immigration should be increased, decreased, or kept at its present level.[13] At that time, only 7 percent preferred an increase in immigration, 39 percent preferred immigration to remain at its present level, and 33 percent wanted to see immigration decreased.[14] At no point in the time trend has a preference for increasing immigration surpassed a penchant to maintain or decrease current levels. When we look at immigration preferences only among white Americans in more recent years, we observe similar patterns. Figure 6.2 presents attitudes about immigration levels between 1992 and 2016 among whites in the ANES Time Series. While support for decreasing immigration has declined somewhat since a peak in 1994, most whites still prefer that fewer immigrants cross the country's borders. In 2016, approximately 49 percent of whites wanted to see immigration decreased.

An impressive body of research has sought to explain what drives opposition to immigration, especially among whites, who are far more opposed to immigration than other Americans (Abrajano and Hajnal 2015; Espenshade and Hempstead 1996; Kinder and Sanders 1996; Schuman et al. 1985).[15] Generally, explanations fall into two camps. The first focuses on the economic burdens immigrants place on the nation's citizens. It examines increased opposition to immigration at the aggregate level during economic downturns (Burns and Gimpel 2000; Espenshade and Calhoun 1993; Foner 1964; Higham 1955; Lapinski et al. 1997; Olzak 1992; Simon and Alexander 1993). Other work uncovers beliefs about immigrants burdening the welfare state, increasing taxation and social welfare spending (Calavita

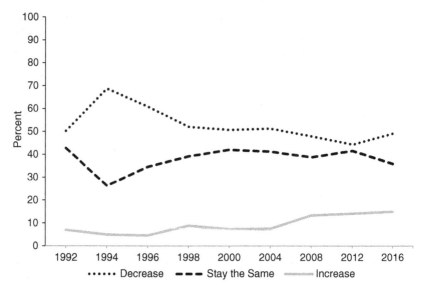

Figure 6.2 Support for Immigration over Time

Note: Lines represent the percentage of respondents who hold each preference on immigration.

Source: ANES Cumulative File. Data are weighted.

1996; Coenders and Scheepers 1998; Quillian 1995). Still other work has found some evidence that at the individual level, more economically vulnerable individuals tend to support more restrictive immigration policies (Abowd and Freeman 1991; Borjas and Freeman 1992). Much of the research in this vein argues that individuals in occupational sectors or positions most likely to experience competition from immigrants are far more opposed to immigration (Clark and Legge 1997; Pettigrew, Wagner, and Christ 2007; Scheve and Slaughter 2001). Some of the evidence with respect to the role of economic concerns in predicting opposition to immigration has been, however, inconsistent. For instance, political scientists Hainmueller and Hiscox (2010) find little indication that individuals who are more likely to experience labor market competition with immigrants are significantly more opposed to immigration. They also find minimal support for the argument that wealthy citizens oppose immigration from low-skilled workers, who are more likely to burden the social welfare system and increase taxes. These results cast doubt on the claim that economic concerns are the driving force behind immigration attitudes (Hainmueller and Hopkins 2014).

A second line of work argues that opposition to immigration is not a product of real economic concerns, but instead a function of symbolic attitudes. This research argues that the same negative evaluations of groups that motivate public opinion in other domains apply to immigration opinion as well (Citrin et al. 1997; Nelson and Kinder 1996). For instance, Citrin and colleagues (1997) find that beliefs about the state of the national economy and feelings about Hispanics and Asians – the main immigrant groups – are far more powerfully associated with immigration opinion than are individual economic circumstances. Sides and Citrin (2007) find that cultural and national identity, as well as references for cultural unity, outweigh the effect of economic dissatisfaction when it comes to explaining opposition to immigration across Europe. Other predispositions, like SDO and authoritarianism, appear to be related to immigration opinion as well (Pettigrew, Wagner, and Christ 2007).

Much of the scholarship on immigration opinion focuses overwhelmingly on how *out-group* attitudes or hostilities motivate opposition to immigration. In other words, when whites dislike the specific groups they believe comprise the immigrant population, they are less supportive of immigration. There is certainly powerful evidence for this claim. Kinder and Kam (2010) demonstrate that in the 1990s, ethnocentrism – or prejudice toward racial out-groups writ large – was one of the most potent predictors of white opposition to immigration. Elsewhere, my colleagues and I demonstrated that in more recent years, the media's focus on Latino immigrants in particular has narrowed the effect of prejudicial attitudes; now hostility toward Hispanics (and less toward other groups) underlies support for more restrictive immigration policy (Valentino, Brader, and Jardina 2013).

Unsurprisingly, the group-centric nature of immigration opinion means that hostility toward immigrants is not uniformly distributed. The trends described earlier in this chapter showed that Americans seem to have markedly different preferences for immigrants by region of origin. White Americans seem far less hostile to newcomers from places like England and Scandinavia – immigrants who look physically and culturally similar to themselves. Brader, Valentino, and Suhay (2008) corroborate this argument; they find that news about the costs of immigration is far more likely to trigger anxiety and opposition among whites when the immigrants are Latino than when they are European.

The claims I make here are consistent with much of this work, but they depart from previous efforts in a central way. Rather than focusing on how out-group hostility fuels immigration opinion, I instead focus on how whites' anxiety and concern for their in-group plays a fundamental role in opinion. Whites do not merely endorse more restrictive immigration policy out of animus toward Latinos, I argue; they are also concerned that the large influx of non-white immigrants threatens their dominance over America's culture and its political and economic institutions. It follows that immigrants from many European countries, therefore, seem far less threatening since they identify as (and are identified as) white. Of course, not all whites are especially opposed to immigration. What accounts for differences in opinion? If I am right, then even after accounting for out-group attitudes, we should find that whites with higher levels of racial identity possess far more restrictive attitudes toward immigration.

Testing the Link between White Identity and Immigration Opinion

To examine the relationship between white racial identity and immigration opinion, I turn to multiple sources: The 2010 KN Study, the 2012 ANES, the 2013 SSI Study, the 2016 ANES Pilot, and the 2016 ANES. If white racial identity is as central to immigration opinion as I claim, then we should observe a strong relationship between the two in multiple years, across samples, and with different measures of identity. We should also observe an even stronger link between immigration opinion and racial consciousness. And we should see these trends when it comes to a range of different immigration policies or efforts to limit immigration, as well as with respect to beliefs about the negative consequences of immigration. Employing multiple sources of evidence allows me to demonstrate the robustness of these claims.

In order to determine that white identity is in fact significantly associated with immigration opinion, all else equal, I account for several potentially competing explanations when appropriate measures are available. First, I consider the possibility that more economically vulnerable individuals, or those who are more likely to compete with immigrants for jobs or who may potentially feel financial strain from immigration, will be more supportive of restricting immigration. Accordingly, I control for employment status (employed or unemployed), and subjective evaluations of how one's immediate family is doing financially. Yet, individual economic circumstances often play little to no role in public opinion (Sears and Funk 1990). Instead, to the extent that economic evaluations matter, it is usually with respect to the national economy; thus, I control for these types of appraisals as well.

I also include a measure of Hispanic affect (measured with the 101-point feeling thermometer), since today, when most Americans think of immigrants, they are thinking of those of Hispanic origin (Pérez 2016; Valentino, Brader, and Jardina 2013).[16] And of course, we might expect how whites feel about Hispanics to factor into their opinion on immigration. Furthermore, I include opinion about the scope of government, on the idea that those who prefer less government involvement might also prefer that the government stay out of regulating immigration. Finally, I control for other demographic characteristics, including levels of education, age, and gender. These models are consistent with the "standard" model of public opinion I introduced in Chapter 3.

I begin by examining attitudes toward increasing, decreasing, or maintaining current levels of immigration in the 2012 ANES. Americans' attention to immigration grew dramatically in 2014, and as I will discuss more in Chapter 8, immigration remained near the top of the list of America's most important problems moving into 2016 with the presidential candidacy of Donald Trump.[17] In 2012, however, Americans in general were not especially concerned with immigration compared to other matters, such as the state of the national economy.[18] Nevertheless, we might still expect that high white identifiers were disproportionately opposed to immigration compared to low-identifiers, even when immigration did not feel like a particularly pressing national problem.

The first panel (A) in Figure 6.3 summarizes the results of a model in which white identity is regressed on attitudes about immigration levels, coded such that higher levels of the dependent variable indicate more restrictive views on immigration.[19] All variables in the model are coded to range from zero to one, and the model includes the control variables described above. The shaded bars represent the coefficients associated with each variable in the model, and the capped lines present the 95 percent confidence intervals. The coefficients reveal whether differences in white identity are systematically related to

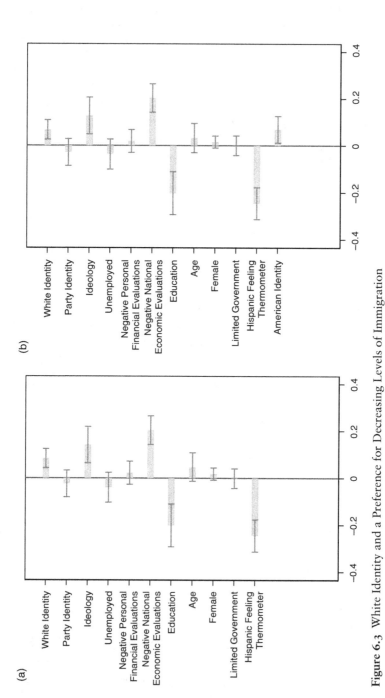

Figure 6.3 White Identity and a Preference for Decreasing Levels of Immigration

Note: Panel (A) shows the effect without controlling for American identity (B). Bars represent the coefficient for each variable in the OLS model. The lines represent the 95 percent confidence intervals. Model also controls for race of interviewer. Estimates from full model appear in Online Appendix 6A.

Source: 2012 ANES (face-to-face).

differences in opinion on immigration, while holding constant other considerations, like party identity, ideology, employment status, and so forth.

We can see in Figure 6.3, by the fact that the confidence intervals for the white identity variable do not cross zero, that the coefficient on white identity is statistically distinguishable from zero. The magnitude of the effect is relatively modest – it is smaller than what we observe for other significant variables in the model, including political ideology, evaluations of the national economy, education, and attitudes toward Hispanics. Nevertheless, it is still a substantively meaningful effect. Moving from the lowest to the highest level of white identity is associated with a 10 percent increase in preferences for decreasing levels of immigration.

White identity, however, might not be the main identity through which Americans are filtering their immigration attitudes. Work on immigration opinion has suggested that Americans also view immigration as a threat to their national identity, and so perhaps it is this attachment that is mainly driving opinion (Citrin 2001; Citrin and Sears 2014; Citrin and Sides 2008; Citrin et al. 2007). Does white identity maintain its predictive power with respect to immigration opinion even after controlling for the extent to which whites think that their identity as an American is important? Panel (B) in Figure 6.3 suggests that it does. Including American identity, which also significantly predicts immigration opinion, only slightly reduces the effect of white identity. These results suggest that white identity and American identity are not one and the same, and they independently influence whites' immigration opinion.

Next, I ask whether white identity maintains its predictive power when it comes to other attitudes about immigrants and immigration over time and across other sources of evidence. To find out, I examine the link between identity and a host of immigration attitudes across seven data sources. These studies include general questions about whether immigration should be increased or decreased, attitudes toward immigrants themselves, and opinions on policies intended to address immigration in some way. In each case, we would expect that white identifiers are far less supportive of increasing immigration than those whites who do not possess a racial identity. Importantly, we would expect that white consciousness is even more strongly linked to opposition to immigration than is white identity.

Table 6.1 presents the coefficients on white identity and white consciousness when the two items are included in separate models predicting a range of ten different immigration attitudes. In this table I focus on how whites feel about immigration and immigrants more generally. The first thing to note is the remarkable consistency with which white identity and white consciousness are associated with immigration opinion, all else equal. Across every study, both forms of racial solidarity are linked with a preference for decreasing immigration. White identifiers are also more likely to think that immigration is an especially important issue, would prefer to increase federal spending to tighten border security, and support laws checking the status of immigrants. Whites with higher levels of racial solidarity also feel less warm toward "illegal" immigrants, and they favor building a wall with Mexico. What is more, in each case, we see that the magnitude of the coefficient on consciousness is even greater than it is for white identity. Whites with higher levels of racial consciousness are especially unfavorable toward immigration.

I note that if there is any ambivalence when it comes to immigration attitudes on the part of these whites, it is with respect to issues concerning the status of children. We see in the 2012 ANES that white identity is not significantly related to attitudes about allowing children brought to the United States illegally to become citizens. The coefficients are insignificant and close to zero. The results are also somewhat less consistent across studies when it comes to eliminating birthright citizenship for children of immigrants. These results may reflect more uncertainty about the issue of birthright citizenship generally – although I note that whites with higher levels of white consciousness even support changing the Constitution to eliminate the policy – or they may also reflect a degree of sympathy for children, who have little control over their immigrant status.

Table 6.2 reveals the relationship between white identity, white consciousness, and beliefs about the consequences of immigration. We should observe that those high on identity view immigration as having a largely negative effect on American citizens and society. Whites high on racial consciousness should take an even more pessimistic view. The results in Table 6.2 paint a portrait of impressive consistency. In each case, even after accounting for a number of alternative explanations, both white identity and white consciousness are powerful predictors of opinion. Whites with higher levels of racial solidarity are more inclined

Table 6.1 *The Relationship between White Identity, White Consciousness, and Attitudes toward Immigrants and Immigration*

Dependent Variable	KN 2010	ANES 2012		SSI 2013		ANES 2016 Pilot		ANES 2016			
		(Face-to-face)	(Web)					(Face-to-face)		(Web)	
	ID	ID	ID	ID	Consc.	ID	Consc.	ID	Consc.	ID	Consc.
Decrease number of immigrants	0.148** (0.058)	0.107*** (0.035)	0.083*** (0.021)	0.054* (0.030)	0.107*** (0.037)	0.064** (0.029)	0.198*** (0.041)	0.014 (0.035)	0.113*** (0.036)	0.085*** (0.025)	0.192*** (0.038)
Importance of immigration level issue	0.131*** (0.041)										
Increase federal spending on tightening border security	0.100*** (0.032)			0.113*** (0.024)	0.282*** (0.029)						
Support law checking immigration status		0.121*** (0.043)	0.101*** (0.029)								
Illegal immigrant feeling thermometer		−0.040 (0.029)	−0.053*** (0.017)					−0.106*** (0.029)	−0.141*** (0.038)	−0.040 (0.023)	−0.053* (0.031)
Oppose allowing children brought illegally to become citizens		0.045 (0.048)	0.003 (0.032)								
Support changing US Constitution so that children of unauthorized immigrants do not get citizenship if born in the United States						0.086 (0.067)	0.208** (0.090)	0.067 (0.051)	0.155* (0.080)	0.056** (0.026)	0.138*** (0.043)

(continued)

Table 6.1 (*cont.*)

Dependent Variable	KN 2010	ANES 2012 (Face-to-face)	ANES 2012 (Web)	SSI 2013		ANES 2016 Pilot		ANES 2016 (Face-to-face)		ANES 2016 (Web)	
	ID	ID	ID	ID	Consc.	ID	Consc.	ID	Consc.	ID	Consc.
Oppose children of unauthorized immigrants automatically getting citizenship if born in the United States						0.084 (0.052)	0.229*** (0.071)				
Favor sending back children brought illegally								0.057* (0.033)	0.129*** (0.036)	0.037 (0.027)	0.100** (0.040)
Favor building a wall along border with Mexico								0.064 (0.044)	0.178*** (0.063)	0.091*** (0.026)	0.234*** (0.039)

Note: Table entries are OLS coefficients. Standard errors in parentheses. All variables in model coded to range from zero to one. KN and ANES data are weighted. Model also controls for party identity, ideology, employment status, negative personal and national economic evaluations, education, age, gender, and the Hispanic feeling thermometer. Estimates from full models available in Online Appendix 6B.
***p<0.01, **p<0.05, *p<0.1, two-tailed.
Source: 2010 KN, 2012 ANES, 2013 SSI, 2016 ANES Pilot, 2016 ANES.

Table 6.2 The Relationship between White Identity, White Consciousness, and Beliefs about the Consequences of Immigration

Dependent Variable	KN 2010	ANES 2012 (Face-to-face)	ANES 2012 (Web)	SSI 2013		ANES 2016 Pilot		ANES 2016 (Face-to-face)		ANES 2016 (Web)	
	ID	ID	ID	ID	Consc.	ID	Consc.	ID	Consc.	ID	Consc.
Immigrants don't make Americans open to new ideas and culture	0.197*** (0.037)										
Immigrants change American culture and values				0.203*** (0.037)	0.352*** (0.046)						
America's culture is harmed by immigrants								0.107** (0.039)	0.256*** (0.051)	0.145*** (0.022)	0.287*** (0.030)
Immigration is generally bad for the United States						0.135*** (0.035)	0.275*** (0.052)				
Immigrants take jobs away from American citizens	0.215*** (0.043)	0.124*** (0.038)	0.073*** (0.025)	0.234*** (0.035)	0.499*** (0.042)			0.114** (0.045)	0.333*** (0.050)	0.109*** (0.028)	0.330*** (0.035)
Immigrants are bad for the US economy								0.070** (0.032)	0.196*** (0.041)	0.064*** (0.022)	0.159*** (0.033)
Immigrants increase crime rates								0.075** (0.034)	0.244*** (0.033)	0.136*** (0.023)	0.305*** (0.034)
Concern about changing ethnic makeup of United States	0.281*** (0.052)			0.298*** (0.035)	0.563*** (0.041)						

Note: Table entries are OLS coefficients. Standard errors in parentheses. All variables in model coded to range from zero to one. KN and ANES data are weighted. Model also controls for party identity, ideology, employment status, negative personal and national economic evaluations, education, age, gender, and the Hispanic feeling thermometer. Estimates from full models available in Online Appendix 6B.

***p<0.01, **p<0.05, *p<0.1, two-tailed.

Source: 2010 KN, 2012 ANES, 2013 SSI, 2016 ANES Pilot, 2016 ANES.

to believe that immigrants do not make America open to new ideas and culture, and that immigrants change American culture and values, but not for the better. They also think that immigration is generally bad for the United States.

Popular narratives about the influence of immigration do not merely focus on the potentially detrimental effect of immigration on American culture. Immigration opponents also claim that competition over jobs in the United States is a zero-sum game, and one that immigrants are winning. Whites with higher levels of racial solidarity, it seems, are inclined to believe these narratives. They agree that immigrants take jobs away from American citizens and that immigrants are bad for the US economy. They also believe that immigrants increase crime rates and are generally concerned about the changing ethnic makeup of the country.

These relationships are robust to controlling for both personal economic circumstances and sociotropic evaluations of the national economy. I find, as have others, that economic self-interest is only sporadically associated with immigration opinion – even when it comes to attitudes about the economic consequences of immigration – and the effect is often minimal. I also find, consistent with prior work, that negative *national* economic evaluations matter. Whites who believe the national economy has performed relatively poorly in recent years tend to be more opposed to immigration and to believe it has negative consequences. Republicans and conservatives tend to hold more anti-immigrant sentiments than Democrats and liberals, although the effects of partisanship and ideology are not always consistent or powerful. Whites on either end of the partisan aisle tend to have more anti-immigrant attitudes. And of course, whites with more negative evaluations of Hispanics are far more opposed to immigration.

Immigration opinion is also often a function of levels of education, suggesting that a more parochial view of the world might increase more anti-immigrant sentiment. Immigration attitudes seem to be driven less by age and attitudes about the scope of government. Gender matters on occasion, although the effects are generally small. To the extent that it does have an effect, women are often somewhat more opposed to immigration and likely to worry more about its consequences.

Even after taking these other factors into consideration, both white identity and white consciousness remain powerful predictors of immigration opinion. The magnitude of the effect of white solidarity on immigration opinion is noteworthy; moving from the lowest levels to the highest levels of racial solidarity usually shifts immigration in a more negative direction by at least 10 percentage points, if not more. More importantly, the effect of both types of racial solidarity rival or exceed some of the most powerful predictors of immigration attitudes. White identity and white consciousness are often as, if not more strongly, tied to immigration opinion than negative national economic evaluations, education, and attitudes toward Hispanics.

To illustrate the strength of these relationships more clearly, in Figure 6.4, I plot, using the 2016 ANES, the predicted level of opinion, across levels of consciousness, for four immigration attitudes: preferences for increasing or decreasing immigration, support for building a wall along the border with Mexico, endorsement of the belief that immigrants take jobs from American citizens, and support for the notion that immigrants increase crime. We can see that in each case, moving from the lowest levels of consciousness to the highest produces a marked shift in immigration opinion. For instance, compared to whites low on consciousness, whites at the highest level of consciousness more greatly prefer to decrease immigration on an order of eighteen points. Scanning across the figure, we can see that the effect of white consciousness on each immigration opinion is a similar order of magnitude. In short, white consciousness has a potent effect on anti-immigrant attitudes.

Immigration Opinion over Time

The evidence presented here makes it difficult to deny that white identity and white consciousness play a significant role in how white Americans arrive at their immigration attitudes. Across studies conducted between 2010 and 2016, we see that both measures of racial solidarity consistently, strongly, and significantly predict immigration opinion. As expected, white identifiers are far more opposed to immigration and more likely to believe that immigration has negative consequences. Are these attitudes a recent phenomenon? Perhaps, if we were to step back in time, we would not necessarily observe such a strong link between identity and immigration.

Unfortunately, we cannot step too far back in time with available data. We can, however, get some purchase on the idea that white

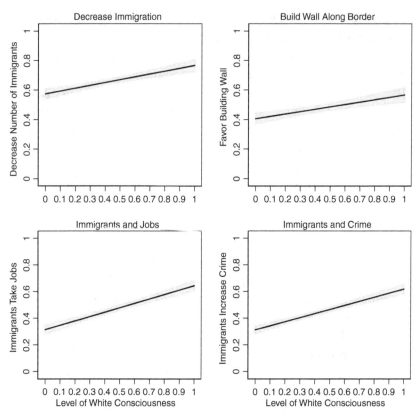

Figure 6.4 The Effect of White Consciousness on Immigration Opinion

The lines represent the predicted opinion on immigration at each level of white consciousness. The shaded region represents the 95 percent confidence interval. Predicted values generated by holding gender constant at female and all other variables at their mean. Model also controls for party identity, ideology, employment status, personal and national financial economic evaluations, education, age, gender, attitudes toward the scope of government, and affect toward Hispanics. Estimates from full models available in Online Appendix 6B5.

Source: 2016 ANES (Web).

in-group attitudes have played an increasingly powerful role in immigration opinion by turning to the ANES and exploring the relationship between white in-group affect – measured with the 101-point feeling thermometer – and immigration opinion between 1992 and 2016. The thermometer measure is an admittedly imperfect measure of identity – it does not capture the centrality of a group identity as much as it does positive feelings toward the in-group. Nevertheless, we would expect that whites who feel especially favorable toward their own in-group should have notably different opinions on factors that might be detrimental to their group relative to whites who hold more ambivalent or even negative attitudes.

If the extent to which white in-group attitudes are brought to bear on opinion is in part related to growing perceptions of threat, then we ought to expect that the relationship between white identity and immigration opinion should increase as levels of immigration in the United States grew. If we turn back to Figure 6.1 and remind ourselves of trends in the rate of immigration to the United States, we see that while there was certainly an uptick in immigration between 1980 and 1990, it was not until 2000 that immigration rates leapt, approaching levels we had not seen since the early 1900s. Thus, we might not expect to see white in-group attitudes especially related to immigration opinion until after the year 2000, when immigration rates truly began to soar.

Surely, you might say, most white Americans were not so attuned to trends in immigration that they could describe the pattern outlined in Figure 6.1. Certainly not. But what we would expect is that as the size of the immigrant population grew, news coverage of immigration ought to have increased as well. Valentino, Brader, and Jardina (2013) show, for instance, that the number of articles about Hispanic and Asian immigrants – groups considered non-white – increased between 1980 and 2011, but grew especially in the 2000s. What is more, Pérez (2010) shows that much of the immigration coverage about Latinos over this period was decidedly negative, and focused frequently on *illegal* immigration, especially in the mid 2000s.

We can also see that coverage of immigration generally, regardless of the group in question or the tone of that coverage, grew markedly over time. Figure 6.5 plots the proportion of articles on immigration that appeared in the *New York Times*, *Los Angeles Times*, and *Washington Post* – three of the top newspapers in the country by circulation.[20] The rate at which these papers published articles mentioning immigration increased over the period, and especially as rates of immigration were peaking in the early to mid 2000s.

Does the relationship between white in-group attitudes and immigration opinion follow patterns in the salience of the immigration issue? To see, I regressed attitudes about our now familiar dependent variable – whether immigration levels should be increased, decreased, or kept the same – on whites' feeling thermometer evaluations of their own

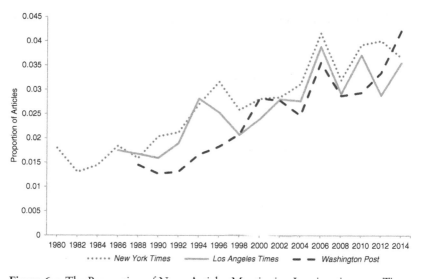

Figure 6.5 The Proportion of News Articles Mentioning Immigration over Time
The lines represent the proportion of articles, out of the total number of articles
published in a year, mentioning immigrant or immigration, over time.
Source: www.newyorktimes.com, www.washingtonpost.com, Proquest Historical
Archive (*Los Angeles Times*).

group in each year the items were available between 1992 and 2016.
For each model, when possible, I controlled for affect toward Hispanics,
as well as for age, education level, employment status, personal financial
assessments, national economic evaluations, party identity, ideology,
and attitudes toward the size and scope of government.

Figure 6.6 presents the coefficients on both the white and
Hispanic feeling thermometers for each model in each year, beginning
in 1992. The lines running through the points represent the 95 percent
confidence intervals. We can see that in 1992, the effect of the thermometer on opinion was fairly small. In 1994 and 1996, it was also
relatively minimal, and statistically insignificant. By 2000, the effect
was much larger, and remained significant in each year through 2016.

The results fit the expected pattern. The relationship between
white in-group affect and immigration opinion was weak and inconsistent in the 1990s, before becoming more consistent and substantively
effective in the mid to late 2000s.[21] In each year analyzed between
2004 and 2016, rating whites more positively on the thermometer was
associated with greater support for decreasing levels of immigration,
even after controlling for out-group attitudes.

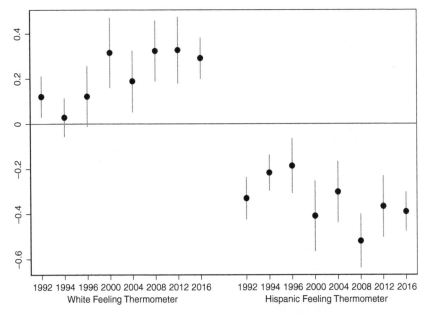

Figure 6.6 The Relationship between White and Hispanic Affect and Support for Decreasing Levels of Immigration

The points represent the coefficient on the white feeling thermometer and the Hispanic feeling thermometer in each year (separate models). The lines represent the 95 percent confidence intervals. Model also controls for party identity, ideology, employment status, personal and national economic evaluations, education, age, and gender. Estimates from full models appear in Online Appendix 6C.

Source: ANES Time Series Cumulative File.

The significant effect in 1992, however, is slightly unexpected. Why might we have observed this relationship in 1992 in particular? Because immigration was likely a salient political topic in 1992, especially with regards to the presidential election. It was in this year, now over two decades ago, that Patrick J. Buchanan campaigned for the Republican nomination for president of the United States. Buchanan's campaign message feels remarkably familiar in today's political climate. He, like Donald Trump, railed against immigration, even advocating for the building of a fence along the southern border of the United States. It is therefore unsurprising that an election study picked up these associations when Buchanan was publicly arguing, even in 1992, that immigration was a threat to America's culture, and that immigration would eventually result in white Americans becoming a minority.

Are Whites Threatened Where There Are More Immigrants?

While the results of the immigration analysis are compelling, they do not quite help us uncover whether the relationship between white identity and opposition to immigration is a result of group threat. How might we draw more direct conclusions in test of my broader theory? One way in which previous work tests the relationship between threat and moderating attitudes on outcomes or preferences is by experimentally introducing threat and demonstrating the subsequent activation of the relevant attitudes. When it comes to immigration opinion, however, white identity is *already* activated; in observational data, it appears as a strong and significant predictor in line with many of my theoretical expectations.

But we might not expect all white identifiers in all circumstances to feel that out-groups pose a challenge to their group. In fact, a long line of work on racial threat has proposed that the racial context in which individuals reside can influence perceptions of threat. Much of this research argues that a sizeable and proximate population of non-whites can increase perceptions of out-group threat or competition among whites. Generally, studies in this vein employ measures of the size of the non-white population as a measure of threat (Blalock 1967; Campbell, Wong, and Citrin 2006; Glaser 1994; Key 1949; Oliver and Mendelberg 2000; Oliver and Wong 2003; Quillian 1996; Taylor 1998). Implicit in this research is the assumption that when proximate non-white populations are large, whites feel increasingly threatened, which subsequently influences the salience of whites' identity with their racial group. This identity is then linked to higher levels of racial hostility. The majority of this work, however, rarely demonstrates that whites possess an identification with their racial group, therefore missing an important step in a broader theoretical account.

Here, however, we can test these relationships directly, allowing us to further assess whether group threat is indeed an important moderator of opinion. Specifically, we can ask whether white identity is more strongly associated with opposition to immigration among whites who live in more racially diverse locales. To determine if we can in fact observe this relationship, I again turn to the 2012 ANES, which includes for each respondent, a geo-code that can be matched to Census data on various characteristics at the county level. Specifically, I want to know if the effect of white identity on opposition to immigration is more powerful in counties with a greater change in the immigrant population.

I measure change in the immigrant population for each county between 2000 and 2010 using US Census estimates for the foreign-born population. The dependent variable for this analysis is the standard measure of immigration opinion – a preference for increasing, decreasing, or keeping levels of immigration the same. As usual, immigration opinion is coded such that higher values are associated with more restrictive preferences. In addition to accounting for the change in the immigrant population, I also control for demographic characteristics, out-group attitudes, personal economic circumstances, national economic evaluations, party identity, ideology and a prefer-ence for more limited government.[22]

Does the effect of white identity on immigration opinion become more potent as the change in the county-level foreign-born population increases? Figure 6.7 suggests that is the case. The chart plots the marginal effect of white identity at each degree of change in the foreign-born population between 2000 and 2010. As the popula-tion becomes more diverse, white identity is associated with greater support for decreasing levels of immigration. Thus, the results provide some provocative evidence for the claim that white identity is brought to bear on opinions, in response to threat, in a manner consistent with protecting the group and its status.

Do Demographic Changes Threaten White Identifiers?

The US Census and demographers from other institutions have made a number of projections about the future racial and ethnic composition of the country. News coverage of these trends often focuses on the fact that whites will be a racial and ethnic minority by sometime around the year 2042.[23] Prior research has already demonstrated that whites feel threatened by this information (Alba, Rumbaut, and Marotz 2005; Albertson and Gadarian 2013; Craig and Richeson 2014b; Myers and Levy 2018). My argument, however, is that it is whites high on racial solidarity who ought to be especially threatened by information about the loss of their majority status and about increasing immigration.

One observable implication of experiencing threat to one's group comes from Intergroup Emotions Theory, which argues that individuals will experience emotions on behalf of their collective group

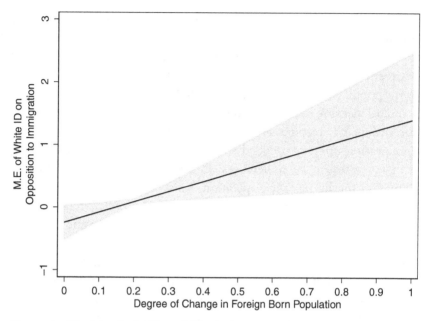

Figure 6.7 The Marginal Effect of White Identity on Opposition to Immigration by Each Level of Change in the County-Level Foreign-Born Population

The line represents the marginal effect of white identity at each level of the foreign-born population, by county. The shaded region represents the 95 percent confidence interval. Predicted values generated by holding gender constant at female and all other variables at their mean. Model also controls for party identity, ideology, employment status, personal and national economic evaluations, education, age, gender, attitudes toward government, and affect toward Hispanics. Estimates from full model in Online Appendix 6D.

Source: 2012 ANES (Face-to-face).

based on their appraisal of the group's security (Mackie, Devos, and Smith 2000; Smith, Seger, and Mackie 2007). Events that are assessed as threatening to one's in-group should produce a negative emotional response (Albertson and Gadarian 2015). Specifically, individuals should report feeling angry when they believe that their group is losing valuable resources or that their goals are being obstructed. They should feel fear when they perceive uncertainty about their group's well-being (Cottrell and Neuberg 2005). Thus, we might observe that the impending relative loss of status due to demographic shifts or to increasing immigration should produce negative emotional reactions among whites who feel attached to their racial group.[24] Previous work demonstrates that emotional reactions have political implications;

people tend to behave in ways consistent with their emotional reactions by, for example, by becoming more opposed to immigration and by seeking more information about the issue (Brader 2006; Brader, Valentino, and Suhay 2008).

To determine whether white identifiers respond more negatively to information about demographic change, as part of the 2016 YouGov Study, I included an experimental component which presented subjects with information about whites' numerical status in the US population or about the changing immigrant population. The study was conducted over the two waves of the survey, and was comprised only of non-Hispanic white adult US citizens. In wave 1 of the study, conducted in October before the 2016 election, respondents were asked about their white identity and racial consciousness. Then at the beginning of wave 2 of the study, conducted just after the presidential election in November, respondents were randomly assigned to one of four experimental conditions. Respondents in each condition read between two and four sentences that described a chart pictured below the text. In each condition, care was taken to create parallelism between the provided text and the aesthetics of the graphs.

In the control condition, subjects viewed a (fictitious) chart accompanied by two sentences claiming that the number of cellphone-only households in the United States was on the rise. Subjects in the first treatment condition, or what I call the "white majority" condition, were presented with a similar graph, but this one described the projected population of whites and non-whites in the United States over the next forty years, claiming that whites will continue to comprise a majority of the population for the foreseeable future. Again, the chart and data were fictitious, and are inconsistent with current population projections. The graph was intended to present whites with non-threatening information about their group's status. In this condition, whites ought to be assured that their group will maintain its numerical majority. The second treatment condition, called the "white minority condition," was intended to exacerbate whites' concerns about the status of their group. Whites were presented with a graph that, consistent with real population projections, indicated their group would be a minority by 2042.[25] Finally, in the last treatment condition, referred to as the "increasing immigrants" condition, subjects viewed a graph illustrating that the number of foreign-born individuals in the United States was expected to rise sharply over the next several decades. This condition allowed me to parse out any potential differences in reactions to demographic change generally compared to immigration, although my expectation is that the two conditions were prompt similar reactions.[26]

Following the implications of intergroup emotions theory, whites should report more negative emotions in response to the threatening "white displacement" and "increasing immigration" information compared to the control. We should not expect, however, that *all* whites feel negatively toward this information. Instead, it should be whites with higher levels of racial identity who are most reactive. Immediately following the presentation of the graphs, respondents were asked to indicate the extent to which they "felt" a number of emotions in reaction to the treatment. For analytical purposes, I scaled together the emotions into three categories: fear (uneasy, afraid, anxious), anger (angry, disgusted), and enthusiasm (happy, proud, hopeful).[27]

To determine whether my expectations with respect to white identifiers come to fruition, I regressed each emotion scale on white identity, indicators for the experimental treatments (with the control as the excluded category), and the interaction between white identity and the treatments. I find that compared to the control condition, in the "white majority" condition, whites, regardless of their level of racial identity, do not display any differences in their emotional reactions. There are, however, notable effects for whites who read the article indicating their group would become a minority, and for those who were told that immigration to the United States was increasing. I illustrate these effects in Figure 6.8, which plots the predicted emotional response, across levels of white identity, for respondents in either the "white minority" or in the "increasing immigrants" condition.

In the "white minority" condition, whites with higher levels of racial identity reported notably higher levels of anger. Note that compared to those in the control, whites low on racial identity were less angry, and whites high on identity were more so. White identifiers were also more fearful, although the effect does not achieve statistical significance. By comparison, whites high on identity who were told that their group was becoming a minority, were also relatively less enthusiastic compared to those in the control. The effects among those who were told that the number of immigrants to the United States was expected to steadily increase were similar. Whites high on racial identity were much more angry and fearful in response to

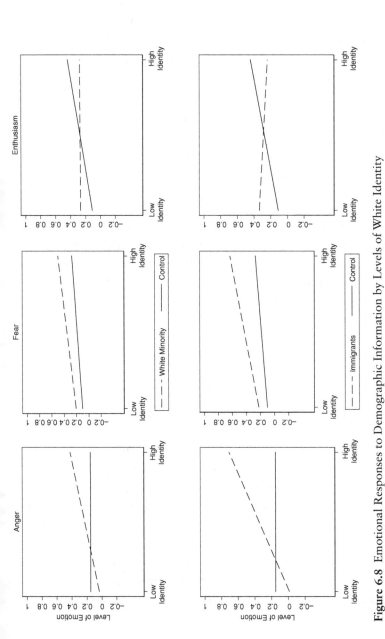

Figure 6.8 Emotional Responses to Demographic Information by Levels of White Identity

The solid represents the predicted level of each emotion the control condition. The dashed lines represent the predicted level of each emotion in the treatment conditions. Estimates from full models available in Online Appendix 6F.

Source: 2016 YouGov.

this information, and far less enthusiastic, compared to those in the control.[28]

These results provide provocative evidence that whites high on racial identity are responding to threatening information about demographic change and immigration in a manner quite distinct from whites who possess lower levels of racial solidarity. The findings here are consistent not only with intergroup emotions theory, but with my larger theoretical framework, which argues that dominant group members who identify with their group will respond especially negatively to threats to their groups' position.

Conclusion

I have argued that immigration is especially tied to white racial identity. From the time the first European settlers arrived on American soil, the country has been dominated by individuals of white, Anglo-Saxon heritage. This means that the social, economic, and political power and very identity of the nation is inextricably tied up in the cultural and racial identity of white Americans. The wave of new immigrant groups that have sought refuge in this country, who have looked to build their own lives, and to raise families, have also led many whites to feel as if their racial group has been threatened. White identifiers perceive these immigrants as arriving with darker skin, foreign languages, and with unfamiliar traditions. They view immigrants as having come to this country in great numbers, and believe they threaten to alter the racial and ethnic composition of the United States. In short, immigration, by its very nature, is seen by some whites as provoking a challenge to whiteness.

Despite the great American myth that our country is a "nation of immigrants," American citizens have never looked especially favorably upon rising levels of immigration. This dismay for new waves of immigrants was true in the 1920s, and it is no less true today. Not all Americans are equally opposed to opening our borders and welcoming newcomers from abroad. White Americans are far more opposed to increasing immigration than are blacks or Hispanics. Not all whites, however, view immigration unfavorably. A number of factors drive some whites to adopt more negative immigration attitudes, including their national economic evaluations, partisanship and political ideology, education, and attitudes toward Hispanics. What I have demonstrated is that there is another important component to this story; whites who identify more with their racial group, and who possess a sense of racial consciousness, are far more opposed to immigration, all else equal. These same whites are also much more likely to believe that immigration introduces negative consequences for the nation.

This finding is powerful and robust. It holds across time and over multiple sources of evidence. What is more, regardless of the nature of the question white Americans are asked about immigration, it is clear they are viewing the issue through the lens of their racial identity. These results are consistent with my overarching expectations about the role of white racial solidarity in American politics. Immigration is an issue that deeply challenges the status of white Americans. Population changes as a result of immigration threaten to displace whites numerically, and immigrants challenge the notion of America as a prototypically white nation. The issue is a fundamental source of status threat for whites in the United States. Therefore, as expected, white racial solidarity is tightly linked to whites' immigration attitudes.

One implication of what I have described is that the extent to which white identity is brought to bear on public opinion ought to be contingent on how salient or significant the issue of immigration becomes in the public mind (Hopkins 2010). I have shown that as immigration rates in the United States grew between the early 1990s and the present, so did national news coverage of immigration. When the news media turns its attention to immigration, or when a politician capitalizes on anti-immigrant sentiment in order to mount a campaign, we ought to see the link between white identity and immigration opinion strengthen. The over-time analysis presented here provides some evidence that the power of white identity has expanded as levels of immigration to the United States have climbed. As the United States continues to diversify, and as the white population shrinks relative to the non-white population in the United States, we might see the impact of white identity and white consciousness grow.

The results from the diversity experiment demonstrate that white identifiers do indeed respond to information about immigration and demographic changes in a manner quite distinct from whites with moderate to low levels of white identity. When faced with information about their pending loss of majority status or of increased immigration, white identifiers report feeling significantly angrier and less enthusiastic. They are also somewhat more fearful. Taken together, these results suggest that whites who are more attached to their racial group do see immigration as a threat to their group, and consequently, their racial identity is an important component of their opinions, fueling their anti-immigrant and immigration attitudes.

7 POLICIES THAT PROTECT THE GROUP

In his much-lauded analysis of the nature of belief systems in mass publics, political scientist Philip Converse argued that most individuals do not arrive at their positions on political issues via abstract ideological principles (1964). Instead, he claimed people use a much simpler means by which to understand the political world and to form policy opinions; they turn to "visible social groupings," making judgments about which groups in society receive the benefits or pay the costs of particular policies. Put in psychological terms, organizing one's political thinking around groups serves as a heuristic, or mental shortcut – one that helps reduce the complexities of politics (Nisbett and Ross 1980; Sniderman, Brody, and Tetlock 1991).

Converse's claim about the group-centric nature of politics has been well established (Achen and Bartels 2016; Kinder 1998; Nelson and Kinder 1996). Not only do individuals often bring their attitudes about specific social groups to bear on their policy preferences, but politicians and policymakers often use this feature of public opinion to their advantage, framing issues around groups to garner support or opposition for policies. And many policies in the United States have been deliberately constructed to benefit or exclude certain groups (Lieberman 1995; Weir, Orloff, and Skocpol 1988).

My purpose in this chapter is to investigate the ways in which whites' thinking about their own group informs their opinions on a broad range of policies. I extend my efforts from the previous chapter, where I demonstrated that white racial solidarity is a powerful predictor of attitudes toward immigration. Here, I show that white identity is associated with a much broader range of policy preferences. I also suggest that prior efforts to understand the political consequences of white identity have too narrowly focused on policies associated with racial out-groups – especially blacks – rather than examining the relationship between white identity and opinion on policies that are more closely tied to benefiting or harming whites as a group.

When white racial solidarity is viewed in this way – as a social identity where those who identify with the group are motivated to protect its collective interests – we see that it is far more politically consequential than previous work suggests. White racial solidarity, it turns out, powerfully predicts opinion on many policies, including attitudes toward social welfare and entitlement programs like Social Security and Medicare. I also show, as others have, that white racial solidarity is *not* linked to racialized policies associated with benefiting blacks, such as affirmative action in college admissions or welfare. Whites with higher levels of racial solidarity are, however, more supportive of policies like college legacy admissions programs, which disproportionately benefit their racial group.

Finally, I demonstrate that white racial solidarity predicts opinion on policies related to the nation's interdependence with an increasingly globalized world. White Americans with high levels of white identity, I argue, are not merely threatened by domestic concerns related to the nation's growing diversity; they also are worried about their status globally. Consequently, white identity is linked to more protectionist opinions on the outsourcing of jobs, on trade, and on the country's role in the affairs of other nations.

White Prejudice and Public Opinion

Race is one of the most central social cleavages in American life. It is therefore unsurprising that it is with respect to racial issues that the group-centric nature of public opinion is readily apparent.[1] Social scientists have now amassed a significant body of work demonstrating how major policies have been racialized, either because they were designed with certain racial groups in mind, or because they have been strategically linked with certain racial or ethnic groups. A great deal of this literature has focused on how means-tested social welfare policies like welfare, food stamps, and Medicaid are especially tied in the public mind to certain racial groups (Gilens 1999; Kinder and Sanders 1996; Quadagno 1994). These are programs designed to redistribute resources and provide aid to poor individuals and families, regardless of race or ethnicity. Yet whites believe these policies primarily serve African Americans, and support for such programs among whites is minimal. Public assistance of this sort is viewed as a handout to the undeserving poor, and to those who eschew hard work in favor of exploiting government's generosity (Gilens 1999). For example, most Americans are now familiar with the disparaging image, popularized by Ronald Reagan, of the welfare queen. This stereotype paints welfare recipients as predominately black, female, and intent on fraudulently taking advantage of government assistance.

The racialization of these social programs means that whites' opinions on them are largely tied to their racial attitudes; more racially conservative whites are far less supportive of policies like welfare and other forms of public assistance than are more racially tolerant whites. But white Americans' racial animosities extend to other racialized domains as well, including issues like affirmative action in college admissions, racial quotas in hiring and promotions, fair housing, school desegregation, and more (Kinder and Sanders 1996; Kuklinski, Cobb, and Gilens 1997; Sears and Kinder 1985).

It is in these policy domains where previous scholars have generally looked to see if whites' in-group attitudes might play a role in opinion, often comparing their predictive power to out-group attitudes (Kinder and Winter 2001; Sears and Savalei 2006; Wong and Cho 2005). The rationale for expecting white in-group attitudes to matter for these types of issues comes from a body of social psychological work on intergroup conflict and prejudice. As I discussed in Chapters 1 and 2, work within this paradigm views in-group and out-group attitudes as a natural byproduct of social groups interacting in society. Much of the research on race and politics in the United States in this tradition has been largely influenced by realistic group conflict theory (Jackson 1993; Sumner 1906). According to this theory, animosity between groups in society is the product of real struggles over scarce resources. Conflict between whites and other racial and ethnic groups, Giles and Evans argue, is the result of groups engaged in "on-going competition for control of economic, political, and social structures" (1985, p. 50). One important proposition of this approach is that external threat boosts in-group solidarity, which is, in turn, directly related to out-group hostility and to opposition to policies that benefit racial and ethnic minorities. In other words, work in this tradition views racial prejudice as a cause of whites' sense of racial identity. It argues that if whites not only dislike racial and ethnic minorities, but also oppose policies that help these groups, it is because they view such policies as a threat to their group and its collective interests.

Yet evidence that strong in-group attachments among whites leads to white racial prejudice, or to opposition to policies that benefit racial and ethnic minorities (especially blacks) is weak, especially when the effects of white identity are compared to that of racial resentment (Kinder and Sears 1981; Kinder and Winter 2001; Sears and Savalei 2006; Wong and Cho 2005). There is little indication, for example, that white identity is associated with attitudes regarding government assistance to blacks, government efforts to promote racial equality, or affirmative action policies. Instead, opinion on these sorts of policies seems largely driven by racial resentment, independent of in-group sentiments.

Reconsidering the Relationship Between White Racial Solidarity and Racialized Policies

One reason we might not observe a relationship between white identity and opinion on these specific policies is because whites do not actually view such policies as threats to their group or its status. With the exception of affirmative action, which I will discuss in more detail later in the chapter, policies like welfare or other forms of means-tested government assistance have not been described routinely as threats to whites' position atop the racial hierarchy. Instead, they have been framed very much in the way that we conceive of the nature of contemporary white racial hostility more generally – as indicative of some moral or cultural failing on the part of black Americans. Popular arguments against welfare, for instance, hardly reflect some belief about the economic success of blacks as a threat to the dominance of white Americans. Rather, welfare and related programs are disparaged as a government handout, and as free money for the lazy and undeserving.

The association between these policies and white prejudice, especially in the form of white racial resentment, is unsurprising. After all, as Kinder and Sanders (1996) explain, whites' contemporary racial attitudes are a product of elite efforts to frame blacks not as a threat to whites' status, but rather as a group which fails to live up to American values. They describe how politicians like Wallace, Nixon, Reagan, and others helped to create this new form of racial animus:

> They did not promote biological racism: they were not white supremacists; they did not allege genetic impairments; they did not promote a return to segregation; they did not imply that blacks were second-class citizens or that they should be treated differently than anyone else. Their message was subtle, rather than blatant: it was that blacks should behave themselves. They should take quiet advantage of the ample opportunities now provided them. Government had been too generous, had given blacks too much, and blacks, for their part, had accepted these gifts all too readily. Discrimination was now illegal, opportunities were plentiful. Blacks should work their way up without handouts or special favors in a society that was now color-blind.
>
> *(p. 105)*

As these very same politicians were legitimizing this new form of prejudice, they were simultaneously incorporating certain policies, like welfare, into their argument, helping to racialize them in this very vein. Consequently, certain social welfare policies are deeply implicated in the nature and construction of modern prejudice.

At the same time, while political elites have not framed many racialized policies as a challenge to whites' resources, power, or privileges, the very fact that certain policies are associated with some racial groups and not others facilitates whites' ability to determine which policies might benefit or harm their own group. Whites who identify with their racial group might not view policies that help racial and ethnic minorities as a threat, but there are a number of other policies that whites might see as potentially beneficial or harmful to their in-group. It is with respect to these policies – those that whites do interpret as serving their group's interests – that we ought to observe a relationship between white racial solidarity and public opinion. My aim is to consider such policies across three domains: social welfare programs, affirmative action, and issue positions related to globalization.

Social Security and Medicare as Policies for Whites

The Great Depression of the 1930s was devastating to America's aging population. With record unemployment and a dramatic decline in the national income, many Americans saw their entire lifetime savings disappear. For older Americans near the end of their prime working years, this loss meant that they would spend their old age in destitution. As part of the New Deal programs meant to provide a social safety net that would protect Americans from such losses in the future, the Roosevelt administration proposed a federal old-age insurance program, one that would include all working individuals regardless of occupation. When the legislation that ultimately became the Social Security Act of 1935 reached congressional deliberations, however, Southern Democrats in Congress moved to restrict farm and domestic workers from the program. In doing so, they effectively blocked African Americans, who disproportionately worked in those sectors, from receiving these government benefits (DeWitt 2010; Gordon 1994; Lichtenstein et al. 2000; Lieberman 1995).[2] Thus, for much of Social Security's history, it was white Americans who disproportionately benefited.[3]

Over time, the policy was modified to expand coverage to all citizens. In fact, political scientist Robert Lieberman argues that today, Social Security is "perhaps the closest thing to a race-blind social program that the United States has ever known" (1995, p. 513). While the administration of the program may now be race-neutral, however, Social Security is nevertheless a racialized policy – one primarily associated with whiteness. In making this claim, I join company with political scientist Nicholas Winter and others, who argue that both Social Security and Medicare have been framed by elites and subsequently understood by the American public as two policies that are for whites and that benefit whites (Kinder and Kam 2010; Winter 2006, 2008).

Winter makes a compelling argument that even though public dialogue does not overtly suggest that Social Security disproportionately benefits white people, the way political elites and the media discuss the program is nevertheless racialized (2006). He describes how policymakers were especially deliberate in crafting a frame for Social Security as an individual social insurance program. They wanted to secure public acceptance of the program, and believed that deeming it an insurance program implied a return for work, preserving the self-respect of its beneficiaries (Derthick 1979; Winter 2006).

This framing is racialized because it is structurally part of a schema – or a pattern of thought – on race that first ascribes stereotypes to blacks as poor, dependent, and lazy, and then attributes unequal outcomes between blacks and whites to individual effort and merit. Social Security stands in stark contrast to other social welfare programs in that it is seen as just reward for hard work and is not tied to need. In other words, Social Security has been intentionally contrasted with welfare as a return for hard work (a stereotype associated with whites), rather than as a handout for the dependent (a stereotype associated with blacks). As Winter writes,

> this association with whiteness likely makes Social Security more popular among white Americans than a universal program would otherwise be; after all, Social Security is not for "everyone" – in important ways for white Americans, it is for "us."
>
> *(2008, p. 117)*

According to Winter, political leaders have also routinely described Social Security using in-group rhetoric. For example, in the 1980s, President Reagan would often refer to "*our* elderly" and "*our* senior citizens" (emphasis mine) when discussing Social Security but would say "those people" when mentioning welfare or food stamps.

Medicare has been similarly framed; it was proposed as a social insurance program to provide health insurance for Americans reaching retirement age and was modeled on Social Security. It too is a program whose benefits are viewed as compensation for work; people pay into the program over the course of their lives via payroll taxes (Altman and Frist 2015). Thus, compared to other social welfare programs, especially the need-based insurance program Medicaid, Medicare has been described in such a way that we might also expect it to be associated with whiteness.

Consistent with the argument that Social Security and Medicare are viewed as programs that benefit whites – even if they are not explicitly described as such – Winter (2006, 2008) and Kinder and Kam (2010) find that in-group attitudes play an important role in whites' support for these policies. Whites who rate their in-group more warmly on a 101-point feeling thermometer are significantly more supportive of Social Security and Medicare, even after accounting for a host of alternative hypotheses. Accordingly, we should also expect to find that white identity and white consciousness are powerfully associated with favorable attitudes toward these two social programs.

To determine whether these relationships are borne out, I turn to three sources of evidence – the 2012 ANES Time Series, my own 2013 SSI Study, and the 2016 ANES Time Series. Across each of these studies, I test the proposition that white identity and white consciousness should predict more favorable attitudes toward Social Security and Medicare, measured in the ANES studies with a question asking respondents whether federal spending on Social Security should be increased, decreased, or kept the same – or, in the case of the SSI Study, the extent to which they support or oppose the programs.

In my analysis, I control for party identity, ideology, education, employment status, personal and national economic evaluations, age, gender, and attitudes about the size of government. I also account for racial resentment, paying special attention to how racial resentment and white racial solidarity predict opinion on these two social welfare policies, compared to more notoriously racialized policies like welfare. We might find that racial resentment is linked to opinion on Social Security and Medicare, but it should not be as closely tied to these policies as it is for ones that have been linked with blacks in the United States.

What is the relationship between whites' in-group and out-group attitudes when it comes to these social welfare programs? I find that in most cases, white identity and white consciousness do in fact predict support for Social Security spending.[4] Table 7.1 shows the effect of white racial solidarity on preferences for increasing Social Security across each of the three surveys. I note that the effect of identity falls short of statistical significance in the 2016 ANES Time Series, although it is in the expected direction, such that whites with higher levels of racial solidarity are inclined to favor more Social Security spending. We see the effects are significant in the other surveys and some differences may be explained by the question wording for the measure in the ANES compared to the SSI survey. The ANES question wording conflates overall support for Social Security with a preference for spending on the program. That is, some individuals might favor Social Security, but nonetheless may not want to spend more on it. Nevertheless, there is some evidence that white racial solidarity is tied to support for Social Security, all else equal.

Table 7.1 *White Identity, White Consciousness, and Support for Increasing Social Security Spending/Expanding Medicare*

	Support for Social Security				Support for Medicare	
	ANES 2012 (Face-to-face)	SSI 2013	ANES 2016 (Web)		SSI 2013	
	(1)	(2)	(1)	(2)	(1)	(2)
White identity	0.064** (0.033)	0.105*** (0.027)	0.015 (0.025)		0.100*** (0.027)	
White consciousness			0.176*** (0.037)	0.044 (0.039)		0.075* (0.038)
Racial resentment	0.155* (0.06)	−0.011 (0.042)	−0.071 (0.046)		−0.091** (0.043)	−0.092* (0.047)
Observations	782	678	678	1,819	1,824	677	677
R-squared	0.130	0.122	0.130	0.128	0.130	0.115	0.104

Note: Table entries are OLS coefficients. Standard errors in parentheses. All variables in model coded to range from zero to one. ANES data are weighted. Model also controls for party identity, ideology, negative personal and national economic evaluations, employment status, education, age, gender, attitudes about the scope of government. The race of the interviewer is also controlled for in the 2012 face-to-face data. Estimates from full model available in Online Appendix 7A.
*** $p<0.01$, ** $p<0.05$, * $p<0.1$, two-tailed.
Source: 2012 ANES, 2013 SSI, 2016 ANES.

We can see in Table 7.1 that white identity and white consciousness are associated with support for Medicare as well. Whites with higher levels of white identity and white consciousness are more supportive of expanding Medicare than are those with lower levels of racial solidarity. To be clear, the size of the effects I have uncovered are not monumental, but they are notable; among respondents in the SSI studies, for instance, the effect of moving from the lowest level of consciousness to the highest produces close to a twenty-point change in opinion in a more favorable direction for Social Security. With respect to Medicare, the effect is slightly less than a one-point change in a more favorable direction. These relationships are, however, remarkable when we consider how subtly both Social Security and Medicare have been racialized; such results are indicative of the fact that both programs have been symbolically linked with whiteness.

It is also worth noting that racial resentment is inconsistently related to opinion on Social Security. It achieves marginal significance in the 2012 ANES, where more racially resentful whites are somewhat more supportive of Social Security. In the 2013 SSI Study, racial resentment is negatively associated with opinion on Medicare, potentially reflecting the fact that while the policy is associated with whiteness, we may also be observing the beginnings of the policy's association with out-group animus. In 2013, when the SSI survey was conducted, health care policy more generally was being linked to whites' racial prejudice due to its association with Obama and the passage of the Affordable Care Act (Henderson and Hillygus 2011; Tesler 2012b).

Opposition to Racialized Social Welfare Policies Associated with Racial and Ethnic Minorities

In the United States, welfare – a term that refers to state-run assistance programs for the poor like the Temporary Assistance for Needy Families (TANF) and food stamps – is deeply unpopular. For instance, when asked whether they would like to decrease, increase, or keep federal spending on welfare the same, 49 percent of white respondents in the 2016 ANES indicated they would like to decrease spending.[5] By comparison, only 6 percent of whites wanted to reduce spending on Social Security, and 61 percent preferred spending increased.

Welfare has been shunned since its inception. In his 1935 State of the Union Address, even Franklin Roosevelt spoke disparagingly about the first federal welfare programs his administration established to address the country's severe economic woes:

> The lessons of history, confirmed by the evidence immediately before me, show conclusively that continued dependence upon relief induces a spiritual and moral disintegration fundamentally destructive to the national fiber. To dole out relief in this way is to administer a narcotic, a subtle destroyer of the human spirit. It is inimical to the dictates of sound policy. It is in violation of the traditions of America. Work must be found for able-bodied but destitute workers. The Federal Government must and shall quit this business of relief.[6]

Today, opposition to welfare draws on similar themes, and is rooted in beliefs about individual responsibility that are now also tinged by attitudes toward racial groups (Desante 2013; Kinder and Mendelberg 2000). In his thorough investigation of Americans' opinion on welfare, political scientist Martin Gilens (1999) finds that a majority of the American public believes that most welfare recipients do not really need the support they receive. They also believe (incorrectly) that most welfare recipients are black.[7] Gilens goes on to explain how white opinion on welfare is strongly tied to whites' racial attitudes toward blacks, partly because of the way in which poverty in the United States was racialized by the media in the late 1960s when race riots drew attention to the black urban poor (Gilens 1996).[8] He shows that in only three years, the percentage of newsmagazine stories on poverty featuring images of blacks leapt from 27 percent in 1964 to 72 percent in 1967.

Today, whites' opinion on welfare and other similarly racialized policies, like Medicaid, and on general federal spending on racial and ethnic minorities, remains strongly tied to their racial attitudes, particularly those they hold with respect to blacks.[9] But one line of reasoning might propose that opinion on these matters is similarly linked to whites' in-group attachments as well. Indeed, as I already alluded to above, one interpretation of group hierarchy theories is that blacks' demands, ostensibly through programs of racial redistribution, threaten whites' sense of privilege. Consequently, we ought to observe a direct relationship between whites' in-group attitudes and opposition to race-targeted policies. Yet, the evidence for such an effect is scarce, and public opinion on these sorts of issues seems much more strongly related to whites' racial resentments (Kinder and Winter 2001; Sears and Savalei 2006).

One reason why scholars may have failed to observe a relationship between white racial solidarity and opinion on race-targeted policies is because they often had only proximate measures of white identity – a problem we can lay to rest with the analyses to come. Alternatively, the failure to find such a link may instead be because race-targeted policies have seldom been overtly framed as a threat to whites' racial dominance. Welfare, for instance, has rarely been described as a policy that will elevate the position of blacks at the expense of whites. Thus, if whites do not perceive such policies as a threat to their group, we would not expect to find that white racial solidarity is related to these issues.

Like several scholars before me, I look to see whether white racial solidarity matters on opinion in these domains, beginning with support for welfare and Medicaid, using the 2012 ANES, the 2013 SSI

Study, and the 2016 ANES Time Series. In these models, I also control for racial resentment and a number of other potentially related factors, including party identity, ideology, negative personal and national economic evaluations, employment status, education, age, gender, and attitudes about the scope of government.

The results, presented in Table 7.2, are remarkably consistent. With the exception of a marginally significant and negative relationship between white identity and opposition to Medicaid, white identity is unrelated to opinion on these policies. What is more, for the most part, the direction of the effect is negative, such that whites with higher levels of racial solidarity are actually less opposed to welfare and Medicaid. The coefficients are, however, relatively small and statistically indistinguishable from zero. In short, white identity is not an important ingredient of whites' attitudes toward these two social welfare programs.

In contrast, as expected, racial resentment is strongly, significantly, and consistently related to opinion on each of these policies. Among respondents in the 2016 ANES, for example, moving from the lowest to highest level of racial resentment is associated with an increase in opposition of welfare that accounts for over half of the opinion scale. Racial resentment is clearly a potent predictor of these attitudes, just as previous work has indicated.

Welfare and Medicaid are racially coded, but neither policy is intended to directly benefit one particular racial group over another. What if, however, we were to ask whites how they feel about government efforts to aid specific groups more directly? Perhaps in this case some whites might see government assistance in more zero-sum terms. To find out, I look to a question routinely posed on the ANES Time Series surveys. Respondents are asked to indicate, on a seven-point scale, whether they believe "government should help blacks" or if, instead, "blacks should help themselves." Does white racial solidarity predict responses to this question? Table 7.3 shows that it does not. Whites high on racial solidarity are not more (or less) opposed to providing aid to blacks than are whites lower on the racial identity scale. Note, however, that as we would expect, racial resentment is doing the heavy lifting. Whites higher on the resentment scale are far more opposed to government providing aid to blacks.

We can make a similar comparison by examining white attitudes toward increasing federal spending to not only blacks, but

Table 7.2 *White Identity, White Consciousness, and Opposition to Welfare and Medicaid*

| | Opposition to welfare | | | | | | Opposition to Medicaid | |
| | ANES 2012 (Face-to-face) | SSI 2013 | | ANES 2016 (Web) | | | SSI 2013 | |
	(1)	(2)		(1)	(2)		(1)	(2)
White identity	0.010			-0.029			-0.056*	
	(0.038)			(0.028)			(0.030)	
White consciousness		0.000			-0.035			-0.049
		(0.046)			(0.043)			(0.043)
Racial resentment	0.186***	0.334***		0.374***	0.379***		0.253***	0.258***
	(0.060)	(0.058)		(0.041)	(0.044)		(0.048)	(0.053)
Observations	788	676		1,817	1,822		676	676
R-squared	0.217	0.292		0.343	0.344		0.196	0.193

Note: Table entries are OLS coefficients. Standard errors in parentheses. All variables in model coded to range from zero to one. ANES data are weighted. Model also controls for party identity, ideology, negative personal and national economic evaluations, employment status, education, age, gender, attitudes about the scope of government. The race of the interviewer is also controlled for in the 2012 face-to-face data. Estimates from full model available in Online Appendix 7B.

***p<0.01, **p<0.05, *p<0.1, two-tailed.

Source: 2012 ANES, 2013 SSI, 2016 ANES.

Table 7.3 *White Identity, White Consciousness, and Opposition to Government Aid to Blacks*

	ANES 2012	ANES 2016
	(Face-to-face)	(Web)
White identity	0.011	
	(0.028)	
White consciousness		−0.143
		(0.725)
Racial resentment	0.471***	1.246*
	(0.043)	(0.710)
Observations	694	1,822
R-squared	0.388	0.035

Note: Table entries are OLS coefficients. Standard errors in parentheses. All variables in model coded to range from zero to one. Data are weighted. Model also controls for party identity, ideology, negative personal and national economic evaluations, employment status, education, age, gender, attitudes about the scope of government. The race of the interviewer is also controlled for in the 2012 face-to-face data. Estimates from full model available in Online Appendix 7C.
***$p<0.01$, **$p<0.05$, *$p<0.1$, two-tailed.
Source: 2012 ANES, 2016 ANES.

also to other groups. The 2013 SSI Study asked whites how they would feel about increasing federal spending for blacks, Hispanics, Asians, and whites. What happens when whites are asked about federal assistance to not only other racial and ethnic groups, but also to their group as well? Does white identity predict opposition to increasing federal spending for any of these groups? Figure 7.1 provides the answer. It plots the coefficients for white identity, white consciousness, and racial resentment for four separate models, each predicting opinion on federal spending for each of the four groups. As usual, I also control for party identity, ideology, negative personal and national economic evaluations, education, age, gender, and attitudes about the scope of government. Points to the right of zero on the x-axis indicate a positive association between the variable of interest and opinion on spending. Points to the left of zero indicate a negative relationship, or support for decreasing spending.

We can see that for each group, higher levels of white identity and consciousness are actually associated with *greater* support for spending. The effect among whites is especially powerful when it comes to support for increasing spending for their own group. Nevertheless, the point is clear; whites with higher levels of racial solidarity are in

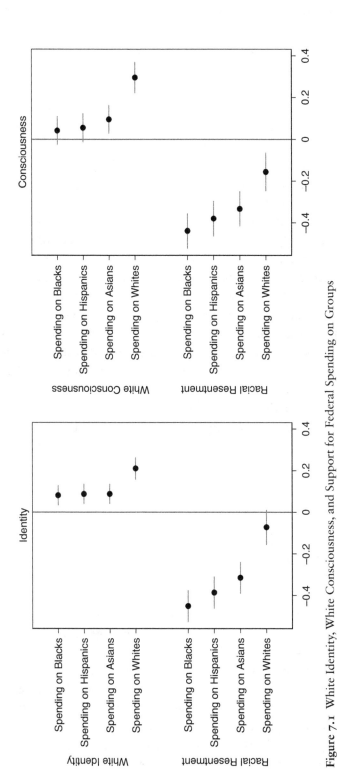

Figure 7.1 White Identity, White Consciousness, and Support for Federal Spending on Groups

The points represent the coefficients on white identity and racial resentment for each model. The lines represent the 95 percent confidence intervals. Model also controls for party identity, ideology, negative personal and national economic evaluations, education, age, gender, and attitudes about the scope of government. Estimates from full model appear in Online Appendix 7D.

Source: 2013 SSI.

favor of more spending, regardless of the group in question, not less. By comparison, racial resentment is associated with support for decreasing spending on all groups, including whites.

These results also provide some important insight as to who white identifiers are and what they support. We know from Chapter 3 that higher levels of white identity are slightly correlated with Republican Party identification. White identifiers are not, however, toeing the Republican Party line by largely rejecting government spending or supporting a reduction in government-funded social safety nets. Furthermore, while they might lean toward the Republican Party, they do not necessarily endorse the party's traditional policy positions. These white Americans like Social Security and Medicare. They would like to see the federal government do more to help their group, not less.

We also see that these whites are somewhat more favorable to spending on other racial groups. Part of the reason we might be observing this effect is because we are looking at the relationship between white identity and spending on other groups while controlling for racial resentment. Thus, the effect of white identity is what we observe above and beyond racial hostility. But the results are also indicative of the fact that many white identifiers do not completely begrudge government assistance toward other racial and ethnic groups; they simply would like more spending and services that they believe benefit whites.

Affirmative Action

Thus far, we have considered white identity's role in motivating support or opposition for certain social welfare policies. Unlike racial resentment, white identity does not predict opposition to racialized policies that are linked with providing social welfare benefits to racial and ethnic minorities. If anything, white racial solidarity is associated with greater support for spending on all racial and ethnic groups. But what about attitudes toward another highly racially charged and controversial policy: affirmative action? Opposition to affirmative action has long been associated with racial resentment (Jacobson 1985; Kinder and Sanders 1996). This relationship is unsurprising, as affirmative action is often framed as a prime example of "undeserving blacks" taking advantage of opportunities they did not earn. But a second frame argues that affirmative action is an example of "reverse discrimination" – a policy that benefits blacks at the expense of whites.[10] Perhaps, therefore, affirmative action is viewed as a threat to whites' status, and is associated not only with racial animus, but with white in-group identity as well.

To explore this possibility, I examine the effect of white identity and white consciousness on attitudes toward affirmative action in the workplace and with respect to college admissions. I employ evidence again from the 2012 and 2016 ANES Studies, the 2013 SSI Study, and the 2016 ANES Pilot. This latter study included a question-wording experiment in which respondents were randomly assigned to be asked their opinion on affirmative action when it comes to university admissions for either blacks, Hispanics or "minorities." These items allow us to also explore whether white identity matters more or less when the target of affirmative action policies changes.

The results of the models predicting opposition to affirmative action are presented in Table 7.4. In each case, higher values of the dependent variable correspond to greater opposition to affirmative action. What is immediately apparent from the results is that, generally, neither white identity nor white consciousness predict *greater opposition* to affirmative action, regardless of whether we are inquiring about affirmative action in the workplace or in university admissions. In only one instance, in the 2016 ANES, is white consciousness associated with more opposition to affirmative action, but the effect is modest. In a few cases, the coefficient on white racial solidarity is actually negative. That is, higher levels of white identity and consciousness are associated with more *support* for (or at least less opposition to) affirmative action, especially when the policy is just described as benefiting "minorities" generally.

While white identity or consciousness do not appear to drive opposition to affirmative action, regardless of the group benefiting from the policy, it is important to note from the results that in every instance, racial resentment was the most powerful predictor of opposition in the models. One way to interpret these results is that even though some critics of affirmative action attempt to frame it as a policy that harms whites, this frame is not always salient when whites consider their opinion on the policy. In other words, when asked to express their opinion on affirmative action, most whites are drawing on their attitudes toward racial out-groups, and toward blacks in particular. When most white Americans think of affirmative action, they

Table 7.4 *White Identity, White Consciousness, and Opposition to Affirmative Action*

	Opposition to affirmative action in universities			Opposition to affirmative action in the workplace			ANES 2016 Pilot					
							Opposition to affirmative action for:					
							Blacks		Hispanics		Minorities	
	ANES 2012 (Face-to-face)	ANES 2016 (Web)		ANES 2012 (Face-to-face)	ANES 2016 (Web)							
		(1)	(2)		(1)	(2)	(1)	(2)	(1)	(2)	(1)	(2)
White identity	-0.017 (0.033)	0.030 (0.020)		0.019 (0.031)	-0.046** (0.023)		-0.094** (0.045)		-0.089** (0.045)		-0.135*** (0.046)	
White consciousness			0.072** (0.034)			-0.055 (0.038)		-0.113 (0.073)		-0.083 (0.074)		-0.126** (0.056)
Racial resentment	0.373*** (0.053)	0.354*** (0.033)	0.339*** (0.034)	0.344*** (0.054)	0.488*** (0.035)	0.495*** (0.036)	0.565*** (0.095)	0.577*** (0.094)	0.498*** (0.092)	0.501*** (0.091)	0.572*** (0.060)	0.589*** (0.065)
Observations	783	1,818	1,823	789	1,807	1,811	386	386	386	386	407	407
R-squared	0.192	0.284	0.287	0.199	0.291	0.290	0.377	0.374	0.392	0.386	0.432	0.418

Note: Table entries are OLS coefficients. Standard errors in parentheses. All variables in model coded to range from zero to one. Data are weighted. Models also control for party identity, ideology, employment status, negative personal and national economic evaluations, education, age, gender, attitudes about the scope of government. The race of the interviewer is also controlled for in the 2012 face-to-face data. Estimates from full model available in Online Appendix 7E.

***p<0.01, ** p<0.05, * p<0.1, two-tailed.

Source: 2012 ANES (face-to-face), 2016 ANES Pilot, 2016 ANES (web).

either do not immediately feel that they or their group are potentially threatened, or their racial resentment outweighs any concerns they have about affirmative action potentially displacing them or a member of their racial group from a job or place at a university. Nevertheless, elite efforts to frame affirmative action as a policy that discriminates against whites may very well activate whites' racial identity.

Legacy Admissions

White racial solidarity is not, it seems, associated with opposition to affirmative action policies that benefit racial and ethnic minorities. Might it instead be associated with similar policies that benefit whites? More specifically, do whites who identify with their racial group favor college legacy admissions policies? These policies grant children of alumni preferences in college and university admissions processes. Legacy admissions policies are also deeply unpopular among the American public. According to the *Chronicle of Higher Education*, some public opinion polls have found that Americans oppose legacy admissions policies by 75 percent (compared to 23 percent who favor).[11]

Historically, legacy admissions were used primarily to give preference to white, male students. Today, while the pool of individuals to which such preferences are given has become much more diverse, historical racial divides in college attendance mean that more whites stand to gain from legacy policies than blacks or other racial and ethnic minorities. These policies also give applicants a real advantage. One study of the impact of legacy status at thirty highly selective colleges in the United States found that legacy applicants got at least a 23.3 percentage point increase in their probability of admission (Hurwitz 2011). The bump was even greater for applicants with parents who attended the college as undergraduates. These potential students received a boost of 45.1 percentage points. Because these policies are so notorious for benefiting white students, they are sometimes referred to as "affirmative action for whites."[12]

Accordingly, I consider the possibility that whites high on racial identity are more supportive of legacy policies. To find out, I employ a new data source. In 2014, I conducted with the firm SSI another study, which included a question allowing me to assess opinion on legacy admissions policies.[13] Respondents were asked the following: "When

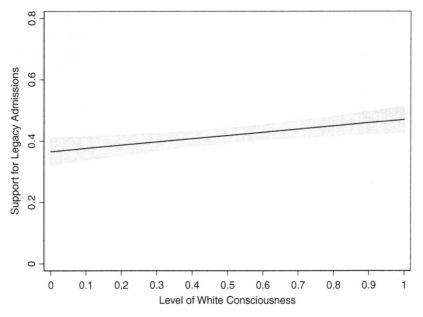

Figure 7.2 White Consciousness and Support for Legacy Admissions

The line represents the predicted level of support for legacy admissions at each level of white consciousness. The shaded area represents the 95 percent confidence intervals. Predicted values are generated by holding gender constant at female and all other variables in the model at their mean. Model also controls for party identity, ideology, employment status, education, age, gender, and racial resentment. Estimates from full model appear in Online Appendix 7F.

Source: 2014 SSI.

admitting students, Colleges and Universities sometimes have 'legacy policies,' which allow these schools to grant admission preferences to individuals whose parents or grandparents attended the school. Do you favor or oppose such policies?" Response options ranged from "Strongly favor" to "Strongly oppose" on a seven-point scale. I estimate attitudes toward legacy policies as a function of white consciousness, party identity, ideology, employment status, education, age, gender, and racial resentment.

The results, presented in Figure 7.2, show that even after accounting for these other factors, white consciousness is clearly associated with support for legacy admissions policies. The coefficient on white consciousness is large, positive, and significant. Moving from the lowest level of white identity to the highest changes the predicted value of supporting or opposing legacy admissions from 0.36 to 0.47

on the zero to one scale. Taken together, these results lend further support for the argument that white racial solidarity influences opinion on policies that benefit whites as a group, but not uniformly on those that help racial and ethnic minorities. For these latter issues, white identity is either unrelated or marginally linked to greater support for such policies.

White Racial Solidarity and Globalization

Outsourcing and Imports

On Monday, November 7, 2016, the day before the presidential election, Donald Trump strolled on stage at a rally in Raleigh, NC.[14] Looking out into a sea of white faces, he told the crowd, "We are going to bring back jobs that have been stolen from you. We're going to bring back wealth taken from this country." Trump had been on the campaign trail for 511 days, and at this point, his message was familiar. It was a message that was also remarkably consistent. When Trump officially announced his candidacy in June of 2015, he said the following:

> And our real unemployment is anywhere from 18 to 20 percent.
> Don't believe the 5.6. Don't believe it. That's right. A lot of
> people up there can't get jobs. They can't get jobs, because there
> are no jobs, because China has our jobs and Mexico has our jobs.
> They all have jobs.

The idea that many Americans were being left behind as jobs moved overseas might certainly stoke a sense of economic anxiety. But Trump was on to something else. In the same speech, he also said,

> Our country is in serious trouble. We don't have victories
> anymore. We used to have victories, but we don't have them.
> When was the last time anybody saw us beating, let's say China
> in a trade deal? They kill us. I beat China all the time. All the
> time. When did we beat Japan at anything? They send their cars
> over by the millions, and what do we do? When was the last time
> you saw a Chevrolet in Tokyo? It doesn't exist folks. They beat
> us all the time. When do we beat Mexico at the border? They're
> laughing at us, at our stupidity. And now they are beating us

economically. They are not our friend, believe me. But they're
killing us economically.

This argument is not merely about individual-level economic
turmoil. It is very much one about the status and standing of the United
States in the world. In this sense, Trump was stoking an additional type
of status threat. If white Americans view themselves as prototypical of
the nation, then they might also see threats to the standing of the nation
as threats to their own standing as a racial group.[15] Thus, whites might
not only perceive status threat via their position within the nation's
racial hierarchy, they may also view challenges to Americans within a
global hierarchy as a threat to their racial group's status.

If you recall from Chapter 3, there is little indication that white
identifiers are especially vulnerable to the economic consequences of
globalization. Therefore, we might not expect to find much support
for the notion that whites' opinions on issues related to globalization,
like their attitudes toward trade or outsourcing, are actually related to
economic self-interest. Indeed, political scientists Mansfield and Mutz
(2009) find that opinion on trade is motivated less by material self-
interest and more by beliefs about how the national economy is doing.
Yet, the threat posed by globalization to American manufacturing, and
to the status of whites in the United States likely to be left behind by
such changes – especially those without a college degree – has become a
popular narrative. Its appeal, however, may lie less in economic anxiety
and may be more deeply rooted in whites' concerns about the standing
of their racial group.

Trump certainly capitalized on these fears, promising to establish tariffs to discourage companies from off-shoring jobs and production, and to abandon the Trans-Pacific Partnership (TPP). He also turned
his attention to the North American Free Trade Agreement (NAFTA).
NAFTA is an agreement signed by the United States, Canada, and
Mexico that reduces barriers to trade between the three countries. It
was crafted in part through the efforts of George H.W. Bush and went
into effect in 1994 after being signed into law by President Bill Clinton.
The bill drew controversy before being passed, especially from presidential candidates Ross Perot, Patrick Buchanan, Jesse Jackson, and
Ralph Nader. Despite their concerns, however, studies have suggested
that on average, US citizens have largely benefited from the agreement
(Burfisher, Robinson, and Thierfelder 2001; Caliendo and Parro 2015).

Nevertheless, NAFTA has been blamed for significant job loss by several groups, including the AFL-CIO, the largest US labor union.[16] On their website, the AFL-CIO cites a study by the Economic Policy Institute, which claims that, to date, NAFTA has cost the United States almost 700,000 jobs, many to Mexico.[17]

During the presidential campaign, Trump claimed that, upon winning office, he would immediately call for the renegotiation of NAFTA. If Canada and Mexico were to disagree with his terms, Trump declared that America would then withdraw from the agreement.[18] This attack on NAFTA, and the idea that it is to blame for the decline in available manufacturing jobs, fits nicely into the narrative of the alienated white, working-class Americans who have been left behind by globalization and free trade. There might be something to this claim, but I suspect that another force is at play here.

Since it was introduced, NAFTA has served as a scapegoat for marginalized Americans from both the left and the right who feel like they are alienated by a rapidly changing and diversifying America. Writing for the *Fort Worth Star-Telegram* in 1993, one of the paper's columnists made a similar point. She noted that the political elites most outspoken against NAFTA – Pat Buchanan, Ross Perot, the AFL-CIO leaders, Ralph Nader, and others – are strange bedfellows.[19] What unites them is that they represent the disaffected in American society, a subset of marginalized Americans who might feel left behind, perhaps economically, but even more so culturally, by a globalizing world. And not just a world in which the barriers between trade and people and cultures are weakened, but one which politicians claim will threaten the dominant culture and the very sovereignty of the United States – and by extension, the power and status of white Americans. In this way, Trump's focus on trade and outsourcing are entirely consistent with the broader fears and motivations of white identifiers in the United States.

Is this a message that therefore appeals to whites who possess a strong level of racial identity? Might they view outsourcing and other trade issues not through the lens of self-interest, but instead through that of group-interests? To see, we can turn to the 2012 and 2016 ANES Time Series studies, which asked several relevant questions. First, respondents on the 2012 ANES were asked the extent to which they thought the federal government should encourage or discourage companies from outsourcing. I model opposition to outsourcing as a function of white identity, party identity, ideology, employment status,

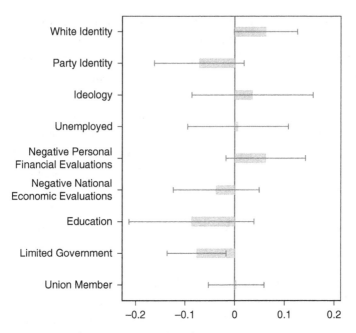

Figure 7.3 White Consciousness and Opposition to Outsourcing

Bars represent the coefficient for each variable in the OLS model. The lines represent the 95 percent confidence intervals. Model also controls for gender and race of interviewer. Estimates from full model appear in Online Appendix 7G.

Source: 2012 ANES (face-to-face).

negative personal and national economic evaluations, education, gender, attitudes about the scope of government, and whether anyone in the respondent's household is a union member. The results are presented in Figure 7.3, which plots the magnitude of each variable of interest in the model. From the figure, we can see that the two factors which emerge as significant are white identity and attitudes about the scope of government. Not surprisingly, individuals who prefer a more limited role for government are also less supportive of government intervention in outsourcing. Somewhat more interestingly, there appears to be no significant relationship between opinion on outsourcing and union membership, employment status, or personal economic evaluations – findings consistent with previous work which argues that self-interest plays only a marginal role in public opinion. Most relevant for the purposes here, however, we also see that whites who feel more strongly attached to their in-group are significantly more opposed to outsourcing.

Do whites bring similar attitudes to bear on their opinion about trade? The 2016 ANES Time Series asked respondents whether they think increasing trade with other countries is good or bad for the United States. They were also asked about the extent to which they favored or opposed the United States making free trade agreements with other countries. We can see from Figure 7.4 that racial solidarity predicts opinion on trade as well.[20] Even after accounting for a host of relevant factors, whites with higher levels of racial consciousness are more opposed to increasing trade with other countries and they are less supportive of free trade policies.[21]

Support for Isolationism

We should also ask how far this propensity to turn inward and protect the nation goes. Do whites high on identity, as the world becomes more globalized, prefer to withdraw from our interactions with other nations? If many whites are eager to protect their in-group, might they be less inclined to involve the nation in external affairs? In short, is white identity linked to greater support for isolationism? The 2016 ANES allows us to investigate this claim with a question that asked respondents whether they agree or disagree with this statement: "This country would be better off if we just stayed home and did not concern ourselves with problems in other parts of the world."

Do whites who adopt a group identity endorse this position? They do. Figure 7.5 presents the predicted probability of agreeing with the statement across levels of white identity and white consciousness. Even after controlling for additional factors, both white identity and white consciousness are strongly associated with support for the United States staying out of matters of the world. Moving from the lowest to the highest level of consciousness, for example, increases the probability of agreeing with the statement from 20 percent to over 40 percent.

Conclusion

Despite strong support for the notion among political scientists that public opinion is group-centric, whites' in-group attitudes have largely been dismissed as an important component of whites' political

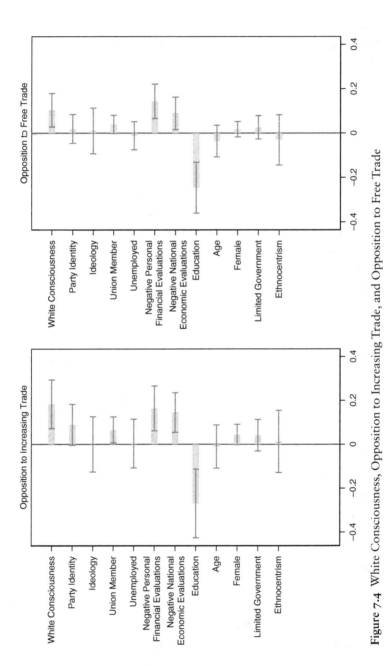

Figure 7.4 White Consciousness, Opposition to Increasing Trade, and Opposition to Free Trade

Bars represent the coefficient for each variable in the OLS model. The lines represent the 95 percent confidence intervals. Estimates from full model appear in Online Appendix 7H.

Source: 2016 ANES (Web).

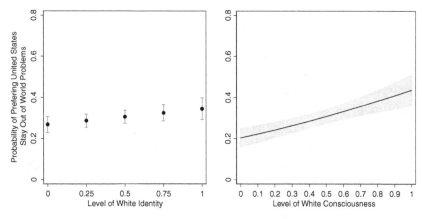

Figure 7.5 White Identity, White Consciousness, and Support for Isolationism

Points and solid line represent the predicted probability of preferring the United States stay out of world problems at each level of white identity or white consciousness. Bars and shaded region represent the 95 percent confidence intervals. Predicted probabilities are calculated by holding gender constant at female and all other variables in the model at their mean. Model also controls for party identification, ideology, employment status, personal and national economic evaluations, education, age, gender, and attitudes toward scope of government. Estimates from full model appear in Online Appendix 7I.

Source: 2016 ANES (Web).

preferences. In this chapter, I provide compelling evidence that part of the reason why white racial solidarity may have been overlooked as an important force in American politics is because social scientists were looking for its effects in the wrong place. White racial solidarity does factor into whites' political thinking, primarily with respect to policies that whites see as benefiting or harming their in-group. Prior work, however, often expected white identity to be implicated in opinion on policies associated with benefiting or harming racial and ethnic minorities. Instead, what we have seen here is that either through schematic links or a growing knowledge of who benefits from the program, white identifiers are much more in favor of policies, such as Social Security, that are framed as benefiting their group. We see a similar trend with respect to Medicare and to support for legacy college admissions policies.

These results also make an important point about the discriminant predictive power of white identity compared to racial animus. As I discussed in Chapter 2, the correlation between white identity or consciousness and resentment was not especially high, and certainly not high enough to conclude that these two constructs are one and the same. Now we have even greater evidence indicating that white identity and white consciousness are quite distinct from racial animus; their predictive power lies primarily in the domain of policies that protect whites and their status, rather than with respect to policies that benefit out-group members. For instance, neither white identity nor white consciousness are implicated in opinion on welfare, Medicaid, or federal government assistance for blacks. Furthermore, white racial solidarity is not tied to opposition to affirmative action policies in college admissions or in the workplace.

Compared to whites low on racial identity, white identifiers are also not more opposed to the federal government aiding blacks, nor do they oppose an increase in federal spending to help blacks, Hispanics, or Asians. They are, however, much more in favor of an increase in federal spending for themselves. In other words, white identifiers are not overtly interested in taking resources away from out-group members, but they do display, as expected, a marked degree of in-group favoritism. Notably, these are not individuals who agree with the traditional position of the Republican Party that federal intervention should be scarce and spending should be limited. If anything, these whites would like the federal government to do more for their group, and they would like the entitlement programs they believe benefit their group to be well-funded.

We also see that white identity is linked to policies associated with globalization, suggesting that white Americans are not merely concerned about their loss of status domestically. The threat of America's status in the world at large is also one about which white Americans who identify with their racial group are especially concerned. Consequently, these whites support policies framed as protecting the nation from the outside world; they are more opposed to outsourcing and increasing trade with other countries. They are also less supportive of free trade policies. What is more, these same whites adopt a more isolationist view about the role of the United States in the world. They prefer the United States stay out of the affairs of other nations.

Taken together, these results confirm that whites with higher levels of racial solidarity favor policies that help to maintain their group's power and privilege, both domestically and abroad. White identity is not, however, synonymous with racial animus. Sometimes, as in the case of immigration opinion, its effects are similar to what we observe among whites who dislike out-group members. In this chapter, however, we see that white identity is more often associated with policies associated with the in-group. Of course, this does not mean that the consequences of white identity are innocuous when it comes to racial equality in the United States. By promoting policies that protect their group, whites are of course seeking to maintain the power and privileges of their group, ultimately preserving a system of inequality. What we can conclude, however, is that in-group attitudes among whites are an important force in American politics, and one that is distinct from racial prejudice, with sometimes different consequences for public opinion.

8 A BLACK MAN IN THE WHITE HOUSE

In 2008, America made history when it elected the nation's first African American president. Barack Obama won the presidency over 138 years after the ratification of the Fifteenth Amendment to the US Constitution, which prohibited government from denying citizens the right to vote based on race, color, or previous condition of servitude.[1] He was sworn into office forty-five years, five months, and fourteen days after President Lyndon Johnson signed into law the Voting Rights Act, which aimed to remove legal barriers that state and local government had put in place to prevent blacks from exercising the right to vote established by the Fifteenth Amendment.[2] Obama's election was a clear indication of the unsteady progress the nation has made in incorporating racial and ethnic minorities into the political system. It was also highly symbolic of a great shift in the nation's political image; Obama followed a succession of forty-three white presidents, marking a break in the total dominance of whiteness at the level of the nation's highest elected office.

In previous chapters, I showed that white racial solidarity is associated with a preference for policies that benefit whites and that protect their group's status. In this chapter, I ask whether white identity is also brought to bear on evaluations of political elites. I begin by examining the relationship between white identity and attitudes toward Obama – a political candidate both deeply symbolic of whites' loss of political power, and one who was reelected by an increasingly diverse electorate. I also evaluate whether whites with higher levels of racial solidarity are less favorable toward Obama specifically, or if they feel more generally ambivalent about non-white candidates, such as a hypothetical Latino president. Then, I explore the relationship between white identity and evaluations of the Tea Party – a conservative political movement comprised largely of white Americans that arose soon after Obama's election. From there, I examine the relationship between white identity and evaluations of Donald Trump, a presidential candidate who not only appealed to whites' racial animosities but also, I argue, to whites' desire to maintain their group's power and status. I also demonstrate that Trump was not alone in his ability to capitalize on these sentiments; long before he appeared on the national stage, other presidential candidates took advantage of whites' interests in protecting their group.

Finally, I examine whether group consciousness is a politically motivating force. The notion that white racial solidarity influences whites' political preferences is important, but less powerful if this identity pulls whites out of the political arena. In keeping with prior work on group consciousness among subordinated groups, like people of color and women, however, I presume that white identity is actually related to greater levels of political participation. I put this claim to the test at the end of the chapter.

Whiteness and the Nation's Highest Office

Barack Obama's victory was initially met with public celebration and optimism about race relations in the United States. The day after the election, the headline on the front page of the *New York Times* read, "Obama," on its own line, in bold letters larger than the paper's masthead. Below, a subtitle to the cover story stated, "Racial barrier falls in decisive victory."[3] Similarly, the cover of the *Washington Post* claimed, "Obama Makes History," and just below stated, "U.S. decisively elects first black president."[4] Even conservative outlet Fox News made note of the momentous occasion with positive and conciliatory words. During the cable news channel's election coverage, Republican political consultant Karl Rove said this of Obama's win: "an African American candidate who was aspirational and inspirational, who appealed to the better angels of our nature, is very powerful." Later that night, in his concession speech, Republican candidate John McCain described Obama's victory as a sign that "America today is a world away from the cruel and prideful bigotry" that it once embraced.[5]

The case for such optimism, however, was short-lived. It was not long before political scientists began chipping away at the presumption that Obama's election was any indication that racial equality in the United States had been realized. Research uncovered little evidence that Obama's victory was accompanied by a marked shift in whites' racial attitudes in a more liberal, tolerant direction. Whites and blacks appeared to be just as divided in their opinions on issues related to race (Hutchings 2009). Studies rolled in revealing the serious impact that racial prejudice had in depressing white votes for Obama in 2008 (Kinder and Dale-Riddle 2012; Lewis-Beck, Tien, and Nadeau 2010; Parker, Sawyer, and Towler 2009; Piston 2010; Tesler and Sears 2010). And work began to ask whether Obama's election had actually awakened more insidious forms of racial prejudice among whites (Tesler 2012a).

In 2012, support for Obama among whites became noticeably more tepid. He was reelected with only 39 percent of the white vote, compared to the 43 percent he received in 2008.[6] In prior presidential elections, modern Democratic presidential candidates have received even fewer votes from whites than Obama did in 2012, although none who did so were victorious. So how did Obama maintain his place in office? He was reelected with strong support from racial and ethnic minorities. In 2012, Obama won 93 percent of the black vote, 71 percent of the Hispanic vote, and 73 percent of the Asian vote. Furthermore, Obama captured the majority of votes among people of color at a time when the share of white voters in the electorate was at a historical low. In 2012, the percentage of white voters, relative to the rest of the electorate, bottomed out at 73.7 percent, compared to 76.3 percent in 2008 and to 81.9 percent a decade earlier in 1998.[7] Whites continue to comprise a solid majority of those voting in US presidential elections, but their share of the total electorate is on a steady decline as more racial and ethnic minorities participate in the political process.

In the aftermath of Obama's reelection, the tone of some news outlets' election coverage was decidedly different from what it had been in 2008. Many conservative news sources once again highlighted the importance of race in the election, but not in celebration of the nation's progress toward racial equality. Instead, many pundits and journalists focused on the notion that Obama and his electoral base posed a threat to white Americans. For instance, conservative talk show host Rush

Limbaugh, complaining to his listeners the day after the election, said the following:

> I went to bed last night thinking we're outnumbered. I went to bed last night thinking all this discussion we'd had about this election being the election that will tell us whether or not we've lost the country. I went to bed last night thinking we've lost the country. I don't know how else you look at this.[8]

Presumably, when Limbaugh said "we," he was referring to conservative white voters. It was not the first time Limbaugh had lamented what he saw as the loss of white Americans' power and status. In 2009, on his radio show, he went on at length:

> How do you get promoted in a Barack Obama administration? By hating white people, or even saying you do, or that they're not good, or whatever. Make white people the new oppressed minority and they are going along with it, because they're shutting up. They're moving to the back of the bus. They're saying I can't use that drinking fountain, ok. I can't use that restroom, ok. That's the modern day Republican Party, the equivalent of the Old South, the new oppressed minority.[9]

Limbaugh was not alone in expressing these concerns. On the evening of the 2012 election, as the vote counts rolling in signaled an Obama victory, Fox News host Bill O'Reilly offered an explanation for the outcome: "The white establishment is now the minority. The demographics are changing. It's not traditional America anymore."[10] A few days later, left-leaning *New York Times* columnist Maureen Dowd penned a piece in which she suggested that the "white male patriarchy" was in a "delusional death spiral."[11]

This narrative continued well after Obama left office and Donald Trump became president. Bill O'Reilly made similar remarks on his television show in March of 2018:

> For a long time, skin color wasn't really much of an issue, in the '80s and '90s we didn't hear a lot. Yeah, you always had your Farrakhans and your Sharptons. We always had those people but – Jackson – they were race hustlers, but it was a money thing, an industry thing. But now, whiteness has become the

issue. Whiteness. All right. So if you're a white American you are a part of a cabal that either consciously or unconsciously keeps minorities down. Therefore, that has to end and whiteness has to be put aside. That's what the border is all about. The open-border people, and believe me this is behind the movement in California and in the Democratic precincts. Let everybody in. Everybody in. All right. That would diminish whiteness because minorities then would take over, as they have in many parts of California. That's what that is all about. Getting whiteness out of power.[12]

It is apparent from these statements that the media were attuned to the idea that a segment of white Americans felt threatened by the election of Obama, by the composition of the electorate that helped keep him in office, by immigration, and by the nation's racial and ethnic diversity. What is more, many conservative pundits were undoubtedly reiterating this perspective to their viewers. But were white Americans viewing the political world through this lens? Did such beliefs influence the way they thought about Barack Obama in 2012 or Donald Trump in 2016?

I test the proposition that white Americans perceived Obama's election as threatening to their group and its relative status. As I posited in Chapter 2, white identity should predict opposition to political candidates that white identifiers view as a threat to their group's dominance. Undoubtedly, Barack Obama serves as the most symbolic displacement of whites' political power by way of his blackness. Theoretically, however, whites high on racial identity should be opposed, in the abstract, to the election of *any* non-white candidate to the nation's highest office, regardless of whether that candidate is black or another non-white race. We should also find, therefore, that whites oppose the possibility of a Latino candidate winning the presidency.

I also argued that white racial identity and consciousness ought to be tied not only to opposition toward candidates they view as threatening, but also to support for political candidates or movements whites see as maintaining or restoring their political power. Shortly after Obama took office, a conservative movement known as the Tea Party gained traction. Initially, the movement branded itself loosely around opposition to government bailouts, lower taxes, and reduced government spending, but eventually it became associated with racism, and deemed part of the backlash to the election of Obama (Parker and Barreto 2013). Given this characterization, we might expect that Tea Party fans are also whites with higher levels of racial solidarity, especially if the movement's goals were in fact thinly veiled efforts to restore whites' political power.

Finally, as Obama's term neared its end and the 2016 election approached, Donald Trump took the stage as a candidate who signaled to whites an intention to restore whites' power and privileges. Unlike any other Republican frontrunner, I suggest that Trump took positions that uniquely and powerfully appealed to white identifiers. His promise to promote "white" social welfare policies, his strong position on immigration, and even his campaign slogan all seemed like well-crafted efforts to target whites who desired to protect their racial group's collective interests.

Donald Trump is not the only presidential candidate who has exploited the concerns whites might have regarding their group's status in a racially and ethnically changing nation. Other candidates have made similar appeals, and in doing so, they have drawn favor from whites with higher levels of racial solidarity. Most recently, Pat Buchanan ran for president in 1992 on a platform that looked very similar to Donald Trump's. He too chose immigration as a central issue and campaigned for more restrictive immigration policies while appealing to whites' fear over a changing nation.

Long before Buchanan made his presidential bid, Alabama Governor George Wallace, Jr. repeatedly campaigned for president, running in 1964, 1968, 1972, and 1976. Wallace was known for his notorious stance on racial integration, refusing orders from President John F. Kennedy to enforce the racial integration of the University of Alabama. For this reason, Wallace has certainly gone down in history as a face of racial prejudice. Yet, as I will describe in more detail, Wallace's political appeals did not exclusively focus on hostility toward blacks; they were often framed around protecting and preserving whites' power.

In 1968 and 1972, Richard Nixon followed in Wallace's footsteps, making similar appeals to southern whites who were resentful of integration. The story of Nixon's "Southern Strategy" – or his effort to win over southern white Democrats by exploiting their racial grievances – is undoubtedly one rooted in out-group animus. Nixon was not only appealing to whites' racial hostilities, however, but also arguably to concerns about their group, its power, and its status in the wake of the Civil Rights. If so, we should find that white in-group attitudes are also implicated in support for Wallace and Nixon.

The Threat of the Nation's First Black President

I turn first to considering the relationship between white identity and attitudes toward Barack Obama in 2012. The notion that white identity might be a powerful predictor of vote choice in any election is a provocative one. Choosing a presidential candidate is one of the most visible and most common forms of political participation. It is also a domain where predispositions like party identification and ideology play a powerful and durable role. In addition, we also know that racial prejudice, and especially racial resentment, was powerfully linked to attitudes toward Obama (Kam and Kinder 2012; Kinder and Dale-Riddle 2012; Lewis-Beck, Tien, and Nadeau 2010; Piston 2010; Tesler and Sears 2010). These factors were so obviously potent in driving vote choice that we might think it highly unlikely that any other variable could be meaningfully implicated in whites' voting decisions. Adding yet another account to the fray might reasonably seem like a fool's errand.

Yet the profound symbolic threat Obama may have presented to whites' political power is one that we ought to take seriously. Indeed, I posit that when it comes to attitudes toward Obama, many whites were not exclusively driven by racial animus; some were also independently motivated by a desire to protect their in-group and its status. If I am right, then we should see that white identity is significantly tied to vote choice in 2012, such that white identifiers were much less likely to vote for Obama and much more likely to prefer his Republican opponent, Mitt Romney.[13]

To test this claim, I turn to the 2012 ANES, which included the standard racial importance measure of white racial identity. After the election, ANES survey respondents were asked if they voted and, if so, whether they voted for Romney, Obama, or another candidate. To explore whether white identity was associated with vote choice in this election, I estimate voting for Romney or Obama as a function of levels of white identity.[14] To this model I also add a host of controls, stacking the deck against white identity. First, I account for partisan identification and political ideology. I also include employment status, evaluations of personal economic circumstances, and assessments of national economic conditions. To this list I then add level of education, as well as age and gender. I also control for the possibility that many whites voted against Obama because they worried that he might expand government too much. Accordingly, I also control for a preference for a more limited government. Finally, previous scholarship has made it abundantly apparent that racial animus, especially in the form of racial resentment, was strongly associated with opposition to Obama (e.g., Kinder and Dale-Riddle 2012; Tesler and Sears 2010). I therefore include the standard four-item measure of resentment in the model of vote choice.[15]

The results of the model predicting vote choice are presented in Figure 8.1, and they tell an important story. Not surprisingly, party identity was the most powerful factor in shaping vote choice, with Republicans far more likely to vote for Romney and Democrats far more likely to vote for Obama. Political ideology also played an independent role, with self-identified conservatives more supportive of Romney and liberals more likely to vote for Obama. The condition of the national economy also mattered; voters who rated the national economy as worse off than the previous year were also less likely to vote for Obama. Attitudes about the role of government were implicated as well. Voters who reported preferring a more limited government were less likely to vote for Obama. What is more, as expected, racial resentment was strongly and significantly associated with vote choice, such that more racially conservative whites were less likely to vote for Obama.[16] And finally, we see that neither levels of education, age, nor gender were significantly associated with white voters' preferences, all else equal.

Figure 8.1 also tells us something new about the attitudes voters brought to bear in 2012. Even after controlling for the usual suspects in a model of vote choice, white racial identity also mattered ($p < 0.05$). Whites with higher levels of racial identity were much more likely to vote for Romney over Obama. Figure 8.2 illustrates the magnitude of this effect. Moving from the lowest levels of racial identity to the highest, the predicted probability of voting for Obama declines dramatically, from 0.52 among the low identifiers to 0.25 among the

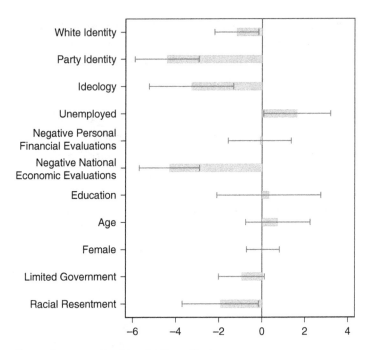

Figure 8.1 2012 Presidential Vote Choice

The bars represent the coefficient for each variable in the model. The lines represent the 95 percent confidence intervals. Model also controls for race of interviewer. Estimation results appear in Online Appendix 8A.

Source: 2012 ANES (face-to-face).

highest identifiers on a scale ranging from zero to one. In other words, whites who reported that their racial identity is extremely important were 50 percent more likely to vote for Romney rather than Obama compared to whites low on identity.

In short, the effect of white racial identity on vote choice in 2012 is powerful and robust, even after accounting for a number of other factors that might explain whites' voting behavior. All else equal, whites with higher levels of racial identity were far less likely to vote for Obama. This relationship represents an important revision to our understanding of electoral behavior. While political scientists have been attentive to the power of racial animus, especially in the Obama era, the results here demonstrate that out-group attitudes are not the only factor, or even necessarily the primary factor, motivating voters. Many whites in 2012 also seem especially concerned with protecting their racial group's status.

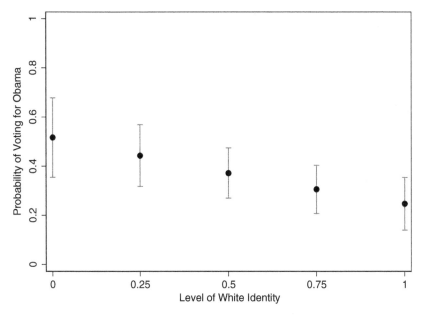

Figure 8.2 The Probability of Voting for Barack Obama in 2012

Points represent the predicted probability of voting for Obama over Romney at each level of white identity. The capped lines represent the 95 percent confidence intervals. Predicted probabilities are calculated by holding gender constant at female and all other variables in the model at their mean. Model also controls for party identification, ideology, negative personal and national economic evaluations, employment status, education, age, gender, attitudes about size of government, and racial resentment. Estimates from full model appear in Online Appendix 8A.

Source: 2012 ANES (face-to-face).

Obama as a Threat to Group Interests

The symbolism of Obama's election as a displacement of whites' political dominance is hard to dismiss. But many whites might also have opposed Obama not merely because he represents their group's political displacement, but also because they worried that Obama might, in practice, favor his own racial group at the expense of whites. In other words, whites high on white identity might see Obama as a real threat to their group's interests and may doubt that Obama represents all groups equally. I investigate this possibility, using the 2012 ANES, which asked respondents to indicate whether they believe Obama favors blacks over whites or whites over blacks. I estimate responses to this question using the same logit model as specified above for vote choice, but this time

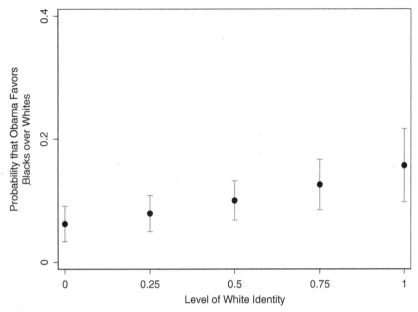

Figure 8.3 The Predicted Probability that Obama Favors Blacks over Whites

Points represent the predicted probability of believing Obama favors whites over blacks at each level of white identity. The capped lines represent the 95 percent confidence intervals. Predicted probabilities are calculated by holding gender constant at female and all other variables in the model at their means. Model also controls for party identification, ideology, negative personal and national economic evaluations, employment status, education, age, gender, attitudes about size of government, and racial resentment. Estimates from full model appear in Online Appendix 8B.

Source: 2012 ANES (face-to-face).

with the dependent variable coded at zero if respondents indicated that Obama favors whites over blacks and one for those that think Obama favors blacks over whites.

Figure 8.3 plots the probability of believing Obama favors blacks over whites at each level of white identity. It is first worth noting that most whites in the United States were not overwhelmingly concerned that Obama would favor blacks over their own group. We can see from Figure 8.3 that regardless of levels of white identity, the probability of endorsing this position is not especially large. Nevertheless, the effect of white identity is statistically significant and noteworthy. For whites low on racial identity, the predicted probability of believing Obama favors blacks over whites is 0.06 on the zero to one scale. Among whites highest on identity, the probability leaps to 0.16. Thus, there is some evidence that part of what may be motivating white identifiers in their negative evaluations of Obama is the belief that Obama will favor blacks, possibly at the expense of whites.

Opposition to a Latino Presidential Candidate

As the first non-white US president, the symbolism of Obama's election was a profound loss to whites' status. If many whites are worried about their group's position, it is likely that any non-white candidate would have been – and will likely continue to be – met with resistance on the part of white identifiers. Whites with higher levels of racial solidarity likely prefer white political representatives. Consistent with this argument, Schildkraut (2015) finds that whites who more strongly identify with their in-group prefer candidates who descriptively represent their group. Additionally, Petrow, Transue, and Vercellotti (2018) find that high white identifiers are less supportive of black candidates. The implication of this argument is especially important when we consider the role of white identity moving forward. As the country becomes increasingly diverse, blacks, Latinos, and Asian Americans will continue to seek political incorporation, and they may very well receive pushback from whites who see the political success of non-whites as a threat to the status quo (McConnaughy et al. 2010).

The 2016 ANES Pilot allows us to test this claim more directly. Do whites who possess either greater levels of identity or consciousness feel more negatively about the prospect of non-white political candidates? For instance, how might these whites respond to a Latino presidential candidate? Respondents on the ANES Pilot were explicitly asked the extent to which they would be pleased (or not) with the idea of a Latino person being president of the United States. I estimate the relationship between responses to this item and levels of white identity, while also controlling for attitudes toward Hispanics, demographic traits, party identity, ideology, employment status, and national economic evaluations.[17] Figure 8.4 provides the predicted response to this question across levels of white identity and white consciousness, both of which are significantly associated with lower levels of displeasure over a Latino president. Moving from the lowest level of white identity or white consciousness to the highest produces an approximately

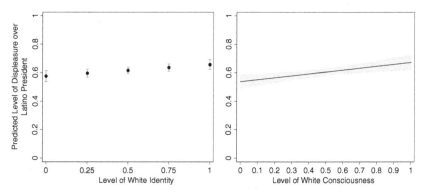

Figure 8.4 White Racial Solidarity and Displeasure over a Latino President

Points and solid line represent the predicted level of displeasure about a Latino president at each level of white identity or white consciousness. The capped lines and shaded region represent the 95 percent confidence intervals. Predicted probabilities are calculated by holding gender constant at female and all other variables in the model at their means. Model also controls for party identification, ideology, negative personal and national economic evaluations, employment status, education, age, gender, and affect toward Hispanics. Estimates from full model appear in Online Appendix 8C.

Source: 2016 ANES Pilot Study.

ten-point change in dismay over a Latino president on the zero to one scale.

The Tea Party Movement as a Backlash to Obama

When Obama took office, the country was reeling from the economic turmoil caused by the financial crisis of 2007 to 2008. Many Americans were dismayed by the massive bailouts banks and auto companies had received as part of the recovery efforts, and they were even more resistant to the costly economic stimulus package Obama and Democrats in Congress passed in 2009.[18] In February of 2009, a CNBC television reporter gave these Americans, most of whom identified with the Republican Party, a rallying cry for their consternation. Referencing the historic Boston Tea Party, he invited individuals who wanted to protest the government bailout to a Chicago Tea Party, and the Tea Party movement was born.[19]

The movement attracted disaffected members of the Republican Party who largely claimed to be focused on economic issues and who supported a more limited government, lower taxes, and a reduction in government spending. It is now apparent, however, that Tea Party supporters had adopted political beliefs that went beyond fiscal conservatism and anti-big government. They helped revitalize and remake a brand of right-wing conservatism in the United States that also marginalizes immigrants and people of color.

What motivated Tea Party supporters at the grassroots level? Several accounts have honed in on a running theme espoused by individuals who identified with the movement: the desire to "take the country back" (Hochschild 2016; Parker and Barreto 2013; Williamson, Skocpol, and Coggin 2011). Scholars and commentators studying the Tea Party noted that this mantra was likely a racially charged dog-whistle in response to the election of Obama. In their important book on the rise of the Tea Party movement, political scientists Christopher Parker and Matthew Barreto make this argument directly:

> We believe that people are driven to support the Tea Party from the anxiety they feel as they perceive the America they know, the country they love, slipping away, threatened by the rapidly changing face of what they believe is the "real" America: a heterosexual, Christian, middle-class, (mostly) male, white country. We think it likely that they perceive such change is subverting their way of life, everything they hold dear. They not only wish to halt change; if we are correct, Tea Party supporters actually wish to turn the clock back. They hope to return to a point in American life before Barack Obama held the highest office in the land, before a Latina was elevated to the Supreme Court, and when powerful members of Congress were all heterosexual (at least publicly).
>
> (2013, p. 3)

My own claims about the circumstances that have led to the politicization of white identity are similar to the sentiments Parker and Barreto describe as motivating the Tea Party. Is Tea Party support as much about in-group anxiety as it is about out-group animus? Do whites who feel anxious about changes to the racial order in the United States also endorse the Tea Party movement, or are Tea Party sympathizers driven more by their dislike of non-whites?

To see, I examine support for the Tea Party movement using the KN 2010 study, the 2012 ANES, and the 2016 ANES. I model support for the Tea Party – measured either with 101-point feeling thermometer items or questions that ask about respondents' degree of support – as a function of white identity, party identity, ideology, employment status, negative personal and national economic evaluations, education, age, gender, attitudes about the size of government, and racial resentment. The results are presented in Table 8.1.

What we see, consistently, is that white racial solidarity is *not* associated with greater support for the Tea Party. If anything, it is marginally linked to less support, but the effect across each survey is relatively small and often insignificant. In contrast, racial resentment emerges repeatedly as a powerful predictor of Tea Party opinion. More racially resentful whites are far more likely to say they support the Tea Party and rate it more positively. What is more, when controlling for Tea Party support in my model of vote choice in 2012, I find that including this measure only slightly reduces the effect of white identity, but greatly reduces the impact of racial resentment.[20] Thus, while Tea Party support may very well come from disaffected whites who are angry with the racial changes the country has experienced, their feelings are being channeled not through their in-group anxieties, but rather through their racial hostilities.

A White Backlash and the Rise of Donald Trump

If the election of Obama represented a challenge to the racial hierarchy, then we might expect that some whites wanted to see a return to order. Such a reversion to the status quo does not necessarily mean, however, that any white political candidate would be appealing. In order for a political candidate to stand out from a field of other white politicians, and for white identity to be brought to bear on attitudes, such a person would likely need to appear to be prioritizing the interests of whites.

Writing in 2005, Wong and Cho noted that when they analyzed the relationship between white identity and whites' attitudes toward racialized policies, they found little to report. But they were prescient about the potential relationship between white identity and political preferences. They described one interpretation of their results in this way:

> The identity exists and is related to ingroup attitudes, but it has
> yet to become a politicized identity. If White identity is indeed

Table 8.1 *White Identity, Racial Resentment, and Support for the Tea Party*

	KN 2010	ANES 2012 (Face-to-face)		ANES 2012 (Web)		ANES 2016 (Face-to-face)	(Web)
	Tea Party support	Tea Party support	Tea Party thermometer	Tea Party support	Tea Party thermometer	Tea Party thermometer	Tea Party thermometer
White identity	0.016	−0.082**	−0.011	−0.049**	−0.040**	−0.023	0.001
	(0.041)	(0.033)	(0.022)	(0.021)	(0.016)	(0.025)	(0.018)
Racial resentment	0.328***	0.200***	0.157***	0.193***	0.177***	0.042	0.155***
	(0.073)	(0.054)	(0.037)	(0.032)	(0.025)	(0.032)	(0.025)
Observations	570	706	692	2,323	1,952	591	1,571
R-squared	0.520	0.468	0.361	0.488	0.415	0.355	0.385

Note: Table entries are OLS coefficients. Standard errors in parentheses. All variables in model coded to range from zero to one. Data are weighted. Models also controls for party identity, ideology, employment status, negative personal and national economic evaluations, education, age, gender, and attitudes about the size of government. Estimates from full models appear in Online Appendix 8D.

***p<0.01, **p<0.05, *p<0.1, two-tailed.

Source: 2010 KN, 2012 ANES, 2016 ANES.

> unstable but easily triggered, the danger is that a demagogue
> could influence the salience of these identities to promote
> negative outgroup attitudes, link racial identification more
> strongly to policy preferences, and exacerbate group conflict.
>
> (p. 716)

In 2016, Donald Trump mounted a surprisingly successful campaign for the presidential nomination. He drew a great deal of attention for his racially charged remarks, many of which were explicit and disparaging. For instance, Trump made broad and offensive generalizations about undocumented immigrants from Mexico, referring to them as rapists smuggling illegal drugs.[21] He called for an outright ban on Muslims entering the country, uniformly linking members of this group to terrorism.[22] He was one of the most vocal leaders of the birther movement, which questioned whether Obama was born in the United States – a belief largely endorsed by more racially conservative whites (Hughey 2012; Jardina and Traugott in press; Pasek et al. 2015). One need not dig very deep to find examples of Trump making offensive remarks about Jews or Native Americans, either.[23] There is little doubt that Trump appealed to whites' racial prejudices, and that whites with higher levels of racial animus were among some of his strongest supporters.[24]

Trump was certainly unusual in that his racial rhetoric was explicit and overt (Valentino, Neuner, and Vandenbroek 2018), but the notion that a political candidate would attempt to strategically appeal to whites' racial hostilities is now a forgone conclusion in American politics (Mendelberg 2001). What sets Trump further apart from the long line of politicians who have used race to win white votes is that he capitalized on more than white voters' animosity for racial and ethnic minorities. He also made pointed appeals that very well may have resonated with whites concerned about their group's status. Many journalists certainly proposed that support for Trump was motivated by whites' anxiety about their loss of status in an increasingly diverse nation.[25] They suggested that Trump's campaign slogan – "Make America Great Again" – was really dog-whistle politics for restoring power to white Americans.[26] Some even likened this slogan and Trump's political rhetoric more broadly to the language traditionally employed by the Ku Klux Klan.[27] Troublingly, Trump even gained public support from bona fide white nationalists and white supremacists – groups overtly interested in both maintaining white dominance and in denigrating non-whites.[28]

Trump's appeal extends well beyond those individuals who consider themselves members of white nationalist or white supremacist organizations. Nevertheless, we should recognize that many of the same issue positions adopted by members of these more marginalized groups are also held by a broader set of white Americans (Swain 2002; Swain and Nieli 2003). For example, as I described in Chapter 6, like white nationalists (Swain and Nieli 2003), many white Americans more generally are especially concerned with the issue of immigration. Trump began his campaign focusing exclusively on immigration, an issue I argue is central to the increased salience of white identity. Early analysis of Trump supporters showed he had especially strong support among whites who were significantly opposed to immigration.[29] In fact, immigration was so central to Trump's initial presidential agenda that near the end of August 2015, it was the *only* issue on Trump's campaign website.[30] What is more, I find that whites high on racial consciousness were significantly more likely than those low on consciousness to indicate that immigration was one of their top two issues when they were determining which political candidate to support during the presidential primaries.[31]

Trump's stance on immigration was quite clear. He promised to end illegal immigration to the United States, and to build a wall along the southern border of the country to restrict the flow of immigrants from Mexico. Speaking before a crowd of supporters at a campaign rally in Phoenix, Arizona, Trump claimed:

> We will build a great wall along the southern border. And Mexico will pay for the wall. One hundred percent. They don't know it yet, but they're going to pay for it. And they're great people and great leaders but they're going to pay for the wall. On day one, we will begin working on an impenetrable, physical, tall, power [*sic*], beautiful southern border wall.[32]

Trump's strident attention to immigration continued well into the first year of his presidency. In January of 2018, he complained about a bipartisan immigration deal that would protect immigrants from Haiti, El Salvador, and African countries. After deriding immigrants from these countries, he then suggested that the United States should bring more people from Norway, eerily echoing the very sentiments expressed in the early twentieth century by many lawmakers, who advocated for preserving the "Nordic" character of the nation.[33]

Trump also appealed to white identifiers in a second important way. He departed from the traditional Republican Party agenda aimed at cutting social spending and reducing the social safety net. Meanwhile, most of his Republican primary opponents adopted the anti-big government position the party has touted for years. At one Republican primary debate, candidate Marco Rubio claimed that he would fight anyone who wanted to expand government. John Kasich boasted that they had shrunk the government in his state of Ohio. Ted Cruz described government as a problem, and argued that less government means more freedom and prosperity. Ben Carson supported raising the minimum age to receive Social Security benefits. In contrast, Trump rejected benefits cuts and promised his supporters that he would preserve Social Security and Medicare.[34] In May of 2015, Trump claimed via Twitter, "I was the first and only potential GOP candidate to state there will be no cuts to Social Security, Medicare, and Medicaid. Huckabee copied me."[35]

Of course, we know from Chapter 7 that Social Security and Medicare are the very sort of racialized policies white identifiers support. By departing from the traditional Republican position of less government, and by loudly and attentively turning to immigration reform as one of the main issues of his campaign, Trump touted a unique and unusual combination of policy positions – ones that happen to align exceptionally well with the preferences of white identifiers.

In light of Trump's racial ploys and policy positions, it is perhaps unsurprising that in the months before and after the 2016 presidential election, many journalists proposed that Trump was tapping into "white identity politics." It is worth noting, however, that a number of these articles equated "white identity politics" with racism.[36] As I demonstrate, however, white identity politics is not the expression of racial animus, and we should not simply equate it with Trump's appeals to whites' racial hostilities; rather, Trump capitalized on white identity because many white voters saw him as restoring and protecting their group's power and resources.

If this assessment is correct, we would expect to find a strong relationship between levels of white identity, white consciousness, and support for Trump. We should also expect to observe these relationships above and beyond measures of racial prejudice.[37] But the notion that Trump supporters were driven largely by racial prejudice is not the only competing hypothesis of concern here. Many also proposed that Trump support could be found among aggrieved working-class whites, and so I also account for individual economic circumstances in my analyses. I note, however, that there has never been support for the notion that Americans vote with their "pocketbook" (Sears and Funk 1990), and previous work has already demonstrated that individual change in financial well-being had little impact on candidate preferences in 2016 (Mutz 2018).[38] Finally, as I describe in more detail below, I also examine whether Trump support was primarily driven by authoritarianism and populism.

To evaluate these relationships, I turn first to the 2016 ANES Pilot Study, which was conducted in January 2016 just prior to the presidential primaries. The study includes the racial importance identity measure and the two items that when combined with identity, serve as a valid measure of racial consciousness. Since consciousness captures a more politicized identity, we would expect it to be a stronger predictor of political preferences than identity alone.

White Identity and Positive Evaluations of Trump before the Primaries

In the general election, we might expect to find that when faced with two candidate choices, Americans were driven primarily by their partisan identities. Considering attitudes toward Trump well before the general election, however, allows me to compare the factors associated with attitudes toward a range of Democratic and Republican political candidates. Thus, I am able to determine whether white racial identity and consciousness were uniquely linked with support for Trump.

I first examine the relationships between identity, consciousness, and affective evaluations of Trump using the 101-point feeling thermometer measure, where respondents are asked to rate how warm or cold they feel toward a particular political figure. At the lowest end of the scale, zero represents the most unfavorable or cold feelings. At the high end of the scale, 100 represents the most positive or warm feelings.

Ratings around fifty degrees capture more neutral assessments.[39] What predicts warmer evaluations of Trump? To find out, I regress thermometer evaluations of Trump on white identity and white consciousness (as two separate models). I also control for party identification, political ideology, employment status, evaluations of the national economy, education, age, and gender.[40] Finally, I account for racial hostility with the standard measure of racial resentment.

The results of the regressions are presented in Figure 8.5. We can see that even after controlling for other factors, white identity was a significant predictor of affect toward Trump in January of 2016. To be clear, racial animus mattered as well, as others have indicated (Schaffner, Macwilliams, and Nteta 2018). But all else equal, whites with higher levels of racial identity evaluated Trump more warmly. Furthermore, when in-group solidarity is measured with the consciousness item, the effect is more potent. Whites high on racial consciousness gave Trump a thermometer score eighteen points higher than did those with the lowest levels of consciousness.[41]

Perhaps, however, Trump was not alone in appealing to racially conscious whites. My speculation might be wrong, and it could be that any Republican candidate, or possibly any white candidate, might draw favor from this subset of whites. In mid to late January of 2016, when the ANES Pilot Study was conducted, the campaign field was littered with potential presidential candidates. Voters had many options from which to choose, and it was not evident that Trump would secure the nomination. Given a choice between all of the Republican candidates competing in the primaries, would high white identifiers prefer Trump over other Republican candidates? To find out, I examine whether white identity and consciousness were associated with choosing Trump above and beyond the other Republican candidates.

I present in Figure 8.6 the predicted probability from two logit models – one with white identity and one with white consciousness – of preferring Trump in the primary over the other nine leading Republican candidates.[42] Just as I did in the previous model predicting affect toward Trump, I control for party identity, ideology, employment status, national economic evaluations, education, age, gender, and racial resentment. In the first panel, we can see that those higher on racial identity were indeed more likely to prefer Trump. Moving from the lowest level of identity to the highest increases the probability

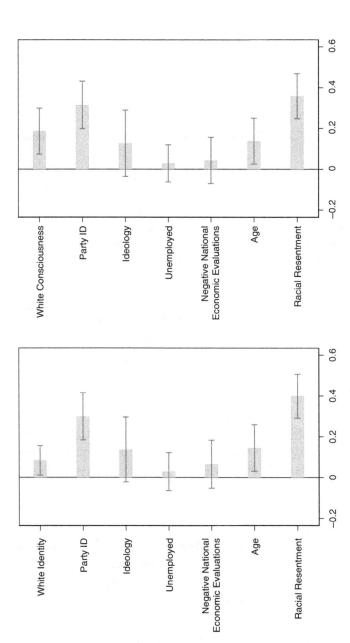

Figure 8.5 Affective Evaluations of Donald Trump

The bars represent the coefficient for each variable in the OLS model. The lines represent the 95 percent confidence intervals. Estimates from full models appear in Online Appendix 8E.

Source: 2016 ANES Pilot Study.

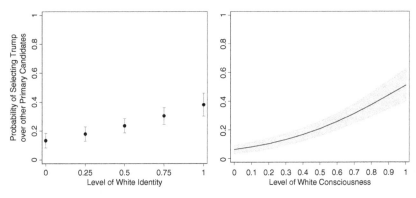

Figure 8.6 The Probability of Choosing Trump over Other Republican Primary Candidates

Points and solid line represent the predicted probability of choosing Trump over other Republican primary candidates. The capped lines and shaded region represent the 95 percent confidence intervals. Predicted probabilities are calculated by holding gender constant at female and all other variables in the model at their means. Model also controls for party identity, ideology, employment status, negative national economic evaluations, education, age, gender, and racial resentment. Estimates from full models appear in Online Appendix 8F.

Source: 2016 ANES Pilot Study.

of selecting Trump from 0.13 to 0.38 on the zero to one scale. The right panel in figure 8.6 that the effect among those high on consciousness is even greater than those high on identity alone. Whites high on consciousness are nearly eight times more likely to choose Trump than those lowest on consciousness.[43]

Trump may have been viewed favorably among whites high on racial consciousness, but it is possible that these whites might still have had more positive (or notably negative) feelings toward other candidates, potentially on both sides of the partisan aisle. For instance, some journalists have speculated that Democratic candidate Bernie Sanders was successfully tapping into the same sense of disenchantment among whites as was Trump.[44] Furthermore, some might contend that white identity ought to be negatively associated with support for candidates Ted Cruz and Marco Rubio, who share a Latino identity, and who therefore, according to my analysis above, ought to be penalized by white identifiers. At the same time, both Cruz and Rubio were candidates who had largely distanced themselves from their Hispanic heritage and who were largely unsupportive of undocumented immigrants. Both candidates made a point of downplaying

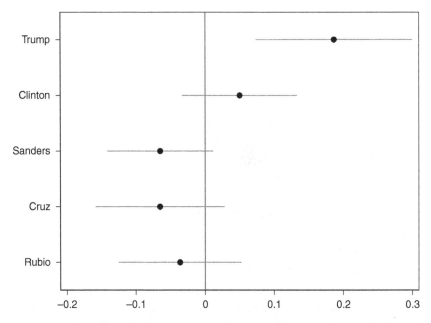

Figure 8.7 The Effect of White Consciousness on Evaluations of 2016 Presidential Candidates

Points represent the coefficient on evaluations of Trump. The lines represent the 95 percent confidence intervals. Model also controls for party identity, ideology, employment status, negative national economic evaluations, education, age, gender, and racial resentment. Estimates from full models appear in Online Appendix 8G.
Source: 2016 ANES Pilot Study.

their ethnic identity, and it is therefore possible that many white voters paid little mind to these candidates' ethnicity.

In Figure 8.7, I present the relationship between white consciousness and feeling thermometer evaluations of the four most successful presidential candidates during the 2016 primary season besides Trump: Hillary Clinton, Bernie Sanders, Ted Cruz, and Marco Rubio. Looking at the figure, it is immediately obvious that Trump was in fact unique in his appeal to racially conscious whites. White racial consciousness is not a significant predictor of evaluations of Hillary Clinton, nor of Republican candidates Ted Cruz or Marco Rubio. The measure marginally predicts evaluations of Sanders, but in the direction opposite of what we might anticipate. Those higher on white consciousness evaluated Sanders *less* favorably, not more. In short, across the landscape of political frontrunners, Trump was unequivocally capitalizing on the politics of white identity.

Alternative Explanations for the Rise of Trump: Testing the Robustness of White Racial Solidarity and Attitudes Toward Trump

A number of other scholars have identified several alternative explanations for Trump's success. One popular and widely covered account for Americans' support for Trump is the prevalence of authoritarianism in the public mind.[45] Authoritarians desire order, especially when they are fearful or threatened (Hetherington and Weiler 2009). What is more, they not only respond to fear threats, but especially to threats from abroad. Over the course of his campaign, Trump frequently mentioned threats to the nation from overseas, particularly from Iran and from terrorist organizations. Perhaps he was exceptionally successful at activating authoritarianism.

Other research has challenged the claim that authoritarianism was driving Trump support. Analysis by political scientists Eric Oliver and Wendy Rahn (2016) suggests that Trump supporters might have instead been motivated by populism. Unlike authoritarians, who align themselves with those in charge, populists are opposed to elites of all kinds. Accordingly, populism is characterized both by anti-elitist sentiments and by mistrust of experts. To put these claims to the test, I included measures of both these sentiments on the 2016 YouGov Study. I measure authoritarianism with a traditional four-item measure gauging attitudes toward child-rearing. Following Oliver and Rahn, I measured anti-elitism by asking respondents the extent to which they agree or disagree with two statements: (1) It doesn't really matter who you vote for because the rich control both political parties, and (2) The system is stacked against people like me. I gauged mistrust of experts with the following item, also presented in an agree or disagree format: "I'd rather put my trust in the wisdom of ordinary people than the opinions of experts and intellectuals."[46]

Finally, some might wonder whether most of the effects I observe with respect to white identity or white consciousness are really being driven by those with especially extreme views. We know from Chapter 3 that the measure of white identity is capturing not just a wide swath of white Americans who feel an attachment to their racial group, but also the much smaller segment of those with especially insidious views – individuals who identify overtly with white nationalist organizations, the alt-right, or white supremacist groups.

To make sure the effects of white racial solidarity I am observing are not primarily driven by these individuals, I also evaluate attitudes toward Trump while controlling for the ratings survey respondents give the Ku Klux Klan (KKK) on a 101-point feeling thermometer measure.

I re-examine Trump support here with two approaches. The first considers the relationship between white racial consciousness, racial animus, populism, and authoritarianism as they relate to affective evaluations of Trump measured with a feeling thermometer. Then, I explore the extent to which each of these factors predicts reported vote choice in the 2016 presidential election. In each case, in addition to accounting for these alternative hypotheses, I also control party identity, political ideology, employment status, education, age, gender, attitudes about the scope of government, and racial animus.

I present in Table 8.2 the results of an ordinary least squares regression controlling for each of these items and white racial consciousness. I focus solely on consciousness, but note that the results for identity are nearly identical. We see in the first columns of the table that, as I have already demonstrated, consciousness is strongly associated with more favorable ratings of Trump, even after controlling for racial resentment. Certainly, resentment matters as well; Trump support is very clearly a product both of white group solidarity *and* racial animus.

In the second column, I replace the measure of racial resentment with a more explicit measure of racial attitudes – a standard stereotype measure of racial animus, coded as the difference between where whites evaluate their group on two dimensions – either hardworking or lazy, and either intelligent or unintelligent – and where they rate blacks, on average, on those scales. We can see that measured this way, racial animus still predicts Trump support, but the effect of white consciousness remains the same.

Next, I measure racial prejudice with an even more explicit attitude: affect toward the KKK. As I mentioned in Chapter 3, whites high on white racial solidarity do rate the KKK more favorably than whites who are less attached to their racial group. The average thermometer rating among those with consciousness scores in the upper quartile of the scale is twenty-one degrees – a still considerably unfavorable score. Nevertheless, there are some individuals in the sample who rate the KKK more warmly. Approximately 9 percent of whites in the sample give the KKK a thermometer rating at fifty-one degrees or above. Are these individuals primarily responsible for the significant relationship we observe between white racial consciousness and attitudes toward Trump? The results of the model in the second column of Table 8.2 suggest not. After controlling for attitudes toward the KKK, the effect of white consciousness on Trump evaluations is reduced only slightly, and the relationship remains statistically significant. I note, however, that warm feelings toward the KKK were also significantly linked to warmer feelings for Trump.

In the fourth column, I examine the relationship between evaluations of Trump while also controlling for authoritarianism. The effect of authoritarianism is small and marginally significant, and accounting for it in the model does not reduce the effect of white consciousness on attitudes toward Trump. We can also see in the fifth column of Table 8.2 that neither anti-elitism nor mistrust of experts significantly explains evaluations of Trump above and beyond consciousness. Furthermore, when I control for all four items together, the relationships are largely the same.[47] The results suggest that white consciousness, partisanship, age, attitudes about the size of government, and racial resentment were what primarily account for positive attitudes toward Trump.

Next, I turn to determining whether white consciousness was related to vote choice in 2016, accounting for the same factors as above. In the 2016 YouGov Study, which was conducted in two waves, respondents were asked after the election to report for whom they voted. Were white racial solidarity, racial resentment, authoritarianism, and populism implicated in whites' vote choice? To find out, I examine the relationship between each of these items and vote choice, and I present the results in Figure 8.8.

Figure 8.8 is generated via the same model as presented in the last column of Table 8.2, except this time I estimate a logit model predicting vote choice in the election, where zero indicates a vote for Clinton and one a vote for Trump. In this model, neither authoritarianism nor populism are significant. Instead, we see that vote choice is a function of white consciousness, party identity, ideology, gender, and attitudes about the size of government.[48] We also observe a small and marginally significant effect for economic self-interest. Unemployed respondents were significantly more likely to report voting for Trump, but the effect does not approach that of white consciousness or party identification.

Table 8.2 *Affective Evaluations of Trump*

	(1)	(2)	(3)	(4)	(5)	(6)
White consciousness	0.260***	0.284***	0.224***	0.241***	0.240***	0.221***
	(0.076)	(0.077)	(0.082)	(0.078)	(0.079)	(0.081)
Party identification (Republican)	0.404***	0.406***	0.436***	0.402***	0.399***	0.397***
	(0.057)	(0.055)	(0.058)	(0.057)	(0.057)	(0.057)
Ideological identification (conservative)	0.128*	0.170**	0.189**	0.110	0.133*	0.119
	(0.073)	(0.069)	(0.074)	(0.075)	(0.074)	(0.075)
Employment status	0.014	-0.000	-0.007	0.015	0.024	0.024
	(0.071)	(0.072)	(0.078)	(0.073)	(0.070)	(0.072)
Education	0.016	0.006	-0.032	0.020	0.030	0.035
	(0.052)	(0.052)	(0.056)	(0.052)	(0.052)	(0.052)
Age	-0.126**	-0.124	-0.031	-0.132**	-0.127**	-0.132**
	(0.063)	(0.066)	(0.067)	(0.062)	(0.062)	(0.062)
Female	-0.032	-0.034	-0.018	-0.029	-0.029	-0.027
	(0.031)	(0.030)	(0.032)	(0.031)	(0.031)	(0.031)
Limited government	0.072**	0.096**	0.082**	0.078**	0.066*	0.073**
	(0.035)	(0.034)	(0.036)	(0.035)	(0.035)	(0.035)
Racial resentment	0.221***			0.215***	0.208***	0.201***
	(0.074)			(0.073)	(0.074)	(0.073)
Racial stereotype index		0.344**				
		(0.159)				
KKK thermometer			0.320***			
			(0.069)			

(continued)

Table 8.2 (*cont.*)

	(1)	(2)	(3)	(4)	(5)	(6)
Authoritarianism				0.081		0.078
				(0.050)		(0.050)
Anti-elitism					0.039	0.056
					(0.069)	(0.069)
Mistrust of experts					0.073	0.062
					(0.084)	(0.084)
Constant	−0.043	−0.137	−0.004	−0.068	−0.104	−0.133
	(0.067)	(0.092)	(0.069)	(0.071)	(0.079)	(0.082)
Observations	543	549	513	542	543	542
R-squared	0.387	0.379	0.397	0.392	0.390	0.395

Note: Table entries are OLS coefficients. Standard errors in parentheses. All variables in model coded to range from zero to one. Data are weighted.
***p<0.01, **p<0.05, *p<0.1, two-tailed.
Source: 2016 YouGov Study.

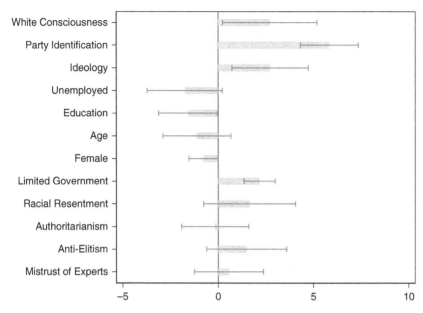

Figure 8.8 White Consciousness and 2016 Presidential Vote Choice
Bars represent the coefficient for each variable in the model. The lines represent the 95 percent confidence intervals. Greater values indicate a preference for Trump. Estimates from full models appear in Online Appendix 8H.
Source: 2016 YouGov Study.

Candidate Evaluations and Threat

Throughout this book, I have argued that as a dominant identity, white racial solidarity's association with political preferences is in part a function of perceived group threat. The results in this chapter lend further support to my argument that politicians can appeal to whites, activating their racial identity, by reminding them of threats to their group's status and by indicating that they will protect this status. The fact that white racial solidarity so strongly predicts evaluations of Trump, and only evaluations of Trump, is strong evidence for this claim. You might also wonder, however, whether information about demographic change or immigration boosts white identifiers' support for Trump even more. Recall that, in Chapter 5, I showed that in response to information about their pending numerical decline and of increased immigration in the future, whites with higher levels of identity reported significant negative emotional reactions. Does information about demographic change effect how white identifiers view

Trump? My examination of this relationship suggests there is some shift, although the results fall short of statistical significance. Whites high on solidarity, when reminded of their impending numerical decline or when told that immigration to the United States is increasing, do tend to rate Trump even more favorably. The effect, however, is not especially large, in part because whites high on racial solidarity already rate Trump so highly. Nevertheless, the confluence of evidence here is important. White racial solidarity is tightly linked to opposition to immigration. It is also significantly tied to attitudes toward Trump, who clearly exploited whites' anti-immigrant sentiment. Trump serves as a prime example of politicians capitalizing on whites' desire to protect their group.

The Civil Rights Movement

Donald Trump exploited whites' concerns in a rapidly diversifying nation, warning them of their impending loss of status due to immigration, globalization, and multiculturalism. Decades before these subtler threats began to bubble to the surface, however, whites were caught in a much more overt, sometimes violent, and certainly explicit fight over their group's power and status. During the Civil Rights movement, whites' dominance over racial and ethnic minorities was directly challenged, especially in the US South. The Civil Rights movement certainly highlighted the persistence of white racial animosity in the United States, but it was also indicative of a shift in whites' absolute power over the nation's political, social, and economic institutions. We might therefore expect to find that both racial animus and white in-group attitudes were politically relevant in the late 1960s and early 1970s.

Unfortunately, public opinion surveys from the time did not include direct measures of white racial identity. Nevertheless, we can turn to more affective measures, comparing the relationship between political preferences and the evaluations whites give their own group above and beyond those they gave to blacks during the time. One way to assess whether whites were bringing their in-group sentiments to bear on attitudes toward the Civil Rights movement is to turn to the ANES Time Series, which asked individuals the following: "Some say that the civil rights people have been trying to push too fast. Others feel they haven't pushed fast enough. How about you: Do you think that civil rights leaders are trying to push too fast, are going too slowly, or are they moving about the right speed?" Respondents were asked this question beginning in 1964. Here, I examine the relationship between white in-group attitudes, measured with the white feeling thermometer measure (where whites are asked on a 100-point scale to rate how warm or cold they feel toward their group), whites' attitudes toward blacks, also measured with the thermometer, and responses to this question during the latter half of the Civil Rights movement and in the years just after its end (1964, 1966, 1968, 1972, and 1974).[49] The dependent variable here is coded to range from zero to one, with "1" representing the belief that leaders were pushing too fast, "0" representing the belief they were moving too slowly, and "0.5" an endorsement that they were moving at the right speed. I also control for party identity, personal financial evaluations, education, gender, age, and residence in the South.[50]

Figure 8.9 plots the coefficients on the white thermometer and black thermometer items from each model for each year. Not surprisingly, how whites felt toward blacks was significantly linked to their belief about Civil Rights leaders. Those who felt warmer toward blacks were also more inclined to report that Civil Rights leaders were going too slowly. It is also important to note, however, that whites' feelings toward their own group mattered as well, even after accounting for attitudes toward blacks. In each year, whites who rated whites more warmly were also significantly more likely to believe that Civil Rights leaders were pushing too fast.

Were politicians prior to Trump able to capitalize on these sentiments, just as I have argued Trump was able to take advantage of whites' perceptions of threat about their status today? To see, I explore whether prominent political figures, beginning with Wallace and Nixon, during and just after the Civil Rights movement, and then later Patrick Buchanan, were able to appeal not only to whites' racial hostilities, but also to their sense of racial solidarity.

George Wallace

Arguably at the forefront of the effort to maintain white power during the Civil Rights movement was Alabama Governor George C. Wallace. He was a strict segregationist, best known for his attempt to block the integration of the University of Alabama as ordered

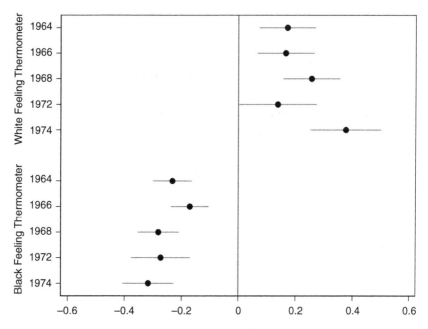

Figure 8.9 The Relationship between White Affect, Black Affect, and Belief that Civil Rights Leaders are Pushing Too Fast

The points represent the coefficient on the white feeling thermometer and black feeling thermometers in each year. The lines represent the 95 percent confidence intervals. Model also controls for party identity, negative personal economic evaluations, education, gender, age, affect toward blacks, and South. Estimates from full model appear in Online Appendix 8I.

Source: ANES Time Series. Analysis was run using the ANES Cumulative File.

by President John F. Kennedy. In this respect, Wallace very overtly attempted to maintain the system of Jim Crow segregation that benefited southern whites.

Wallace was first elected Governor of Alabama in 1962. He was sworn into office on January 14, 1963 in a ceremony marked by brazen symbolism. He took the oath of office while standing in the same spot where almost 102 years prior, Jefferson Davis was sworn in as the provisional president of the Confederate States of America. Wallace's inaugural address was written by Asa Earl Carter, a 1950s leader of the Ku Klux Klan. In the address, Wallace proclaimed, "In the name of the greatest people that have ever trod this earth, I draw the line in the dust and toss the gauntlet before the feet of tyranny ... and I say ... segregation today ... segregation tomorrow ... segregation forever" (Wallace 1963). Of course, when Wallace referred to the "greatest people that have ever trod this earth" he surely meant white Americans.

But Wallace's speech was not, largely, an explicit attempt to denigrate blacks. Instead, much of his address blatantly pandered to whites, echoing language we have heard before. His words were reminiscent of the same appeals made during the congressional debates over immigration reform in the 1920s. Wallace praised his state as the heart of the "Great Anglo-Saxon Southland." Most poignantly, like Senator Durant in the 1920s, like Buchanan in the 1990s, and like Trump and others today, Wallace warned that whites were in jeopardy. He cautioned that they stood to be submerged and persecuted globally by a growing non-white minority:

> It is the "changing world" of which we are told ... it is called "new" and "liberal". It is as old as the oldest dictator. It is degenerate and decadent. As the national racism of Hitler's Germany persecuted a national minority to the whim of a national majority ... so the international racism of the liberals seek to persecute the international white minority to the whim of the international colored majority ... so that we are footballed about according to the favor of the Afro-Asian bloc. (Wallace 1963)

Wallace moved to carry his popularity as governor onto the national scene in 1963, intending to oppose John F. Kennedy for the Democratic presidential nomination. He was unsuccessful, losing the nomination to Lyndon Johnson, who came into office after Kennedy's assassination. Despite his Democratic partisanship, Wallace's campaign mirrored many of the themes of Republican candidate Barry Goldwater, who was also notorious for resisting the efforts of the Civil Rights movement, and who campaigned against strong action by the federal government to enforce civil rights.[51] Wallace ran again in 1968, 1972, and 1976, continuing his anti-integration agenda and concern over the erosion of white privilege. Much like Trump, he railed against the establishment, against liberal elites, and against black protestors. In short, while support for Wallace was surely driven by racial animus, we might also expect that it was motivated by whites who sought to protect their group and its power.

Richard Nixon

Like Wallace, Nixon also sought to win over southern whites who were resistant to civil rights. Nixon, however, adopted some of Wallace's more subtle approaches. Rather than explicitly attacking the efforts of the Civil Rights movement, Nixon focused on preserving states' rights and on "law and order" – terms that, according to scholars, served as dog-whistles, or coded language meant to symbolize a resistance to civil rights (Crespino 2007; Haney-Lopez 2014). Nixon used the language of states' rights to oppose federal government involvement in busing and integration. Today, we see Nixon's efforts as part of a larger story about partisan realignment, one where the Democratic Party became associated with civil rights and racial and ethnic minorities while the Republican Party moved to capture the votes of more racially conservative whites (Carmines and Stimson 1989; Schickler 2016; Valentino and Sears 2005). I propose that part of the story was not merely one of Republican candidates' efforts to appeal to whites' racial animosities, but also one of candidates appealing to whites' in-group interests (Bobo 1983; Bobo and Kluegel 1993).

To determine whether attitudes toward Wallace and Nixon were a function of how whites felt about their own group, I turn to the 1968, 1972, and 1976 ANES Time Series studies. I estimate affect toward the major presidential candidates in each of those years, measured with thermometer ratings, as a function of white in-group attitudes (also measured with the thermometer), party identity, personal financial evaluations, education, gender, age, attitudes toward blacks (measured with the thermometer), and a control for southern residence.[52]

Figure 8.10 illustrates the relationship between whites' ratings of their in-group and attitudes toward each of the major presidential candidates, as well as Wallace, across the three years. In 1968, white in-group attitudes were significantly related to warmer evaluations of both Wallace and Nixon, but not to evaluations of Democratic nominee Hubert Humphrey. In 1972, the ratings whites gave their group on the thermometer were also significantly associated with attitudes toward both Wallace and Nixon, but not with feelings toward Democratic presidential candidate George McGovern. Finally, in 1976, whites who rated their group more warmly still felt more significantly favorable toward Wallace, and not Democratic candidate Jimmy Carter.[53] Interestingly, white thermometer evaluations were also related

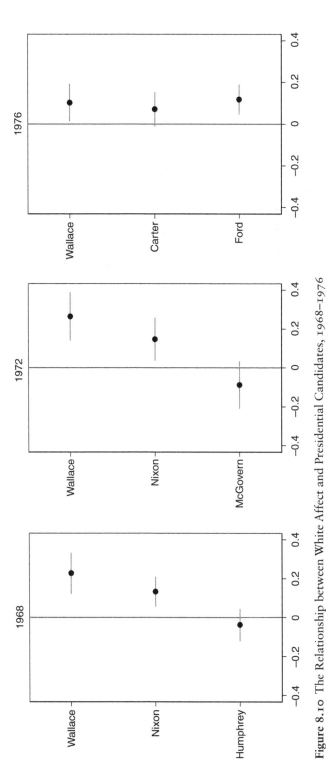

Figure 8.10 The Relationship between White Affect and Presidential Candidates, 1968–1976

The points represent the coefficient on the white feeling thermometer in each model of candidate evaluations. The lines represent the 95 percent confidence intervals. Model also controls for party identity, negative personal economic evaluations, education, gender, age, affect toward blacks, and South. Estimates from full model appear in Online Appendix 8J.

Source: ANES Time Series. Analysis was run using the ANES Cumulative File.

to attitudes toward Republican candidate Gerald Ford, although as Nixon's former vice president, it may not be especially surprising that the same whites who were more favorable toward Nixon also viewed Ford somewhat more positively as well.

Patrick Buchanan

Trump is certainly not the first presidential candidate to make immigration an issue front and center to his campaign. In fact, some have claimed that Trump simply borrowed strategies from conservative political advisor, commentator, and politician, Patrick Buchanan. Even Pat Buchanan expressed surprise at the similarities between Trump's campaign to his own in the 1990s.[54] In an interview, Buchanan remarked about Trump, "I was relatively astonished when he came out against trade and immigration – and to Make America First – that's on my [campaign] hats."[55]

Buchanan, a former senior advisor to Richard Nixon, Gerald Ford, and Ronald Reagan, ran for president in 1992, 1996, and 2000. His 1992 campaign initially posed a serious challenge to Republican incumbent George H.W. Bush, but ultimately Buchanan did not do well enough in the primaries to move forward. He gained more support in the 1996 campaign, when Bill Clinton sought re-election, winning several of the primaries. He fell, however, to Bob Dole on Super Tuesday. While Buchanan never earned the Republican Party's nomination, the level of support he did receive is noteworthy.

Like Trump, Buchanan advocated for stringent immigration restrictions. He called for a fence to be built along the border with Mexico, much like Trump's promise to build a wall that would prevent Mexicans from illegally crossing into the United States. At a political rally speech in Santa Barbara, California in 1996, prior to the Republican Convention, Buchanan said:

> We're going to go to that convention. We're going to go to that convention and we're going to tell that convention we want … a security fence all along the transit points and if the illegal aliens come into the country we're going to have Proposition 187 for the United States of America.[56]
>
> *(Buchanan 1996)*

Buchanan also took a very similar position to Trump on the North American Free Trade Agreement (NAFTA). Trump railed against

NAFTA, arguing that the agreement was to blame for America's slow wage growth, low labor force participation rates, and the decline in employment in manufacturing.[57] In the early 1990s, Buchanan more bluntly expressed the idea that NAFTA was a danger to America's place in the world. He maintained it would introduce "world government" and diminish US sovereignty. He declared that defeating NAFTA would be the "shot heard 'round the world that the Old Republic is back, that we Americans are, once again, looking out for America first."[58] When Buchanan talked about "America first" he was unabashedly speaking about white Americans. In his 1992 speech announcing his presidential candidacy, he remarked, "When we say we will put America first, we mean also that our Judeo-Christian values are going to be preserved, and our Western heritage is going to be handed down to future generations, not dumped onto some land fill called multi-culturalism" (Buchanan 1991). He would go on to write several books lamenting the threat multiculturalism and diversity posed to the status of white Americans. He warned his readers that white Americans would soon be the new minority, displaced by Hispanics and other groups in a rapidly changing country (Buchanan 2011).

Buchanan was largely considered a fringe candidate, relegated and dismissed as a member of the radical right, never achieving the success Trump realized in the 2016 presidential election. Of course, the world in which Buchanan was campaigning looked very different from today's political landscape. At that time, immigration had yet to reach the rates it ultimately achieved in the late 1990s and early 2000s. Buchanan also did not have the opportunity to seize upon the hostility and sense of threat that accompanied the election of the nation's first black president. Nevertheless, Buchanan's message resonated with some voters. Perhaps, therefore, he was able to make white identity a salient component of his support.

To investigate this claim, I again turn to the ANES Times Series to evaluate attitudes toward Pat Buchanan in each year he ran for president: 1992, 1996, and 2000. In each year, I compare the relationship between the white feeling thermometer and evaluations of Buchanan with attitudes toward other presidential candidates, controlling for party identity, personal economic evaluations, education, gender, age, attitudes toward blacks, and whether the respondent lives in the South.

We can see from the results presented in Figure 8.11 that white in-group sentiments were predictive of support for Buchanan in each

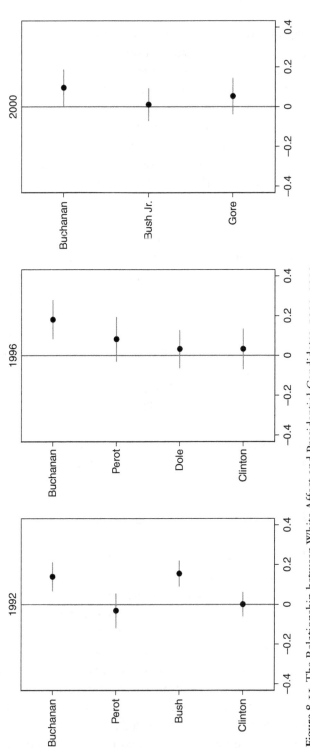

Figure 8.11 The Relationship between White Affect and Presidential Candidates, 1992–2000

Note: The points represent the coefficient on the white feeling thermometer in each model of candidate evaluations. The lines represent the 95 percent confidence intervals. Model also controls for party identity, negative personal economic evaluations, education, gender, age, affect toward blacks, and South. Estimates from full model appear in Online Appendix 8K.

Source: ANES Time Series. Analysis was run using the ANES Cumulative File.

of the years he ran for president. The higher whites rated themselves on the white thermometer item, the more warmly they rated Buchanan. The thermometer evaluations were not predictive of any other presidential candidates – including other Republican candidates – in these years, with the exception of George Bush in 1992. It is not entirely evident why white in-group attitudes would be especially linked to Bush, but it is worth noting that it was in May of 1992 that Bush condemned the race riots in Los Angeles in the wake of the brutal beating African American Rodney King received during his arrest in 1991. He used familiar "law and order" language, pledging to restore order in Los Angeles, potentially appealing both to whites' racial hostilities and their in-group concerns.

This analysis provides some suggestive but important evidence that politicians can make racial appeals that not only take advantage of the hostilities whites feel toward racial and ethnic minorities, but also ones that appeal to whites' desire to protect and preserve their group's power. Trump is not alone in having successfully tapped into whites' in-group sentiments. George Wallace, Richard Nixon, and Pat Buchanan clearly took advantage of both in-group and out-group racial attitudes. We may therefore expect that future political candidates may try to do the same.

Political Mobilization

Over the course of this chapter, I have demonstrated that politicians can successfully exploit whites' sense of racial solidarity. Certainly, for Donald Trump, appealing to whites' animosities and anxieties was an overwhelmingly successful strategy. But were these whites actually more likely to show up at the polls? Are whites with higher levels of racial consciousness more likely to participate in politics? Previous work on group consciousness more broadly indicates that the construct is one of the more powerful predictors of political participation. In fact, this domain is one where the distinction between identity and consciousness clearly emerges, and scholars often use consciousness to predict political participation more generally (Chong and Rogers 2005; Miller et al. 1981). After all, group members high on consciousness believe that their group must work within the political system to address group disparities (Miller et al. 1981). Does this pattern hold for

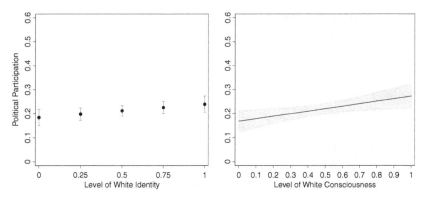

Figure 8.12 The Relationship between White Identity, White Consciousness, and Levels of Political Participation

Points and solid line represent the predicted level of political participation at each level of white identity or white consciousness. The capped lines and shaded region represent the 95 percent confidence intervals. Predicted probabilities are calculated by holding gender constant at female and all other variables in the model at their means. Model also controls for party identity, ideology, employment status, negative national economic evaluations, income, education, political knowledge, age, gender, and racial resentment. Estimates from full model appear in Online Appendix 8L.

Source: 2016 ANES Pilot Study.

whites as well? Previous work would suggest some skepticism, arguing that whites are primarily driven by socioeconomic model of participation, in which their economic resources, levels of education, and political knowledge motivate their political engagement. Here, I examine whether they are driven by a sense of group consciousness as well.

I construct a scale of political participation using six items in the 2016 ANES Pilot. Respondents were asked how likely they were to attend a political meeting, give money to a political organization, and distribute advertisements supporting a political group or figure. They were also asked whether they joined in a protest march or rally in the past four years, and whether in the past two months they wore campaign paraphernalia or donated money to a political party or candidate. The average of these six items forms a reliable measure of political participation.[59]

In Figure 8.12, I present the relationship between white identity, white consciousness, and reported levels of political participation, controlling for other factors likely to be associated with political participation, including partisanship, ideology, employment status, income, education, and political knowledge. We can see that after controlling for these factors, white identity is only marginally significant; consciousness, in contrast, is significantly linked to political participation. Whites high on racial consciousness report an intention to participate in politics at a much greater rate than those low on racial consciousness. Compared to whites with the lowest level of consciousness, those with the highest degree have participation scores 1.6 times higher.

These results add an important nuance to our understanding of political behavior among whites. Political participation among whites, it seems, is not merely a function of socioeconomic resources (Rosenstone and Hansen 1993). Similar to the pattern we observe among blacks (Chong and Rogers 2005; Miller et al. 1981; Verba, Schlozman, and Brady 1995), group consciousness among whites is strongly associated with greater levels of political participation.[60] Racial consciousness, as expected, pulls people into the political world.

Conclusion

The evidence presented in this chapter shows that white identity can play a powerful role in one of the most visible and significant expressions of political preferences – presidential vote choice. In 2012, white identifiers were far more likely to vote for Romney than Obama, even after accounting for racial animus. These results suggest that Obama represented a clear challenge to whites' dominance, and therefore the lack of support for Obama among whites was not merely, exclusively, or even primarily a result of racial hostility. Many whites opposed Obama because he represented their group's loss of power and privileges. White identity was significantly associated with the belief that Obama favors blacks over whites, further indication that Obama was viewed by some whites as a threat to their in-group. Interestingly, however, not all backlashes to Obama are rooted in white racial solidarity. Support for the Tea Party movement, which many consider a direct response to Obama's election, is not associated with whites' in-group attitudes. Instead, more favorable views toward the Tea Party are overwhelmingly linked to white racial resentment.

We also saw that white identity was significantly associated with opposition to a Latino president, providing further evidence that non-white political candidates more generally are viewed as threats to whites' political power. These results suggest that as the electorate becomes more diverse, and more non-white political candidates run for office, whites high on racial identity are likely to be especially discontent.

Obama represents a case in which white identity is brought to bear on evaluations of a political figure viewed as a challenge to whites. But I have also argued that white identity should predict support for political figures whites view as protecting their group, or restoring the racial order. In this chapter, I demonstrated that Donald Trump emerged as a candidate who directly appealed to white identifiers, and even more so to those high on white consciousness. Not only did Trump promise to protect their group by insulating US workers and severely restricting immigration – one of the greatest sources of threat to whites – but he also supported many of the racialized social welfare policies that, as I and others have suggested, whites see as benefiting their group. Throughout his campaign, Trump appealed to these whites by pledging to protect Social Security and Medicare – policies strongly supported by white identifiers.

Trump effectively activated white identity by leveraging threats to whites' status. As a result, white identity predicts support for Trump and only Trump in 2016. Furthermore, I demonstrate that white identity predicted Trump support above and beyond traditional measures of racial animus. Yet one should not walk away with the conclusion that this aspect of Trump's appeal is somehow more innocuous than racially charged language directed at racial and ethnic minorities. Throughout his campaign, and in the early part of his presidency, Trump worked to position himself very much in opposition to Barack Obama. Many of his policy positions seemed intended to dismantle policies and programs that had been established by Obama, including health care reform, climate change, and criminal justice reform. Trump's success came not merely from disparaging people of color, but from positioning himself as the antidote to any threat posed by the nation's first black president. In doing so, he was, and is, seeking to maintain the dominance of whiteness in the United States.

Other politicians have, in the past, been able to make similar appeals. Politicians like George Wallace, Richard Nixon, and Patrick Buchanan sought political support by playing on whites' fears and anxieties over their potentially waning status in the nation and the world. In keeping with this possibility, white in-group sentiments are significant predictors of attitudes toward both these political figures in the years in which they ran for US president. Not only do these results demonstrate the potential for white identity to be leveraged by political candidate, but they also provide important evidence that white identity has mattered politically during periods of time in which whites felt threatened.

These results also offer insight into future elections. It is likely that in the years to come, the electorate will continue to diversify. The same demographic shifts that are putting some whites on edge are only exacerbating the feeling that whites are losing out. Barack Obama would not have won his second term if it were not for the Latinos and blacks who turned out in great numbers to vote for him. All signs suggest that these profound changes to the political and social landscape of the United States will increase, and racial and ethnic minorities will continue to gain more positions of political, economic, and social power. As a result, the power of white racial solidarity is likely to persist well into the future of electoral politics. We can see that whites who feel this sense of attachment to their racial group can be politically mobilized. Whites with higher levels of consciousness also report higher levels of political participation. The political milieu of 2016 suggests that whites will increasingly think of themselves as a political group with cohesive interests, a sentiment that surely other politicians will attempt to exploit long after Donald Trump.

9 THE FUTURE OF WHITE AMERICA

The voice of the people is but an echo.

V.O. KEY (1966)

In the 2016 presidential election, the electorate was one of the most diverse in US history. According to exit poll data from CNN, approximately 30 percent of voters were not white. These trends are certainly a preview of the profound demographic changes that the United States will continue to experience over the coming decades. While white Americans will remain a plurality, their numbers are waning. These changes are indicative, to some extent, of a potential new reality – one in which whites do not maintain a complete monopoly of power over the nation's economic, social, and political institutions.

While projections indicate that whites will not be displaced as the majority of the US population for another two decades, incredible diversity is already upon us. In California, Hawaii, New Mexico, and Texas, non-Hispanic whites are already a minority. Nevada, Maryland, and Georgia are next in line to receive their designation as majority-minority states. White Americans are losing their numerical majority, their stronghold over elective offices, and, perhaps, their ability to define the nation's identity in their image. And they are not going out without a fight. Throughout this book, I have argued that one effect of the perceived waning status of white Americans is the activation of white racial identity and white racial consciousness. In what follows, I summarize what we know about the content of white racial identity and the profound political consequences of its salience in the United

States, but I also briefly consider how white identity might matter in Europe as well. I also discuss what the role of white racial solidarity in politics means for the future strategies of American political parties, before offering speculation about the future of racial attitudes and racial context in the United States.

Summary of Findings

The Nature of White Racial Solidarity

A sizeable percentage of white Americans identify with their racial group. The evidence presented here demonstrates between 30 and 40 percent of the white American population possesses a strong racial identity. Across datasets spanning seven years, levels of white identity have remained relatively stable. What is more, this identity cuts across age groups, gender, region, income levels, occupation, and political identities. There is some indication that whites with higher levels of identity tend to be slightly older, female, situated in blue-collar jobs, and Republican, but these trends are at the margins. White identifiers are a demographically diverse group.

White identity has been politicized. Many whites in the United States do not merely identify with their racial group. Another 20 percent possess strong levels of group consciousness; compared to those whites who merely possess a white identity, these whites feel a sense of discontent over the status of their group. They are more aggrieved, and they believe whites should work together politically to benefit their group's collective interests. Relative to identity, consciousness has even more powerful effects on political attitudes and behavior. The relationship between consciousness and the political outcomes studied here is similar to what we observe with respect to identity, except whites high on consciousness tend to hold more extreme views, and the strength of the relationship between consciousness and political attitudes and behavior is much greater.

From where does white racial solidarity arise? The results here suggest, to some extent, that this identity is rooted in personality. Individuals who prefer a more hierarchical arrangement to the world and who prefer order seem more disposed to adopt a group attachment. Education is also a distinguishing factor. Whites who adopt a racial identity are less likely to have gone to college. They are therefore perhaps less likely to have been exposed to different worldviews, to learn about structural inequality, and to have met diverse groups of people. I make these inferences only with observational data drawn at a single point in time, so we must approach drawing conclusions tentatively. There is still much to be done in order to understand what compels individuals to adopt group identities, particularly dominant ones.

What is apparent is that whites with higher levels of racial solidarity share a common set of beliefs and attitudes. Since the nation's founding, American identity has been inextricably linked with whiteness, and the beliefs white identifiers hold reflect these deep ties. Whites high on racial solidarity are more likely to adopt exclusionary views about what it means to be American, preferring boundaries around the nation's identity that maintain it in their image. "True" Americans, in their minds, are not just more likely to feel American, have American citizenship, or respect America's institutions; they are also those that are English-speaking, Christian, and white.

White identifiers are also proud of their racial group. They seem resentful that they are unable to celebrate and recognize their racial group similar to the ways in which they believe people of color in the country do. This discontent reflects the claim I made in Chapter 2 – namely, that white identity is in part constructed in response to the identities of other racial and ethnic groups in the United States. Many whites believe they should be able to organize around their race or mark the accomplishments of their racial group formally or symbolically, for example via the establishment of a White History month. Part of what underlies some whites' perceptions of racial discrimination is their belief that their racial group is treated unfairly by being maligned for wanting to recognize their racial group in these ways.

White racial solidarity is also associated with perceptions of group competition and alienation. Whites who adopt greater levels of racial identity or consciousness are more likely to see the world in zero-sum terms. They view their own group as in competition with non-whites, and they believe that economic and political gains for these out-groups come at the expense of their own group. These whites also feel a sense of grievance. They believe their group has not gotten its fair share, and that they, as whites, are owed more than they have been given.

At the same time, many white identifiers recognize that their group has captured certain advantages. White identity is defined both by an anxiety about encroachment from other groups, and a recognition that being white has its privileges. It is marked by a tension between recognizing the privileges and power of whites as a group, and by the belief that whites are treated unfairly. The unattributed quote with which I start Chapter 2 helps reconcile these disparate beliefs: "When you're accustomed to privilege, equality feels like oppression."

These whites are not, therefore, especially concerned that these advantages are systematically unfair or harmful to other racial and ethnic minorities. They are not, as some proponents of racial equality would hope, motivated to create a more racially egalitarian society. Instead, whites high on racial solidarity are preoccupied with the possibility that other groups are chipping away at their privileges. White identity, as a dominant group identity, is asserted in the face of group threat because many whites believe and recognize that they have something to lose.

The Political Consequences of White Racial Solidarity

White racial solidarity has profound consequences across several key political domains. For one, it is a central factor in how whites arrive at their opinion on immigration. Over the past several years, immigration has waxed and waned as one of the most important problems facing the United States in the public mind.[1] By some accounts, immigration represents a fundamental threat to white identity; it has the potential to reshape what it means to be "mainstream" American, moving the nation away from one defined by an Anglo-Protestant heritage. Immigration from Asia and Latin America in recent decades serves not only as a perceived threat to whites' numerical majority in the population, but also to whites' ability to define the identity of the nation. I find that white identity and white consciousness are one of the strongest and most consistent predictors of immigration opinion. Whites who possess higher levels of identity are far more supportive of restrictive immigration policies. The effect is even stronger among those whites who possess higher levels of racial consciousness. These same whites are not merely supportive of policies that would restrict the flow of immigration and certain immigrant rights within the country; they are also more likely to believe that immigration introduces negative consequences for the United States and its culture.

Consistent with the argument that in-group solidarity motivates support for policies that benefit the in-group, white identifiers are far more supportive of policies that have been subtly racialized with whiteness. Specifically, whites with higher levels of racial solidarity are more supportive of Social Security and Medicare. These are policies that are associated as rewards for hard work – stereotypes associated with whites. They stand in contrast to negatively racialized policies like welfare, which are associated with special favors and handouts and are stereotypes associated with blacks.

Examining the policy domains in which white identity and consciousness are implicated, and where they are not, provides important evidence that white racial solidarity is distinct from racial animus. Identity and consciousness are not simply alternative measures of racial animosity or prejudice. The whites studied here are very much interested in protecting their in-group and in securing their group's power and privileges. It may be the case that in practice, these efforts come at the expense of out-groups, but that is not the primary intention of white identifiers. One important source of evidence for this claim is that neither white identity nor consciousness predicts opposition to policies that are intended to benefit racial and ethnic minorities. Unlike racial resentment or racial prejudice, white identity is not associated with opposition to affirmative action, or with less support for the federal government providing aid to racial and ethnic minorities. White identifiers are not especially interested in cutting welfare spending either.

This preference for government intervention does not extend outside the country's borders, however. Whites high on identity and consciousness are displeased with the outsourcing of jobs, and they would like the United States to limit imports from other nations. In general, these whites would prefer the United States take a more isolationist stance, withdrawing from intervening in other parts of the world. We have some evidence, then, that whites are also worried about the loss of their status due to the effects of globalization.

The impact of white racial solidarity is not limited to the domains of immigration, social welfare spending, or trade policy. We also see that white identity and consciousness are crucial to understanding one of the most fundamental types of political behavior: vote choice. The election of Obama was profoundly symbolic from the perspective of threats to whites' status. It therefore follows that, in 2012, white identity was one of the strongest predictors of preferring Mitt Romney over

Barack Obama. In 2016, white identity politics were at the center of the national political stage. We cannot understand the rise and success of Donald Trump, one of the most unconventional and unexpected modern presidential candidates, without turning our attention to white racial identity and consciousness. Trump certainly mounted an incredibly successful appeal to this subset of American voters with his draconian stance on immigration and his support for entitlement programs. Whites high on identity and consciousness overwhelmingly threw their support behind Trump in 2016.

European Identity

The demographic changes threatening whites' dominance are not limited to the United States. Western Europe is experiencing a similar decline in white birth rates, and many of these countries have also been subject to decades of increased immigration. Compared to the United States, waves of immigrants to Western Europe arrived much earlier. Between 1950 and 1970, approximately thirty million people entered the region, arriving mostly from non-European countries (Castles, Booth, and Wallace 1984). More recently, in 2015, Western Europe experienced a refugee crisis. A record 1.3 million migrants, primarily from war-torn Iraq, Afghanistan, and Syria, sought asylum across the European Union, Switzerland, and Norway.[2]

When it comes to immigration, most of Europe is distinct from the United States; the notion of a "nation of immigrants" is not woven into the fabric of these countries' origins in the way that it is in the United States. Instead, theories of nationhood in Europe are especially exclusive, defined by bounded ethnic terms around geography, common culture, language, religion, values, and history (Citrin and Sides 2008; Tirkides 2009).[3] It is not surprising, then, that in many European countries, views about diversity are far less positive than they are among Americans. For instance, a Pew Research Center survey in 2016 found that the most common view among many European countries about diversity is ambivalence; no nation reports a majority indicating that diversity yields positive benefits for their country. In some places, like Greece, Italy, Hungary, and Poland, diversity is viewed quite negatively. In contrast, a majority of Americans believe that diversity makes the country a better place to live.[4]

The massive waves of immigrants and refugees to Europe have profoundly affected the composition of many European countries – countries that in many ways were culturally and politically unprepared to absorb these groups. In Norway, Austria, and Sweden, foreign-born individuals made up more than 15 percent of the population in 2016. In the UK, the foreign-born population is estimated at 13.4 percent, and 12.3 percent in France.[5] What is more, many of these European countries experienced over a percentage point increase in the total immigrant share of the population in a single year, between 2015 and 2016. By comparison the United States experienced a one-point increase in the immigrant share of the population over the course of a *decade*.

Significant immigration, coupled with European states' very specific beliefs about national identity and antagonism toward multiculturalism, have meant that native Europeans have been especially hostile to immigrants over the past several decades. Many scholars have turned their attention to understanding xenophobia and anti-immigrant politics among Europeans as a result (Fetzer 2000; Rensmann and Miller-Gonzalez 2010; Sniderman and Hagendoorn 2009). One consequence of these anti-immigrant attitudes has been the rise and relative success of radical right political parties whose candidates have exploited these sentiments (Kitschelt 2007; Mudde 2007; Norris 2005). These parties have been surprisingly popular in many European countries over the past several years in the wake of both the migrant crisis and stagnant economies. Many also attribute the June 2016 vote among UK citizens to leave the European Union (EU) – also known as Brexit, a portmanteau of the words "Britain" and "exit" – to fear and animosity over immigration. Supporters of the Brexit referendum argued that leaving the EU was necessary in order to preserve the country's culture, identity, and place in the world amidst the threat posed by massive immigration.

While xenophobia and anti-immigrant sentiment appear to be rampant in Europe, it is unclear whether racial identity is now salient among white Europeans. On the one hand, identity among Europeans seems to revolve far more around national identity than it does around race. On the other hand, white nationalist organizations have emerged across Europe, helping to organize nationalism around race and throwing their support behind right-wing candidates. Thus, the role of white identity in driving attitudes toward European political candidates and policies deserves serious inquiry.

The Power of Both In-Group Love and Out-Group Hate

The political phenomena I have taken up here, like whites' opposition to Barack Obama and the success of Donald Trump, cannot be explained by turning our attention solely to existing theories of racial conflict, ones that focus exclusively on whites' out-group animus. These theories have two important limitations. For one, many were designed to explain white hostility toward blacks at a time in which racial or ethnic conflict in the United States was very much centered around blacks and whites. But our increasingly multi-racial context requires updated theories and accounts in order for us to accurately understand how racial attitudes motivate political attitudes and behavior today. In making this point, I do not mean to say that existing theories no longer apply. It is undeniably evident that racial resentment and racial prejudice are an important part of the story. Out-group hostilities are undoubtedly at play when it comes to opposition to immigration and to support for political candidates like Donald Trump. But these theories do not account for the fact that whites' racialized attitudes and behaviors are not always out-group oriented. Whites are not necessarily entirely motivated by socialized, negative beliefs about the moral failings of blacks in the United States. The results here demonstrate that for some whites, political attitudes and preferences can also be motivated by their desire to protect their in-group, and to maintain its power and privileges.

In some cases, out-group animus and in-group favoritism are observationally equivalent. Both, for instance, seem to play a role in political candidate evaluations. They also, however, have discriminant predictive power. For example, white identity is not predictive of attitudes toward racialized policies like affirmative action and welfare, which are significantly associated with racial resentment. If we truly seek to understand the nature and origins of political and racial conflict, we would be remiss to treat these constructs as one and the same. Many whites are not motivated to oppose immigration because they dislike Latinos. They are also not inclined to support Donald Trump because they feel negatively about people of color in the United States. Rather, these whites feel, to some extent, that the rug is being pulled out from under them – that the benefits they have enjoyed because of their race, their groups' advantages, and their status atop the racial hierarchy are all in jeopardy.

Understanding the distinction between in-group identity and racial animus is essential, and not only because they have distinct predictive powers or might be activated under different circumstances. We seek to understand the nature of racial conflict because we believe it is detrimental to a functioning and flourishing democracy. If we are to attempt to find ways to ameliorate this conflict, we must be clear about its origins. For instance, students of racial resentment argue that it is a learned predisposition, one acquired through socialization. This account implies that different formative experiences, training, or education would be one route to mitigating racial hostility. But white identity is activated in a very different manner – it is a product of the belief that resources are zero-sum, and that the success of non-whites will come at the expense of whites. Part of limiting the power of white identity may lie in assuaging the belief that whites will be the losers in this game.

At the same time, the findings throughout this book give cause for concern. I have argued that white identity is not synonymous with racial prejudice. White racial solidarity provides a lens through which whites interpret the political and social world that is inward-looking. Nevertheless, my argument is not meant to imply that the preferences and behavior of white identifiers are more innocuous than the consequences of white racial prejudice. White identifiers have coopted the language of racial discrimination and oppression. They not only argue that their group is treated unfairly, but their demands are rooted in a denial of and disregard for inequality in the United States. Their efforts to start white-only student organizations reveal how unaware they are of the misrepresentation and destruction of African American history that warrants a Black History month in the first place. Put bluntly, the politics of white identity is marked by an insidious illusion, one in which whites claim their group experiences discrimination in an effort to reinforce and maintain a system of racial inequality where whites are the dominant group with the lion's share of power and privileges. What is more, to many whites, identifying with their group and protecting its status hardly seems problematic, especially compared to racism. It is likely difficult to convince some whites that there's something normatively objectionable about identifying with one's racial group and wanting to protect its interests.

Even more troublingly, we see that sometimes white identity and racial resentment are working in tandem. For instance, in both 2012 and 2016, white racial solidarity and racial resentment were powerful predictors of vote choice. Obama's lack of support from whites was a result of both racial resentment and white identity. Donald Trump was successful not merely because he appealed to whites' worst racial prejudices, but also because he promised to protect the status of whites. His success is a sign that in the years to come, efforts to achieve racial equality in the United States may now need to be fought on two fronts; one that addresses whites' racial biases, and another that assuages their perception of status threat and its consequences.

White Identity and the Future of Party Politics

Heading into the 2016 election, it was obvious that Donald Trump's supporters were overwhelmingly white. This pattern of support is hardly surprising, as most Republican candidates in recent memory have largely been supported by white voters. In 2012, 59 percent of whites cast their ballot for the Republican presidential candidate Mitt Romney. In 2008, 55 percent of whites supported Republican candidate John McCain and, in 2004, 58 percent of whites cast their ballot for George W. Bush. In short, Republican presidential candidates have been doing well among white voters for quite some time. Conversely, Republicans have fared far less well when it comes to votes among blacks, Hispanics, and Asian Americans. In 2012, Obama won 71 percent of the Hispanic vote, 73 percent of the Asian vote, and a whopping 93 percent of the black vote. He did almost as well in 2008, winning over 60 percent of the Asian and Hispanic vote, and capturing 95 percent of the black vote.[6]

Of course, by way of his race and the historical symbolism of his election, Obama stands as a likely exception in his ability to appeal to racial and ethnic minorities. But even if we return to the 2004 presidential election, when John Kerry ran against George W. Bush, we can see large differences in minority support for Democratic versus Republican candidates. In that year, Kerry won over 50 percent of the Hispanic and Asian vote and 88 percent of the black vote. Our political parties are becoming increasingly polarized around race (Carmines and Stimson 1989; Mason 2018; Schickler 2016).

By many accounts, this process of racial alignment began in the 1960s.[7] In the midst of the Civil Rights movement, when race was the dominant issue in American political life, the two major parties were forced to take positions on civil rights issues. These positions sent a much more direct signal to voters about where the parties would side than what citizens had seen in previous decades. In 1964, the positions became starker when Barry Goldwater became the Republican Party's nominee for president and opposed the Civil Rights Act of 1964. At the time, states in the deep South were traditionally Democratic. But Goldwater's position appealed to racially conservative white Southern Democrats, setting in motion the realignment of white southerners who began over the next decade to identify with the Republican Party (Carmines and Stimson 1989). These lines in the sand were even more clearly demarcated by Richard Nixon during his 1968 campaign, with the help of political strategist Kevin Phillips. They helped develop and implement the Republican Party's "southern strategy," which deliberately sought to play on the racial fears and resentments of whites in order to win elections in the South (Phillips 1969).

The positions Republican elites adopted during the Civil Rights movement, coupled with the implementation of the southern strategy, helped cement the parties' positions on race and, subsequently, set a precedent for how different groups in American society would align themselves when it came to partisan identification. The Republicans became the party for whites, especially those conservative on matters of race, while Democrats appealed to unmarried white women and racial and ethnic minorities. Over the past several decades, whites have become increasingly Republican. According to survey data from the Pew Research Center, in 2017, 51 percent of white voters were affiliated with or leaned toward the Republican Party, compared to 43 percent who leaned toward the Democratic Party.[8]

If 2016 is any sort of bellwether, it suggests that members of the Republican Party see exploiting the politics of both white racial resentment and white racial identity as a winning strategy.[9] The Democratic Party is in a much more precarious position when it comes to issues of race. Appealing to whites in the way Republican candidates are able to do risks alienating the Democrats' base of racial and ethnic minorities. As the country has become more racially and ethnically diverse, however, some commentators have argued that the Republican tactic of winning elections by capturing white voters will soon run its course (Judis and Texeira 2002). For the Democratic Party, many have posited, demographics are destiny. The expectation is that most of the growing number of racial and ethnic minorities entering the electorate will identify as Democrats, and more and more elections will look like Obama's 2012 coalition. This outcome ought to be especially likely if the GOP continues to use race and immigration as wedge issues, further alienating racial and ethnic minorities (Abrajano and Hajnal 2015; Hajnal and Rivera 2014).

This expectation is a reasonable one, but there are several obstacles to demographic changes ensuring greater electoral success for the Democratic Party. For one, Latinos and Asian Americans continue to participate in electoral politics at rates far below the percentage of the electorate they comprise, meaning that at least in the near term, Republicans could ostensibly continue to appeal successfully to whites' racial animosities and to their concerns about their group's waning status without much consequence. Furthermore, a number of social scientists have argued that demographic projections placing whites in the minority before the middle of the century are overstated, since the Census counts anyone of mixed race or ethnicity as a minority (Myers and Levy 2018).[10] For some individuals of mixed race, identities are more fluid, and some of these individuals may become more readily incorporated into definitions of "white" (Lee and Bean 2010). Finally, demographic change is not evenly dispersed geographically across the nation. As a result, the effects of growing diversity are not realized in many Republican strongholds, and therefore, election outcomes are not likely to change dramatically in the foreseeable future. As a result, the GOP very well may continue to exploit successfully whites' fears about the changing nation.

The outcome of the 2016 presidential election demonstrates that Democrats cannot merely rely on the racial and ethnic coalition that carried Barack Obama into office in 2012. In order for Democrats to succeed at the national level, they will need to figure out how to more reliably mobilize blacks, Latinos, Asian-Americans, and other racial and ethnic minorities. Some of these efforts, however, may come at the expense of their already waning base of white voters. Democrats will still have to reckon with some of their white voters and find a way to balance the interests of multiple racial groups. There is some evidence, however, that as the parties have become more polarized on race, Democrats have captured more racially liberal whites, ones who are mobilized by the nativist sentiments espoused by Republican candidates like Trump. These whites may engage more politically as part of a backlash to anti-immigrant and xenophobic appeals.[11]

Democrats could appeal to whites who would like to see government do more for their group, not less. The evidence presented here does suggest that there is an important opening for the Democratic Party when it comes to engaging in white identity politics. Historically, the Republican Party has been antagonistic toward Social Security, to the dismay of the American public. In the 1980s, President Reagan's attempts to cut the program were so wildly unpopular that the outcry led to the characterization of Social Security as the "third rail" of American politics – a policy charged and untouchable. Today, many Republican Party leaders continue to advocate for reducing entitlement programs. As we know from the analysis here, white identifiers disproportionately support these programs. But these programs are also immensely popular among whites more generally. They are especially popular among older Americans who stand to gain the most from these benefits (Campbell 2003; Sherman 1989). As the Republican base of white voters continues to age, they may find themselves at odds with their party's position on this key issue, potentially pushing them toward the Democrats, who have long been associated with protecting Social Security (Petrocik 1996). Democrats might actively appeal to white voters by promoting the funding and protection of Social Security and Medicare without alienating their diverse base.

Trump's presidential victory, and the policy positions he has taken since assuming office, have clearly set the country on a particular path for the time being. Trump was ushered into office by whites concerned about their status, and his political priorities are plainly aimed at both protecting the racial hierarchy and at strengthening its boundaries. His imposition of a travel ban on individuals from Middle Eastern countries, his appointment of Cabinet members ideologically disposed to dismantling the government agencies they run, and his failure to condemn racist attacks in the United States are acts harmful to those most vulnerable in our society. They are, however, unlikely to affect most white Americans in a way that is directly apparent to them. If anything, Trump's efforts to close our borders and to renegotiate trade deals limiting outsourcing and importing of foreign goods, will be viewed favorably, as provisions intended to protect the country, albeit one defined and dominated by whites.

The fact that Trump's success came as a shock to so many suggests that as a nation, we are destined for further turmoil in the coming years. Obama's presidential victory, and his high approval ratings, masked an undercurrent of anxiety about our changing nation. It hid a swell of resistance to multiculturalism, and a growing backlash to immigration. Yet the trends that have given way to these attitudes – the waves of immigrants and the shift in the demographic composition of the country – are tides that are now largely irreversible. America is now racially and ethnically diverse, and the coming years will be defined by our attempts to navigate and negotiate what that means for our understanding of race and of identity.

The Myth of a White Minority

Historically in the United States, immigrant groups have not merely been assimilated into American culture; they have also been woven into the nation's racial hierarchy. The past, then, offers some insight into the future. When non-Anglo-Saxon European immigrants, like the Irish, Italian, Hungarian, and Polish, arrived in the United States, they were considered members of distinct, non-white, races. Eventually, these groups were subsumed under the umbrella of whiteness (Ignatiev 1995; Painter 2003; Roediger 1999). There are hints that Hispanics in the United States will follow a similar path (Gans 2012). Already, a number of Hispanics, especially those of mixed racial background, identify as white. Furthermore, according to a report from the Pew Research Center, lower levels of immigration and high interracial marriage rates diminish Hispanic identity. Thus, by the time current population projections expect whites to be a minority in the United States, many individuals who today might identify (or be identified) as Hispanic may very well then be considered white.[12]

This expectation does not bode well for the future of the color line in the United States, however. It suggests that, just as in the 1920s, by incorporating new immigrant groups into the current racial hierarchy, and eventually into the definition of whiteness, America's pervasive boundaries between black and white will be firmly reasserted (Bonilla-Silva 2010; Lee and Bean 2004, 2007). As a result, America's racial hierarchy will shift, but remain intact, and blacks in the United States will continue to experience discrimination.

In the meantime, many Americans will struggle to navigate this increasingly diverse country – one in which the racial hierarchy feels upended. As such, in the coming years, race relations in the United States may be ever more defined by whites' efforts to assert pro-white policies and practices. Under some circumstances, white identifiers may come to embrace policies that discriminate against minorities in practice.

Furthermore, demographic changes in which whites' relative share of the population continues to decrease may lead whites to feel that their relative power as a group has waned considerably. They may subsequently come to more fully believe that racial equality has been achieved and may therefore become increasingly opposed to policies aimed at reducing structural inequalities between minorities and whites. These whites may take this line of reasoning even further; more may come to believe that their group is actually racially disadvantaged, increasing support for policies that disproportionately benefit their group (Morrison, Plaut, and Ybarra 2010). Other whites may simply believe that acting in a way that is racially self-interested is normatively acceptable. Kaufmann, for instance, finds that when Americans and British people believe that the white majority wants to lower immigration levels to maintain whites' share of the population, such behavior is self-interested, but not racist (Kaufmann 2017). Troublingly, the work here implies that elites have the power to amplify these attitudes among whites by reminding them of impending demographic changes, and the efforts of political elites like Trump indicate that these strategies are already being employed.

The results here also suggest, however, that not all whites will respond negatively to demographic changes, nor do all whites identify strongly with their racial group. In fact, it appears that some low white identifiers are actually quite *supportive* of demographic changes, and additional work needs to be done in order to more fully understand the political preferences and behavior of *both* low and high white identifiers. Furthermore, work has shown that when members of dominant groups recognize that their group is somehow illegitimately privileged, they are more likely to support practices that reduce their relative power (Branscombe, Schmitt, and Schiffhauer 2007). These results provide some indication that reframing white privilege is possible and effective.

The Darkest Side of White Identity

The adoption of white identity and white consciousness is not, for the most part, motivated by racial animus. Nevertheless, history is replete with examples of how in-group favoritism can be a source or component of group hostility, oppression, and violence. Nativism, tribalism, and xenophobia are just a few examples of attitudes and behaviors we see as having in-group origins for out-group animosities. The attachment to whiteness in particular has an especially sordid past. Groups like the Ku Klux Klan, neo-Nazi organizations, and other designated hate groups have all championed the superiority of the white race. They have, very explicitly, sought supreme power for white Americans with European ancestry, very much at the expense of racial and ethnic minorities.

The overwhelming majority of white Americans whose attitudes and behavior I have focused on throughout this text are not card-carrying members of the KKK. They would not consider themselves to be white supremacists and would not think of joining a white nationalist organization. Nevertheless, the same factors that have led to the increased salience of white identity among the general white American population have energized pro-white movements across the country. According to the Southern Poverty Law Center (SPLC), a group that identifies and tracks hate groups across the country, between 2000 and 2010, the number of hate groups in the country rose from 602 to more than 1,000. The SPLC attributes the rise to the country's changing racial demographics and antagonism toward Barack Obama.[13]

Demographic changes have been especially instrumental in spurring existing white nationalist organizations and spawning new ones. White nationalists espouse the belief that white people of European ancestry are of a superior race. They want to instigate a rise in white identity and advocate for the preservation of "Western civilization." The large influx of non-white immigrants and the prospect that whites may soon become a minority, coupled with the ability for whites to access, via the Internet, communities that might promote more extreme ideologies, have led to an environment ripe for the white nationalist movement to thrive (Swain 2002; Swain and Nieli 2003). Most recently, the collection of white nationalists, white supremacists, neo-Nazis, anti-Semitic groups, nativists, and right-wing populists have all been given the umbrella term "alternative right" or "alt-right."[14]

One of the troubling aspects of these groups is their effort to go mainstream. Leaders of the white nationalism and alt-right movements are no longer the ridiculous cliché of a hooded clansman parading on horseback. Instead, many are like Jared Taylor, a Yale-educated leader of the movement and editor for *American Renaissance*, a monthly magazine that seeks to promote the broader development of white identity. Taylor appears high-minded and decorous; his conversations about race avoid slurs, and his academic-like framing about racial conflict disguises his calls for racial purity and eugenics in a façade of reason.

Donald Trump's candidacy appears to have breathed even more life into the alt-right movement. His severe positions on immigrants, disparaging comments about Muslims and other racially charged remarks have appealed to members of these right-wing organizations. Many avowed white supremacists have endorsed his candidacy and donated to his campaign. Jared Taylor, for instance, participated in a robocall to potential voters before the 2016 Iowa and New Hampshire primaries, telling listeners "We don't need Muslims. We need smart, well-educated white people who will assimilate to our culture. Vote Trump."[15] Richard Spencer, president of a white nationalist think tank in the DC area told the *Los Angeles Times*, "Before Trump, our identity ideas, national ideas, they had no place to go." Former KKK leader David Duke remarked, "The fact that Donald Trump's doing so well, it proves that I'm winning. I am winning."[16]

Donald Trump was slow to distance himself from these groups. He initially refused to condemn David Duke's support of his candidacy.[17] Trump also retweeted white supremacists on Twitter and shared memes created by online white nationalist groups, although it is unclear whether he did so with knowledge of the Twitter users' backgrounds or the memes' origins.[18] In short, whether he intended to or not, Trump helped to bring these fringe groups and their claims into everyday politics, blurring the lines between white identity and white supremacism.[19]

It is at this point where in-group favoritism takes an especially dark turn, becoming an overt justification for gross inequality and for extremist endorsement of beliefs that are dangerous to racial and ethnic minorities. What is more, these attitudes are being espoused by groups that have organizational advantages. The nationalist movement has polished leaders who now have practice delivering their messages to national audiences. They have think tanks, and websites, magazines, and online forums. They have spent time clarifying their ideologies and rallying their supporters. In a world where political scientists have worried about the rise in old-fashioned forms of prejudice (Tesler 2012a) and a decline in the adherence to the norm of racial equality, we might also consider the possibility that a broader set of whites might be primed to accept these messages than we would hope, truly moving nationalism from the margins to the mainstream. As one troubling indication of this trend, former KKK leader David Duke polled high enough in his 2016 US Senate seat bid in Louisiana to qualify for a televised debate.

We might think that such fringe movements are temporary and only at the margins. The phenomena I have described here, however, suggest we should make such assumptions with great caution. We like to think of tolerance toward groups as a slow and steady train, moving only in a single direction, toward greater acceptance, leniency, and egalitarianism. The atrocities of the past may feel unimaginable in today's world. But we are not so fundamentally different today from where we were just a few decades ago, when a desire to preserve a strict racial order was carried out with gross violence and oppression under Jim Crow. We still possess the capacity for such behavior.

We should pay careful attention to the fact that many whites do not just feel aggrieved about the loss of their group's status – a status that comes often at the expense of racial and ethnic minorities. They are also turning on their heads the tools used by racial and ethnic minorities to seek and demand equality. Whites wonder, if blacks, Latinos, Asians, and others can organize around their race or ethnicity, why can't we do the same? We must also recognize that whiteness, by its very nature, is still constructed in opposition to other groups. It exists as an identity by way of drawing boundaries around racial and ethnic groups, asserting who belongs, and who does not. Who is granted privilege and status, and who is not. The power and import of white identity politics makes clear that as a nation, we have a long way to go toward achieving racial equality, and race remains one of the most fundamental organizing features of American politics.

The Echo of Elite Voices

It is on this note that I return to the question posed by President Clinton, which I cited at the very beginning of this book. Will the changes upon us unite or divide us? We are at a critical juncture where the choices made by political elites may very well determine the direction of the nation. As Key wrote decades ago, "democracies decay, if they do, not because of the cupidity of the masses, but because of the stupidity and self-seeking of leadership echelons ... the masses do not corrupt themselves; if they are corrupt, they have been corrupted" (Key 1961, pp. 557–8). For Key, the future of a nation's democratic order lies in the "beliefs, standards, and competence of those who constitute the influential, the opinion-leaders, the political activists in the order" (p. 558). Political elites are in the unique position of being able to exploit and exacerbate these sentiments of grievance, racial competition, and divisiveness. Currently, many whites may not identify with groups like the KKK or the alt-right, while they might even recoil at such associations, it is nevertheless the case that these aggrieved whites are a potentially untapped well, one whose resentments are primed, ready to be stoked by politicians willing to go down a potentially very dark path.

Elites need not take their efforts so far to be successful, however. They may make slightly more tempered, but nevertheless direct and even racist claims – ones that suggest the anxieties whites feel about their status are justified. Much of the rhetoric employed by Trump during his campaign and into his first year as president demonstrates that there is an audience of whites receptive to such appeals. Trump has helped preserve his base of enthusiastic white voters with a fervent focus on immigration. He has framed the issue as a pressing national crisis, even though the number of authorized and unauthorized immigrants has been falling in recent years. There is also no evidence that immigrants commit crime at higher rates than native-born Americans, and analysis suggests immigrants have net positive effects on the national economy. Donald Trump, however, has successfully hijacked the national dialogue on immigration, and his positions are most certainly appealing to white Americans who see immigration as a threat to their dominance.

Many might argue that Trump's efforts are beyond the pale. The success of his strategy ought to be cause for concern for advocates of racial and ethnic equality. Trump has managed to garner support even with overtly racialized appeals. The prevalence of whites' discomfort over the loss of their status, however, suggests that even politicians and policy advocates who use nonracist arguments to endorse measures that preserve the status quo are likely to find support. In other words, political elites need not be as brazen as Trump to be successful, and in fact – and troublingly – more subtle efforts might be even more effective. In short, appealing to whites' desire to preserve the nation's racial hierarchy is a powerful tool that politicians have at their disposal.

This argument also implies, however, that elites have the power to quell conflict by reframing policies as non-threatening to whites' status. Furthermore, work by scholars like Gaertner et al. (1997), under the umbrella of aversive racism, proposes that intergroup bias can be reduced by efforts to re-categorize groups under single, super-ordinate identities (see also Sherif (1958) and Transue (2007)). Some work, for instance, has shown that when whites prioritize an American identity over a less exclusive "Caucasian" identity, they tend to be more amenable to policies designed to benefit blacks (Smith and Tyler 1996). Thus, redirecting in-group favoritism may prove to be a powerful strategy for addressing racial biases resulting from whites' in-group identities. A less sanguine view of American politics, however, suggests that such efforts are unlikely to be widely adopted by politicians in the coming years.

The Future of White Racial Solidarity

Is a desire to protect group interests likely to define whites' race-related political attitudes in the very long term? In a sense, yes. But as Sears and Savalei and others propose, "the new immigrant groups may well enter the United States as somewhat alien and therefore stigmatized minority groups, but in the long run are not likely to face the same impermeable color line as blacks" (Sears and Savalei 2006, p. 917). Many of these groups, just as the Irish and Italian immigrants of the early twentieth century, will likely be subsumed under the umbrella of whiteness. When this process is complete, other forms of racial attitudes may more strongly govern opinion. The process of assimilation is an inter-generational one, however, and it still may forever change the now predominantly Anglo-Protestant nature of American culture. Therefore, instead of seeing this identity as only temporary, what we should expect is that its salience will continue to wax and wane over time as whites' dominance fluctuates. Thus, the importance of white identity in the coming decades is not to be dismissed.

For those invested in racial equality, this outcome should be of little comfort. The broader implication of the assertion of white identity we are witnessing now is that racial conflict can be the product of both group interests and individual level predispositions. That means that our efforts to mitigate conflict may require more and different approaches than we have previously considered. In the case of attitudes like racial resentment or racial prejudice, the presumption is that if these are socialized beliefs, we could prevent them, or even undo them with some sort of intervention. Generational differences, increased education, group conflict, and exposure to counter-stereotypical information about out-groups have all been proposed as means by which to eradicate these attitudes.

Yet racial equality in the face of a desire to protect the status of the group is a wholly different challenge. In this case, equality is achieved not merely by changing the negative attitudes whites direct at racial and ethnic minorities; instead, equality is realized by dismantling a system of racial stratification. It requires us to deconstruct the racial hierarchy. This task is, perhaps, far more daunting. It suggests that whites must equitably share control and resources, which many will certainly be wont to do. In the past, when faced with this challenge, white Americans have responded not by leveling the field; instead, they have expanded the scope of who is considered white, allowing the racial hierarchy to remain more firmly in place, organized such that whites are at the top, blacks are at the bottom, with other non-white groups falling roughly somewhere in between. But a truly egalitarian approach would not expand the scope of power at the margins, while leaving some groups at the bottom. Instead, it would work to eradicate racial stratification.

How might a more egalitarian arrangement of groups be achieved? Several social psychologists have argued that we must first make whites aware of their unearned privileges. In doing so, they presume, many whites who otherwise endorse egalitarianism, will recognize structures of inequality, see them as inconstant with their egalitarian beliefs, and subsequently reject their privilege and the institutions that foster it. I am less optimistic of this approach. As we saw in Chapter 3, many whites who identify with their racial group do recognize their privileged status, and yet they express no interest in relinquishing it. Instead, a more viable approach may be to work to frame equality in less zero-sum terms. Growing diversity and the political, economic, and social success of racial and ethnic minorities need not be framed as occurring at the expense of whites.

An alternative approach is to tackle resistance to an upending of the racial hierarchy head on. There is some small indication in the size and fervor of the protests that have unfolded since Trump took office that a proportion of Americans endorse the image of a more egalitarian country. These organized efforts to hold elected officials accountable, to resist efforts to make our country more insular and less equitable, are an important part of this story as well. As political scientist Taeku Lee writes, "Transformative social change requires the presence of an institutionalized, indigenous countervailing force, wrought from the wellsprings of a robust civil society" (2013, p. 48). There is evidence that a countervailing force is bubbling to the surface. As older generations of whites leave this world, and as education levels among whites continue to rise, we might find that this countervailing force will grow more powerful.

It is apparent that racial conflict in the United States is and will continue to be a complicated, knotty problem. The evidence presented here indicates that race relations are indeed multidimensional. Our solutions for equality, therefore, need to be nuanced and multi-faceted. They must address not only individual animosities, but they must take seriously the way in which the hierarchical arrangement of race has deeply influenced American politics.

APPENDIX

Variable Measures

Unless noted, variables employed on the KN, SSI, and YouGov 2016 surveys are identical to the items as they appear on the ANES surveys.

AGE. Respondents' actual ages, rescaled to range from zero to one. Dem_age_r_x (ANES 2012); birthyr (ANES 2016 Pilot); V161267 (ANES 2016); VCF0101 (ANES Cumulative).

AMERICAN IDENTITY. A five-category variable ranging from 0 (being American is not at all important to identity) to 1 (being American is extremely important to identity). Patriot_amident (ANES 2012); amer_ident (ANES 2016 Pilot); V162332 (ANES 2016). In the KN 2010 study, this variable is a four-category variable ranging from 0 (strongly disagree that being American is a very important part of how I see myself) to 1 (strongly agree that being American is a very important part of how I see myself).

ANTI-ELITISM. An index variable made up of the extent to which the respondent agrees or disagrees with three items: (1) It doesn't really matter who you vote for because the rich control both political parties; (2) Politics usually boils down to a struggle between the people and the powerful; and (3) The system is stacked against people like me. The scale ranges from 0 (disagree strongly) to 1 (agree strongly). YouGov 2016.

ATTITUDES TOWARD RACIAL OUT-GROUPS. Average thermometer rating of out-groups (blacks, Hispanics, and Asians), rescaled to range from 0 (coldest) to 1 (warmest).

AUTHORITARIANISM. An additive index ranging from 0 (least authoritarian) to 1 (most authoritarian). Items included in the index measure which trait respondents believe to be more important for a child to have for four trait-pairs: (1) Independence-Respect for elders (auth_ind, ANES 2012; V162239, ANES 2016); (2) Curiosity-Good manners (auth_cur, ANES 2012; V162240, ANES 2016); (3) Obediance-Self-reliance (auth_obed, ANES 2012; V162241, ANES 2016); and (4) Being considerate-Being well behaved (auth_consid, ANES 2012; V162242, ANES 2016).

BIBLICAL INNERACY. An indicator variable with values 1 (bible is the actual word of god) and 0 (bible is not the actual word of god). Relig_wordgod (ANES 2012)

BIG FIVE PERSONALITY TRAITS.

Extraversion: An additive index ranging from 0 (least extraverted) to 1 (most extraverted). Tipi_extra and tipi_resv (ANES 2012); V162333 and V162338 (ANES 2016)

Agreeableness: An additive index ranging from 0 (least agreeable) to 1 (most aggreable). Tipi_warm and tipi_crit (ANES 2012); V162334 and V162339 (ANES 2016)

Conscientiousness: An additive index ranging from 0 (least conscientious) to 1 (most conscientious). Tipi_dep and tipi_disorg (ANES 2012); V162335 and V162340 (ANES 2016)

Emotional Stability: An additive index ranging from 0 (least emotionally stable) to 1 (most emotionally stable). Tipi_calm and tipi_anx (ANES 2012); V162336 and V162341 (ANES 2016)

Openness: An additive index ranging from 0 (least open) to 1 (most open). Tipi_open and tipi_conv (ANES 2012); V162337 and V162342 (ANES 2016)

BLUE COLLAR. An indicator variable from the ANES occupation data indicating respondent occupation type with values 0 (non-blue-collar worker) and 1 (blue-collar worker). Coded from dem_occpast (ANES 2012).

CENSUS REGIONS. An indicator variable with values 0 (not in census region [Northeast/Midwest/South/West]) and 1(in census region

[Northeast/Midwest/South/West]). Sample_region (ANES 2012); state (ANES 2016 Pilot); state (ANES 2016).

CLERICAL WORKER. An indicator variable from the ANES occupation data indicating respondent occupation type with values 0 (nonclerical worker) and 1 (clerical worker). Coded from dem_occpast (ANES 2012).

DEEP SOUTH. An indicator variable with values 0 (non-deep-South state) and 1 (deep South state). States included in the definition of "deep South" are Alabama, Georgia, Louisiana, Mississippi, and South Carolina. State (ANES 2012; ANES 2016 Pilot; ANES 2016).

ECONOMIC MOBILITY. A seven-category variable measuring how much easier or harder it is today to move up the economic ladder compared to twenty years ago. The variable ranges from 0 (a great deal easier) to 1 (a great deal harder). V162136x (ANES 2016); ladder (ANES 2016 Pilot).

EDUCATION. Respondents' highest level of education, rescaled to range from zero to one. Dem_edu (ANES 2012); educ (ANES 2016 Pilot); V161270 (ANES 2016); VCF0110 (ANES Cumulative).

EGALITARIANISM.

ANES 2012: An additive index constructed from responses to six survey items, with response options ranging from Agree Strongly to Disagree Strongly for each. The six survey items are: (1) society should make sure everyone has an equal opportunity to succeed (egal_equal); (2) we have gone too far in pushing equal rights in this country (egal_toofar); (3) one of the big problems in this country is that we don't give everyone an equal chance (egal_bigprob); (4) this country would be better off if we worried less about how equal people are (egal_worryless); (5) it is not really that big a problem if some people have more of a chance in life than others (egal_notbigprob); (6) if people were treated more equally in this country we would have many fewer problems (egal_fewerprobs). The index is rescaled to range from zero to one, with higher values indicating more egalitarian attitudes.

ANES 2016: An additive index constructed from responses to four survey items, with response options ranging from Agree Strongly to Disagree Strongly for each. The four survey items are: (1) our society should do whatever is necessary to make sure that everyone has an equal opportunity to succeed (V162243); (2) this country would be better off if we worried less about how equal people are (V162244); (3) it is not really that big a problem if some people have more of a chance in life than others (V162245); (4) if people were treated more equally in this country we would have many fewer problems (V162246). The index is rescaled to range from zero to one, with higher values indicating more egalitarian attitudes.

YouGov 2016: An additive index constructed from responses to three survey items, with response options ranging from Strongly Agree to Strongly Disagree for each. The three survey items are: (1) If people were treated more equally we would have many fewer problems; (2) society should do whatever necessary to make sure that everyone has an equal opportunity to succeed; (3) the country would be better off if we worried less about how equal people are. The index is rescaled to range from zero to one, with higher values indicating more egalitarian attitudes.

ETHNOCENTRISM. Difference between the white feeling thermometer rating and the average feeling thermometer rating for other racial groups (blacks, Hispanics, Asians). Ftcasi_white, ftcasi_black, ftcasi_hisp, ftcasi_asian (ANES 2012)

EVANGELICAL. An indicator variable with values 0 (not evangelical) and 1 (evangelical). Relig_7cat_x (ANES 2012).

GENDER. Indicator variable taking on a value of 1 (female) or 0 (male). Gender_respondent (ANES 2012); gender (ANES 2016 Pilot); V161342 (ANES 2016); VCF0104 (ANES Cumulative).

HOME OWNERSHIP. An indicator variable with values 0 (respondent (does not own their home) or 1 (respondent owns their home). Dem3_ownhome (ANES 2012); V161334 (ANES 2016).

IDEOLOGY. Respondents' self-placement on ideological scale ranging from 0 (extremely liberal) to 1(extremely conservative). Libcpo_self (ANES 2012); ideo5 (ANES 2016 Pilot); V161126 (ANES 2016); VCF0803 (ANES Cumulative).

INCOME. Annual household income of respondent, rescaled to range from zero to one. Inc_ingroup_pre (ANES 2012); faminc (ANES 2016 Pilot); V161361x (ANES 2016); VCF0114 (ANES Cumulative).

LABORER. An indicator variable from the ANES occupation data indicating respondent occupation type with values 0 (non-laborer) and 1 (laborer). Coded from dem_occpast (ANES 2012).

LIMITED GOVERNMENT SCALE.

ANES 2012: An additive index constructed from responses to three survey items. (1) government has become bigger because it has gotten involved in things people should do for themselves; (2) need a strong government to handle today's complex economic problems; and (3) the less government the better. The scale ranges from zero to one, with higher values indicating a stronger preference for limited government. The three variables that make up the scale are govrole_big, govrole_market, and govrole_lessmore.

YouGov 2016: Dummy variable indicating response to question of whether the less government the better (1), or there are more things government should be doing (0).

MIDDLE CLASS. An indicator variable with values 0 (respondent does not think of themselves as being a member of the middle class) or 1 (respondent thinks of themselves as being a member of the middle class). Dem_whichclass (ANES 2012); V162129 (ANES 2016).

MISTRUST OF EXPERTS. An index variable that is made up of the extent to which the respondent agrees or disagrees with two items: (1) I'd rather put my trust in the wisdom of ordinary people than the opinions of experts and intellectuals; and (2) ordinary people are perfectly capable of deciding for themselves what's true and what's not. The variable ranges from 0 (disagree strongly) to 1 (agree strongly). YouGov 2016.

NEGATIVE ECONOMIC EVALUATIONS. A five-category variable ranging from 0 ([The US economy/Personal finances] is much better off than it was a year ago) to 1 ([The US economy/Personal finances]) is much worse off than it was a year ago). Econ_ecpast_x and finance_finpast_x (ANES 2012); econnow (ANES 2016 Pilot); V162280 (ANES 2016); VCF0880 (ANES Cumulative).

PARTY IDENTIFICATION. Respondents' self-identified party identification, rescaled to range from 0 (Strong Democrat) to 1 (Strong Republican). Pid_x (ANES 2012); pid7 (ANES 2016 Pilot); V161158x (ANES 2016); VCF0301 (ANES Cumulative).

POLITICAL KNOWLEDGE. In 2012, this is measured as a scale consisting of factual questions about politics, including preknow_prestimes, preknow_sizedef, preknow_senterm, preknow_medicare, preknow_leastsp. In the ANES 2016 Pilot, the scale consists of items pk_spend, pk_sen, and pk_deficit. The 2016 ANES scale consists of items V161513, V161514, V161515, and V161516.

POPULATION PERCENTAGES. Percentage of population within a FIPS region that is [black/Latino/non-white/foreign-born]. 2012 ANES data merged with 2010 Census estimates using FIPS codes.

PROFESSIONAL. An indicator variable from the ANES occupation data indicating respondent occupation type with values 0 (non-professional worker) or 1 (professional worker). Coded from dem_occpast (ANES 2012).

PROTESTANT. An indicator variable with values 0 (not mainline Protestant) and 1 (mainline Protestant). Relig_7cat_x (ANES 2012); religpew (ANES 2016 Pilot); V161247a (ANES 2016).

RACIAL RESENTMENT. An additive index constructed from responses to four survey items, with response options ranging from Strongly Agree to Strongly Disagree for each. The survey items ask respondents if they agree/disagree that (1) blacks should work their way up without any special favors; (2) generations of slavery and discrimination make it difficult for blacks to work their way out of the lower class; (3) blacks have gotten less than they deserve; (4) black must try harder to get ahead. The index is scaled to range from 0 (least resentful) to 1 (most resentful).

ANES 2012: resent_workway, resent_slavery, resent_deserve, resent_try
ANES 2016 Pilot: rr1, rr2, rr3, rr4
ANES 2016: V162211, V162212, V162213, V162214

RURAL. An indicator variable with values 0 (non-rural) and 1 (rural) based on USDA rural–urban continuum codes matched with ANES 2012 FIPS codes.

SEMI-SKILLED WORKER. An indicator variable from the ANES occupation data indicating respondent occupation type with values 0 (non-semi-skilled worker) and 1 (semi-skilled worker). Coded from dem_occpast (ANES 2012).

SOCIAL DOMINANCE ORIENTATION. An additive index ranging from 0 (lowest social dominance orientation) to 1 (highest social dominance orientation). Survey items included in the index ask respondent to indicate the extent to which they agree with the following: (1) we should try to get ahead by any means necessary;

(2) sometimes war is necessary to put other nations in their place; (3) winning is more important than how the game is played; (4) inferior groups should stay in their place. SSI 2013.

SOUTH. An indicator variable with values 0 (non-southern state) and 1 (southern state). States included in the definition of "southern" are South Carolina, Mississippi, Florida, Alabama, Georgia, Louisiana, Texas, Virginia, Arkansas, Tennessee, and North Carolina. State (ANES 2012; ANES 2016 Pilot; ANES 2016); VCF0112 (ANES Cumulative).

STEREOTYPE INDEX. Average difference between respondents' stereotype endorsements for whites and blacks on two of three seven-point scales: (1) Hardworking-Lazy, (2) Intelligent-Unintelligent (ANES 2012), and (3) Peaceful-Violent (ANES 2016 Pilot and ANES 2016). Variable ranges from zero to one.

ANES 2012: stype_hwkblack, stype_hwkwhite, stype_intblack, stype_intwhite

ANES 2016 Pilot: lazyb, lazyw, violentb, violentw

ANES 2016: V162345, V162346, V162349, V162350

THERMOMETER RATINGS. A 101-point rating rescaled to range from zero (coldest) to one (warmest).

Black Feeling Thermometer: ftcasi_black (ANES 2012); ftblack (ANES 2016 Pilot); V162312 (ANES 2016); VCF0206 (ANES Cumulative); group_therm_blacks_w2 (YouGov 2016)

Hispanic Feeling Thermometer: ftcasi_hisp (ANES 2012); fthispanic (ANES 2016 Pilot); V162311 (ANES 2016); VCF0217 (ANES Cumulative)

Asian Feeling Thermometer: ftcasi_asian (ANES 2012); V162310 (ANES 2016); VCF0227 (ANES Cumulative)

Muslim Feeling Thermometer: ftgr_muslim (ANES 2012) ftmuslim (ANES 2016 Pilot); V162106 (ANES 2016)

UNEMPLOYED. Indicator variable for which 1 represents "unemployed" and 0 represents "not unemployed." Dem_empstatus_ initial (ANES 2012); employ (ANES 2016 Pilot); V161276x (ANES 2016); VCF0116 (ANES Cumulative).

UNION MEMBERSHIP. An indicator variable with values 0 (nobody in household is a member of a union) or 1 (somebody in household is a member of a union). Dem_unionhh (ANES 2012); V161302 (ANES 2016).

WHITE GUILT. An additive index ranging from 0 (least white guilt) to 1 (most white guilt). Survey items included in the index asked respondents to indicate how often they feel each of the following: (1) guilty about the benefits and privileges that you receive as a white American; (2) guilty about the past and present social inequality of black Americans; (3) guilty about social inequality between white and black Americans; and (4) guilty because you are white. SSI 2013.

WHITE PRIVILEGE. An additive index ranging from 0 (least white privilege) to 1 (most white privilege). Survey items included in the index asked respondents to indicate the extent to which they agree with each of the following: (1) your status as a white person grants you unearned privileges in today's society; (2) white people have benefits or privileges due to their race; (3) having white skin in the United States opens doors for whites during their everyday lives; (4) having white skin is an asset to you in your everyday life; and (5) white Americans have certain advantages that minorities do not have in this society. SSI 2013.

WORKING CLASS. An indicator variable with values 0 (respondent does not think of themselves as being a member of the working class) or 1 (respondent thinks of themselves as being a member of the working class). Dem_whichclass (ANES 2012); V162129 (ANES 2016).

Dependent Variables

2012 VOTE CHOICE. An indicator variable with values 0 (voted Romney in 2012 election) or 1 (voted Obama in 2012 election). Presvote2012_x (ANES 2012).

2016 VOTE CHOICE. An indicator variable with values 0 (voted Clinton in 2016 election) or 1 (voted Trump in the 2016 election).

AID TO BLACKS. A 7-category variable ranging from 0 (Blacks should help themselves) to 1 (Government should help blacks). Aidblack_self (ANES 2012); V161198 (ANES 2016).

ATTITUDES TOWARD AFFIRMATIVE ACTION.

University: A 7-category variable ranging from 0 (favor university affirmative action a great deal) to 1 (oppose university affirmative action a great deal). aa_uni_x (ANES 2012); V161204x (ANES 2016).

Workplace: A 7-category variable ranging from 0 (favor workplace affirmative action a great deal) to 1 (oppose workplace affirmative action a great deal). aa_work_x (ANES 2012).

Affirmative Action – Blacks: A 7-category variable ranging from 0 (favor affirmative action for blacks a great deal) to 1 (oppose affirmative action for blacks a great deal). aa1 (ANES 2016 Pilot).

Affirmative Action – Hispanics: A 7-category variable ranging from 0 (favor affirmative action for Hispanics a great deal) to 1 (oppose affirmative action for Hispanics a great deal). aa2 (ANES 2016 Pilot).

Affirmative Action – Minorities: A 7-category variable ranging from 0 (favor affirmative action for underrepresented minorities a great deal) to 1 (oppose affirmative action for underrepresented minorities a great deal). aa3 (ANES 2016 Pilot).

ATTITUDES TOWARD LEGACY ADMISSIONS. A variable ranging from 0 (Extremely disapprove of legacy admissions) to 1 (Extremely approve of legacy admissions). SSI 2014.

ATTITUDES TOWARD IMMIGRATION.

Decrease number of immigrants: A variable ranging from 0 (immigration levels should be increased a lot) to 1 (immigration levels should be decreased a lot). Immigpo_level (ANES 2012); immig_number (ANES 2016 Pilot); V161257 (ANES 2016)

Importance of immigration level issue: A five-category variable ranging from 0 (immigration level issues is not at all important) to 1 (immigration level is extremely important).

Increase federal spending on tightening border security: A variable ranging from 0 (spending on tightening border security should be cut out entirely) to 1 (spending on tightening border security should be increased a great deal).

Support law checking immigration status: A three-category variable ranging from 0 (oppose law that requires immigration status checks) to 1 (favor law that requires immigration status checks), with the midpoint indicating the respondent neither favors nor opposes the law. Immig_checks (ANES 2012).

Illegal immigrant feeling thermometer: A 101-point rating rescaled to range from zero (coldest) to one (warmest). Ftcasi_illegal (ANES 2012); V162313 (ANES 2016)

Support changing Constitution so that children of unauthorized immigrants do not get citizenship if born in United States: A seven-category variable ranging from 0 (Oppose a great deal) to 1 (Support a great deal). birthright_a (ANES 2016 Pilot); V161193 (ANES 2016)

Oppose children of unauthorized immigrants automatically getting citizenship if born in the United States: A seven-category variable ranging from 0 (Favor a great deal) to 1 (Oppose a great deal). birthright_b (ANES 2016 Pilot).

Favor sending back children brought illegally. A seven-category variable ranging from 0 (favor a great deal allowing children to stay) to 1 (favor a great deal sending children back) that measures response to the question, "What should happen to immigrants who were brought to the US illegally as children and have lived here for at least 10 years and graduated high school here?" V161195x (ANES 2016).

Favor building a wall along the border with Mexico. A seven-category variable ranging from 0 (oppose a great deal) to 1 (favor a great deal) that measures response to the question, "Do you favor, oppose, or neither favor nor oppose building a wall on the US border with Mexico?" V161196x (ANES 2016).

Immigrants make Americans more open to new ideas and culture: A four-category variable ranging from 0 (Strongly agree) to 1 (Strong disagree). KN 2010.

Immigrants change American culture and values: A five-category variable ranging from 0 (Not likely at all) to 1 (Extremely likely). SSI 2013.

Immigration is generally bad for the United States: A seven-category variable ranging from 0 (Extremely good) to 1 (Extremely bad). Immig_legal (ANES 2016 Pilot).

Immigrants take jobs away from American citizens: A variable ranging from 0 (Strongly disagree) to 1 (Strongly agree). Immigpo_jobs (ANES 2012); V162158 (ANES 2016).

Concern about changing ethnic makeup of the United States: A variable ranging from 0 (Not at all worried) to 1 (Very/Extremely worried). KN 2010, SSI 2013.

Immigrants are generally good for America's economy. A five-category variable ranging from 0 (Agree strongly) to 1 (Disagree strongly). V162268 (ANES 2016).

Immigrants increase crime rates in the United States. A five-category variable ranging from 0 (Disagree strongly) to 1 (Agree strongly). V162270 (ANES 2016).

America's culture is generally harmed by immigrants. A five-category variable ranging from 0 (Disagree strongly) to 1 (Agree strongly). V162269 (ANES 2016).

ATTITUDES TOWARD SOCIAL PROGRAMS.

Social Security: A three-category variable ranging from 0 (social security spending should be decreased) to 1 (social security spending should be increased), with the midpoint indicating spending on social security should be kept the same. Fedspend_ss (ANES 2012); V161205 (ANES 2016). On the SSI 2013 survey, this variable is an eight-category variable ranging from 0 (spending should be cut out entirely) to 1 (spending should be increased a great deal).

Medicare: A seven-category variable ranging from 0 (oppose expanding Medicare program a great deal) to 1 (Support expanding Medicare program a great deal).

Welfare: A three-category variable ranging from 0 (welfare spending should be decreased) to 1 (welfare spending should be increased), with the midpoint indicating spending on welfare should be kept the same. Fedspend_welfare (ANES 2012); V161209 (ANES 2016). On the SSI 2013 survey, this variable is a seven-category variable ranging from 0 (oppose welfare programs a great deal) to 1 (support welfare programs a great deal).

Medicaid: A seven-category variable ranging from 0 (oppose Medicaid program a great deal) to 1 (support Medicaid program a great deal).

CIVIL RIGHTS LEADERS ARE PUSHING TOO FAST. A three-category variable with values 0 (civil rights leaders are moving too slowly), .5 (civil rights leaders are moving at the right speed), or 1 (civil rights leaders are moving too fast). VCF0814 (ANES Cumulative).

FEDERAL SPENDING ON [BLACKS/HISPANICS/ASIANS/ WHITES]. An eight-category variable ranging from 0 (spending on the group should be cut out entirely) to 1 (spending on the group should be increased a great deal).

GOVERNMENT HELP TO WHITES. A five-category variable ranging from 0 (federal government should be doing nothing at all to help whites) to 1 (federal government should be doing a great deal to help whites).

LIMIT IMPORTS. A three-category variable ranging from 0 (oppose placing limits on imports) to 1 (favor placing limits on imports), with the midpoint indicating that the respondent hasn't thought much about this issue. Imports_limit (ANES 2012); V162152 (ANES 2016).

OBAMA FAVORS BLACKS OVER WHITES. An indicator variable with values 0 (Obama does not favor whites over blacks) of 1 (Obama favors whites over blacks). Nonmain_bias (ANES 2012).

OPPOSE FREE TRADE AGREEMENTS. A seven-category variable ranging from 0 (favor a great deal the United States making free trade agreements with other countries) to 1 (oppose a great deal the United States making free trade agreements with other countries). V162176x (ANES 2016).

OPPOSE INCREASING TRADE. A three-category variable ranging from 0 (increasing trade with other countries is bad) to 1 (increasing trade with other countries is good). V162175 (ANES 2016).

OPPOSE OUTSOURCING. A five-category variable ranging from 0 (government should encourage outsourcing a great deal) to 1 (government should discourage outsourcing a great deal). outsoruce_ enc_x (ANES 2012); V162177 (ANES 2016).

OPPOSITION TO LATINO PRESIDENT. A five-category variable indicating the extent to which the idea of a Latino president makes the respondent pleased or not pleased. The variable ranges from 0 (extremely pleased) to 1 (not at all pleased). Lpres_pleased (ANES 2016 Pilot).

PERCEPTIONS OF DISCRIMINATION.

Discrimination against Blacks. A five-category variable ranging from 0 (none at all) to 1 (a great deal) that measures respondents' perceptions of how much discrimination blacks face in the United States today. Discrim_blacks (ANES 2012); Disc_b (ANES 2016 Pilot); V162357 (ANES 2016).

Discrimination against Hispanics. A five-category variable ranging from 0 (none at all) to 1 (a great deal) that measures respondents' perceptions of how much discrimination Hispanics face in the United States today. Discrim_hispanics (ANES 2012); Disc_h (ANES 2016 Pilot); V162358 (ANES 2016).

Discrimination against Whites. A five-category variable ranging from 0 (none at all) to 1 (a great deal) that measures respondents' perceptions of how much discrimination whites face in the United States today. Discrim_whites (ANES 2012); Disc_w (ANES 2016 Pilot); V162360 (ANES 2016).

POLITICAL INFLUENCE.

White Political Influence. A three-category variable ranging from 0 (whites have too much influence) to 1 (whites have too little influence). Racecasi_infwhite (ANES 2012); V162322 (ANES 2016).

Black Political Influence. A three-category variable ranging from 0 (blacks have too much influence) to 1 (blacks have too little influence). Racecasi_infblacks (ANES 2012); V162323 (ANES 2016).

Hispanic Political Influence. A three-category variable ranging from 0 (Hispanics have too much influence) to 1 (Hispanics have too little influence). Racecasi_infhips (ANES 2012); V162324 (ANES 2016).

Asian Political Influence. A three-category variable ranging from 0 (Asians have too much influence) to 1 (Asians have too little influence). V162325 (ANES 2016).

POLITICAL PARTICIPATION. An additive index scaled to range from 0 to 1, with higher values indicating higher levels of political participation. Survey items in the index asked respondents (1) the likelihood they would attend a meeting to talk about political or social concerns (meet, ANES 2016 Pilot; V162011, ANES 2016); (2) likelihood they would give money to an organization concerned with political or social issues (givefut, ANES 2016 Pilot; V162018d, ANES 2016); (3) likelihood they would distribute information or advertisements support a political or social issue (info, ANES 2016

Pilot;); (4) whether they had joined in a protest march, rally, or demonstration during the past four years (march, ANES 2016 Pilot; V162018a); (5) whether they had worn a campaign button, put a campaign sticker on their car, or placed a campaign sign in their yard (sign, ANES 2016 Pilot; V162012, ANES 2016); and (6) whether they had given money to any candidate during the past twelve months (give12mo, ANES 2016 Pilot; V162014, ANES 2016).

RACIAL ALIENATION. An index measure consisting of three items: (1) American society owes [White/Black/Hispanic] people a better chance in life than we currently have; (2) American society has provided [White/Black/Hispanic] people a fair opportunity to get ahead in life; and (3) American society just hasn't dealt fairly with [White/Black/Hispanic] people. For each item, respondents indicate the extent to which they agree on a scale ranging from Strongly Disagree to Strongly Agree. The items are indexed to create a measure of racial alienation in which higher values indicate higher levels of perceived alienation. SSI 2013.

SUPPORT FOR ISOLATIONISM. A three-category variable ranging from 0 (county would not be better off if we just stayed home) to 1 (county would be better off if we just stayed home. Usworld_stay (ANES 2012); V161153 (ANES 2016)

SUPPORT FOR WHITE HISTORY MONTH. A seven-category variable ranging from 0 (oppose a great deal) to 1 (support a great deal). The variable measures responses to the question, "To what extent would you support or oppose Congress passing a law which would designate one month of the year as White History Month?"

TEA PARTY SUPPORT. A seven-category variable ranging from 0 (strongly oppose the Tea Party) to 1 (strongly support the Tea Party). Tea_supp_x (ANES 2012).

THERMOMETER RATINGS. A 101-point rating rescaled to range from zero (coldest) to one (warmest).

Donald Trump Feeling Thermometer: fttrump (ANES 2016 Pilot); V161087 (ANES 2016)
Hillary Clinton Feeling Thermometer: fthrc (ANES 2016 Pilot); V161086 (ANES 2016)
Bernie Sanders Feeling Thermometer: ftsanders (ANES 2016 Pilot)
Ted Cruz Feeling Thermometer: ftcruz (ANES 2016 Pilot)

Patrick Buchanan Feeling Thermometer: VCF0472 (ANES Cumulative)

George Wallace Feeling Thermometer: VCF0439 (ANES Cumulative)

Black Feeling Thermometer. VCF0206 (ANES Cumulative); ftcasi_black (ANES 2012)

Richard Nixon Feeling Thermometer. VCF0442 (ANES Cumulative)

Hubert Humphrey Feeling Thermometer. VCF0432 (ANES Cumulative)

George McGovern Feeling Thermometer. VCF0435 (ANES Cumulative)

Jimmy Carter Feeling Thermometer. VCF0446 (ANES Cumulative)

Gerald Ford Feeling Thermometer. VCF0441 (ANES Cumulative)

Ross Perot Feeling Thermometer. VCF0449 (ANES Cumulative)

George H.W. Bush Feeling Thermometer. VCF0438 (ANES Cumulative)

Bill Clinton Feeling Thermometer. VCF0447 (ANES Cumulative)

Robert Dole Feeling Thermometer. VCF0445 (ANES Cumulative)

George W. Bush Feeling Thermometer. VCF0426 (ANES Cumulative)

Al Gore Feeling Thermometer. VCF0448 (ANES Cumulative)

Tea Party Feeling Thermometer. ftgr_tea (ANES 2012); V162109 (ANES 2016)

TRUMP OVER OTHERS IN PRIMARY. An indicator variable with values 0 (did not vote for Trump in Republican primary) and 1 (voted for Trump in Republican primary). Repcand (ANES 2016 Pilot)

WHITE CONSCIOUSNESS. An additive index comprised of the white identity variable(s) as well as perceived likelihood that many whites are unable to find jobs because employers are hiring minorities (whitejob, ANES 2016 Pilot; V162317, ANES 2016) and the importance of whites working together to change laws that are unfair to whites (whitework, ANES 2016 Pilot; V162316, ANES 2016). Rescaled to range from 0 (lowest white consciousness) to 1 (highest white consciousness).

WHITE IDENTITY. A five-category variable ranging from 0 (being white is not at all important to my identity) to 1 (being white is extremely important to my identity). Ident_whiteid (ANES 2012); race_ident (ANES 2016 Pilot); V162327 (ANES 2016).

YouGov 2016: An additive index comprised of three survey items. The three items measure importance of white identity, white pride, and white commonality. Item is rescaled to range from 0 to 1.

WHITE LINKED FATE. A five-category variable ranging from 0 (what happens to other white people has no effect at all on my life) to 1 (what happens to other white people affects my life a lot). Link_white and link_whiteamt (ANES 2012).

ZERO-SUM ECONOMIC COMPETITION. A four-category variable ranging from 0 (strongly disagree that the more good jobs for blacks/Hispanics, the fewer good jobs for members of other groups) to 1 (strongly agree that the more good jobs for blacks/Hispanics, the fewer good jobs for members of other groups).

ZERO-SUM POLITICAL COMPETITION. A four-category variable ranging from 0 (strongly disagree that the more influence blacks/Hispanics have in politics, the less influence members of other groups have) to 1 (strongly agree that the more influence blacks/Hispanics have in politics, the less influence members of other groups have). Racecasi_infblacks and racecasi_infhisp (ANES 2012); V162323 and V162324 (ANES 2016).

NOTES

Chapter 1   The New American Minority

1 Alba, Rumbaut, and Marotz (2005) found that as of the year 2000, roughly half of Americans believed that whites had already become a numerical minority. More information about population projections from the U.S. Census are available at www.census.gov/programs-surveys/popproj.html.

2 Sonia Sotomayor is the first US Supreme Court Justice of Hispanic heritage and the first Latina appointed to the court.

3 To be clear, despite reaching unprecedented levels of racial and ethnic diversity, this Congress as a whole was still disproportionately white compared to the US population.

4 Throughout this book, by white Americans, I mean non-Hispanic whites in the United States.

5 Jacquellena Carrero. 2013. "Texas State Legislators Seek to Limit Ethnic History Studies in College Requirements." *NBC Latino*. www.nbclatino.com/2013/03/15/texas?state?legislators?seek?to?limit?ethnic?history?in?college?requirements/. Colleen Flaherty. 2017. "White Is the Word." *Inside Higher Ed*. https://insidehighered.com/news/2017/01/18/arizona?lawmakers?failed?ban?divisive?college?courses?highlights?new?criticism?white%0AProposed.

6 An effort to pass legislation requiring presidential candidates to produce birth certificates rose after many politicians and citizens questioned whether Barack Obama was born in the United States. This skepticism grew, eventually becoming known as "the birther movement" (Jardina and Traugott in press).

7 Robert P. Jones, Daniel Cox, Betsy Cooper, and Rachel Lienesch. 2015. *Anxiety, Nostalgia, and Mistrust: Findings from the 2015 American Values Survey*. Washington DC: Public Religion Research Institute. www.prri.org/research/survey-anxiety-nostalgia-and-mistrust-findings-from-the-2015-american-values-survey/.

8 By prejudice, I mean negative affective feelings that whites might possess toward members of other racial or ethnic groups.

9 Others, like Bierstedt (1948), made similar observations. Bierstedt wrote that, "nowhere is there a similar or even comparable concern for majorities and majority groups" (p. 700).

10 Over a decade ago, Swain and Nieli (2003) wrote about what they saw as the inevitable rise and mainstreaming of white nationalism as a consequence of immigration.

11 The term "alt-right" is short for "alternative right." An exposé of prominent individuals who identify with the alt-right and white nationalism was featured in the December 10, 2016 *New York Times* at www.nytimes.com/2016/12/10/us/alt-right-national-socialist-movement-white-supremacy.html.

12 During the 2016 presidential election, Donald Trump was endorsed by David Duke, former grand wizard of the Ku Klux Klan.

13 This act was the beginning of what Omni and Winant describe as a long history of national efforts to enact racial policy with the main objective, they argue, of repression and exclusion (1986, p. 75).

14 In the two decades prior, between approximately 800,000 and one million Irish immigrated to the United States in order to take advantage of the shortage of wage laborers in manufacturing. Most of these immigrants in this earlier period, however, were Presbyterian or Anglican, and most were not poor (Ignatiev 1995).

15 Animosity was also likely fueled by the fact that these immigrants often worked with and lived in the same neighborhoods as blacks in the United States.

16 The movement began as a secret society in which members, when asked about the movement, were instructed to say "I know nothing" or "I don't know," giving the party its appellation.

17 Chin (1996) describes how some scholars and commentators viewed the 1965 Act as a Trojan Horse, and a key example of unintended consequences. Many commentators, he explains, argue that the legislation never would have passed had Congress, at the time, known that the majority of the post-1965 immigrants would be non-white. Chin disagrees, however, and argues that many members of Congress knew more Asians would immigrate as a result of the law but supported the idea that race should no longer be a factor in the country's immigration laws.

18 A dominant group is one which possesses a disproportionate share of a society's privileges, resources, and power (Knowles and Peng 2005).

19 Jackman (1994) provides an elegant overview of the different traditions in the study of group conflict and group prejudice. She points out that while social psychologists focused on identity and prejudice, sociologists focused more on realistic conflict.

20 The notion that the progress of the Civil Rights movement was in part a product of a significant sense of racial sympathy among whites is advanced by Kinder and Sanders (1996), but it is not an argument universally accepted by scholars. We might also consider the fact that this sympathy was rather limited, and that white hostility and indifference to blacks is what gave rise to black riots in the first place.

Chapter 2 Making the Invisible Visible

1 Bobo (2004) is a particularly strong advocate of adopting a sociological view of race relations that considers how racial hierarchies shape whites' racial attitudes. He argues that whites' racial attitudes today can be characterized by what he calls laissez-faire racism. He argues that this racism is a product of the current era, in which whites persistently and negatively stereotype blacks, blame blacks for the racial gap in socioeconomic status between blacks and whites, and resist efforts to ameliorate structural inequality.

2 It is also the "normalization" of dominant group identities that make them understudied in the first place (Mannheim 2013).

3 Citrin and Sears (2014) make a similar distinction, calling what I refer to as "intergroup oriented" theories part of the "politicized group consciousness

paradigm" (p. 33), which they distinguish from their symbolic politics approach. They place the latter approach under the umbrella of a "black exceptionalism" paradigm. Sears and Savalei (2006) parse these theories somewhat differently, comparing "group hierarchy" theories to the symbolic politics approach. They place social dominance orientation under the same umbrella as social identity theory and other group theories, arguing that these approaches share the common claim that a static racial hierarchy shapes race relations in the United States.

4   See Altemeyer (1981) and Duckitt (1992) for a discussion of problems with the empirical evidence for and psychometric properties of Adorno et al.'s (1950) original measure of authoritarianism.

5   There has been some push to consider both authoritarianism and SDO, not as personality dimensions, but instead as attitudes or ideological belief dimensions (Duckitt 2001, 2003). In a 1994 article, however, Sidanius and colleagues refer to SDO as a "personality variable" and an "individual-difference variable" (Pratto et al. 1994).

6   Despite SDO and authoritarianism predicting similar attitudes and behaviors, the two scales seem to operate independently and are only weakly correlated with one another (Altemeyer 1998). Moreover, according to Duckitt (2003), authoritarianism and SDO seem to fall onto two orthogonal dimensions. The authoritarianism dimension corresponds to social conservatism, collectivism and traditionalism (as opposed to personal freedom, individualism, and openness). The SDO dimension corresponds to economic conservatism, support for inequality, and power distance (as opposed to social welfare, egalitarianism, and humanitarianism).

7   There are some conceptual differences between these constructs, but they are often measured using the same or similar survey items, and their general theoretical approaches are complementary.

8   As I described in Chapter 1, symbolic racism arguably dominates our understanding of race relations between blacks and whites in the United States today. As I also mentioned, some scholars are critical of this framework. While they generally agree that white prejudice toward blacks lingers in American society, they argue that racial resentment entangles conservative principles, like individualism, with racial prejudice (Feldman and Huddy 2005; Sniderman and Tetlock 1986; Tetlock 1994). With this critique in mind, one alternative approach adopted by many racial attitudes scholars is to substitute measures of racial resentment with measures of whites' subscription to negative stereotypes about blacks. Usually, when such measures are employed on public opinion surveys, they ask whites to assess whites and blacks, on average, on dimensions like hardworking versus lazy, intelligent versus unintelligent, and trustworthy versus untrustworthy. To be clear, while these items surely capture the relatively negative attitudes whites may possess toward blacks, relative to their own group, they are not especially grounded in a theoretical framework. We can consider them simply as another set of beliefs whites may possess about blacks, likely acquired through socialization.

9   There is also some evidence that in the Obama era, overt racism may have become more politically relevant (Tesler 2012a).

10 Empirical evidence has supported the notion that white attitudes toward blacks, compared to other minority groups, are unique. For instance, Bobo and Hutchings (1996) find that whites were more likely to view blacks as competitive threats compared to Hispanics or Asians.

11 See also Turner's (1985) self-categorization theory.

12 This argument is in keeping with claims by Key (1949), Blalock (1967), and Giles and Evans (1985), who argue that whites residing in areas with greater

numbers of blacks feel threatened politically and economically, and subsequently express greater out-group antipathy.

13 Allport (1954) speculated that minority groups would develop a strong sense of racial solidarity as a way to cope with prejudice. He wrote that "Misery finds balm through the closer association of people who are miserable for the same reason. Threats drive them to seek protective unity within their common membership" (p. 148).

14 Specifically, this work posits that whites residing in areas with large black populations likely feel especially threatened economically or politically by blacks; this threat increases the salience of white identity, which then ought to be associated with prejudice and political preferences antagonistic to blacks (Blalock 1967; Key 1949; Taylor 1998). Most of this work, however, excludes white identity from its empirical tests and instead directly examines the relationship between the racial composition of neighborhoods in which whites reside and their levels of prejudice or their political preferences, largely overlooking the moderating role of identity.

15 Many of the intergroup oriented studies sidestep examining white racial identity, perhaps in part because appropriate measures were not historically included on major public opinion surveys. Instead, these theories were applied using measures of a sense of group position (Bobo 1999), or on whites' sense of group-interest, self-interest, or collective racial threat (see Bobo and Hutchings (1996) and Bobo and Johnson (2000) for exceptions).

16 For exceptions, see Bush(2004); Croll (2007); Hartmann, Gerteis, and Croll (2009); Helms (1990).

17 In the article cited here, Sears and Kinder are challenging work by Bobo (1983), who argued that group interests – as opposed to self-interest or symbolic racism – were what best account for whites' opposition to busing.

18 Even work more clearly situated in the domain of social identity theory focused on out-group animus, attending to the idea that racial stereotypes were a consequence of the normal social categorization processes (Pettigrew 1979).

19 Part of the difference in how we treat white identity versus black identity is surely normative. White identity was viewed as part of the way in which whites discriminated against people of color. Indeed, my own claims here are in keeping with this perspective, with important nuances. But the expectation for blacks is that racial identity is a preservation tactic, one that helps their group fight oppression and seek equality, and not as a way to express derogation.

20 To be clear, the question of whether black racial pride is the same coin as black hostility to out-groups is in fact at the center of Sniderman and Piazza's (2002) book. They find, however, that generally the two attitudes are not interchangeable.

21 Sometimes salience is conceived of as the readiness to adopt an identity, but here, by salience, I mean the relevance of an identity to a given situation (Huddy 2013).

22 See Huddy (2003) for a fuller discussion of these different approaches.

23 The exact direction of the relationship between deprivation, group identity, and political behavior is difficult to untangle. Some studies have found that identity moderates the political consequences of deprivation, such that more strongly identifying group members are more likely to alter their political preferences or behavior in response to feelings of deprivation (Hinkle et al. 1996). Other work, however, finds that the strength of group identification can actually affect feelings of deprivation (Gurin and Townsend 1986). For example, Hutchings et al. (2011) found that whites who preferred an identification with their racial group were more likely to view relations with blacks,

Latinos and Asians in zero-sum terms. Thus, the relationship between identity and shared grievances may be bi-directional (Simon and Klandermans 2001).

24 Sears and Valentino (1997) make a compelling argument that major political events can be especially instrumental with respect to political socialization.

25 Klinkner and Smith (1999) might argue that many of these same events are moments in time when serious progress toward racial equality was made. But of course, those same efforts toward equality ought to trigger a backlash among whites who do not want to see a change in the racial hierarchy.

26 See McDermott and Samson (2005) for a comprehensive review.

27 Yet some of these same scholars are revising their understanding of whiteness as invisible in light of the shrinking size of the white population and the increased presence of non-whites in the United States (Frankenberg 2001).

28 The particulars of Helms' theory and scale have been subject to noteworthy debate and criticism (Leach, Behrens, and Lafleur 2002; Rowe, Bennett, and Atkinson 1994).

29 Some work responding to Helms has discussed the development of "white racial consciousness" (LaFleur, Rowe, and Leach 2002; Leach, Behrens, and Lafleur 2002; Rowe, Bennett, and Atkinson 1994). These scholars do not define consciousness in a politicized sense (Miller et al. 1981), however. Instead, they define consciousness as the common constellation of attitudes whites hold about racial out-group members.

Chapter 3   The Measurement and Meaning of Group Ties

1 See Gleason (1983) for a comprehensive history of the term identity.

2 See Abdelal et al. (2001) and Fearon (1999) for a quantification of work done on identity in the social sciences over time.

3 See Dawson (2009) for a strong critique of Brubaker and Cooper's (2000) characterization of the identity literature, particularly that on racial identity and racial hierarchies in the United States.

4 See Abdelal et al. (2009) for a review of methods for measuring identity.

5 Knowles and Peng (2005) argue that the social sensitivity of race makes many whites reluctant to express a racial identity. They create an implicit measure of identity as a way to circumvent this social desirability problem, while still capturing the extent to which whiteness is important to individuals' self-concepts. It is important to note, however, that work on implicit and explicit attitudes has argued that we should not necessarily view implicit attitudes as revealing individuals "true" or latent preferences, nor are implicit attitudes necessarily linked to explicit preferences or behavior (Ditonto, Lau, and Sears 2013; Kalmoe and Piston 2013). Thus, we should not necessarily treat implicit measures as a similar but more optimal way to measure racial identity.

6 Special thanks go to Vincent Hutchings, Robert Mickey, and the late Hanes Walton, Jr. at the University of Michigan for allowing me to use these data.

7 I applied to have these items included on the survey through the ANES Online Commons.

8 SSI's panel closely matches the characteristics of the larger white, adult, American citizen population based on 2010 Census data. For more information on this sampling approach see Berrens et al. (2003) and Best et al. (2001).

9 The re-interview rate does not reflect a problem with attrition, but was simply a decision about how many respondents to re-interview given cost constraints.

10 In a few instances throughout the text, I will also draw from other years of the ANES Time Series, and other sources of data. I describe the attributes of those sources at the time they are presented in the text.

11 Demographic characteristics of each dataset are provided in Online Appendix 3A.

12 See most University of Michigan graduates for an exception.

13 Note that this attribute of identity is often referred to as salience. Within the study of identity, however, the term salience can mean either the strength and significance of a group identity, or it can refer to the strength of the relationship between identity and political behavior or preferences due to the relevance and accessibility of that identity (Huddy 2013). For the purpose of clarity, when using the term salience, I mean in the latter sense.

14 The exact wording used by Hooper (1976) is as follows: "Is it important to you to think of yourself as a [group name placed here]?"

15 Some work has conceptualized this aspect as a sense of emotional closeness. One of the measures previously used to proximate group identity on opinion surveys like the ANES was a measure of group closeness. Conceptualizing group cohesion in this way, however, has a significant shortcoming: it does not distinguish between group identity and sympathy toward or liking of a particular group (Conover 1984; Herring, Jankowski, and Brown 1999). Huddy points out that the way this question has been previously asked only adds to its limitations (Huddy 2013). She notes that on the ANES, the closeness question asks respondents to choose, from a list, the groups toward which they feel close. If a respondent chooses more than one group, they are asked toward which group they feel closest. While this approach allows researchers to capture some degree of strength of identification, it otherwise makes only crude distinctions between "close" and "closest." To this list of critiques, I add that the closeness measure also conflates closeness with salience. An individual might feel attached, for instance, both to their racial group and to their religious group. But because they are forced to pick a single identity within the context of the survey, they might select the one that feels most accessible or relevant in that particular moment, even if both have the potential to significantly influence political attitudes and behavior.

16 It is worth noting that one of the most central variables in the study of public opinion, party identification, is measured with a single item, although see Huddy and Khatib (2007) for a critique of this practice.

17 As an additional test of what is lost by using only the single-item measure of identity, I compare, in Online Appendix 3J, the effect of white identity measured with the one item, to the effect when measured with the three items across four dependent variables, using the 2016 YouGov data. As one would expect, the three-item measure is more strongly and significantly associated with the variables of interest. Nevertheless, the direction and substantive effect of white identity when using the single-item measure is the same.

18 I proposed these items via the ANES Online Commons, and they were selected for inclusion on the 2016 ANES Pilot and 2016 ANES Time Series study by the principal investigators and board of the ANES.

19 Ideally, a measure of consciousness would include the three identity items combined with the two additional consciousness items. The YouGov 2016 survey is the only dataset analyzed throughout this text that includes all five items. Most of the time, consciousness is measured with the single racial importance identity item combined with the two consciousness items to form a three-item measure.

20 The distribution for the white identity and white consciousness items in the 2016 ANES Time Series often departs from what we observe in the previous datasets. Investigating the reasons for this shift is beyond the scope of the work here, but my own preliminary analysis suggests that the attention that race and white identity received around the election produced some social

desirability effects when it came to respondents answering these particular survey questions immediately after the election. We shall see, however, in the chapters to come, that while levels of white racial solidarity look a bit different in the 2016 ANES, the effect of both identity and consciousness on political preferences is nevertheless consistent with other sources of evidence.

21 There are fewer response options provided for the racial importance item on the LACSS than would be preferred given standard survey practices today. The fewer options truncate responses, which very likely explains why there are more whites scoring in the highest two categories of identity on the LACSS compared to the ANES. The rest of the distribution is as follows: "not at all important" (26 percent), "not very important" (30 percent).

22 My intention is not to claim definitively that levels of white identity have not fluctuated markedly since the 1990s. That might be true, but the racial and ethnic diversity and racial tensions present in LA in the 1990s might also have simply served as a bellwether for the levels of racial identity we can observe in more recent years at the national level. Unfortunately, a lacuna of public opinion data on the topic makes it difficult to determine whether levels of racial identity elsewhere or nationally mirrored those found among whites in LA in the 1990s.

23 Results for the importance item across datasets and for both groups are presented in Online Appendix 3B.

24 It is worth noting that the distribution of the collective orientation item is somewhat lower among the representative samples, regardless of mode, compared to the opt-in surveys. Even the more conservative figures, however, indicate that support for whites working together to change laws unfair to their group is prevalent.

25 The distribution of consciousness across each dataset in which it is available is presented in Online Appendix 3D. The distribution is fairly similar across datasets, although average levels of consciousness are a bit lower among the nationally representative samples compared to the opt-in survey samples.

26 Mean levels of white identity and white consciousness, across each dataset and with both the truncated and multi-item measures, are presented in Online Appendix 3C.

27 When constructing a measure with multiple survey items, we worry not only about the external reliability of our measure, but also its internal reliability. Specifically, the items that comprise the scale should each be measuring the same basic trait, producing a high item-to-item correlation. We can assess the inter-item reliability of the measures of white identity and white consciousness by calculating the Cronbach's alpha. Possible alpha scores range from zero to one, with 0 indicating complete unreliability and 1 meaning perfect reliability. The threshold for deciding when a measure is reliable based on alpha is somewhat arbitrary, but generally scales with alpha coefficients less than 0.5 are considered unreliable, and those with coefficients above 0.7 are considered acceptable (Jackman 2008). Here, I report the Cronbach's alpha for my measures of consciousness, with the caveat that alpha calculations are sensitive to the number of items in a scale, and are only one piece of information important to assessing the overall validity of a measure.

To calculate the Cronbach's alpha of the three-item white identity scale, which again is comprised of the racial importance item, the question gauging pride in whites, and the item about perceptions of commonality among whites, I turn to the 2016 YouGov Study. Among this sample, the Cronbach's alpha is an acceptable 0.73. The measure is internally reliable. I follow the same procedure for determining the inter-item reliability of the measure of consciousness. In the YouGov 2016 study, the five-item measure, which includes the three identity items combined with the two consciousness items, produces an acceptable alpha of 0.79. The three-item version, comprised of just the racial importance identity item and the two consciousness items, yields an alpha of 0.71. Among respondents in the 2016 ANES Pilot, the Cronbach's alpha for the three-item measure of consciousness was a somewhat lower but still acceptable 0.66.

28 During the 2012 face-to-face interview, the white identity measure was asked using a Computer-Aided Self-Interview (CASI) format, whereby the interviewer handed a tablet computer to the respondent and the respondent answered the questions privately. This method was implemented to reduce social desirability bias, but one could argue that the setting, where the interviewer remained in the room, would not necessarily reduce bias in the same way that taking the entire survey anonymously on the Internet might.

29 Previous work has shown that Internet survey modes reduce social desirability biases that accompany sensitive questions (Chang and Krosnick 2009).

30 In the 2012 ANES, mean levels of white identity among respondents were 0.44 in the face-to-face sample and 0.45 in the web sample. The difference is not statistically significant. In the 2016 ANES, mean levels of white identity among respondents in the face-to-face study were 0.40 and 0.42 in the web study. This difference is also not statistically significant.

31 On the 2012 ANES, interviewers self-report their race, and the options available are limited to white, black, or other. The analysis here uses the race of the interviewer from the post-test survey, since the white identity question was asked on the post-test survey.

32 The mean difference (0.095) in white identity when the interviewer is black compared to white is significant at $p = 0.022$, two-tailed.

33 Mean levels by race of interviewer are reported in Online Appendix 3E.

34 This study was conducted only with the racial importance item.

35 The open-ended responses reproduced here are taken word for word from the survey, and therefore typos or grammatical errors are not corrected.

36 Some might wonder whether identity and consciousness are distinct from one another, seeking confirmation via factor analysis. Conceptually, we would not expect these constructs to have two distinct underlying latent factors as consciousness is a subset of identity, and the measure itself is in part comprised of group identity. Nevertheless, if I force two factors with oblique rotation on the two scales using the YouGov 2016 data, two factors, correlated at 0.62, do emerge. Using an SEM approach with confirmatory factor analysis shows that all the items load well on a single factor, but forcing the constituent items into two separate models does improve the overall fit. Nevertheless, the two factors are overwhelmingly correlated at 0.82 with one another.

37 Across each survey, partisanship is a seven-point scale, recoded from zero to one, with zero representing "strong Democrat" and one representing "strong Republican."

38 The correlations between these items and consciousness are reported in Online Appendix 3F.

39 The 2012 ANES allows me to make similar comparisons when it comes to where whites rate Hispanics and Asians on these same dimensions. The correlation among white respondents in the face-to-face sample between white identity and the anti-Hispanic stereotype index is 0.32. The correlation between white identity and the anti-Asian stereotype index 0.24. Again, in neither case would we consider white identity to simply be a measure of animus toward these groups.

40 These results are reported in Online Appendix 3F.

41 The racial importance item was included on the 2012 ANES Time Series, the 2016 ANES Pilot Study, and the 2016 ANES Time Series as a measure of racial identity among whites, blacks, and Hispanics.

42 When using the feeling thermometers, particularly those that measure attitudes toward racial groups, researchers often construct a measure by taking the difference between where whites rate themselves and where they rate other racial groups. The advantage of this approach is that it accounts for any individual survey-taker's propensity to rate all groups warmly or coldly, on average. I avoid this strategy for two reasons. For one, in their operationalization of the concept ethnocentrism, Kinder and Kam (2010) use the difference between where whites rate themselves and their average ratings of non-white groups. This method is consistent with their claim that ethnocentrism is a preference for the in-group coupled with prejudice toward out-groups, writ large. But their operationalization means that adopting the difference-measure approach to measure white identity for empirical reasons also results in unintentional conceptual overlap with ethnocentrism. Thus, I let the feeling thermometer do the heavy lifting on its own, while acknowledging that the difference measure might produce crisper effects. Second, Kinder and Kam (2010) provide evidence that for some opinion domains, like immigration, the white feeling thermometer as a measure of in-group attitudes explains opinion better than the out-group thermometers. Their finding is theoretically consistent with my claims, and my measurement approach allows direct comparison and corroboration with their findings.

43 In the 2012 ANES, the correlation between white identity, measured with the racial importance item, and the white feeling thermometer is 0.27 ($p<0.05$).

44 In this analysis, high white identifiers were those with a score of 0.75 or 1 on the racial importance item, which was recoded to range from zero to one. Low identifiers were those with a score of 0.25 or 0. The mean thermometer evaluation of whites among high identifiers was 81 degrees. Among low identifiers it was 67 degrees.

45 Percentage calculated among face-to-face respondents using survey weights.

46 Sanchez and Vargas (2016) examine the relationship between linked fate and group consciousness across racial groups, and reach a conclusion that is consistent with Dawson's. They argue that linked fate operates differently for blacks than it does for whites.

47 These are the percentage of respondents of each racial group that indicated that what happens to other members of their racial group will affect them "a lot." When combining "a lot" with the next highest category, "some," 71.7 percent of blacks possess some degree of linked fate, compared to 50.3 percent of whites.

48 Results are presented in Online Appendix 3G. I do note that in a few instances, the correlation between white linked fate and some of these items is statistically significant in the 2012 ANES web sample, but the magnitude of the effect is still very small.

49 White linked fate is in fact positively correlated with white identity, as measured by the racial importance item, in the 2012 ANES. Nevertheless, the correlation is relatively small (0.13, $p<0.05$), suggesting that these two items are capturing very different sentiments.

50 Online Appendices 3H and 3I present estimates of several models in which white linked fate is regressed on political attitudes and preferences.

51 Following Zaller (1992), I coded those respondents who could not place themselves ideologically as moderates.

52 Some work has found a small link between unemployment status and preference for the Democratic Party (Kiewiet 1983; Schlozman and Verba 1979),

but others have failed to find a link between employment status and political attitudes (Feldman 1982; Kinder and Mebane 1983).

53 I do not control for income across most of my models. Survey respondents frequently feel uncomfortable reporting their income, and thus the variable often suffers from a non-trivial degree of non-response error. Second, I find that controlling for income usually has little to no effect on the variables of interest here, and so I exclude it to reduce the non-response error it otherwise would introduce into the models.

Chapter 4   Who Identifies as White?

1 Analyses are replicated across all the main data sources used in the book and available in Online Appendix 4.

2 These data come from analysis of US Census data conducted by Howard Rosenthal and reported in the *Washington Post*. See Howard Rosenthal. 2016. "Why Do White Men Love Donald Trump so Much?" *Washington Post*. www .washingtonpost.com/news/monkey-cage/wp/2016/09/08/why-do-white-men-love-donald-trump-so-much/?noredirect=on&utm_term=.d1b94d14c1a6.

3 Analysis by Croll (2008) is consistent with this expectation; he finds that more educated whites are less likely to report that their racial identity is important.

4 Jackman's argument is similar to the system of "legitimizing myths" described by the authors of SDO (Sidanius and Pratto 1999).

5 Work using the closeness item to measure white identity has suggested that education is positively correlated with identity, such that *more* educated individuals possess stronger levels of white racial identity (Wong and Cho 2005)

6 As a reminder, whites high on identity are those who score at 0.75 and above on the zero to one scale. Low identifiers are those who score at 0.25 or below.

7 The relationship between white consciousness, age, gender, and education is provided in Online Appendix 4A4.

8 The correlation between age and other items discussed in this chapter are available in Online Appendix 4F.

9 Parsing age into generational cohorts does not indicate that whites born in a specific decade are primarily driving the positive correlation between age and white identity.

10 The correlations between identity, consciousness, and geography are provided in Appendices 4H and 4I.

11 The distribution of consciousness by geography is available in Online Appendix 4B.

12 States are categorized into four Census regions. Northeast: Connecticut, Maine, Massachusetts, New Hampshire, New Jersey, New York, Pennsylvania, Rhode Island, Vermont; North Central: Indiana, Illinois, Iowa, Kansas, Michigan, Minnesota, Missouri, Nebraska, North Dakota, Ohio, South Dakota, Wisconsin; South: Alabama, Arkansas, Delaware, DC, Florida, Georgia, Kentucky, Louisiana, Maryland, Mississippi, North Carolina, Oklahoma, South Carolina, Tennessee, Texas, Virginia, West Virginia; West: Alaska, Arizona, California, Colorado, Hawaii, Idaho, Montana (no respondents), Nevada, New Mexico, Oregon, Utah, Washington, Wyoming.

13 One might have specific hypotheses about levels of white identity within states. Unfortunately, the limited sample sizes of the surveys analyzed here make it difficult to make any state comparisons.

14 I define rural as non-metro (www.ers.usda.gov/data-products/rural-urban-continuum-codes/).

15 The racial and ethnic composition of the county is determined using Census American Community Survey five-year estimates from 2010 to 2014. The percent foreign born comes from the 2010 Census, and the change in the foreign-born population is calculated using data from the 2000 and 2010 Censuses.

16 This finding is not necessarily inconsistent with the work under the umbrella of the power-threat hypothesis, which argues that the relative size of the non-white population serves as a threat to whites. The composition may in fact activate identity, but not necessarily influence the acquisition of this identity.

17 Correlations provided in Online Appendix 4H.

18 Hochschild (2016) and Vance (2016).

19 Correlations between white identity, white consciousness, and income are provided in Appendices 4F and 4G. Examining the relationship between white identity, white consciousness, and income separated into quintiles reveals little of interest. There are no consistent differences across income groups, with the exception of the fact that the correlation is more consistently significant at the highest levels of income.

20 I also consider the interaction between income and education, hypothesizing that it is higher income by lower educated whites who are more likely to adopt a white identity. I find, however, no significant effect.

21 Job loss in the manufacturing industry was paired to county codes using US Census American Community Survey five-year and three-year estimates. Overall changes in unemployment were paired with county codes with data on local area unemployment statistics via the Bureau of Labor Statistics (www.bls .gov/lau/).

22 The Bureau of Labor Statistics provides information about union membership: www.bls.gov/news.release/union2.nr0.htm.

23 A 2012 Gallup Survey, for instance, found that 42 percent of Americans placed themselves in the working class: http://news.gallup.com/poll/159029/americans-likely-say-belong-middle-class.aspx.

24 Coding responses to these open-ended questions into categories is an imprecise effort. Many respondents do not answer the question, and many who do choose not to provide enough information to make the task of categorizing their occupation straightforward. Thus, we should view this analysis as an especially noisy examination of the relationship between occupation and racial identity.

25 The results for white consciousness are presented in Online Appendix 4D.

26 Results presented in Online Appendix 4E.

27 Silvestri and Richardson (2001) find that agreeableness is associated with white racial identity, but they use the conceptualization of identity formulated by Helms (1995), which involves an understanding and rejection of privilege and oppression. This notion of identity is very different from the way I theorize about white identity in this book.

28 Results presented in Online Appendix 4J.

29 Results presented in Online Appendix 4K.

30 In the 2012 and 2016, authoritarianism is measured with four items assessing attitudes about child-rearing scaled together. The Cronbach's coefficient alpha among whites in the face-to-face sample is 0.61. The correlation coefficient reported here is among whites in the face-to-face sample, N=859.

31 I note that we should consider this result with some caution. SDO was not measured on any of the other surveys employed throughout this text, so we have no other point of comparison. Furthermore, the SSI Study was an opt-in survey, and so it is unclear whether this relationship would hold among nationally representative probability samples.

32 Results in Online Appendix 4M.

33 Results available in Online Appendix 4N.

34 These findings also run counter to the relationship between education and white linked-fate, further demonstrating that linked fate is not capturing the same latent construct.

Chapter 5 The Content and Contours of Whiteness

1 Act of March 26, 1790, ch. 3, 1 Stat. 103.

2 Levels of identity here are split by the highest and lowest two categories, with those in the middle excluded. That is, "high identifiers" are those who reported that their identity was either "very" or "extremely important." "Low identifiers" are those who reported their identity was either "a little" or "not at all important."

3 The quotes from survey respondents are presented throughout this chapter verbatim, and therefore contain a number of grammatical or spelling errors that I have chosen not to correct.

4 Schildkraut (2007) and Citrin, Reingold, and Green (1990) make similar distinctions. The former contrast liberal (civic) orientations with nativist (ethnic) views. In other work, Wright and colleagues (2012) distinguish between civic and ascriptive views. Schildkraut compares assimilationist and ethnocultural conceptions. There is, however, disagreement over what items belong on what dimension, and empirically, the factor loadings for these items can shift significantly depending on what items are included in the scale and across datasets.

5 This finding is in keeping with work that shows that the two dimensions of these items are often highly correlated. See Wright, Citrin, and Wand (2012) for a discussion of this point.

6 The pairwise correlation between these items and the white identity measure is as follows: To have American citizenship (0.38); To be a Christian (0.38); To be able to speak English (0.35); To feel American (0.27); To have American ancestry (0.18); To have been born in America (0.17); To have lived in America most of one's life (0.10); To respect America's political institutions and laws (0.45); To be white (0.45). In each case $p < 0.05$.

7 Following Theiss-Morse (2009), I combine "to have American citizenship," "to feel American," and "to respect America's laws and institutions" to create the soft boundaries scale (alpha=0.76). I combine "to be Christian," "to be able to speak English," "to have American ancestry," "to have been born in America," "to have lived in America most of one's life," and "to be white" into the hard boundaries scale (a=0.74). I note that there is disagreement over what items should comprise these separate subscales, but the choices I have made here are consistent with the factor loadings for these items in this particular dataset. I also note that scaling these items together into a single scale (a=0.85) is in keeping with Wong (2010) who, using General Social Survey data, combines the same items into a single measure, with the exception of the "to be white" question. Wong advocates for a single scale because, empirically, these items do not consistently load onto separate scales.

8 Wright, Citrin, and Wand (2012) argue that a superior measurement strategy is to have respondents rank these qualities, rather than rate their importance individually. Nevertheless, they still argue that using the ratings method, as I have done here, is valid. Furthermore, my intent here is not to use these items as predictors, but instead to explore their general relationship with white identity.

9 The results when white consciousness is included in the model instead of white identity are presented in Online Appendix 5A.

10 Only a few mentioned disparaging stereotypes associated with the white working class like "Hillbilly, redneck, low intelligence" or "NASCAR."

11 Interestingly, a few whites who scored low on racial identity discussed privilege as a reason for their lack of identity. One said, "I'm privileged enough to be in the majority so I don't have to define myself by that parameter" (MTurk). A second wrote, "As a member of the majority (well, according to most people, anyway), I have the privilege of not having my skin color define me" (MTurk). Another explained, "White people in this country have the luxury of not thinking about race, because we are the majority and are identified with having power. I know there are privileges I enjoy because of my race, but on a daily basis I rarely have to think about them. I can choose to ignore my race in most situations" (MTurk).

12 Alpha=0.92.

13 The mean White Guilt Scale score is 0.28 (standard deviation=0.009) on the scale recoded to range from zero to one.

14 Alpha=0.94.

15 Models showing the effect of white consciousness are available in Online Appendix 5B.

16 Rich Epstein. 2015. "'White History Month' Sign Stirs up Flemington." *Hunterdon County Democrat.* www.nj.com/hunterdon-county-democrat/index.ssf/2015/03/white_history_month_sign_stirs_up_flemington.html.

17 John Blake. 2011. "Are Whites Racially Oppressed?" *CNN.* www.cnn.com/2010/US/12/21/white.persecution/index.html.

18 The results from the 2010 KN Study are replicated in the 2013 SSI Study and presented in Online Appendix 5D.

19 These measures were based on items previously used by Bobo (1999) and Bobo and Hutchings (1996) to examine perceptions of competition between racial groups.

20 The results for these models when consciousness is included in the model instead of white identity are provided in Online Appendix 5D2.

21 I replicate these results using the 2012 ANES and the 2013 SSI Study. The results are provided in Online Appendix 5E.

22 Results of models from other datasets are available in Online Appendix 5G.

23 Alpha=0.73 (KN 2010); alpha=0.40 (SSI).

24 Results from these multivariate models are available in Online Appendix 5H.

25 One person who reported that their racial identity was extremely important in the YouGov survey did mention their white power tattoo.

26 Croll (2007) distinguishes between a defensive and a progressive white identity.

Chapter 6   The Preservation of Whiteness

1 The link between race and naturalization was not newly introduced in 1924. In fact, the import of race in defining immigration policy appeared much earlier in American history: The US Naturalization Law of March 26, 1790 limited naturalization to immigrants who were "free white persons" (Daniels 2002).

2 Americans were also much less enthusiastic about German immigrants, which is hardly surprising given the anti-German sentiments fostered by World War II. Results from Gallup poll reported by the Roper Center at https://ropercenter.cornell.edu/huddled-masses-public-opinion-and-the-1965-u-s-immigration-act/.

3 The Roper Center. 2015. "Huddled Masses: Public Opinion & the 1965 U.S. Immigration Act." https://ropercenter.cornell.edu/huddled-masses-public-opinion-and-the-1965-u-s-immigration-act/.

4 C.P. Trussell. 1964. "New Alien Quotas Urged by Kennedy." *New York Times.*

5 The Roper Center. 2015. "Huddled Masses: Public Opinion & the 1965 U.S. Immigration Act." https://ropercenter.cornell.edu/huddled-masses-public-opinion-and-the-1965-u-s-immigration-act/.

6 "U.S. Senate, Subcommittee on Immigration and Naturalization of the Committee on the Judiciary." 1965. US Government Print Office. https://catalog.hathitrust.org/Record/101745189.

7 Pew Research Center. 2015. *Modern Immigration Wave Brings 59 Million to U.S., Driving Population Growth and Change Through 2065.* www.pewhispanic.org/2015/09/28/modern-immigration-wave-brings-59-million-to-u-s-driving-population-growth-and-change-through-2065/.

8 In 1960, most immigrants to the United States came from Italy, followed by Canada and Germany.

9 For more information on projections, see www.pewhispanic.org/2015/09/28/modern-immigration-wave-brings-59-million-to-u-s-driving-population-growth-and-change-through-2065/.

10 To be clear, concern expressed by these individuals regarding identity politics is not with respect to white identity politics, but instead to the increased salience of group identities among racial and ethnic minorities.

11 Samuel P. Huntington. 2009. "The Threat of White Nativism." *Foreign Policy.* www.foreignpolicy.com/articles/2004/03/01/the_threat_of_white_nativism.

12 A number of scholars have suggested that Hispanics will eventually be viewed as white (e.g., Sears and Savalei 2006; Warren and Twine 1997).

13 The Roper Center. 2015. "Huddled Masses: Public Opinion & the 1965 U.S. Immigration Act." https://ropercenter.cornell.edu/huddled-masses-public-opinion-and-the-1965-u-s-immigration-act/.

14 The remaining percent had no opinion. Historical trends in immigration opinion from Gallup are available here: https://news.gallup.com/poll/1660/immigration.aspx.

15 Carroll Doherty. 2006. "Attitudes Toward Immigration: In Black and White." *Pew Research Center.*

16 Results are robust to controlling for affect toward blacks and Asians. They are also robust to controlling for racial resentment, but I do not do this here since, theoretically, we would not expect racial resentment to be the most relevant out-group attitude associated with immigration opinion.

17 Rebecca Riffkin. 2015. "Government, Economy, Immigration Seen as Top U.S. Problems." *Gallup.* https://news.gallup.com/poll/185504/government-economy-immigration-seen-top-problems.aspx. For additional information about Americans views on the nation's most important problems, see Gallup survey results available at https://news.gallup.com/poll/1675/most-important-problem.aspx.

18 Lydia Saad. 2014. Gallup *One in Six Say Immigration Most Important U.S. Problem.* http://news.gallup.com/poll/173306/one-six-say-immigration-important-problem.aspx.

19 I use OLS to model opinion here, rather than ordered probit, for ease of comparison across different measures of immigration opinion. The results, however, are consistent with estimating with ordered probit.

20 The proportion of articles for each paper was calculated by taking the number of articles returned in a given year with the search term "immigra*" and dividing it by the total number of articles returned via the search engine for the paper that year. The article counts for the *New York Times* and the *Washington Post* were retrieved from each paper's own archive available on their websites. The article counts for the *Los Angeles Times* were retrieved via Proquest.

21 Analysis including fixed effects of years indicates that the effect of the white feeling thermometer on immigration opinion is, for instance, significantly different in 2000 than in 1992.

22 I use clustered standard errors in this analysis to account for including data at the geographic level. I also could have estimated the model hierarchically, and doing so yields substantively similar results.

23 Myers and Levy (2018) offer an important discussion about the nature of the projections and their inclusive and exclusive definitions of "white."

24 Outten et al. (2012) and Myers and Levy (2018) have demonstrated that when exposed to information about demographic changes, white Americans do report feeling more negative emotions. This work does not, however, consider differences in responses by levels of in-group identity, nor does it explore the political implications of these effects. Furthermore, this work focuses on negative reactions to out-groups, rather than negative reactions more broadly.

25 While the general information provided to subjects in this condition is correct, the values plotted on the graph are fabricated; they do not reflect actual annual population projections from the US Census.

26 Images of the treatments are provided in Online Appendix 6E.

27 Scaling these items together in this way is consistent with other work on emotions (Brader, Valentino, and Suhay 2008). I analyze fear and anger here separately but note that they actually emerge as a common factor, and it is difficult to distinguish them. Thus, one could also interpret the emotion scales as negative and positive affect, rather than specifically as anger, fear, and enthusiasm.

28 One might wonder whether these treatments had any effect on attitudes toward immigration more generally. There are some limitations to uncovering an effect of this sort. For one, white identity is already powerfully associated with immigration opinion, and white identifiers' attitudes toward immigration are, on average, near the maximum point on many of the immigration measures (i.e., there are ceiling effects). There is some evidence, however, that the treatments had an effect on immigration opinion conditioned on white identity. For instance, white identifiers who received the "increasing immigrants" treatment were more likely to report that immigration is one of the top problems facing the United States – a notable finding and also a useful manipulation check. Unfortunately, the YouGov Study did not include a general measure of attitudes toward immigration. Instead, it asked respondents two separate immigration questions about their preference for increasing or decreasing immigration, identically worded, except one item asked about immigrants from Latin America, and the other about immigrants from Europe. Even though the order of the items was randomized, there are likely some notable social desirability and response biases here, where respondents are using their response to one question to inform their response to the other. Either way, white identifiers do become marginally more opposed to immigrants from either location upon receiving the "increasing immigrants" treatment. They respond no differently, relative to the control, in the "white majority" or "white minority" conditions.

Chapter 7 Policies that Protect the Group

1 Converse (1964) noted the significance of race as a social group, pointing out that groups delimited by physical characteristics are "highly visible" (p. 42).

2 According to Lichtenstein et al. (2000), southern employers worried that the federal benefits would discourage blacks from taking low-paying jobs in factories, fields, and in homes. But DeWitt (2010) argues that southern racism was not the reason for excluding these workers from the program. Rather, he posits, lobbyists from those industries opposed the tax burden, and southern Democrats and relevant congressional committees had little opinion on the matter. There remains, however, disagreement about this point.

3 Even today, there is some evidence that Social Security disproportionately benefits whites in the United States. Researchers at the Urban Institute find that

Social Security tends to redistribute income from blacks, Hispanics, and other people of color to whites (Steuerle, Smith, and Quakenbush 2013). According to their analysis, for every $100 that white beneficiaries pay in taxes, they receive $113 in Social Security benefits. Meanwhile, blacks receive a return of $89, and Hispanics receive $58. The disparities are not intentional, but likely the result of a number of factors, including different life expectancies across racial groups and the fact that Hispanics are more likely to have immigrated recently, meaning they are paying into the system now rather than currently receiving benefits.

4 I estimate the effect here using OLS, but the results are robust to estimating with ordered probit. I also exclude income from these models, even though some might argue it is a likely control. I find no effect for income when I do include it in the model nor does including it substantively change the relationship between any of the other covariates and the dependent variable. Because of the number of non-responses on the income question, however, I exclude it from the model.

5 Calculated via the 2016 ANES Time Series face-to-face sample. Data are weighted. Thirty percent of respondents indicated they would like to keep spending the same, and 21 percent indicated they would like to increase spending.

6 Roosevelt's Annual Message to Congress, delivered on January 4, 1935, can be read in its entirety via the American Presidency Project's website at www .presidency.ucsb.edu/ws/index.php?pid=14890.

7 While a larger proportion of blacks receive some sort of government assistance than whites, there are more white people receiving some type of means-tested aid.

8 Gilens (1996) demonstrates that whites' racial attitudes are the most important influence on whites' welfare opinions.

9 Because it is only tangential to my main argument here, I do not address a second debate in the literature, which suggests that opposition to welfare and other race-conscious programs is less about racial animus and more about the principles of individualism (Feldman and Huddy 2005; Sniderman and Carmines 1997).

10 Kinder and Sanders (1996) find some evidence that whites' group interests do matter in predicting affirmative action opinion. They measure group interests, however, with questions that specifically ask what the chances are that whites will not get admitted to a school or won't get a job while an equally or less qualified black person gets one instead. That is, their questions designed to measure group interest are directly related to the policy at hand. Thus, it is not surprising that responses to these questions are especially tied to whites' opinion on affirmative action.

11 Richard D. Kahlenberg. 2010. "10 Myths About Legacy Preferences in College Admissions." *The Chronicle of Higher Education.*

12 Edmund Zagorin. 2014. "Race-Blind Admissions Are Affirmative Action for Whites." *The American Prospect.* http://prospect.org/article/race-blind-admissions-are-affirmative-action-whites.

13 The 2014 SSI Study was conducted in July of 2014 and included 1,900 non-Hispanic white adult US citizens.

14 The account of the Trump rally in Raleigh is from the author's own observations.

15 Mutz (2018) makes a similar argument.

16 James Politi. 2013. "Contentious Nafta Pact Continues to Generate a Sparky Debate." *Financial Times.* www.ft.com/content/b7230156-4c51-11e3-923d-00144feabdc0.

17 Jeff Faux,. 2014. "NAFTA, Twenty Years After: A Disaster." *The Huffington Post.* www.huffingtonpost.com/jeff-faux/nafta-twenty-years-after_b_4528140 .html.
18 Vicki Needham. 2016. "Trump Says He Will Renegotiate or Withdraw from NAFTA." *The Hill.* http://thehill.com/policy/finance/285189-trump-says-he-will-renegotiate-or-withdraw-from-nafta-without-changes.
19 Pat Truly et al. 1993. "What's Really Interesting Is Who's Opposing Nafta." *The Orlando Sentinel.* http://articles.orlandosentinel.com/1993-09-06/news/ 9309050654_1_american-liberty-nafta-perot.
20 Results are robust to controlling for American identity.
21 The effect of white identity on opinion on increasing trade and opposition to free trade is also significant in the 2016 ANES web study. These results are presented in Online Appendix 7H1.

Chapter 8 A Black Man in the White House

1 The Fifteenth Amendment to the United States Constitution was ratified on February 3, 1870.
2 The Voting Rights Act of 1965 was signed into law on August 6, 1965.
3 Adam Nagourney. 2008. "Obama Elected President as Racial Barrier Falls." *New York Times.* www.nytimes.com/2008/11/05/us/politics/05elect .html?pagewanted=all&_r=0.
4 Robert Barnes and Michael D. Shear. 2008. "Obama Makes History." *Washington Post.* www.washingtonpost.com/wp-dyn/content/article/2008/11/ 05/AR2008110501769.html.
5 A transcript of McCain's acceptance speech is available at www.npr.org/ templates/story/story.php?storyId=96631784.
6 Information about how racial and ethnic groups voted in these elections was obtained from a summary of exit poll data provided by the Roper Center.
7 Information on the racial composition of the electorate comes from the US Census Bureau Current Population Survey. Values are corrected to account for vote over-report and non-response errors by Dr. Michael McDonald. www .electproject.org/home/voter-turnout/demographics.
8 Thomas B. Edsall. 2012. "Is Rush Limbaugh's Country Gone?" *New York Times.* https://campaignstops.blogs.nytimes.com/2012/11/18/is-rush-limbaughs-country-gone/.
9 Limbaugh made these comments on his radio show on May 29, 2009. A transcription can be found on his website: www.rushlimbaugh.com/daily/2009/05/ 29/america_s_pi_ata_strikes_back_we_won_t_shut_up_on_sotomayor/.
10 Brett LoGiurato. 2012. "Bill O'Reilly Goes Off: 'The White Establishment Is the Minority.'" *Business Insider.* www.businessinsider.com/bill-oreilly-election-obama-white-minority-establishment-romney-2012-11.
11 Maureen Dowd. 2012. "Romney Is President." *New York Times.* www.nytimes .com/2012/11/11/opinion/sunday/dowd-romney-is-president.html.
12 O'Reilly made these remarks on his show on March 28, 2018. A video record can be found at his website: www.billoreilly.com/b/Targeting-White-Males/-219730060400420369.html.
13 White identity may very well have been associated with attitudes toward Obama in 2008, but a lack of valid measures of white identity on public opinion surveys prevents me from examining this possible relationship.
14 The dependent variable is coded such that 0 indicates voting for Romney, and 1 indicates voting for Obama. Respondents who reported not voting or who voted for a third-party candidate were not included in the analysis.

15 Kam and Kinder (2012) demonstrate that ethnocentrism, or a propensity to divide the world into "us" versus "them," drove opposition to Obama in 2008. We might very well expect ethnocentrism to matter in 2012 as well, and so I include it in the model of vote choice as an alternative measure of racial animus to racial resentment. Following Kam and Kinder (2012), I measure ethnocentrism as the difference in the feeling thermometer evaluations whites give themselves and their average evaluations of blacks, Hispanics, and Asians. Kinder and Kam (2010) also argue that racial stereotype measures also capture ethnocentrism, and while I do not include those in the analysis presented here, the model is robust to employing those items instead of the thermometer measure. I present the results for the model including the ethnocentrism measure in Online Appendix 8A.

16 The results here and in the analysis of attitudes toward Trump are robust to controlling for traditional stereotype measures of racial animus as well.

17 Results are robust to controlling for racial resentment, but because the dependent variable is about Latinos and not blacks, I control for attitudes toward Hispanics using the 101-point feeling thermometer measure.

18 The American Recovery and Reinvestment Act was signed into law by Obama in February 2009.

19 Associating resistance to government bailout efforts to the Tea Party was not CNBC commentator Rick Santelli's idea, but he helped popularize the sentiment.

20 Analysis not included here, but available upon request.

21 Jenée Desmond-Harris 2016. "Racism Is Real: Trump Helps Show It." *New York Times*.

22 Jane C. Timm. 2015. "Trump Calls for Discrimination against Muslims." *MSNBC.com*. www.msnbc.com/msnbc/trump-calls-discrimination-against-muslims.

23 Lydia O'Connor. 2016. "Here Are 9 Examples Of Donald Trump Being Racist." *The Huffington Post*. The *New York Times* keeps a running list of Trump's racist remarks at www.nytimes.com/interactive/2018/01/15/opinion/leonhardt-trump-racist.html.

24 Christopher Ingraham. 2016. "Two New Studies Find Racial Anxiety Is the Biggest Driver of Support for Trump." *Washington Post*. www.washingtonpost.com/news/wonk/wp/2016/06/06/racial-anxiety-is-a-huge-driver-of-support-for-donald-trump-two-new-studies-find/?utm_term=.d5b948634a2e. Michael Tesler. 2016. "A Newly Released Poll Shows the Populist Power of Donald Trump." *Washington Post*. www.washingtonpost.com/news/monkey-cage/wp/2016/01/27/a-newly-released-poll-shows-the-populist-power-of-donald-trump/.

25 Michael M. Phillips. 2016. "Anxiety Fuels Donald Trump's Supporters." *Wall Street Journal*. Waleed Shahid. 2016. "Donald Trump and the Disaffected, White, Working Class Voter." *Colorlines*. Derek Thompson. 2016. "Donald Trump and the Twilight of White America." *The Atlantic*. www.theatlantic.com/politics/archive/2016/05/donald-trump-and-the-twilight-of-white-america/482655/.

26 Bryce Covert. 2016. "Make America Great Again for the People It Was Great for Already." *New York Times*. Heather Digby Parton. 2015. "Donald Trump Will Make America White Again: 'White Working-Class Anxiety' Is a Dog-Whistle for Racism." *Salon.com*.

27 Kelly J. Baker. 2016. "Make America White Again?" *The Atlantic*.

28 Peter Holley and Sarah Larimer. 2016. "How America's Dying White Supremacist Movement Is Seizing on Donald Trump's Appeal." *Washington Post*. Beth Reinhard. 2016. "White Nationalists See Advancement Through Donald Trump's Candidacy." *Wall Street Journal*.

29 Michael Tesler. 2015. "How Anti-Immigrant Attitudes Are Fueling Support for Donald Trump." *The Washington Post Monkey Cage*. www.washingtonpost .com/news/monkey-cage/wp/2015/11/24/how-anti-immigrant-attitudes-are-fueling-support-for-donald-trump/.

30 An archived version of Trump's website from August 24, 2015 is available via the Internet Archive: https://web.archive.org/web/20150824010152/https://www.donaldjtrump.com/positions.

31 Analysis presented in Online Appendix 8M.

32 Travis Dove. 2016. "Transcript of Donald Trump's Immigration Speech." *New York Times*. www.nytimes.com/2016/09/02/us/politics/transcript-trump-immigration-speech.html.

33 Josh Dawsey. 2018. "Trump Derides Protections for Immigrants from 'Shithole' Countries." *Washington Post*. www.washingtonpost.com/politics/trump-attacks-protections-for-immigrants-from-shithole-countries-in-oval-office-meeting/2018/01/11/bfc0725c-f711-11e7-91af-31ac729add94_story .html?utm_term=.2dec60a21d06. It is important to note that Trump never officially acknowledged making these comments. Furthermore, he is certainly not the only president to make racially charged comments behind closed doors.

34 Emily Gurnon. 2016. "Where Trump And Clinton Stand On Health Care And Medicare." *Forbes (Online)*. www.forbes.com/sites/nextavenue/2016/08/12/where-trump-and-clinton-stand-on-health-care-and-medicare/#491cc4ca1eb0.

35 Trump's tweet can be found on his Twitter account on May 7, 2015, and at the following URL: https://twitter.com/realdonaldtrump/status/596338364187602944?lang=en.

36 For instance, an article from *FiveThirtyEight* discussed white identity politics in the context of a white nationalist protest over the removal of Confederate Statutes in Charlottesville, Virginia. Perry Bacon, Jr. 2017. "Charlottesville and the Rise of White Identity Politics." *FiveThirtyEiight*: 1–5. https://fivethirtyeight.com/features/charlottesville-and-the-rise-of-white-identity-politics/.

37 Using different measures of white racial identity, others have also demonstrated a relationship between white identity and support for Donald Trump (Knowles and Tropp 2018; Major, Blodorn, and Major Blascovich 2018).

38 Mutz (2018) argues that white Americans were instead driven to vote for Trump out of a concern for status threat, an argument very much in keeping with my own. My analysis here helps clarify *which* whites were most concerned with threats to their group's position.

39 In my analysis, thermometer evaluations were re-coded to range from zero to one, rather than from 0 to 100.

40 The 2016 Pilot did not include a measure of subjective personal economic evaluations or attitudes about the role of government.

41 The predicted effect ranges from 0.29 among those with a consciousness score of zero to 0.47 among those with a consciousness score of one on the zero to one thermometer scale.

42 The dependent variable is coded as "1" for choosing Trump and "0" for selecting any other response option.

43 The predicted probability of choosing Trump in the primary over other candidates among those with a consciousness score of "0" is 0.06. Among those with a consciousness score of "1," the predicted probability is 0.51.

44 John Leland. 2016. "Bernie Sanders and Donald Trump Voters Share Anger, but Direct It Differently." *New York Times*. www.nytimes.com/2016/01/31/us/bernie-sanders-and-donald-trump-voters-share-anger-but-direct-it-differently .html.

45 Amanda Taub. 2016. "The Rise of American Authoritarianism." *Vox*. www
.vox.com/2016/3/1/11127424/trump-authoritarianism%5Cnhttp://blogs
.lse.ac.uk/usappblog/2016/01/27/donald-trump-is-attracting-authoritarian-
primary-voters-and-it-may-help-him-to-gain-the-nomination/.

46 The correlation between anti-elitism and white identity is 0.05 (p=0.22). The
correlation between mistrust of experts and white identity is 0.2 (p=0.00).

47 One might wonder whether introducing each of these items into a model simultaneously produces a problem of multi-collinearity. Neither consciousness,
authoritarianism, anti-elitism, or mistrust of experts is so strongly correlated,
however, that multi-collinearity appears to be a problem.

48 These results generally replicate using the 2016 ANES, but only in the face-
to-face sample. I do not employ the 2016 ANES analysis here because as
I mentioned in Chapter 3, there was a notable drop in levels of white identity
immediately after the 2016 election (when white identity was measured on the
ANES), perhaps due to the significant and negative association the media made
between white identity and Trump support. White identity was measured on
the YouGov Study prior to the election, and was therefore less influenced by
whatever effect the political context had on individuals' propensity to identify
as white.

49 I estimate the relationship using ordinary least squares for ease of interpretation, but the results are robust to modeling with ordered probit.

50 South is defined here as the eleven secession states.

51 We might expect to see a similar relationship between white identity and
support for Goldwater. Unfortunately, the 1964 ANES did not include a thermometer evaluation of Goldwater, and so I am unable to conduct a comparative
analysis.

52 Unlike in other models throughout the book, I control for South in these analyses (a dummy representing residence in one of the eleven Confederate secession states), because during the time in which these data were collected, the
South was still arguably quite politically distinct, even after accounting for
partisanship (Hillygus and Shields 2008; Schickler 2016). In more recent years,
however, in-migration to the South has made the region a less distinct voting
bloc (Hillygus, McKee, and Young 2017).

53 The magnitude of the effect of white identity on evaluations is similar for
Wallace and Carter in 1976, but the relationships fall short of significance at
conventional levels for Carter.

54 Eleanor Clift. 2016. "Pat Buchanan: Donald Trump Stole My Playbook."
The Daily Beast: 1–7. www.thedailybeast.com/pat-buchanan-donald-trump-
stole-my-playbook.

55 Eleanor Clift. 2016. "Pat Buchanan: Donald Trump Stole My Playbook."
The Daily Beast: 1–7. www.thedailybeast.com/pat-buchanan-donald-trump-
stole-my-playbook.

56 The California Proposition was an approved ballot item intended to make
illegal aliens ineligible for public benefits. It was never enforced.

57 *New York Times*. 2016. "Transcript: Donald Trump on NATO, Turkey's Coup
Attempt and the World." www.nytimes.com/2016/07/22/us/politics/donald-
trump-foreign-policy-interview.html.

58 Patrick J. Buchanan. 1993. "America First, NAFTA Never." *Washington
Post*: 8–11. www.washingtonpost.com/archive/opinions/1993/11/07/america-
first-nafta-never/c8450c08-b14b-4a25-abe8-0b7cfc992e11/?utm_
term=.061c3c310b7d.

59 Alpha=0.83 among whites.

60 It is worth noting that in this analysis, racial resentment is strongly and significantly associated with *lower* levels of political participation. Previous literature

does not offer expectations about the relationship between resentment and participation, so this finding is unexpected. Speculating about why it appears here is a potential avenue for future exploration.

Chapter 9   The Future of White America

1   Lydia Saad. 2014. Gallup *One in Six Say Immigration Most Important U.S. Problem.*   http://news.gallup.com/poll/173306/one-six-say-immigration-important-problem.aspx.
2   Philip Connor. 2016. "Number of Refugees to Europe Surges to Record 1.3 Million in 2015." *Pew Research Center*: 1–7. www.pewglobal.org/2016/08/02/number-of-refugees-to-europe-surges-to-record-1-3-million-in-2015/.
3   George Friedman. 2005. "A Question of Integration." *Stratfor*.
4   Bruce Drake and Jacob Poushter. 2016. "In Views of Diversity, Many Europeans Are Less Positive than Americans." *Pew Research Center*: 1–2. www.pewresearch.org/fact-tank/2016/07/12/in-views-of-diversity-many-europeans-are-less-positive-than-americans.
5   Phillip Connor and Jens Manuel Krogstad. 2016. "Immigrant Share of Population Jumps in Some European Countries." *Pew Research Center*: 1–5. www.pewresearch.org/fact-tank/2016/06/15/immigrant-share-of-population-jumps-in-some-european-countries/.
6   Each of these estimates was provided by the Roper Center for Public Opinion Research, and come from their presidential election exit polls, available at the following URL: http://ropercenter.cornell.edu/polls/us-elections/how-groups-voted.
7   Schickler (2016) makes a compelling argument that racial realignment actually began in the 1930s, and that it was driven largely by state parties and rank-and-file members of Congress, rather than national party elites.
8   Results are available at www.people-press.org/2018/03/20/1-trends-in-party-affiliation-among-demographic-groups/.
9   Mason (2018) also argues that the Republican Party is more sorted and polarized along racial, religious, and ideological identities, making them more sensitive to identity appeals.
10   Richard D. Alba. 2015. "The Myth of a White Minority." *New York Times*. www.nytimes.com/2015/06/11/opinion/themythofawhiteminority.html%0Ahttps://nyti.ms/1TcP4KQ.
11   Howard Lavine and Wendy Rahn. 2018. "What If Trump's Nativism Actually Hurts Him Politically?" *New York Times*. https://nyti.ms/2lOVCp6.
12   Mark Hugo Lopez, Ana Gonzalez-Barrera, and Gustavo Lopez. 2017. Pew Research Center *Hispanic Identity Fades Across Generations as Immigrant Connections Fall Away*. www.pewhispanic.org/2017/12/20/hispanic-identity-fades-across-generations-as-immigrant-connections-fall-away/.
13   Kim Severson. 2012. "Number of U.S. Hate Groups Is Rising, Report Says." *New York Times*.   www.nytimes.com/2012/03/08/us/number-of-us-hate-groups-on-the-rise-report-says.html.
14   Paul Gottfried. 2008. "The Decline and Rise of the Alternative Right." www.unz.com/article/the-decline-and-rise-of-the-alternative-right/.
15   Beth Reinhard. 2016. "White Nationalists See Advancement Through Donald Trump's Candidacy." *Wall Street Journal*. www.wsj.com/articles/white-nationalists-see-advancement-through-donald-trumps-candidacy-1463523858.
16   Lisa Mascaro. 2016. "David Duke and Other White Supremacists See Trump's Rise as Way to Increase Role in Mainstream Politics." *Los Angeles Times*.

www.latimes.com/politics/la-na-pol-trump-david-duke-20160928-snap-story
.html.

17 Alan Rappeport. 2016. "Donald Trump Wavers on Disavowing David Duke."
    New York Times. www.nytimes.com/politics/first-draft/2016/02/28/donald-
    trump-declines-to-disavow-david-duke/.

18 Ben Kharakh and Dan Primack. 2016. "Donald Trump's Social Media Ties
    to White Supremacists." *Fortune*. http://fortune.com/donald-trump-white-
    supremacist-genocide/.

19 The popular white supremacist website Stormfront claimed that it had to
    upgrade its servers to accommodate the increased traffic Trump drove to its
    website (Ben Schreckinger. 2015. "White Supremacist Groups See Trump
    Bump." *Politico*. www.politico.com/story/2015/12/donald-trump-white-
    supremacists-216620). Prior to Trump, the day that saw the biggest increase
    in Stormfront's membership, however, was November 5, 2008, the day after
    Obama was elected as reported in Seth Stephens-Davidowitz. 2014. "The Data
    of Hate." *New York Times*. www.nytimes.com/2014/07/13/opinion/sunday/
    seth-stephens-davidowitz-the-data-of-hate.html. The SPLC also reports that
    the number of hate groups rose by 14 percent in 2015 as reported in Niraj
    Chokshi. 2016. "The Year of 'Enormous Rage': Number of Hate Groups Rose
    by 14 Percent in 2015." *Washington Post*.

REFERENCES

Abascal, Maria. 2015. "Us and Them: Black-White Relations in the Wake of Hispanic Population Growth." *American Sociological Review* 80(4): 789–813.

Abdelal, Rawi, Yoshiko M. Herrera, Alastair Iain Johnston, and Rose McDermott. 2009. "Introduction." In *Measuring Identity: A Guide for Social Scientists*, eds. Rawi Abdelal, Yoshiko M. Herrera, Alastair Iain Johnston, and Rose McDermott. New York: Cambridge University Press, 1–13.

Abdelal, Rawi, Yoshiko M. Herrera, Alastair Iain Johnston, and Terry Martin. 2001. "Treating Identity as a Variable: Measuring the Content, Intensity, and Contestation of Identity." In *Annual Meeting of the American Political Science Association*, San Francisco, 695–711.

Abowd, John M., and Richard B. Freeman. 1991. "Introduction and Summary." In *Immigration, Trade, and the Labor Market*, eds. John M. Abowd and Richard B. Freeman. Chicago: University of Chicago Press, 1–25.

Abrajano, Marisa, and Zoltan L. Hajnal. 2015. *White Backlash: Immigration, Race, and American Politics*. Princeton: Princeton University Press.

Abrams, Dominic, and Michael A. Hogg. 1988. "Comments on the Motivational Status of Self-Esteem in Social Identity and Intergroup Discrimination." *European Journal of Social Psychology* 18(4): 317–34.

Achen, Christopher H., and Larry M. Bartels. 2016. *Democracy for Realists*. Princeton: Princeton University Press.

Adorno, Theodor W., Else Frenkel-Brunswik, Daniel J. Levinson, and R. Nevitt Sanford. 1950. *The Authoritarian Personality*. New York: Harper.

Alba, Richard D. 1990. *Ethnic Identity: The Transformation of White America*. New Haven: Yale University Press.

Alba, Richard D., Rubén G. Rumbaut, and Karen Marotz. 2005. "A Distorted Nation: Perceptions of Racial/Ethnic Group Sizes and Attitudes toward Immigrants and Other Minorities." *Social Forces* 84(2): 901–19.

Albertson, Bethany, and Shana Kushner Gadarian. 2013. "Who's Afraid of Immigration? The Effects of Pro- and Anti-Immigrant Threatening Ads among Latinos, African Americans, and Whites." In *Immigration and Public Opinion in Liberal Democracies*, eds. Gary P. Freeman, Randall Hansen, and David L. Leal. New York: Routledge, 286–304.

2015. *Anxious Politics: Democratic Citizenship in a Threatening World*. New York: Cambridge University Press.

Allen, Theodore W. 1997. *The Invention of the White Race: The Origin of Racial Oppression in Anglo-America*. New York: Verso.

Allport, Gordon Willard. 1935. "Attitudes." In *Handbook of Social Psychology*, ed. Carl Murchison. New York: Russell & Russell, 798–811.

1954. *The Nature of Prejudice*. Oxford: Addison-Wesley.

Almond, Gabriel Abraham, and Sidney Verba. 1963. *The Civic Culture*. Princeton: Princeton University Press.

Altemeyer, Bob. 1981. *Right-Wing Authoritarianism*. Winnipeg: University of Manitoba Press.

1998. "The Other 'Authoritarian Personality'" ed. Mark P. Zanna. *Advances in Experimental Social Psychology* 30(1): 47–92.

Altman, Drew, and William H. Frist. 2015. "Medicare and Medicaid at 50 Years." *Journal of the American Medical Association* 314(4): 384–95.

Anderson, Barbara A., Brian D. Silver, and Paul R. Abramson. 1988. "The Effects of Race of the Interviewer on Measures of Electoral Participation by Blacks in SRC National Election Studies." *Public Opinion Quarterly* 52(1): 53–83.

Baker, Donald G. 1975. "Race, Power and White Siege Cultures." *Social Dynamics* 1(2): 143–57.

Baldwin, James. 1976. *The Devil Finds Work*. New York: Vintage International.

Barreto, Matt A., and Francisco I. Pedraza. 2009. "The Renewal and Persistence of Group Identification in American Politics." *Electoral Studies* 28(4): 595–605.

Benedict, Ruth. 1945. *Race: Science and Politics*. New York: Viking Press.

Bentele, Keith Gunnar, and Erin E. O'Brien. 2013. "Jim Crow 2.0? Why States Consider and Adopt Restrictive Voter Access Policies." *Perspectives on Politics* 11(4): 1088–116.

Berelson, Bernard R., Paul F. Lazarsfeld, and William N. McPhee. 1954. *Voting: A Study of Opinion Formation in a Presidential Campaign*. Chicago: University of Chicago Press.

Berinsky, Adam J., Gregory A. Huber, Gabriel S. Lenz, and R. Michael Alvarez. 2012. "Evaluating Online Labor Markets for Experimental Research: Amazon.Com's Mechanical Turk." *Political Analysis* 20(3): 351–68.

Berrens, Robert P., Alok K. Bohara, Hank Jenkins-Smith, Carol Silva, and David L. Wiemer. 2003. "The Advent of Internet Surveys for Political Research: A Comparison of Telephone and Internet Samples." *Political Analysis* 11(1): 1–22.

Best, Samuel J., Brian Krueger, Clark Hubbard, and Andrew Smith. 2001. "An Assessment of the Generalizability of Internet Surveys." *Social Science Computer Review* 19(2): 131–45.

Bettencourt, B. Ann, Nancy Dorr, Kelly Charlton, and Deborah L. Hume. 2001. "Status Differences and In-Group Bias: A Meta-Analytic Examination of the Effects of Status Stability, Status Legitimacy, and Group Permeability." *Psychological Bulletin* 127(1972): 520–42.

Bierstedt, Robert. 1948. "The Sociology of Majorities." *American Sociological Review* 13(6): 700–10.

Billington, Ray Allen. 1938. *The Protestant Crusade, 1800–1860.* New York: Macmillan.

Blalock, Hubert M. 1956. "Economic Discrimination and Negro Increase." *American Sociological Review* 21(5): 584–8.

    1967. *Toward a Theory of Minority-Group Relations.* New York: Wiley.

Blumer, Herbert. 1958. "Race Prejudice as a Sense of Group Position." *The Pacific Sociological Review* 1(1): 3–7.

Bobo, Lawrence D. 1983. "Whites' Opposition to Busing: Symbolic Racism or Realistic Group Conflict?" *Journal of Personality and Social Psychology* 45(6): 1196–210.

    1999. "Prejudice as Group Position: Microfoundations of a Sociological Approach to Racism and Race Relations." *Journal of Social Issues* 55(3): 445–72.

    2004. "Inequalities That Endure? Racial Ideology, American Politics, and the Peculiar Role of the Social Sciences." In *The Changing Terrain of Race and Ethnicity*, eds. Maria Krysan and Amanda E. Lewis. New York: Russell Sage Foundation, 13–42.

Bobo, Lawrence D., and Vincent L. Hutchings. 1996. "Perceptions of Racial Group Competition: Extending Blumer's Theory of Group Position to a Multiracial Social Context." *American Sociological Review* 61(6): 951–72.

Bobo, Lawrence D., and Devon Johnson. 2000. "Racial Attitudes in a Prismatic Metropolis: Mapping Identity, Stereotypes, Competition, and Views on Affirmative Action." In *Prismatic Metropolis: Inequality in Los Angeles: A Volume in the Multi-City Study of Urban Inequality*, eds. Lawrence D. Bobo, Melvin L. Oliver, James H. Johnson Jr., and Abel Valenzuela Jr. New York: Russell Sage Foundation, 81–163.

Bobo, Lawrence D., and James R. Kluegel. 1993. "Opposition to Race-Targeting: Self-Interest, Stratification Ideology, or Racial Attitudes?" *American Sociological Review* 58(4): 443.

Bobo, Lawrence D., and Frederick C. Licari. 1989. "Education and Political Tolerance: Testing the Effects of Cognitive Sophistication and Target Group Affect." *Public Opinion Quarterly* 53(3): 285–308.

Bonilla-Silva, Eduardo. 2010. *Racism without Racists: Color-Blind Racism and the Persistence of Racial Inequality in America*. 2nd ed. Lanham: Rowman & Littlefield.

Borghans, Lex, Angela Lee Duckworth, James J. Heckman, and Bas ter Weel. 2008. "The Economics and Psychology of Personality Traits." *Journal of Human Resources* 43(4): 972–1059.

Borjas, George J., and Richard B. Freeman. 1992. *Immigration and the Work Force: Economic Consequences for the United States and Source Areas*. Chicago: University of Chicago Press.

Brader, Ted. 2006. *Campaigning for Hearts and Minds*. Chicago: University of Chicago Press.

Brader, Ted, Nicholas A. Valentino, and Elizabeth Suhay. 2008. "What Triggers Public Opposition to Immigration? Anxiety, Group Cues, and Immigration Threat." *American Journal of Political Science* 52(4): 959–78.

Branscombe, Nyla R., Michael T. Schmitt, and Kristin Schiffhauer. 2007. "Racial Attitudes in Response to Thoughts of White Privilege." *European Journal of Social Psychology* 37(2): 203–15.

Brewer, Marilynn B. 1979. "In-Group Bias in the Minimal Intergroup Situation: A Cognitive-Motivational Analysis." *Psychological Bulletin* 86(2): 307–24.

———. 1999. "The Psychology of Prejudice: Ingroup Love or Outgroup Hate?" *Journal of Social Issues* 55(3): 429–44.

Brewer, Marilynn B., and Roderick M. Kramer. 1985. "The Psychology of Intergroup Attitudes and Behavior." *Annual Review of Psychology* 36(1): 219–43.

Brimelow, Peter. 1996. *Alien Nation: Common Sense About America's Immigration Disaster*. New York: HarperCollins.

Brodkin, Karen. 1998. *How Jews Became White Folks: And What That Says About Race in America*. New Brunswick: Rutgers University Press.

Brown, Robert A., and Todd C. Shaw. 2002. "Separate Nations: Two Attitudinal Dimensions of Black Nationalism." *Journal of Politics* 64(1): 22–44.

Brown, Rupert. 2000. "Social Identity Theory: Past Achievements, Current Problems and Future Challenges." *European Journal of Social Psychology* 30(6): 745–78.

Brubaker, Rogers, and Frederick Cooper. 2000. "Beyond 'Identity'." *Theory and Society* 29(1): 1–47.

Buchanan, Patrick J. 1991. "Pat Buchanan 1992 Announcement Speech." December 10, 1991. New Hampshire. www.4president.org/speeches/buchanan1992announcement.htm

1996. "Rally Speech in Santa Barbara, CA." March 24, 1996. https:// buchanan.org/blog/rally-speech-in-santa-barbara-ca-184

2011. *Suicide of a Superpower: Will America Survive to 2025?* New York: Macmillan.

Burfisher, Mary E., Sherman Robinson, and Karen Thierfelder. 2001. "The Impact of NAFTA on the United States." *Journal of Economic Perspectives* 15(1): 125–44.

Burns, Peter, and James G. Gimpel. 2000. "Economic Insecurity, Prejudicial Stereotypes, and Public Opinion on Immigration Policy." *Political Science Quarterly* 115(2): 201–25.

Bush, Melanie E.L. 2004. *Breaking the Code of Good Intentions: Everyday Forms of Whiteness.* Lanham: Rowman & Littlefield.

Calavita, Kitty. 1996. "The New Politics of Immigration: 'Balanced-Budget Conservatism' and the Symbolism of Proposition 187." *Social Problems* 43(3): 284–305.

Caliendo, Lorenzo, and Fernando Parro. 2015. "Estimates of the Trade and Welfare Effects of NAFTA." *Review of Economic Studies* 82(1): 1–44.

Cameron, James E. 2004. "A Three-Factor Model of Social Identity." *Self and Identity* 3(3): 239–62.

Campbell, Andrea Louise. 2003. "Participatory Reactions to Policy Threats: Senior Citizens and the Defense of Social Security and Medicare." *Political Behavior* 25(1): 29–49.

Campbell, Andrea Louise, Cara Wong, and Jack Citrin. 2006. "'Racial Threat', Partisan Climate, and Direct Democracy: Contextual Effects in Three California Initiatives." *Political Behavior* 28(2): 129–50.

Campbell, Angus, Philip E. Converse, Warren E. Miller, and Donald E. Stokes. 1960. *The American Voter.* Chicago: University of Chicago Press.

Carmines, Edward G., and James A. Stimson. 1989. *Issue Evolution.* Princeton: Princeton University Press.

Castles, Stephen, Heather Booth, and Tina Wallace. 1984. *Here for Good: Western Europe's New Ethnic Minorities.* London: Pluto Press.

Chang, Linchiat, and Jon A. Krosnick. 2009. "National Surveys via RDD Telephone Interviewing Versus the Internet: Comparing Sample Representativeness and Response Quality." *Public Opinion Quarterly* 73(4): 641–78.

Chin, Gabriel J. 1996. "The Civil Rights Revolution Comes to Immigration Law: A New Look at the Immigration and Nationality Act of 1965." *North Carolina Law Review* 75(1): 273–345.

Chong, Dennis, and Reuel Rogers. 2005. "Racial Solidarity and Political Participation." *Political Behavior* 27(4): 347–74.

Citrin, Jack. 2001. "The End of American Identity?" In *One America?* ed. S. Renshon. Washington, DC: Georgetown University Press, 285–307.

Citrin, Jack, and David O. Sears. 2014. *American Identity and the Politics of Multiculturalism*. New York: Cambridge University Press.

Citrin, Jack, and John Sides. 2008. "Immigration and the Imagined Community in Europe and the United States." *Political Studies* 56(1): 33–56.

Citrin, Jack, Beth Reingold, and Donald P. Green. 1990. "American Identity and the Politics of Ethnic Change." *The Journal of Politics* 52(4): 1124–54.

Citrin, Jack, Cara Wong, and Brian Duff. 2001. "The Meaning of American National Identity: Patterns of Ethnic Conflict and Consensus." In *Social Identity, Intergroup Conflict, and Conflict Reduction*, eds. Richard D. Ashmore, Lee Jussim, and David Wilder. New York: Oxford University Press, 71–100.

Citrin, Jack, Donald P. Green, Christopher Muste, and Cara Wong. 1997. "Public Opinion Toward Immigration Reform: The Role of Economic Motivations." *The Journal of Politics* 59(3): 858–81.

Citrin, Jack, Amy Lerman, Michael Murakami, and Kathryn Pearson. 2007. "Testing Huntington: Is Hispanic Immigration a Threat to American Identity?" *Perspectives on Politics* 5(1): 31–48.

Clark, John A., and Jerome S. Jr. Legge. 1997. "Economics, Racism, and Attitudes toward Immigration in the New Germany." *Political Research Quarterly* 50(4): 901–17.

Coenders, Marcel, and Peer Scheepers. 1998. "Support for Ethnic Discrimination in the Netherlands 1979–1993: Effects of Period, Cohort, and Individual Characteristics." *European Sociological Review* 14(4): 405–22.

Colby, Sandra L., and Jennifer M. Ortman. 2014. U.S. Census Bureau Current Population Reports *Projections of the Size and Composition of the US Population: 2014 to 2060*.

Conover, Pamela Johnston. 1984. "The Influence of Group Identifications on Political Perception and Evaluation." *Journal of Politics* 46(3): 760–85.

1988. "The Role of Social Groups in Political Thinking." *British Journal of Political Science* 18(1): 51–76.

Conover, Pamela Johnston, and Stanley Feldman. 1981. "The Origins and Meaning of Liberal/Conservative Self-Identifications." *American Journal of Political Science* 25(4): 617–45.

Converse, Philip E. 1964. "The Nature of Belief Systems in Mass Publics." In *Ideology and Discontent*, ed. David E. Apter. New York: Free Press, 1–74.

Coser, Lewis A. 1956. *The Functions of Social Conflict*. New York: Simon & Schuster.

Cottrell, Catherine A., and Steven L. Neuberg. 2005. "Different Emotional Reactions to Different Groups: A Sociofunctional Threat-Based Approach to 'Prejudice'." *Journal of Personality and Social Psychology* 88(5): 770–89.

Craig, Maureen A., and Jennifer A. Richeson. 2014a. "More Diverse yet Less Tolerant? How the Increasingly-Diverse Racial Landscape Affects White Americans' Racial Attitudes." *Personality and Social Psychology Bulletin* 40(6): 750–61.

2014b. "On the Precipice of a 'Majority-Minority' America: Perceived Status Threat from the Racial Demographic Shift Affects White Americans' Political Ideology." *Psychological Science* 25(6): 1189–97.

Cramer, Katherine J. 2016. *The Politics of Resentment: Rural Consciousness in Wisconsin and the Rise of Scott Walker*. Chicago: University of Chicago Press.

Crespino, Joseph. 2007. *In Search of Another Country: Mississippi and the Conservative Counterrevolution*. Princeton: Princeton University Press.

Crocker, Jennifer, and Riia Luhtanen. 1990. "Collective Self-Esteem and Ingroup Bias." *Journal of Personality and Social Psychology* 58(1): 60–7.

Croll, Paul R. 2007. "Modeling Determinants of White Racial Identity: Results from a New National Survey." *Social Forces* 86(2): 613–42.

2008. "A New Look at Racial Attitudes in America: Incorporating Whiteness by Examining White Privilege." Unpublished Ph. D. Dissertation, The University of Minnesota.

Danbold, Felix, and Yuen J. Huo. 2015. "No Longer 'All-American'? Whites' Defensive Reactions to Their Numerical Decline." *Social Psychological and Personality Science* 6(2): 210–18.

Daniels, Roger. 2002. *Coming to America: A History of Immigration and Ethnicity in American Life*. 2nd ed. New York: HarperCollins.

Dawson, Michael C. 1994. *Behind the Mule: Race and Class in African-American Politics*. Princeton: Princeton University Press.

2001. *Black Visions: The Roots of Contemporary African-American Political Ideologies*. Chicago: University of Chicago Press.

2009. "Black and Blue: Black Identity and Black Solidarity in an Era of Conservative Triumph." In *Measuring Identity: A Guide for Social Scientists*, eds. Rawi Abdelal, Yoshiko M. Herrera, Alastair Iain Johnston, and Rose McDermott. New York: Cambridge University Press, 175–99.

Delgado, Richard. 2013. "Precious Knowledge: State Bans on Ethnic Studies, Book Traffickers (Librotraficantes), and a New Type of Race Trial." *North Carolina Law Review* 91: 1513–54.

Delgado, Richard, and Jean Stefancic. 1997. *Critical White Studies: Looking Behind the Mirror*. Eds. Richard Delgado and Jean Stefancic. Philadelphia: Temple University Press.

Derthick, Martha. 1979. *Policymaking for Social Security*. Washington, DC: Brookings Institution.

Desante, Christopher D. 2013. "Working Twice as Hard to Get Half as Far: Race, Work Ethic, and America's Deserving Poor." *American Journal of Political Science* 57(2): 342–56.

Devos, Thierry, and Mahzarin R. Banaji. 2005. "American = White?" *Journal of Personality and Social Psychology* 88(3): 447–66.

DeWitt, Larry. 2010. "The Decision to Exclude Agricultural and Domestic Workers from the 1935 Social Security Act." *Social Security Bulletin* 70(4): 49–68.

Ditonto, Tessa M., Richard R. Lau, and David O. Sears. 2013. "AMPing Racial Attitudes: Comparing the Power of Explicit and Implicit Racism Measures in 2008." *Political Psychology* 34(4): 487–510.

Doane, Ashley W. 1997. "Dominant Group Ethnic Identity in the United States: The Role of 'Hidden' Ethnicity in Intergroup Relations." *The Sociological Quarterly* 38(3): 375–97.

2003. "Rethinking Whiteness Studies." In *White Out: The Continuing Significance of Racism*, eds. Ashley W. Doane and Eduardo Bonillva-Silva. New York: Routledge, 3–20.

Doane, Ashley W., and Eduardo Bonilla-Silva. 2003. *White Out: The Continuing Significance of Racism*. New York: Routledge.

Doosje, Bertjan, Russell Spears, and Naomi Ellemers. 2002. "Social Identity as Both Cause and Effect: The Development of Group Identifica ..." *The British Journal of Social Psychology* 41: 57–76.

Doosje, Bertjan, Nyla R. Branscombe, Russell Spears, and Antony S. R. Manstead. 1998. "Guilty by Association: When One's Group Has a Negative History." *Journal of Personality and Social Psychology* 75(4): 872–86.

Du Bois, W.E.B. 1935. *Black Reconstruction in America: Toward a History of the Part Which Black Folk Played in the Attempt to Reconstruct Democracy in America 1860–1880*. New York: Harcourt, Brace, and Company.

Duckitt, John H. 1989. "Authoritarianism and Group Identification: A New View of an Old Construct." *Political Psychology* 10(1): 63–84.

1992. *The Social Psychology of Prejudice*. New York: Praeger.

2001. "A Dual-Process Cognitive-Motivational Theory of Ideology and Prejudice" ed. Mark P. Zanna. *Advances in Experimental Social Psychology* 33(1): 41–113.

2003. "Prejudice and Intergroup Hostility." In *Oxford Handbook of Political Psychology*, eds. David O. Sears, Leonie Huddy, and Robert Jervis. Oxford: Oxford University Press, 559–600.

Effron, Daniel A., and Eric D. Knowles. 2015. "Entitativity and Intergroup Bias: How Belonging to a Cohesive Group Allows People to Express Their Prejudices." *Journal of Personality and Social Psychology* 108(2): 234–53.

Ellemers, Naomi, Ad van Knippenberg, and Henk Wilke. 1990. "The Influence of Permeability of Group Boundaries and Stability of Group Status on Strategies of Individual Mobility and Social Change." *British Journal of Social Psychology* 29(3): 233–46.

Ellemers, Naomi, Paulien Kortekaas, and Jaap W. Ouwerkerk. 1999. "Self-Categorisation, Commitment to the Group and Group Self-Esteem as Related But Distinct Aspects of Social Identity." *European Journal of Social Psychology* 29(2–3): 371–89.

Erikson, Erik H. 1966. "The Concept of Identity in Race Relations: Notes and Queries." *Daedalus* 95(1): 145–71.

Espenshade, Thomas J., and Charles A. Calhoun. 1993. "An Analysis of Public Opinion toward Undocumented Immigration." *Population Research and Policy Review* 12(3): 189–224.

Espenshade, Thomas J., and Katherine Hempstead. 1996. "Contemporary American Attitudes Toward U.S. Immigration." *The International Migration Review* 30(2): 535–70.

Fearon, James D. 1999. "What Is Identity (As We Now Use the Word)?" Unpublished paper. Stanford.

Feldman, Stanley. 1982. "Economic Self-Interest and Political Behavior." *American Journal of Political Science* 26(3): 446–66.

2003. "Enforcing Social Conformity: A Theory of Authoritarianism." *Political Psychology* 24(1): 41–74.

Feldman, Stanley, and Leonie Huddy. 2005. "Racial Resentment and White Opposition to Race-Conscious Programs: Principles or Prejudice?" *American Journal of Political Science* 49(1): 168–83.

Feldman, Stanley, and Karen Stenner. 1997. "Perceived Threat and Authoritarianism." *Political Psychology* 18(4): 741–70.

Feldman, Stanley, and John Zaller. 1992. "The Political Culture of Ambivalence: Ideological Responses to the Welfare State." *American Journal of Political Science* 36(1): 268–307.

Ferber, Abby L. 1998. *White Man Falling: Race, Gender and White Supremacy.* Lanham: Rowman & Littlefield.

Fetzer, Joel S. 2000. *Public Attitudes toward Immigration in the United States, France, and Germany.* New York: Cambridge University Press.

Finkel, Steven E., Thomas M. Guterbock, and Marian J. Borg. 1991. "Race-of-Interviewer Effects in a Preelection Poll Virginia 1989." *Public Opinion Quarterly* 55(3): 313–30.

Flagg, B.J. 1993. "Was Blind, but Now I See: White Race Consciousness and the Requirement of Discriminatory Intent." *Michigan Law Review* 91(5): 953.

Foner, Philip Sheldon. 1964. *History of the Labor Movement in the United States: The Policies and Practices of the American Federation of Labor 1900–1909.* New York: International Publisher.

Franco, Juan N. 1985. "Intelligence Tests and Social Policy." *Journal of Counseling and Development* 64(4): 278–9.

Frankenberg, Ruth. 1993. *White Women, Race Matters: The Social Construction of Whiteness*. Minneapolis: University of Minnesota Press.

2001. "Mirage of An Unmarked Whiteness." In *The Making and Unmaking of Whiteness*, eds. Birgit Brander Rasmussen, Eric Klinenberg, Irene J. Nexica, and Matt Wray. Durham, NC: Duke University Press, 72–96.

Fukuyama, Francis. 1993. "Immigrants and Family Values." *Commentary* 95(5): 26–32.

Gabennesch, Howard. 1972. "Authoritarianism as World View." *American Journal of Sociology* 77(5): 857–75.

Gaertner, Samuel L., and John F. Dovidio. 2005. "Categorization, Recategorization, and Intergroup Bias." In *On the Nature of Prejudice: Fifty Years after Allport*, eds. John F. Dovidio, Peter Glick, and Laurie A. Rudman. Hoboken: Wiley-Blackwell, 71–88.

Gaertner, Samuel L., John F. Dovidio, Brenda S. Banker, Marcy C. Rust, Jason A. Nier, Gary R. Mottola, and Christine M. Ward. 1997. "Does White Racism Necessarily Mean Antiblackness?" In *Off White: Readings on Power, Privilege, and Resistance*. New York: Routledge, 167–78.

Gallagher, Charles A. 1997. "White Racial Formation: Into the Twenty-First Century." In *Critical White Studies: Looking Behind the Mirror*, eds. Richard Delgado and Jean Stefancic. Philadelphia: Temple University Press, 6–11.

Gans, Herbert J. 2012. "'Whitening' and the Changing American Racial Hierarchy." *Du Bois Review: Social Science Research on Race* 9(2): 267–79.

Gay, Claudine, Jennifer Hochschild, and Ariel White. 2016. "Americans' Belief in Linked Fate: Does the Measure Capture the Concept?" *The Journal of Race, Ethnicity, and Politics* 1(1): 117–44.

Gerber, Alan S., Gregory A. Huber, David Doherty, Conor M. Dowling, and Shang E. Ha. 2010. "Personality and Political Attitudes: Relationships across Issue Domains and Political Contexts." *American Political Science Review* 104(1): 111–33.

Gerber, Alan S., Gregory A. Huber, David Doherty, and Conor M. Dowling. 2012. "Personality and the Strength and Direction of Partisan Identification." *Political Behavior* 34(4): 653–88.

Gest, Justin. 2016. *The New Minority: White Working Class Politics in an Age of Immigration and Inequality*. New York: Oxford University Press.

Gilens, Martin. 1996. "'Race Coding' and White Opposition to Welfare." *The American Political Science Review* 90(3): 593–604.

1999. *Why Americans Hate Welfare: Race, Media, and the Politics of Antipoverty Policy*. Chicago: University of Chicago Press.

Giles, Michael W., and Arthur S. Evans. 1985. "External Threat, Perceived Threat, and Group Identity." *Social Science Quarterly* 66(1): 50–66.

Giles, Michael W., and Kaenan Hertz. 1994. "Racial Threat and Partisan Identification." *The American Political Science Review* 88(2): 317–26.

Glaser, James M. 1994. "Back to the Black Belt: Racial Environment and White Racial Attitudes in the South." *The Journal of Politics* 56(1): 21–41.

Gleason, Philip. 1983. "Identifying Identity: A Semantic History." *The Journal of American History* 69(4): 910–31.

Goldman, Seth K. 2012. "Effects of the 2008 Obama Presidential Campaign on White Racial Prejudice." *Public Opinion Quarterly* 76(4): 663–87.

Goodwin, Renee D., and Howard S. Friedman. 2006. "Health Status and the Five-Factor Personality Traits in a Nationally Representative Sample." *Journal of Health Psychology* 11(5): 643–54.

Gordon, Linda. 1994. *Pitied But Not Entitled: Single Mothers and the History of Welfare, 1890–1935.* New York: Free Press.

Gould, Stephen Jay. 1981. *The Mismeasure of Man.* New York: W.W. Norton & Company.

Grant, Peter R., and Rupert Brown. 1995. "From Ethnocentrism to Collective Protest: Responses to Relative Deprivation and Threats to Social Identity." *Social Psychology Quarterly* 58(3): 195–212.

Green, Donald P., Bradley Palmquist, and Eric Schickler. 1998. "Macropartisanship: A Replication and Critique." *The American Political Science Review* 92(4): 883–99.

2002. *Partisan Hearts and Minds: Political Parties and the Social Identities of Voters.* New Haven: Yale University Press.

Greene, Steven. 1999. "Understanding Party Identification: A Social Identity Approach." *Political Psychology* 20(2): 393–403.

Gurin, Patricia. 1983. "Women's Gender Consciousness." *Public Opinion Quarterly* 49(2): 143–63.

Gurin, Patricia, and Aloen Townsend. 1986. "Properties of Gender Identity and Their Implications for Gender Consciousness." *British Journal of Social Psychology* 25(2): 139–48.

Gurin, Patricia, Arthur H. Miller, and Gerald Gurin. 1980. "Stratum Identification and Consciousness." *Social Psychology Quarterly* 43(1): 30–47.

Hainmueller, Jens, and Michael J. Hiscox. 2010. "Attitudes toward Highly Skilled and Low-Skilled Immigration: Evidence from a Survey Experiment." *American Political Science Review* 104(1): 61–84.

Hainmueller, Jens, and Daniel J. Hopkins. 2014. "Public Attitudes Toward Immigration." *Annual Review of Political Science* 17(1): 225–49.

Hajnal, Zoltan, and Taeku Lee. 2011. *Why Americans Don't Join the Party: Race, Immigration, and the Failure (of Political Parties) to Engage the Electorate*. Princeton: Princeton University Press.

Hajnal, Zoltan, and Michael U. Rivera. 2014. "Immigration, Latinos, and White Partisan Politics: The New Democratic Defection." *American Journal of Political Science* 58(4): 773–89.

Haney-Lopez, Ian. 2006. *White by Law: The Legal Construction of Race*. 10th ed. New York: New York University Press.

2014. *Dog Whistle Politics: How Coded Racial Appeals Have Reinvented Racism and Wrecked the Middle Class*. New York: Oxford University Press.

Hannaford, Ivan. 1996. *Race: The History of an Idea in The West*. Washington, DC: Woodrow Wilson Center Press.

Hanson, Victor Davis. 2003. *Mexifornia: A State of Becoming*. San Francisco: Encounter Books.

Harris, Cheryl I. 1993. "Whiteness as Property." *Harvard Law Review* 106(8): 1707–91.

Hartigan Jr., John. 1997. "Establishing the Fact of Whiteness." *American Anthropologist* 99(3): 495–505.

Hartmann, Douglas, Joseph Gerteis, and Paul R. Croll. 2009. "An Empirical Assessment of Whiteness Theory: Hidden from How Many?" *Social Problems* 56(3): 403–24.

Hatchett, Shirley, and Howard Schuman. 1975. "White Respondents and Race-of-Interviewer Effects." *The Public Opinion Quarterly* 39(4): 523–28.

Helms, Janet E. 1984. "Toward a Theoretical Explanation of the Effects of Race on Counseling A Black and White Model." *The Counseling Psychologist* 12(4): 153–65.

1990. *Black and White Racial Identity: Theory, Research, and Practice*. Westport: Greenwood Press.

1995. "An Update of Helms' White and People of Color Racial Identity Models." In *Handbook of Multicultural Counseling*, eds. Joseph G. Ponterotto, J. Manuel Casas, Lisa A. Suzuki, and Charlene M. Alexander. Thousand Oaks: Sage Publications, 181–98.

Henderson, Michael, and D. Sunshine Hillygus. 2011. "The Dynamics of Health Care Opinion, 2008–2010: Partisanship, Self-Interest, and Racial Resentment." *Journal of Health Politics, Policy and Law* 36(6): 945–60.

Herberg, Will. 1955. *Protestant-Catholic-Jew: An Essay in American Religious Sociology*. Garden City: Doubleday.

Herring, Mary, Thomas B. Jankowski, and Ronald E. Brown. 1999. "Pro-Black Doesn't Mean Anti-White: The Structure of African-American Group Identity." *Journal of Politics* 61(2): 363–86.

Hetherington, Marc J., and Jonathan D. Weiler. 2009. *Authoritarianism and Polarization in American Politics*. New York: Cambridge University Press.

Higham, John. 1955. *Strangers in the Land: Patterns of American Nativism, 1860–1925*. New Brunswick: Rutgers University Press.

Hillygus, D. Sunshine, and Todd Shields. 2008. "Southern Discomfort? Regional Differences in Voter Decision Making in the 2000 Presidential Election." *Presidential Studies Quarterly* 38(3): 506–20.

Hillygus, D. Sunshine, Seth C. McKee, and McKenzie Young. 2017. "Reversal of Fortune: The Political Behavior of White Migrants to the South." *Presidential Studies Quarterly* 47(2): 354–64.

Hinkle, Steve, Lee Fox-Cardamone, Julia A. Haseleu, Rupert Brown, and Lois M. Irwin. 1996. "Grassroots Political Action as an Intergroup Phenomenon." *Journal of Social Issues* 52(1): 39–51.

Hinkle, Steve, Laurie A. Taylor, D. Lee Fox-Cardamone, and Kimberly F. Crook. 1989. "Intragroup Identification and Intergroup Differentiation: A Multicomponent Approach." *British Journal of Social Psychology* 28(4): 305–17.

Hochschild, Arlie Russell. 2016. *Strangers in Their Own Land*. New York: The New Press.

Hofstadter, Richard. 1992. *Social Darwinism in American Thought*. Boston: Beacon Press.

Hooper, Michael. 1976. "The Structure and Measurement of Social Identity." *Public Opinion Quarterly* 40(2): 154–64.

Hopkins, Daniel J. 2010. "Politicized Places: Explaining Where and When Immigrants Provoke Local Opposition." *American Political Science Review* 104(1): 40–60.

Huddy, Leonie. 2003. "Group Identity and Political Cohesion." In *Oxford Handbook of Political Psychology*, eds. David O. Sears, Leonie Huddy, and Robert Jervis. Oxford and New York: Oxford University Press, 511–58.

2013. "From Group Identity to Political Cohesion and Commitment." In *The Oxford Handbook of Political Psychology*, eds. Leonie Huddy, David O. Sears, and Jack S. Levy. New York: Oxford University Press, 737–73.

Huddy, Leonie, and Nadia Khatib. 2007. "American Patriotism, National Identity, and Political Involvement." *American Journal of Political Science* 51(1): 63–77.

Huddy, Leonie, Lilliana Mason, and Lene Aarøe. 2015. "Expressive Partisanship: Campaign Involvement, Political Emotion, and Partisan Identity." *American Political Science Review* 109(1): 1–17.

Hughes, Everett C. 1948. "The Study of Ethnic Relations." *Dalhousie Review* 27(4): 477–85.

Hughey, Matthew W. 2012. "Show Me Your Papers! Obama's Birth and the Whiteness of Belonging." *Qualitative Sociology* 35(2): 163–81.

Huntington, Samuel P. 2004. *Who Are We? The Challenges to America's National Identity.* New York: Simon & Schuster.

Hurwitz, Michael. 2011. "The Impact of Legacy Status on Undergraduate Admissions at Elite Colleges and Universities." *Economics of Education Review* 30(3): 480–92.

Hutchings, Vincent L. 2009. "Change or More of the Same? Evaluating Racial Attitudes in the Obama Era." *Public Opinion Quarterly* 73(5): 917–42.

Hutchings, Vincent L., Cara J. Wong, James S. Jackson, and Rupert J. Brown. 2011. "Explaining Perceptions of Competitive Threat in a Multiracial Context." In *Race, Reform, and Regulation of the Electoral Process*, eds. Guy-Uriel E. Charles, Heather K. Gerken, and Michael S. Kang. New York: Cambridge University Press, 52–74.

Hyman, Herbert Hiram. 1954. *Interviewing in Social Research.* Chicago: University of Chicago Press.

Hyman, Herbert Hiram, and Charles Robert Wright. 1979. *Education's Lasting Influence on Values.* Chicago: Chicago University Press.

Ignatiev, Noel. 1995. *How the Irish Became White.* New York: Routledge.

Ignatiev, Noel, and John Garvey. 1996. *Race Traitor.* New York: Routledge.

Jackman, Mary R. 1994. *The Velvet Glove: Paternalism and Conflict in Gender, Class, and Race Relations.* Berkeley: University of California Press.

Jackman, Mary R., and Michael J. Muha. 1984. "Education and Intergroup Attitudes: Moral Enlightenment, Superficial Democratic Commitment, or Ideological Refinement?" *American Sociological Review* 49(6): 751–69.

Jackman, Simon. 2008. "Measurement." In *The Oxford Handbook of Political Methodology*, eds. Janet M. Box-Steffensmeier, Henry E. Brady, and David Collier. New York: Oxford University Press, 119–51.

Jackson, Jay W. 1993. "Realistic Group Conflict Theory: A Review and Evaluation of the Theoretical and Empirical Literature." *The Psychological Record* 43(3): 395–414.

Jackson, Jay W., and Eliot R. Smith. 1999. "Conceptualizing Social Identity: A New Framework and Evidence for the Impact of Different Dimensions." *Personality and Social Psychology Bulletin* 25(1): 120–35.

Jackson II, Ronald L., and Susan M. Heckman. 2002. "Perceptions of White Identity and White Liability: An Analysis of White Student Responses to a College Campus Racial Hate Crime." *Journal of Communication* 52(2): 434–50.

Jacobson, Cardell K. 1985. "Resistance to Affirmative Action: Self-Interest or Racism?" *The Journal of Conflict Resolution* 29(2): 306–29.

Jacobson, Matthew Frye. 1999. *Whiteness of a Different Color: European Immigrants and the Alchemy of Race.* Cambridge, MA: Harvard University Press.

Jardina, Ashley E., and Michael Traugott. "The Genesis of the Birther Rumor: Partisanship, Racial Attitudes, and Political Knowledge." *Journal of Race, Ethnicity, and Politics* (in press).

Judis, John B., and Ruy Texeira. 2002. *The Emerging Democratic Majority*. New York: Simon & Schuster.

Junn, Jane, and Natalie Masuoka. 2008. "Asian Status American and Identity: Shared Racial Political Context." *Perspectives on Politics* 6(4): 729–40.

Kalmoe, Nathan P., and Spencer Piston. 2013. "Is Implicit Prejudice Against Blacks Politically Consequential? Evidence from the AMP." *Public Opinion Quarterly* 77(1): 305–22.

Kam, Cindy D., and Donald R. Kinder. 2012. "Ethnocentrism as a Short-Term Force in the 2008 American Presidential Election." *American Journal of Political Science* 56(2): 326–40.

Kaufmann, Eric P. 2000. "Ethnic or Civic Nation? Theorizing the American Case." *Canadian Review of Studies in Nationalism* 27: 1–45.

2004. *The Rise and Fall of Anglo-America*. Cambridge, MA: Harvard University Press.

2017. *"Racial Self-Interest" Is Not Racism: Ethno-Demographic Interests and the Immigration Debate*. London: Policy Exchange.

Key, V.O. 1949. *Southern Politics in State and Nation*. New York: Knopf.

1961. *Public Opinion and American Democracy*. New York: Knopf.

1966. *The Responsible Electorate: Rationality in Presidential Voting, 1936–1960*. Cambridge, MA: Harvard University Press.

Kiewiet, D. Roderick. 1983. *Macroeconomics and Micropolitics: The Electoral Effects of Economic Issues*. Chicago: University of Chicago Press.

Kim, Claire Jean. 2000. *Bitter Fruit: The Politics of Black Korean Conflict in New York*. New Haven: Yale University Press.

Kinder, Donald R. 1998. "Opinion and Action in the Realm of Politics." In *The Handbook of Social Psychology*, eds. Daniel T. Gilbert, Susan T. Fiske, and Gardner Lindzey. New York: Oxford University Press, 778–867.

Kinder, Donald R., and Allison Dale-Riddle. 2012. *The End of Race? Obama, 2008, and Racial Politics in America*. New Haven: Yale University Press.

Kinder, Donald R., and Nathan P. Kalmoe. 2017. *Neither Liberal Nor Conservative: Ideological Innocence in the American Public*. Chicago: University of Chicago Press.

Kinder, Donald R., and Cindy D. Kam. 2010. *Us Against Them: Ethnocentric Foundations of American Opinion*. Chicago: University of Chicago Press.

Kinder, Donald R., and D. Roderick Kiewiet. 1981. "Sociotropic Politics: The American Case." *British Journal of Political Science* 11(2): 129–61.

Kinder, Donald R., and Walter R. Mebane. 1983. "Politics and Economics in Everyday Life." In *The Political Process and Economic Change*, eds. Kristen R. Monroe and Bruno S. Frey. New York: Agathon Press, 141–80.

Kinder, Donald R., and Tali Mendelberg. 2000. "Individualism Reconsidered." In *Racialized Politics: The Debate About Racism in America*, eds. David O. Sears, Jim Sidanius, and Lawrence Bobo. Chicago: University of Chicago Press, 44–74.

Kinder, Donald R., and Lynn M. Sanders. 1996. *Divided by Color*. Chicago: University of Chicago Press.

Kinder, Donald R., and David O. Sears. 1981. "Prejudice and Politics: Symbolic Racism Versus Racial Threats to the Good Life." *Journal of Personality and Social Psychology* 40(3): 414–31.

Kinder, Donald R., and Nicholas J.G. Winter. 2001. "Exploring the Racial Divide: Blacks, Whites, and Opinion on National Policy." *American Journal of Political Science* 45(2): 439–56.

King, Desmond S. 2000. *Making Americans: Immigration, Race, and the Origins of the Diverse Democracy*. Cambridge, MA: Harvard University Press.

King, Gary, Robert O. Keohane, and Sidney Verba. 1994. *Designing Social Inquiry: Scientific Inference in Qualitative Research*. Princeton: Princeton University Press.

Kitschelt, Herbert. 2007. "Growth and Persistence of the Radical Right in Postindustrial Democracies: Advances and Challenges in Comparative Research." *West European Politics* 30(5): 1176–206.

Klinkner, Philip A., and Rogers M. Smith. 1999. *The Unsteady March: The Rise and Decline of Racial Equality in America*. Chicago: University of Chicago Press.

Kluegel, James R., and Eliot R. Smith. 1982. "Whites' Beliefs about Blacks' Opportunity." *American Sociological Review* 47(4): 518–32.

Knowles, Eric D., and Kaiping Peng. 2005. "White Selves: Conceptualizing and Measuring a Dominant-Group Identity." *Journal of Personality and Social Psychology* 89(2): 223–41.

Knowles, Eric D., and Linda R. Tropp. 2018. "The Racial and Economic Context of Trump Support: Evidence for Threat, Identity, and Contact Effects in the 2016 Presidential Election." *Social Psychological and Personality Science* 9(3): 275–84.

Knowles, Eric D., Brian S. Lowery, Rosalind M. Chow, and Miguel M. Unzueta. 2014. "Deny, Distance, or Dismantle? How White Americans Manage a Privileged Identity." *Perspectives on Psychological Science* 9(6): 594–609.

Krysan, Maria. 1998. "Privacy and the Expression of White Racial Attitudes: A Comparison Across Three Contexts." *Public Opinion Quarterly* 62(4): 506–44.

Kuklinski, James H., Michael D. Cobb, and Martin Gilens. 1997. "Racial Attitudes and the 'New South'." *The Journal of Politics* 59(2): 323–49.

LaFleur, N. Kenneth, Wayne Rowe, and Mark M. Leach. 2002. "Reconceptualizing White Racial Consciousness." *Journal of Multicultural Counseling and Development* 30(3): 148–52.

Lane, Robert Edwards. 1959. *Political Life: Why and How People Get Involved in Politics*. Glencoe: The Free Press.

Lapinski, John S., Pia Peltola, Greg Shaw, and Alan Yang. 1997. "Trends: Immigrants and Immigration." *The Public Opinion Quarterly* 61(2): 356–83.

Lasswell, Harold D. 1936. *Politics: Who Gets What, When and How.* New York: Whittlesey House.

Lau, Richard R. 1989. "Individual and Contextual Influences on Group Identification." *Social Psychology Quarterly* 52(3): 220–31.

Lazarsfeld, Paul Felix, Bernard R. Berelson, and Hazel Gaudet. 1944. *The People's Choice: How the Voter Makes up His Mind in a Presidential Campaign*. New York: Columbia University Press.

Leach, C.W., Martijn van Zomeren, Sven Zebel, Michael L.W. Vliek, Sjoerd F. Pennekamp, Bertjan Doosje, Jaap W. Ouwerkerk, and Russell Spears. 2008. "Group-Level Self-Definition and Self-Investment: A Hierarchical (Multicomponent) Model of in-Group Identification." *Journal of Personality and Social Psychology* 95(1): 144–65.

Leach, Mark M., John T. Behrens, and N. Kenneth Lafleur. 2002. "White Racial Identity and White Racial Consciousness: Similarities, Differences, and Recommendations." *Journal of Multicultural Counseling and Development* 30(2): 66–80.

Lee, Jennifer, and Frank D. Bean. 2004. "America's Changing Color Lines: Immigration, Race/Ethnicity, and Multiracial Identification." *Annual Review of Sociology* 30(1): 221–42.

2007. "Reinventing the Color Line: Immigration and America's New Racial/ Ethnic Divide." *Social Forces* 86(2): 561–86.

2010. *The Diversity Paradox: Immigration and the Color Line in Twenty-First Century America*. New York: Russell Sage Foundation.

Lee, Taeku. 2013. "Déjà Vu All Over Again? Racial Contestation in the Obama Era." In *The New Black: What Has Changed—And What Has Not—With Race in America*, eds. Kenneth W. Mack and Guy-Uriel E. Charles. New York: The New Press, 34–48.

Levin, Shana, and Jim Sidanius. 1999. "Social Dominance and Social Identity in the United States and Israel: Ingroup Favoritism or Outgroup Derogation?" *Political Psychology* 20(1): 99–126.

Levin, Shana, Jim Sidanius, Joshua L. Rabinowitz, and Christopher M. Federico. 1998. "Ethnic Identity, Legitimizing Ideologies, and Social

Status: A Matter of Ideological Asymmetry." *Political Psychology* 19(2): 373–404.

LeVine, Robert Alan, and Donald Thomas Campbell. 1972. *Ethnocentrism: Theories of Conflict, Ethnic Attitudes, and Group Behavior.* Hoboken: John Wiley & Sons.

Levitin, Teresa E., and Warren E. Miller. 1979. "Ideological Interpretations of Presidential Elections." *The American Political Science Review* 73(3): 751–71.

Lewis-Beck, Michael S., Charles Tien, and Richard Nadeau. 2010. "Obama's Missed Landslide: A Racial Cost?" *PS: Political Science and Politics* 43(1): 69–76.

Lichtenstein, Nelson, Susan Strasser, Roy Rosenzweig, Stephen Brier, and Joshua Brown. 2000. *Who Built America? Since 1877.* 2nd ed. New York: Bedford/St. Martin's.

Lieberman, Robert C. 1995. "Race, Institutions, and the Administration of Social Policy." *Social Science History* 19(4): 511–42.

Lipsitz, George. 1998. *The Possessive Investment in Whiteness: How White People Profit from Identity Politics.* Philadelphia: Temple University Press.

Lowery, Brian S., Eric D. Knowles, and Miguel M. Unzueta. 2007. "Framing Inequity Safely: Whites' Motivated Perceptions of Racial Privilege." *Personality & Social Psychology Bulletin* 33(9): 1237–50.

Lowery, Brian S., Miguel M. Unzueta, Eric D. Knowles, and Phillip Atiba Goff. 2006. "Concern for the In-Group and Opposition to Affirmative Action." *Journal of Personality and Social Psychology* 90(6): 961–74.

Luhtanen, Riia, and Jennifer Crocker. 1992. "A Collective Self-Esteem Scale: Self-Evaluation of One's Social Identity." *Personality and Social Psychology Bulletin* 18(3): 302–18.

Mackie, Diane M., Thierry Devos, and Eliot R. Smith. 2000. "Intergroup Emotions: Explaining Offensive Action Tendencies in an Intergroup Context." *Journal of Personality and Social Psychology* 79(4): 602–16.

Major, Brenda, Alison Blodorn, and Gregory Major Blascovich. 2018. "The Threat of Increasing Diversity: Why Many White Americans Support Trump in the 2016 Presidential Election." *Group Processes & Intergroup Relations* 21(6): 931–40.

Mannheim, Karl. 2013. *Ideology and Utopia.* London: Routledge.

Mansfield, Edward D., and Diana C. Mutz. 2009. "Support for Free Trade." *International Organization* 63(3): 425–57.

Markus, Gregory B. 2001. "American Individualism Reconsidered." In *Citizens and Politics: Perspectives from Political Psychology*, ed. James H. Kuklinski. Cambridge: Cambridge University Press, 401–32.

Mason, Lilliana. 2018. *Uncivil Agreement*. Chicago: University of Chicago Press.

Massey, Douglas S. 2007. *Categorically Unequal: The American Stratification System*. New York: Russell Sage Foundation.

Masuoka, Natalie, and Jane Junn. 2013. *The Politics of Belonging: Race, Public Opinion, and Immigration*. Chicago: University of Chicago Press.

Matthews, Donald Rowe, and James Warren Prothro. 1966. *Negroes and the New Southern Politics*. New York: Harcourt, Brace, and World.

Mazie, Margery, Phyllis Palmer, Mayuris Pimentel, Sharon Rogers, Stuart Ruderfer, and Melissa Sokolowski. 1993. "To Deconstruct Race, Deconstruct Whiteness." *American Quarterly* 45(2): 281–94.

McClain, Paula D., Monique L. Lyle, Niambi M. Carter, Victoria M. DeFrancesco Soto, Gerald F. Lackey, Kendra Davenport Cotton, Shayla C. Nunnally, Thomas J. Scotto, Jeffrey D. Grynaviski, and J. Alan Kendrick. 2007. "Black Americans and Latino Immigrants in a Southern City." *Du Bois Review* 4(1): 97–117.

McClain, Paula D., Jessica Johnson Carew, Eugene Walton Jr., and Candis S. Watts. 2009. "Group Membership, Group Identity, and Group Consciousness: Measures of Racial Identity in American Politics?" *Annual Review of Political Science* 12(1): 471–85.

McConahay, John B. 1983. "Modern Racism and Modern Discrimination: The Effects of Race, Racial Attitudes, and Context on Simulated Hiring Decisions." *Personality and Social Psychology Bulletin* 9(4): 551–8.

McConahay, John B., and Joseph C. Hough. 1976. "Symbolic Racism." *Journal of Social Issues* 32(2): 23–45.

McConnaughy, Corrine M., Ismail K. White, David L. Leal, and Jason P. Casellas. 2010. "A Latino on the Ballot: Explaining Coethnic Voting Among Latinos and the Response of White Americans." *The Journal of Politics* 72(4): 1199–211.

McDermott, Monica, and Frank L. Samson. 2005. "White Racial and Ethnic Identity in the United States." *Annual Review of Sociology* 31(1): 245–61.

McIntosh, Peggy. 1989. "White Privilege: Unpacking the Invisible Knapsack." *Peace and Freedom* July/August.

McKee, Seth C., and Jeremy M. Teigen. 2016. "The New Blue: Northern In-Migration in Southern Presidential Elections." *PS: Political Science & Politics* 49(2): 228–33.

Mendelberg, Tali. 2001. *The Race Card: Campaign Strategy, Implicit Messages, and the Norm of Equality*. Princeton: Princeton University Press.

Miller, Arthur H., Patricia Gurin, Gerald Gurin, and Oksana Malanchuk. 1981. "Group Consciousness and Political Participation." *American Journal of Political Science* 25(3): 494–511.

Mills, Charles. 1997. *The Racial Contract*. Ithaca, NY: Cornell University Press.

Mondak, Jeffery J. 2010. *Personality and the Foundations of Political Behavior*. New York: Cambridge University Press.

Montagu, Ashley. 1942. *Man's Most Dangerous Myth: The Fallacy of Race*. New York: Columbia University Press.

Morris, R.C., Sheldon Stryker, and Richard T. Serpe. 1994. "Identity Salience and Psychological Centrality: Equivalent, Overlapping, or Complementary Concepts?" *Social Psychology Quarterly* 57(1): 16–35.

Morrison, Kimberly Rios, Victoria C. Plaut, and Oscar Ybarra. 2010. "Predicting Whether Multiculturalism Positively or Negatively Influences White Americans' Intergroup Attitudes: The Role of Ethnic Identification." *Personality & Social Psychology Bulletin* 36(12): 1648–61.

Morton, William Lewis. 1961. *The Canadian Identity*. Madison: University of Wisconsin Press.

Mudde, Cass. 2007. *Populist Radical Right Parties in Europe*. Cambridge: Cambridge University Press.

Mullen, Brian, Rupert Brown, and Colleen Smith. 1992. "Ingroup Bias as a Function of Salience, Relevance, and Status: An Integration." *European Journal of Social Psychology* 22(2): 103–22.

Mullin, Barbara-Ann, and Michael A. Hogg. 1999. "Motivations for Group Membership: The Role of Subjective Importance and Uncertainty Reduction." *Basic and Applied Social Psychology* 21(2): 91–102.

Mullinix, Kevin J., Thomas J. Leeper, James N. Druckman, and Jeremy Freese. 2014. "The Generalizability of Survey Experiments." *Journal of Experimental Political Science* 2(2): 109–38.

Mutz, Diana C. 2018. "Status Threat, Not Economic Hardship, Explains the 2016 Presidential Vote." *Proceedings of the National Academy of Sciences of the United States of America* 115(19): 4330–9.

Myers, Dowell, and Morris Levy. 2018. "Racial Population Projections and Reactions to Alternative News Accounts of Growing Diversity." *Annals of the American Academy of Political and Social Science* 677(May): 215–28.

Myrdal, Gunnar. 1944. *An American Dilemma: The Negro Problem and Modern Democracy*. New York: Harper.

Nelson, Thomas E., and Donald R. Kinder. 1996. "Issue Frames and Group-Centrism in American Public Opinion." *The Journal of Politics* 58(4): 1055–78.

Neuberg, Steven L., and Jason T. Newsom. 1993. "Personal Need for Structure: Individual Differences in the Desire for Simple Structure." *Journal of Personality and Social Psychology* 65(1): 113–31.

Nisbett, Richard E., and Lee Ross. 1980. *Human Inference: Strategies and Shortcomings of Social Judgment*. Englewood Cliffs: Prentice-Hall.

Norris, Pippa. 2005. *Radical Right: Voters and Parties in the Electoral Market*. New York: Cambridge University Press.

Norton, Michael I., and Samuel R. Sommers. 2011. "Whites See Racism as a Zero-Sum Game That They Are Now Losing." *Perspectives on Psychological Science* 6(3): 215–18.

Oliver, J. Eric, and Tali Mendelberg. 2000. "Reconsidering the Environmental Determinants of White Racial Attitudes." *American Journal of Political Science* 44(3): 574–89.

Oliver, J. Eric, and Wendy M. Rahn. 2016. "Rise of the Trumpenvolk: Populism in the 2016 Election." *The Annals of the American Academy of Political and Social Science* 667(1): 189–206.

Oliver, J. Eric, and Janelle Wong. 2003. "Intergroup Prejudice in Multiethnic Settings." *American Journal of Political Science* 47(4): 567–82.

Oliver, Melvin L., and Thomas M. Shapiro. 2006. *Black Wealth / White Wealth*. New York: Taylor & Francis.

Olzak, Susan. 1992. *The Dynamics of Ethnic Competition and Conflict*. Palo Alto: Stanford University Press.

Omni, M., and Howard Winant. 1986. *Racial Formation in the United States*. New York: Routledge and Kegan Paul.

Outten, H. Robert, Michael T. Schmitt, Daniel A. Miller, and Amber L. Garcia. 2012. "Feeling Threatened About the Future: Whites' Emotional Reactions to Anticipated Ethnic Demographic Changes." *Personality & Social Psychology Bulletin* 38(1): 14–25.

Painter, Nell Irvin. 2003. "Why White People Are Called 'Caucasian?'" In *Proceedings of the Fifth Annual Gilder Lehrman Center International Conference at Yale University*, 1–37.

Parker, Christopher S., and Matt A. Barreto. 2013. *Change They Can't Believe In: The Tea Party and Reactionary Politics in America*. Princeton: Princeton University Press.

Parker, Christopher S., Mark Q. Sawyer, and Christopher Towler. 2009. "A Black Man in the White House? The Role of Racism and Patriotism in the 2008 Presidential Election." *Du Bois Review* 6(1): 193–217.

Pasek, Josh, Tobias H. Stark, Jon A. Krosnick, and Trevor Tompson. 2015. "What Motivates a Conspiracy Theory? Birther Beliefs, Partisanship, Liberal-Conservative Ideology, and Anti-Black Attitudes." *Electoral Studies* 40: 482–9.

Patterson, James T. 1996. *Grand Expectations: The United States, 1945–1974*. New York: Oxford University Press.

Patterson, Meagan M., and Rebecca S. Bigler. 2007. "Effects of Physical Atypicality on Children's Social Identities and Intergroup Attitudes." *International Journal of Behavioral Development* 31(5): 433–44.

Pérez, Efrén O. 2010. "Explicit Evidence on the Import of Implicit Attitudes: The IAT and Immigration Policy Judgments." *Political Behavior* 32(4): 517–45.

2016. *Unspoken Politics*. New York: Cambridge University Press.

Perreault, Stephane, and Richard Y. Bourhis. 1999. "Ethnocentrism, Social Identification, and Discrimination." *Personality & Social Psychology Bulletin* 25(1): 92–103.

Perry, Pamela. 2001. "White Means Never Having to Say You're Ethnic." *Journal of Contemporary Ethnography* 30(1): 56–91.

2002. *Shades of White: White Kids and Racial Identities in High School*. Durham, NC: Duke University Press.

2007. "White Universal Identity as a 'Sense of Group Position'." *Symbolic Interaction* 30(3): 375–93.

Petrocik, John R. 1996. "Issue Ownership in Presidential Elections, with a 1980 Case Study." *American Journal of Political Science* 40(3): 825–50.

Petrow, Gregory A., John E. Transue, and Timothy Vercellotti. 2018. "Do White In-Group Processes Matter, Too? White Racial Identity and Support for Black Political Candidates." *Political Behavior* 40(1): 197–222.

Pettigrew, Thomas F. 1979. "The Ultimate Attribution Error: Extending Allport's Cognitive Analysis of Prejudice." *Personality and Social Psychology Bulletin* 5(4): 461–76.

Pettigrew, Thomas F., Ulrich Wagner, and Oliver Christ. 2007. "Who Opposes Immigration? Comparing German with North American Findings." *Du Bois Review* 4(1): 19–39.

Phillips, Kevin P. 1969. *The Emerging Republican Majority*. New Rochelle: Arlington House.

Phinney, Jean S. 1990. "Ethnic Identity in Adolescents and Adults: Review of Research." *Psychological Bulletin* 108(3): 499–514.

Piston, Spencer. 2010. "How Explicit Racial Prejudice Hurt Obama in the 2008 Election." *Political Behavior* 32(4): 431–51.

Pratto, Felicia, Jim Sidanius, Lisa M. Stallworth, and Bertram F. Malle. 1994. "Social Dominance Orientation: A Personality Variable Predicting Social and Political Attitudes." *Journal of Personality and Social Psychology* 67(4): 741–63.

Quadagno, Jill S. 1994. *The Color of Welfare: How Racism Undermined the War on Poverty*. New York: Oxford University Press.

Quillian, Lincoln. 1995. "Prejudice as a Response to Perceived Group Threat: Population Composition and Anti-Immigrant and Racial Prejudice in Europe." *American Sociological Review* 60(4): 586–611.

1996. "Group Threat and Regional Change in Attitudes Toward African-Americans." *American Journal of Sociology* 102(3): 816–60.

Rensmann, Lars, and Jennifer Miller-Gonzalez. 2010. "Xenophobia and Anti-Immigrant Politics." In *The International Studies Encyclopedia*, ed. Robert A. Denemark. Hoboken: Wiley-Blackwell, 7628–53.

Rivers, Douglas. 2006. Polimetrix White Paper Series *Sample Matching: Representative Sampling from Internet Panels.* www.ncbi.nlm.nih.gov/pubmed/20804407.

Roediger, David R. 1994. *Toward the Abolition of Whiteness.* New York: Verso.

1999. "The Pursuit of Whiteness: Property, Terror, and Expansion, 1790–1860." *Journal of the Early Republic* 19(4): 579–600.

2006. *Working Toward Whiteness: How America's Immigrants Became White: The Strange Journey from Ellis Island to the Suburbs.* New York: Basic Books.

Rosaldo, Renato. 1989. *Culture and Truth: The Remaking of Social Analysis.* Boston: Beacon Press.

Rosenstone, S., and J.M. Hansen. 1993. *Mobilization, Participation and Democracy in America.* New York: Macmillan.

Rothwell, Jonathan, and Pablo Diego-Rosell. 2016. SSRN Electronic Journal *Explaining Nationalist Political Views: The Case of Donald Trump.*

Rowe, Wayne, Sandra K. Bennett, and Donald R. Atkinson. 1994. "White Racial Identity Models: A Critique and Alternative Proposal." *The Counseling Psychologist* 22(1): 129–46.

Sanchez, Gabriel R. 2006. "The Role of Group Consciousness in Political Participation Among Latinos in the United States." *American Politics Research* 34(4): 427–50.

Sanchez, Gabriel R., and Edward D. Vargas. 2016. "Taking a Closer Look at Group Identity: The Link between Theory and Measurement of Group Consciousness and Linked Fate." *Political Research Quarterly* 69(1): 160–74.

Saxton, Alexander. 1975. *The Indispensable Enemy: Labor and the Anti-Chinese Movement in California.* Berkeley: University of California Press.

Schaffner, Brian F., Matthew C. Macwilliams, and Tatishe Nteta. 2018. "Understanding White Polarization in the 2016 Vote for President: The Sobering Role of Racism and Sexism." *Political Science Quarterly* 133(1): 9–34.

Scheepers, Daan, and Naomi Ellemers. 2005. "When the Pressure Is Up: The Assessment of Social Identity Threat in Low and High Status Groups." *Journal of Experimental Social Psychology* 41(2): 192–200.

Scheve, Kenneth F., and Matthew J. Slaughter. 2001. "Labor Market Competition and Individual Preferences Over Immigration Policy." *Review of Economics and Statistics* 83(1): 133–45.

Schickler, Eric. 2016. *Racial Realignment.* Princeton: Princeton University Press.

Schildkraut, Deborah J. 2005. "The Rise and Fall of Political Engagement among Latinos: The Role of Identity and Perceptions of Discrimination." *Political Behavior* 27(3): 285–312.

2007. "Defining American Identity in the Twenty-First Century: How Much 'There' Is There?" *The Journal of Politics* 69(3): 597–615.

2015. "White Attitudes about Descriptive Representation in the US: The Roles of Identity, Discrimination, and Linked Fate." *Politics, Groups, and Identities* 5(1): 84–106.

Schlozman, Kay Lehman, and Sidney Verba. 1979. *Injury to Insult: Unemployment, Class and Political Response.* Cambridge, MA: Harvard University Press.

Schuman, Howard, Charlotte Steeh, Lawrence D. Bobo, and Maria Krysan. 1985. *Racial Attitudes in America: Trends and Interpretations.* Cambridge, MA: Harvard University Press.

Sears, David O. 1993. "Symbolic Politics: A Socio-Psychological Theory." In *Explorations in Political Psychology*, eds. Shanto Iyengar and William J. McGuire. Durham, NC: Duke University Press, 113–49.

Sears, David O., and Carolyn L. Funk. 1990. "The Limited Effect of Economic Self-Interest on the Political Attitudes of the Mass Public." *Journal of Behavioral Economics* 19(3): 247–71.

Sears, David O., and P.J. Henry. 2005. "Over Thirty Years Later: A Contemporary Look at Symbolic Racism." *Advances in Experimental Social Psychology* 37(1): 95–150.

Sears, David O., and Donald R. Kinder. 1985. "Whites' Opposition to Busing: On Conceptualizing and Operationalizing Group Conflict." *Journal of Personality and Social Psychology* 48(5): 1141–7.

Sears, David O., and Victoria Savalei. 2006. "The Political Color Line in America: Many 'Peoples of Color' or Black Exceptionalism?" *Political Psychology* 27(6): 895–924.

Sears, David O., and Nicholas A. Valentino. 1997. "Politics Matters: Political Events as Catalysts for Preadult Socialization." *The American Political Science Review* 91(1): 45–65.

Sellers, Robert M., Stephanie A.J. Rowley, Tabbye M. Chavous, J. Nicole Shelton, and Mia A. Smith. 1997. "Multidimensional Inventory of Black Identity: A Preliminary Investigation of Reliability and Construct Validity." *Journal of Personality and Social Psychology* 73(4): 805–15.

Sellers, Robert M., J. Nicole Shelton, Deanna Y. Cooke, Tabbye M. Chavous, Stephanie A.J. Rowley, and Mia A. Smith. 1998. "A Multidimensional Model of Racial Identity: Assumptions, Findings, and Future Directions." In *African American Identity Development: Theory, Research, and Intervention*, ed. R.L. Jones. Hampton: Cobb and Henry, 275–305.

Shapiro, Thomas M. 2004. *The Hidden Cost of Being African American.* New York: Oxford University Press.

Sherif, Muzafer. 1958. "Superordinate Goals in the Reduction of Intergroup Conflict." *American Journal of Sociology* 63(4): 349–56.

1961. *Intergroup Conflict and Cooperation: The Robbers Cave Experiment.* Norman: University of Oklahoma Press.

Sherif, Muzafer, and Carolyn W. Sherif. 1953. *Groups in Harmony and Tension.* New York: Harper.

Sherman, Sally R. 1989. "Public Attitudes Toward Social Security, 1935–1965." *Social Security Bulletin* 52(12): 2–16.

Shingles, Richard D. 1981. "Black Consciousness and Political Participation: The Missing Link." *The American Political Science Review* 75(1): 76–91.

Sidanius, Jim, and Felicia Pratto. 1999. *Social Dominance: An Intergroup Theory of Social Hierarchy and Oppression.* Cambridge: Cambridge University Press.

Sidanius, Jim, Felicia Pratto, and Lawrence D. Bobo. 1996. "Racism, Conservatism, Affirmative Action, and Intellectual Sophistication: A Matter of Principled Conservatism or Group Dominance?" *Journal of Personality and Social Psychology* 70(3): 476–90.

Sidanius, Jim, Felicia Pratto, and Michael Mitchell. 1994. "In-Group Identification, Social Dominance Orientation, and Differential Intergroup Social Allocation." *Journal of Social Psychology* 134(2): 151–67.

Sidanius, Jim, Felicia Pratto, and Joshua L. Rabinowitz. 1994. "Gender, Ethnic Status, and Ideological Asymmetry: A Social Dominance Interpretation." *Journal of Cross-Cultural Psychology* 25(2): 194–216.

Sidanius, Jim, Seymour Feshbach, Shana Levin, and Felicia Pratto. 1997. "The Interface Between Ethnic and National Attachment: Ethnic Pluralism or Ethnic Dominance?" *The Public Opinion Quarterly* 61(1): 102–33.

Sidanius, Jim, Felicia Pratto, Colette van Laar, and Shana Levin. 2004. "Social Dominance Theory: Its Agenda and Method." *Political Psychology* 25(6): 845–80.

Sides, John, and Jack Citrin. 2007. "European Opinion About Immigration: The Role of Identities, Interests and Information." *British Journal of Political Science* 37(3): 477–504.

Silvestri, Timothy J., and Tina Q. Richardson. 2001. "White Racial Identity Statuses and NEO Personality Constructs: An Exploratory Analysis." *Journal of Counseling & Development* 79(1): 68–76.

Simien, E.M. 2005. "Race, Gender, and Linked Fate." *Journal of Black Studies* 35(5): 529–50.

Simon, Bernd, and Bert Klandermans. 2001. "Politicized Collective Identity: A Social Psychological Analysis." *The American Psychologist* 56(4): 319–31.

Simon, Rita, and Susan Alexander. 1993. *The Ambivalent Welcome*. Westport: Praeger.

Smedley, Audrey. 1998. "'Race' and the Construction of Human Identity." *American Anthropologist* 100(3): 690–702.

Smedley, Audrey, and Brian D. Smedley. 2004. "Race as Biology Is Fiction, Racism as a Social Problem Is Real." *The American Psychologist* 60(1): 16–26.

Smith, Eliot R., Charles R. Seger, and Diane M. Mackie. 2007. "Can Emotions Be Truly Group Level? Evidence Regarding Four Conceptual Criteria." *Journal of Personality and Social Psychology* 93(3): 431–46.

Smith, H.J., and T.R. Tyler. 1996. "Justice and Power: When Will Justice Concerns Encourage the Advantaged to Support Policies Which Redistribute Economic Resources and the Disadvantaged to Willingly Obey the Law?" *European Journal of Social Psychology* 26(2): 171–200.

Sniderman, Paul M., and Edward G. Carmines. 1997. "Reaching Beyond Race." *PS: Political Science & Politics* 30(3): 466–71.

Sniderman, Paul M., and Louk Hagendoorn. 2009. *When Ways of Life Collide: Multiculturalism and Its Discontents in the Netherlands*. Princeton: Princeton University Press.

Sniderman, Paul M., and Thomas L. Piazza. 2002. *Black Pride and Black Prejudice*. Princeton: Princeton University Press.

Sniderman, Paul M., and Philip E. Tetlock. 1986. "Symbolic Racism: Problems of Motive Attribution in Political Analysis." *Journal of Social Issues* 42(2): 129–50.

Sniderman, Paul M., Richard Brody, and Philip E. Tetlock. 1991. *Reasoning and Choice: Explorations in Political Psychology*. New York: Cambridge University Press.

Sniderman, Paul M., Louk Hagendoorn, and Markus Prior. 2004. "Predisposing Factors and Situational Triggers: Exclusionary Reactions to Immigrant Minorities." *American Political Science Review* 98(1): 35–49.

Steele, Shelby. 1990. "White Guilt." *The American Scholar* 59(4): 497–506.

Stenner, Karen. 2005. *The Authoritarian Dynamic*. New York: Cambridge University Press.

Speech by Ellison DuRant Smith. April 9, 1924. *Congressional Record*, 68th Congress, 1st Session. Washington DC: Government Printing Office, vol. 65, 5961–2.

Stephan, Walter G., and Cookie White Stephan. 1996. "Predicting Prejudice." *International Journal of Intercultural Relations* 20(3): 409–26.

Steuerle, C. Eugene, Karen E. Smith, and Caleb Quakenbush. 2013. "Has Social Security Redistributed to Whites from People of Color?" *Program on Retirement Policy* 38.

Stokes-Brown, Atiya Kai. 2012. "America's Shifting Color Line? Reexamining Determinants of Latino Racial Self-Identification." *Social Science Quarterly* 93(2): 309–32.

Stouffer, Samuel A. 1955. *Communism, Conformity, and Civil Liberties: A Cross-Section of the Nation Speaks Its Mind.* New Brunswick: Transaction Publishers.

Struch, Naomi, and Shalom H. Schwartz. 1989a. "Intergroup Aggression: Its Predictors and Distinctness from In-Group Bias." *Journal of Personality and Social Psychology* 56(3): 364–73.

1989b. "Intergroup Aggression: Its Predictors and Distinctness From In-Group Bias." *Journal of Personality and Social Psychology* 56(3): 364–73.

Sumner, William Graham. 1906. *Folkways: A Study of the Sociological Importance of Usages, Manners, Customs, Mores, and Morals.* Boston: Ginn.

Swain, Carol M. 2002. *The New White Nationalism in America: Its Challenge to Integration.* New York: Cambridge University Press.

Swain, Carol M., and Russell Nieli. 2003. *Contemporary Voices of White Nationalism in America.* New York: Cambridge University Press.

Swim, Janet K., and Deborah L. Miller. 1999. "White Guilt: Its Antecedents and Consequences for Attitudes Toward Affirmative Action." *Personality and Social Psychology Bulletin* 25(4): 500–14.

Tajfel, Henri. 1970. "Experiments in Intergroup Discrimination." *Scientific American* 223(5): 96–103.

1974. "Social Identity and Intergroup Behavior." *Social Science Information* 13(2): 65–93.

1978. "Social Categorization, Social Identity and Social Comparison." In *Differentiation Between Social Groups: Studies in the Social Psychology of Intergroup Relations*, ed. Henri Tajfel. London: Academic Press, Inc., 61–76.

1982. "Social Psychology of Intergroup Relations." *Annual Review of Psychology* 33(1): 1–39.

Tajfel, Henri, and John C. Turner. 1979. "An Integrative Theory of Intergroup Conflict." In *The Social Psychology of Intergroup Relations*, eds. William G. Austin and Stephen Worchel. Monterrey: Brooks/Cole Publishing Co., 33–47.

1986. "The Social Identity Theory of Intergroup Behavior." In *Psychology of Intergroup Relations*, eds. S. Worchel and W.G. Austin. Chicago: Nelson-Hall, 7–24.

Tate, Katherine. 1993. *From Protest to Politics: The New Black Voters in American Elections*. Cambridge, MA: Harvard University Press.

Tatum, Beverly Daniel. 1992. "Talking about Race, Learning about Racism: The Application of Racial Identity Development Theory in the Classroom." *Harvard Educational Review* 62(1): 1–25.

Taylor, Marylee C. 1998. "How White Attitudes Vary with the Racial Composition of Local Populations: Numbers Count." *American Sociological Review* 63(4): 512–35.

Terry, Robert W. 1981. "The Negative Impact on White Values." In *Impacts of Racism on White American*, eds. Benjamin P. Bowser and Raymond G. Hunt. Beverly Hills: Sage, 119–51.

Tesler, Michael. 2012a. "The Return of Old-Fashioned Racism to White Americans' Partisan Preferences in the Early Obama Era." *The Journal of Politics* 75(1): 110–23.

2012b. "The Spillover of Racialization into Health Care: How President Obama Polarizes Public Opinion By Racial Attitudes and Race." *American Journal of Political Science* 56(3): 690–704.

Tesler, Michael, and David O. Sears. 2010. *Obama's Race: The 2008 Election and the Dream of a Post-Racial America*. Chicago: University of Chicago Press.

Tetlock, Philip E. 1994. "Political Psychology or Politicized Psychology: Is the Road to Scientific Hell Paved with Good Moral Intentions?" *Political Psychology* 15(3): 509–29.

Theiss-Morse, Elizabeth. 2009. *Who Counts as an American? The Boundaries of National Identity*. Cambridge, MA: Cambridge University Press.

Tirkides, Yiannis. 2009. "Europe's Demographic Challenge and Immigration." *Think Global – Act European* (Part 1: Prospects for Economic Growth): 59–66.

Transue, John E. 2007. "Identity Salience, Identity Acceptance, and Racial Policy Attitudes: American National Identity as a Uniting Force." *American Journal of Political Science* 51(1): 78–91.

Turner, John C. 1975. "Social Comparison and Social Identity: Some Prospects for Intergroup Behavior." *European Journal of Social Psychology* 5(1): 5–34.

1985. "Social Categorization and Self-Concept: A Social Cognitive Theory of Group Behavior." In *Advances in Group Process: Theory and Research*, ed. E.J. Lawler. Greenwich: JAI Press, 77–121.

Valentino, Nicholas A., and David O. Sears. 2005. "Old Times There Are Not Forgotten: Race and Partisan Realignment in the Contemporary South." *American Journal of Political Science* 49(3): 672–88.

Valentino, Nicholas A., Ted Brader, and Ashley E. Jardina. 2013. "Immigration Opposition Among U.S. Whites: General Ethnocentrism or Media Priming of Attitudes About Latinos?" *Political Psychology* 34(2): 149–66.

Valentino, Nicholas A., Fabian G. Neuner, and L. Matthew Vandenbroek. 2018. "The Changing Norms of Racial Political Rhetoric and the End of Racial Priming." *The Journal of Politics* 80(3): 757–71.

Vance, J.D. 2016. *Hillbilly Elegy.* New York: HarperCollins.

Vanneman, Reeve D., and Thomas F. Pettigrew. 1972. "Race and Relative Deprivation in the Urban United States." *Race & Class* 13(4): 461–86.

Verba, Sidney, and Norman H. Nie. 1972. *Political Participation in America.* New York: Harper & Row.

Verba, Sidney, Kay Lehman Schlozman, and Henry E. Brady. 1995. *Voice and Equality: Civic Voluntarism in American Politics.* Cambridge, MA: Harvard University Press.

Voss, Kim, Irene Bloemraad, and Taeku Lee. 2011. "The Protests of 2006: What Were They, How Do We Understand Them, Where Do We Go?" In *Rallying for Immigrant Rights: The Fight for Inclusion in 21st Century America*, eds. Irene Bloemraad and Kim Voss. Berkeley: University of California Press, 3–43.

Wallace, George. 1963. "Inaugural Address." January 14, 1963. Montgomery, Alabama. Available at http://digital.archives.alabama.gov/cdm/ref/collection/voices/id/2952

Walsh, Katherine Cramer. 2012. "Putting Inequality in Its Place: Rural Consciousness and the Power of Perspective." *American Political Science Review* 106(3): 517–32.

Warren, Jonathan W., and France Winddance Twine. 1997. "White Americans, the New Minority? Non-Blacks and the Ever-Expanding Boundaries of Whiteness." *Journal of Black Studies* 28(2): 200–18.

Warren, Robert Penn. 1965. *Who Speaks for the Negro?* New York: Random House.

Waters, Mary C. 1990. *Ethnic Options: Choosing Identities in America.* Berkeley: University of California Press.

Weir, Margaret, Anna Shola Orloff, and Theda Skocpol. 1988. *The Politics of Social Policy in the United States.* Princeton: Princeton University Press.

Weisberg, Herbert F., and Jerrold G. Rusk. 1970. "Dimensions of Candidate Evaluation." *The American Political Science Review* 64(4): 1167–85.

Weller, Nicholas, and Jane Junn. 2018. "Racial Identity and Voting: Conceptualizing White Identity in Spatial Terms." *Perspectives on Politics* 16(2): 436–48.

White, Theodore H. 1982. *America in Search of Itself: The Making of the President 1956–1980.* New York: Harper & Row.

Wilkins, Clara L., Joseph D. Wellman, and Cheryl R. Kaiser. 2013. "Status Legitimizing Beliefs Predict Positivity toward Whites Who

Claim Anti-White Bias." *Journal of Experimental Social Psychology* 49(6): 1114–19.

Williamson, Vanessa, Theda Skocpol, and John Coggin. 2011. "The Tea Party and the Remaking of Republican Conservatism." *Perspectives on Politics* 9(1): 25–43.

Winter, J. Alan. 1996. "Symbolic Ethnicity or Religion among Jews in the United States: A Test of Gansian Hypotheses." *Review of Religious Research* 37(3): 233–47.

Winter, Nicholas J. G. 2006. "Beyond Welfare: Framing and the Racialization of White Opinion on Social Security." *American Journal of Political Science* 50(2): 400–20.

———. 2008. *Dangerous Frames: How Ideas About Race and Gender Shape Public Opinion*. Chicago: University of Chicago Press.

Wohl, Michael J.A., Nyla R. Branscombe, and Stephen Reysen. 2010. "Perceiving Your Group's Future to Be in Jeopardy: Extinction Threat Induces Collective Angst and the Desire to Strengthen the Ingroup." *Personality and Social Psychology Bulletin* 36(7): 898–910.

Wong, Cara J. 2010. *Boundaries of Obligation in American Politics: Geographic, National, and Racial Communities*. New York: Cambridge University Press.

Wong, Cara, and Grace E. Cho. 2005. "Two-Headed Coins or Kandinskys: White Racial Identification." *Political Psychology* 26(5): 699–720.

Wong, Janelle S. 2018. *Immigrants, Evangelicals, and Politics in an Era of Demographic Change*. New York: Russell Sage Foundation.

Wong, Janelle S., Pei-te Lien, and M. Margaret Conway. 2005. "Group-Based Resources and Political Participation among Asian Americans." *American Politics Research* 33(4): 545–76.

Woodward, C. Vann. 1958. "The Search for Southern Identity." *Virginia Quarterly Review* 34(Summer): 321–38.

Wright, Matthew, Jack Citrin, and Jonathan Wand. 2012. "Alternative Measures of American National Identity: Implications for the Civic-Ethnic Distinction." *Political Psychology* 33(4): 469–82.

Zaller, John R. 1992. *The Nature and Origins of Mass Opinion*. New York: Cambridge University Press.

Zepeda-Millán, Chris, and Sophia J. Wallace. 2013. "Racialization in Times of Contention: How Social Movements Influence Latino Racial Identity." *Politics, Groups and Identities* 1(4): 510–27.

INDEX

Books in the Series

CPSIA information can be obtained
at www.ICGtesting.com
Printed in the USA
LVHW092022310120
645471LV00005B/110